The Problem of
CRIME

Edited by

John Muncie and
Eugene McLaughlin

SAGE Publications
London • Thousand Oaks • New Delhi

in association with

TheOpen
University

This book is the first in a series published by Sage Publications in association with The Open University.

The Problem of Crime
edited by John Muncie and Eugene McLaughlin

Controlling Crime
edited by Eugene McLaughlin and John Muncie

Criminological Perspectives: A Reader
edited by John Muncie, Eugene McLaughlin and Mary Langan

The books are part of The Open University course D315 *Crime, Order and Social Control.*
Details of this and other Open University courses can be obtained from the Central Enquiry Service,
PO Box 200, The Open University, Milton Keynes MK7 6YZ. For availability of other course components,
including video- and audio-cassette materials, contact Open University Educational Enterprises Ltd,
12 Cofferidge Close, Stony Stratford, Milton Keynes MK11 1BY.

The Open University, Walton Hall, Milton Keynes MK7 6AA

SAGE Publications Ltd
6 Bonhill Street
London EC2A 4PU

SAGE Publications Inc
2455 Teller Road
Thousand Oaks
California 91320

SAGE Publications India Pvt Ltd
32, M-Block Market
Greater Kailash - I
New Delhi 110 048

British Library Cataloguing in Publication data
A catalogue record for this book is available from The British Library

ISBN 0 7619 5004-4
ISBN 0 7619 5005-2 (pbk)

Library of Congress catalog card number 95-071321

Edited, designed and typeset by The Open University

Printed in Great Britain by Butler & Tanner Ltd, Frome and London

Contents

Preface

The Problem of Crime is the first of three volumes in a new series of introductory criminology texts published by Sage in association with The Open University. The series, entitled *Crime, Order and Social Control*, explores key issues in the study of crime and criminal justice systems by examining the *diverse* nature of crime, the *varied* formal and informal means designed to effect its control, and the *multiplicity* of approaches and interpretations that criminologists have brought to bear on this study. Each volume, however, is free-standing and introduces readers to different aspects of the complex body of knowledge that makes up contemporary criminology. By emphasizing diversity – both in the nature of criminological knowledge and in its object of study – the series engages with taken-for-granted notions of the meaning, extent and causes of crime and of the role and function of criminal justice. Above all, we maintain that the study of crime cannot be divorced from the study of social order. Definitions of crime, and the ways in which it is understood and responded to, are not universal and unchanging. Crucially, the recognition of, and reaction to, crime are contingent on social, political and economic circumstances.

The main aim of these volumes is to chart and redraw the parameters of a contemporary criminological imagination. They provide an interdisciplinary overview of 'classic' and current scholarly work in crime, criminal justice and criminology by drawing on the approaches and modes of analysis found in such subjects as sociology, psychology, socio-legal studies, gender studies, social geography and political science. This again alerts us to the potentially disparate and diverse nature of our subject matter.

The three volumes are core components of an Open University course with the same title as that of the series. This volume, *The Problem of Crime*, focuses on the shifting ways in which crime is defined. The second volume, *Controlling Crime*, examines the changing and expanding parameters of criminal justice. The third, *Criminological Perspectives: A Reader*, explores the contested knowledges of criminology itself. Each is distinctive, not only in its chosen subject matter, but also because, unlike a majority of edited collections, it is primarily intended as a resource to aid teaching and student understanding.

To this end, this volume has been designed as an interactive teaching text. The chapters should be read sequentially, as each builds on those that have gone before, and each concludes with suggestions for further and more in-depth reading. The following features have also been built into the overall structure of the book:

- activities: these are exercises in which students are encouraged to take an active part whilst working through the text, in order to test understanding and develop critical thinking;

- comments: these provide feedback on activities and an opportunity for students to check their own responses;

- shorter questions: these are designed to encourage the reader to pause and reflect back on what has just been read;

- key concepts: concepts that are core to each chapter and central to the study of criminology are highlighted in the margins.

In addition, the majority of chapters include a number of short readings – newspaper articles, or extracts from academic books and articles – which are integral to the discussion as it develops and are designed both to encourage self-reflection and to aid in the application of central ideas and concepts to contemporary social developments and political ideologies. While each volume in the series is self-contained, there are also a number of references back and forward to the other volumes, and for those readers who wish to use the books for an integrated exploration of issues in crime, criminal justice and criminology, the references to chapters in the other volumes are printed in bold type. The aim of all these features is to help readers more readily to understand and examine critically the principal arguments not only of each chapter, but of each book and the series as a whole.

The production of this volume – and the series – has been made possible not simply through the work of its editors and chapter authors but through the collective endeavours of an entire Open University Course Team. Each chapter has gone through three drafts whereby content and teaching strategy have been modified and refined. In this respect, we are indebted to our consultants, tutor-testers and assessors who have given invaluable advice; a course manager who, against all odds, has ensured that all our efforts have been co-ordinated and that deadlines have been met; a course secretary who has suffered more than most from being asked to do the impossible; and a supportive team of production editors, designers, graphic artist and media librarian who have made sure the final product looks as good as it does. We thank them all.

John Muncie
(on behalf of The Open University Course Team)

Introduction

The focus of this book is the exploration of the nature and extent of the problem of crime in contemporary society. Its empirical detail is drawn, in the main, from the study of crime in the UK, but the issues it raises are of a wider – even global – significance. Such issues include: How and why do different societies come to define certain behaviours as criminal whilst other behaviours are considered acceptable? Where are the boundaries between the disreputable and the respectable drawn? Where in the social formation are we most likely to find the 'undesirable', the 'troublesome' and the transgressors of criminal law?

The book is less concerned with trying to unravel specific causes of crime and more with revealing the various 'sites' in which crime is experienced, made sense of and understood. Without such contextualization, crime tends to retain some unitary meaning and a power to assign a common denominator to all aspects of law-breaking. Yet, quite clearly, if we subject the concept of crime to even a rudimentary analysis, it is evident that we are dealing with a potentially infinite number and type of behaviours. In this respect the concept obscures more than it reveals. Whatever it is that such behaviours as murder, shoplifting or fraud have in common, it is clear that their differences are more significant.

The study of crime is complicated by a number of issues. Should we study crime as a form of behaviour or as a type of legal sanction? Is there any behaviour that is intrinsically 'criminal', or is it more a matter of studying why and how certain behaviours, at certain times, come to be criminalized? Is crime a moral, or a legal, issue? Can we say anything meaningful about crime without prior knowledge of a social order and its legal apparatus which has the power to confer the label of criminality on specific acts or people? As a result, the title of this book has a double meaning. The 'problem of crime' is not only a matter of the harms and injuries that crime inflicts, it is also a matter of the limited and limiting nature of any debate which talks about 'crime' as if its meaning is self-evident. All the chapters explore questions of how and why it is not simply crime (as behaviour) but also 'crime' (as a conceptual category) that make up the 'problem of crime'. The point can be illustrated simply enough by noting how crime appears to be simultaneously something to condemn (the fear of being a victim?) and something to be used for entertainment (the morbid fascination of the television viewer?). Crime denotes 'pain', but it is also 'pleasure'. It is typically portrayed as pathological, but is a core element of popular culture. Similarly, it is widely assumed to be 'abnormal', yet also appears to be one of the most characteristic and enduring features of social order. Consequently, 'crime' attracts multiple and contradictory meanings and emotions. It is only by revealing how it comes to find expression in particular discourses, at particular times and in particular localities that we can begin to move to a more reasoned analysis of exactly how the 'problem of crime' is framed and constituted.

Chapter 1 begins this process by asking the seemingly straightforward questions: What is crime? How extensive is crime? How serious is crime? When subjected to sustained analysis none of these questions is capable of delivering unequivocal and incontestable answers. Much depends on how 'crime' is defined. If we restrict ourselves to a legal definition and rely on official statistical measures of recorded crime, a common-sense picture emerges of crime being closely correlated with a particular age (the young), a particular gender (male), and a particular social position (low socio-economic). However, if we define 'crime' as an ideological *censure* – the means by which only a small and specific selection of social harms are criminalized – then we are forced to confront the uncomfortable notion not only that crime is widespread, but that it is practised at all levels in the social formation. Expanding the concept of 'crime' in this way reveals that law-breaking is not the preserve of working-class young men, but is prevalent in some of our most cherished institutions – the nuclear family, the democratic state, the free market economy. As John Muncie makes clear, 'crime' is a problem, not simply in its damaging consequences, but also in the way in which the 'problem of crime' is commonly understood and conceptualized. Above all, the constitution of crime is never self-evident; it remains a controversial and contested concept in its own right.

In trying to unravel the meaning of 'crime' there are dangers, too, in continually locating it within the discourse of 'a problem'. In Chapter 2 John Clarke explores how crime is not just something to be feared, but is also a major source of popular entertainment, amusement and diversion. By focusing on how crime and its detection are *represented* in different types of detective novel, the chapter underlines the point that our knowledge of crime is also significantly affected by particular sets of definitions, interpretations and images that circulate widely in the media and fictional entertainment. Moreover, detective novels are not simply stories of criminals, victims and 'whodunnit', they also tell stories about the relationship between types of crime and types of social order – ranging from familial murders in English country houses to the rank corruption of the American underworld. The social orders imagined in the novel provide us with different ways of seeing crime and the social relationships in which it is enmeshed. Rather than crime being simply an object of repulsion, the study of fictional representations reveals how it can also be an object of fascination and seduction. This ambiguity is a telling reminder of the extent to which we are capable of finding pleasure in the morbid and gratification in the 'unthinkable'.

Chapter 3 details another important point of entry into the study of crime: namely, research into social history. History is important not simply as a consequence of our curiosity about the past, but because it reveals that crime is not a fixed and universal phenomenon. It changes through history. More significantly, as Jim Sharpe reveals, what a society defines as 'crime' depends on social, political and economic factors that are specific to *particular* societies at *particular* stages of their development. By focusing on how transformations in the definition and control of crime occurred in English society in the eighteenth and early nineteenth centuries, it becomes possible to extend our understanding of crime as something historically relative and context-bound. Above all, the chapter alerts us to the idea that the frames of reference through which we so readily understand and make sense of crime – such as notions of a criminal class and the juvenile delinquent – are relatively recent in origin and are the product of particular sets of economic, political and ideological relations. Moreover, studying the history of crime and punishment reminds us that our current ways of thinking about these problems are not the only ways that are understandable and defensible.

Chapter 4 focuses on the familiar site of the city as a place of crime and disorder. However, it is designed not simply to describe such elements, but to account for the emergence and perseverance of particular sets of images which have helped to cement the notion that the city is intrinsically a dangerous place. By tracing the tension between representations of progress and danger, from the mid nineteenth century through to visions of the twenty-first century city, Peggotty Graham and John Clarke note how ideas of crime have tended to circulate continually through such peculiarly urban images as the 'dangerous classes', the 'casual poor', the 'social residuum', the 'disorganized', the 'slum family', the 'underclass', the 'rioter' and so on. Woven throughout the chapter is the idea of struggle – struggle not simply about the causes of crime, but struggle about the city as an arrangement of space, and struggle over who has rights of access to its shifting configurations of public and private places. Questions of crime and criminalization are always at the centre of such disputes because every attempt to change the social and spatial organization of the city poses key questions for social order. What sort of social order is envisaged in urban reform, renewal and reconstruction? How are challenges to such order conflated with images of undesirability and criminality? Above all, Chapter 4 notes how the obsession with the city as a dangerous place forms an enduring element of the public debate about crime. However, the focus of such debate rarely stretches further than a concern for such problems as street crime and vandalism. As a result, the city–crime couplet typically produces a peculiarly one-dimensional view of the problem of crime.

The remaining three chapters of the book concentrate on various 'sites' of crime which have traditionally been absent from political and public debate. Chapter 5 focuses on the largely hidden crimes of violence and abuse in the domestic sphere; Chapter 6 explores how corporate 'crime' is not only hidden but has also, in no small measure, been traditionally considered as a legitimate and respectable element of competitive market economies; and Chapter 7 examines the nature and extent of violence in society as expressed not only in political challenges to state authority, but also in the state's own monopoly on the use of legitimate force. Collectively, they contribute to a broader understanding of the problem of crime by revealing the significance of the 'presence of absences' – how everyday assumptions about crime are implicitly framed through a partial and narrow vision of crime's extent and meaning. These final chapters bring questions that have long remained on the margins of the crime debate into the centre of a criminological agenda.

In Chapter 5, Esther Saraga addresses the key questions of to what extent, and why, crime is characteristically defined as a public phenomenon. The implications of such a definition for understanding instances of violence and abuse in the home are discussed, in particular noting how the family occupies an ambiguous position in contemporary crime discourse. In contrast to the public world of the city, the family is often viewed as a private place of safety and protection. Yet, on the other hand, the family is also seen as fragile, at risk of breakdown and as the breeding ground for adult crime. In short, the family is typically viewed as both the cause and the cure of crime. However, both of these dominant public images fail to acknowledge how familial relationships themselves can also contribute to fear and danger, particularly for women, children and older people. Ongoing campaigns to bring instances of domestic violence and child abuse into the centre of public debate once more underline the extent to which the concept of 'crime' is inherently unstable and contestable.

Chapter 6 also moves beyond the sorts of offences that commonly engage the police and the courts to consider a range of property and personal offences committed by financiers and business people, by corporations and small firms and by employees, entrepreneurs and professionals. Whilst 'ordinary crime' appears easily recognizable, these offences often seem remote, complex or obscure and, as a result, have tended to attract a somewhat more ambivalent response from law-enforcement agencies and academic analysts. By focusing on the parallels between legitimate and illegitimate dealings within a competitive and free-market economy, Mary Langan reveals not only the extent of corporate crime, but also limitations of the law, means of detection and punishment in bringing the economically powerful to 'justice'.

Chapter 7 continues to address questions of power and crime, but focuses on issues of political violence, terrorism and crimes of the state. Eugene McLaughlin confronts the many issues of why, when and how certain political movements and nation-states come to be defined as 'terrorist', whilst others seem able to wield a monopoly of violence with impunity. Again, such questions force us to move beyond traditional criminological agendas and into a world occupied by human rights violations, war crimes, torture, genocide and illegal arms dealings. Such 'political' crimes clearly have potentially more damaging social consequences than those behaviours that are commonly considered to be 'criminal', yet rarely (if ever) do they enter public debate as part of the 'problem of crime'. This absence once more underlines the limitations of legal definitions of crime and the remit of the criminal law.

By focusing on issues of how the 'problem of crime' is constructed in public, political and academic discourses, and by revealing the significant absences in those discourses, all the chapters in this book are designed to illustrate how the concept of 'crime' is not as simple as we might be led to believe. The identification and definition of only a selection of social problems, harms and injuries as 'criminal' alerts us to the partial and politically contested nature of the concept. It also alerts us to the proposition that questions of crime can never be divorced from questions of social order. Asking how that social order is structured and how its economic, moral and political interests are protected, will tell us more about what constitutes 'crime' than any simple examination of the characteristics of 'known offenders'.

John Muncie and Eugene McLaughlin
August 1995

Chapter 1
The Construction and Deconstruction of Crime

by John Muncie

Contents

1 Introduction

Crime appears as a constant source of social concern. Escalating crime rates, fear of violence, the threat of public disorder, rioting, household burglary, children out of control, terrorist bombings, football hooligans and mindless vandals are but a few of the enduring images that characterize a society that 'apparently' is drifting further and further into lawlessness. Even if we have no direct experience of crime – as offender, victim or criminal justice practitioner – we are continually reminded of its extent and seriousness. In the late twentieth century, 'law and order' has come to occupy a central position on the agendas of all major political parties in the UK. In political rhetoric, crime is a key signifier of family and national decline: a manifestation of some deeper social and moral malaise. The topic of crime also remains a defining characteristic of what is considered 'news' and newsworthy. All sections of the media rely on crime to fill their news bulletins, documentaries and column inches. Crime, too, is also a constant source of fascination. Police, detective and crime stories are part of the staple diet of film making and television programming and a recurring element of everyday conversation. Indeed, in many ways law enforcement and criminality lie at the very heart of popular culture. It is perhaps unsurprising, then, that crime, law and order have been consistently ranked high in public opinion polls listing the most crucial matters of concern 'facing Britain today' (usually they appear second only to unemployment as *the* major public concern).

But how far are such concerns and preoccupations warranted? Is society on the verge of imminent collapse? Are we becoming less and less law-abiding? Such questions are usually translated into the perennial obsession with the two interrelated issues of what causes crime and what can be done about it. In the popular imagination the topic of crime appears as unfathomable as the weather. Everyone has an opinion but no-one seems to be able to do much about it. For example, low IQ, illegitimacy, lone parenting, television, unemployment, poverty, affluence, lenient courts, drugs, homelessness, recession, and so on, have all been cited as causes of crime; at the same time, hanging, birching, flogging, segregation, imprisonment, more policing (public and private), community service, rehabilitative treatments, better parenting, improved social amenities, full employment, and so on, have all been cited as its remedy. This list of contradictory claims immediately alerts us to some of the complexities and contestations that are intrinsic to the study of crime. However, the obsession with causes and solutions offers a peculiarly partial and short-sighted way of entering into the debate. It assumes that we all know what crime is. Moreover, such 'incessant chatter' is fuelled by a taken-for-granted knowledge that crime is not only a major social problem, but also that it is one of continually growing proportions.

This chapter presents a number of ways in which the 'problem of crime' can be subjected to social scientific inquiry. In particular it asks:

- What is crime? Which forms of behaviour are (or can be) considered criminal and which not?

- How extensive is crime? How can it be measured? How reliable are statistical indices?

- How serious is crime? From where do notions of seriousness emanate?

To ask such questions demands a certain critical distancing from a subject matter which retains the power to evoke highly charged and emotional responses. It requires that we subject the concept of crime to a series of deconstructions. This process can be summarized as:

deconstruction

- Breaking down the concept of 'the problem of crime' into its various constituent elements.

- Revealing the internal contradictions and inconsistencies of those elements.

- Undoing 'common-sense' assumptions and resituating them as but one element in hierarchies of explanation.

- Acknowledging the wide range of interpretations that can legitimately lay claim to the crime debate.

- Recognizing that the problem of crime defies theoretical resolution and is likely to remain a matter of continual dispute and contestation.

Finally, our intention is not to pursue such deconstruction to the extent that we are incapable of saying anything meaningful about the 'crime problem'; neither is the chapter designed to provide definitive and incontestable answers to the numerous questions raised. Rather, its aim is to *reconstruct* the parameters within which a more reasoned and informed assessment of 'the crime problem' can be gained.

2 What is crime?: competing definitions

What is crime? *The Oxford English Dictionary* states that crime is:

crime

> An act punishable by law, as being forbidden by statute or injurious to the public welfare. ... An evil or injurious act; an offence, a sin; *esp.* of a grave character.

At first sight such a definition appears straightforward and uncontroversial. A crime is an illegal act. However, on closer examination things are not so simple. Dictionary definitions neatly avoid complex issues of interpretation by conflating a number of competing meanings. Does crime refer to particular acts and behaviours or to their legal sanction? Is it simply the existence of law that creates crime? What counts as 'injurious', 'sinful' or 'evil'? Who deems some acts to be sinful and evil and others not? Are moral and legal codes inseparable? Are they reflective of any widely held consensus of opinion of the constitution of unlawful activity? Similarly, we can ask what is meant by a 'grave' offence. Grave to whom? Are all crimes grave, or is there some sliding scale of gravity? Finally, is what counts as crime universal and unchanging, or do societies at different historical moments require different kinds of law which in turn create new categories of crime?

In short, dictionary definitions pose questions rather than provide answers. To appreciate fully the complexities of the question, What is crime?, we need to broaden our enquiry to include some understanding of criminal law, social mores and social order.

2.1 Crime as criminal law violation

The most common and frequently applied definition of crime is that which links it to substantive criminal law. In other words, an act is only a crime when it violates the prevailing legal code of the jurisdiction in which it occurs. Michael and Adler are thus able to argue that the most precise and least ambiguous definition of crime is: 'behaviour which is prohibited by the criminal code' (Michael and Adler, 1933, p.5) **[DEFINITION 1]**. Similarly, Williams re-emphasizes the legal foundation of crime by arguing that: 'it is essential that one never forgets that no matter how immoral, reprehensible, damaging or dangerous an act is, it is not a crime unless it is made such by the authorities of the State – the legislature and, at least through interpretation, the judges' (Williams, 1994, p.11).

This logic was taken to its extreme by Tappan's argument that: 'Only those are criminals who have been adjudicated as such by the courts. Crime is an intentional act in violation of the criminal law (statutory and case law), committed without defence or excuse and penalized by the state as a felony or misdemeanor' (Tappan, 1947, p.100) **[DEFINITION 2]**. This black letter law approach – that the application of a legal sanction through court processes and practices must be pursued before a crime can be formally established to have occurred – maintains that no act can be considered criminal before a court has meted out some penalty.

black letter law

Again, this appears clear-cut and uncontroversial, but two important consequences flow from such formulations. First, there would be no crime without criminal law. No behaviour can be considered criminal unless a formal sanction exists to prohibit it. Thus Michael and Adler can logically contend that: 'if crime is merely an instance of conduct which is proscribed by the criminal code, it follows that the criminal law is the formal cause of crime' (Michael and Adler, 1933, p.5). Second, there would be no crime until an offender is caught, tried, convicted and punished. No behaviour or individual can be considered criminal until formally decided upon by the criminal justice system.

As a result, Sutherland and Cressey proposed a definition of crime which (at least up to the 1960s) was adopted by most social scientists and legal scholars:

> Criminal behaviour is behaviour in violation of the criminal law ... it is not a crime unless it is prohibited by the criminal law. The criminal law, in turn, is defined conventionally as a body of specific rules regarding human conduct which have been promulgated by political authority, which apply uniformly to all members of the classes to which the rules refer and which are enforced by punishment administered by the state.
>
> (Sutherland and Cressey, 1970, p.4) **[DEFINITION 3]**

Following this chain of argument, Hartjen (1978, p.4) concludes that at least five conditions must be met before an act can be legally defined as a crime:

1 An act must take place that involves harm inflicted on someone by the actor.

2 The act must be legally prohibited at the time it is committed.

3 The perpetrator must have criminal intent (*mens rea*).

4 There must be a causal relationship between the voluntary misconduct and the resultant harm.

5   There must be some legally prescribed punishment for committal of the
     act.

What this means, of course, is that we can only understand crime by
identifying the distinctive procedural rules of evidence, burdens and
standards of proof and particular forms of trial established within criminal
law. Yet the argument is circular: criminal law and court procedures claim to
respond to crime, yet crime can only be defined by looking to the criminal
law itself. Lacey *et al.* suggest that, to break out of this impasse and to move
towards a more adequate answer to the apparently straightforward question,
What is crime?: 'we must enter upon some broader reflection about how our
society comes to define "deviance"; how it comes to be decided which
deviance calls for a *legal* response; and what determines that legal response
as a criminal as opposed to, or as well as, a civil response' (Lacey *et al.*, 1990,
pp.2–3).

   Asking such questions immediately moves us away from the traditional
assumptions that criminal law constitutes some unitary and discrete category,
divorced from questions of social interaction and social order. Rather, they
lead inevitably to considerations of the political role of criminal law and to a
different set of questions 'about who has the *power* to define criminal
deviance and about the ways in which the legal definition of certain
behaviours as criminal operates as an "objective" depoliticized construction
of those behaviours as deviant' (Lacey *et al.*, 1990, p.7).

   In essence, formal legally based definitions tend to remove law (and
thus crime) from the social, political and economic terrain. Moreover,
because the social creation of criminal law is not subject to any critical
scrutiny it remains assumed (as in Definition 3) that it is applied equally to all
and thus commands and reflects the common assent of the majority. In short,
it is predicated upon the assumption that criminal law is an expression of
widespread public sentiment; that it is a natural outcome of people's views in
general; and that it simply reflects a basic *consensus* on matters of right and
wrong held by most, if not all, members of society.

   We can identify a number of other issues and consequences which flow
from legally based definitions:

1   An act can only be considered a 'crime' once identified by law – thus
     criminals can only be identified once processed and convicted by the
     courts. But not all of those who break criminal laws are caught and
     convicted and many acts that could be considered 'criminal' are rarely
     prosecuted. The study of criminal behaviour is thus severely hampered,
     and may be particularly one-dimensional, if restricted only to those
     persons who are convicted of offences.

2   The approach neglects the basic issues of *why* and *how* some acts are
     legislated as criminal, while others may remain subject only to informal
     control or rebuke.

3   It also tends to suggest a basic continuity in what counts as crime (or at
     least rarely dwells on questions of socio-historical specificity). Yet, quite
     clearly, criminal laws are never static or permanent features of any
     society. For example, customary practices in England, such as poaching
     game, only became criminalized through the convergence of new class
     and power interests in the eighteenth century. Equally, the consumption
     of alcohol in the USA was deemed criminal in the days of prohibition
     between 1920 and 1932. Now it is considered a legal and respectable

social activity. Domestic violence, far from being viewed legally as criminal (or even deviant), has been considered quite legitimate through much of Western history. For example, it was not until 1991 that England was brought into line with France, Sweden, the former USSR, Norway, Denmark, Poland and most US and Australian states by the overturning of a 255-year-old ruling which had given husbands immunity from marital rape. Similarly, what counts legally as crime varies from one jurisdiction to another, even in similar historical periods. An obvious example is that, whilst in England and Wales a person cannot be considered criminally responsible for their actions before the age of 10, in Scotland such responsibility begins at the age of 8. In France the age of criminal responsibility is 13; in Germany 14 and in Spain 16. In these examples crime appears not as a fixed object, the same for all societies and for all times. Rather, it is a historically and socially specific concept.

4   A black letter law approach tends to refer only to the formal constitution and enactment of law and underplays the variable ways in which it is enforced. It divorces the criminal process from its social context, masking the ways in which the law is not simply applied by the courts, but is actively made and interpreted by key court personnel (for example, in plea bargaining, the quality of legal representation, judicial discretion). In turn, this may have important consequences for what kinds of behaviour should be regarded as truly criminal. Are theft and violence more serious than violations of health and safety codes in the work place? Both may be dealt with by the criminal law, but the tendency to view the former as 'real crime' and the latter as 'regulatory offences' may only lead us (unjustifiably?) to exclude these latter behaviours from our legitimate subject matter.

ACTIVITY 1.1

Consider the following behaviours:

1	taking the life of another	7	adultery
2	stealing for personal gain	8	mugging
3	incest	9	racial violence
4	witchcraft	10	pollution of the environment
5	blasphemy	11	vagrancy and begging
6	rape	12	trespass

Now ask yourself:

(a) Which do you think are criminal and which not?
(b) Which are criminal in law?

COMMENT

As behaviours, some or all of these may be considered to be heinous and abhorrent. Most have at one time attracted the severest of penalties, including the death sentence. But equally, each has at some time also been considered quite legitimate. For example, until relatively recently, slavery, non-consensual intercourse within marriage and all forms of execution have received official approval. Similarly, causing the death of another may be particularly odious, but is almost always viewed as justifiable when practised as a part of warfare and 'in defence of the nation'. In the USA, capital punishment was reinstated by the supreme court in 1976. Since then there have been over 300 state-sponsored executions. To add to the confusion, 'mugging' may be popularly considered 'criminal', but is an American media-inspired term for street robbery and not a specific legal offence. Technically, it is still treason and a capital offence in the UK to commit adultery with a sovereign, the heir to the throne and some senior royals (though prosecution is no longer used!). In England, the offence of witchcraft, applied almost exclusively to women and punishable by death, was not repealed until 1736. Begging remains an offence under the 1824 Vagrancy Act. Blasphemy is still forbidden at common law, though restricted to attacks on Christianity – the most recent prosecution was in 1977. At the time of writing, in England racially motivated violence is not a specific offence. On the other hand, mass trespass was made a criminal offence by the 1994 Criminal Justice and Public Order Act.

As Wilkins warns: 'there are no absolute standards. At some time or another, some form of society or another has defined almost all forms of behaviour that we now call "criminal" as desirable for the functioning of that form of society' (Wilkins, 1964, p.46). If there are no clear and unambiguous rules to decide which actions should be subject to legal sanction, can it be argued that any consensus exists in society? Can the law and legal statutes be relied upon to reveal any such consensus?

Crime and law as contested categories: civil rights campaigners mark the enactment of the 1994 Criminal Justice and Public Order Act

2.2 Crime as norm infraction

A black letter law definition of crime has its logic in expediency, since no behaviour can be considered illegal unless a specific statute exists to define it as such. However, some sociologists have argued that, because criminal laws change over time and between different societies, a more 'scientific' and reliable index is needed to delineate the 'criminal' from the 'non-criminal'. For example, Sellin (1938) argued that the concept of crime should be extended beyond legal violations to violations of moral and social codes. He contended that every society has its own standards of behaviour or 'conduct norms', but that these standards may not necessarily all be reflected in law. In this context, terms such as 'deviance', 'non-conformity' and 'anti-social conduct' are preferred to that of 'crime', because the latter is incapable of encompassing all acts of wrong-doing. Accordingly, such diverse activities as income tax avoidance, environmental pollution, juvenile delinquency, insider trading and sexual promiscuity may be considered legitimate topics for criminological inquiry. Of key significance is that this 'normative' approach does not require any reference to the criminal law at all. As Sellin (1938, p.20) argued, if the study of crime is to attain an objective and scientific status it should not allow itself to be restricted to the terms and boundaries of inquiry established by legislators. However, whilst Sellin argued that a universal definition of 'crime' depended on isolating conduct norms that are invariable across all cultural groups, he failed to specify what such universal conduct norms might be. Indeed, given the diversity of human behaviours, moralities and social organizations, it is highly unlikely that any such 'universals' can be found, either inside or outside of the law (Hagan, 1985, p.45).

deviance A similar problem arises with the concept of 'deviance'. Although clearly a social, rather than a legal, category, it can suffer from an extreme cultural relativism and is inextricably related to difficulties in establishing what is 'normal'. As Simmons (1969, p.3) found in public responses to the question, Who's deviant?, the concept can be as readily applied to Christians, pacifists, divorcees, 'know-it-all' professors and the president of the United States, as it can to criminals and law-breakers. Nevertheless, the limitations of legal definitions remain apparent. Sutherland's (1949) research into unethical practices among businessmen and corporate managers in the USA found that, despite their serious and injurious nature, they were often considered non-criminal: as violations of civil, rather than criminal law. As a result, he argued that crime should be defined not on the basis of criminal law, but on the more abstract notions of 'social injury', and 'social harm'. Thus:

> The essential characteristic of crime is that it is behaviour which is prohibited by the state as an *injury* to the state ... The two abstract criteria ... as necessary elements in a definition of crime are legal descriptions of an act as *socially harmful* and legal provision of a penalty for the act.

(Sutherland, 1949, p.31, emphasis added) **[DEFINITION 4]**

Sutherland implied that some moral criteria of social injury must be applied before any comprehensive definition of crime can be formulated. However, whether morality has any more an objective status than law also remains disputed. Just as significantly, such a definition is limiting because it remains tied to whatever a particular political regime and its state practices have deemed to be socially injurious. The Schwendingers thus expand the list of potentially injurious practices to include the systematic violation of basic human rights. Working within a theoretical tradition which maintains that capitalist and imperialist social orders (and their state practices) contain their own criminogenic tendencies, they are able to promote a definition of crime based on a conception of the denial of basic fundamental human rights:

> The abrogation of these rights certainly limits the individual's chance to fulfil himself in many spheres of life. It can be stated that individuals who deny these rights to others are criminal. Likewise social relationships and social systems which regularly cause the abrogation of these rights are also criminal. If the terms imperialism, racism, sexism and poverty are abbreviated signs for theories of social relationships or social systems which cause the systematic abrogation of basic rights, then imperialism, racism, sexism and poverty can be called crimes.
>
> (Schwendinger and Schwendinger, 1970, p.148) **[DEFINITION 5]**

The Schwendingers' formulation is important in so far as it warns us that most traditional concepts of crime – whether legally, socially or morally based – tend to assume the existence of some social consensus. Nevertheless, it maintains that, at least prescriptively, it is possible to reach an objective definition of the concept. It also shares an assumption that 'crime' is to be discovered in certain *behaviours* or *acts*, whether of individuals or of institutions. There is, however, no intrinsic reason why any reference to a particular behaviour or act should be included in a definition at all.

2.3 Crime as social construct

A vast array of behaviours have been (or can be) deemed 'deviant' or 'criminal' because they violate legal, normative or human rights prescriptions. But there is no common behavioural demoninator which ties all of these acts together. Propositions, such as society is based upon a moral consensus or that the criminal law is merely a reflection of that consensus, also remain contentious. An interactionist school of sociology, for example, argues that there is no underlying or enduring consensus in society. Rather, the social order consists of a plurality of social groups each acting in accordance with its own interpretations of reality. Such diversity is as likely to produce conflict as much as consensus. Interpretations of reality are learnt through the ways in which people *perceive* and *react*, either positively or negatively, to the various behaviours of others. Thus, with respect to crime, an interactionist position would argue that defining crime with reference to legal or norm-violating *actions* is seriously limited. Rather, crime is viewed as a consequence of social interaction: that is, as a result of a *negotiated process* that involves the rule-violator, the police, the courts, lawyers and the law-makers who define a person's behaviour as criminal. Behaviour may be *labelled* criminal, but it is not this behaviour in itself that constitutes crime. Rather, behaviour is *criminalized* by a process of social perception and reaction as applied and interpreted by agents of the law. Crime exists only when the label and the law are successfully applied to an individual's behaviour. It is not what people do, but how they are perceived and evaluated by others, that constitutes crime. Whereas law-violation approaches argue that the existence of 'crime' depends on the prior existence of criminal law, interactionism logically contends that, without the *enforcement and enactment* of criminal law (or social reaction to certain

social
construction

behaviours), there would be no crime. As Ditton put it: 'the reaction is constitutive of the criminal (or deviant) act. In fact the reaction *is* the "commission of the act"' (Ditton, 1979, p.20). Just as criminal law is constructed within society, then crime too is a *social construction* (Hester and Eglin, 1992). In this sense society creates crime because it (or at least powerful sections within it) makes the rules, the infraction of which constitutes crime. As Becker explains, the social construct argument is not so much concerned with locating the causes of crime and deviance in social factors or social situations, but in establishing that:

> Social groups create deviance by making the rules whose infraction constitutes deviance, and by applying those rules to particular people and labelling them as outsiders. From this point of view deviance is not a quality of the act a person commits, but rather a consequence of the application by others of rules and sanctions to an 'offender'. The deviant is one to whom that label has been successfully applied; deviant behaviour is behaviour that people so label.

(Becker, 1963, p.9) [DEFINITION 6]

Thus 'crime' has no universal or objective existence, but is relative to the subjective contingencies of social and historical circumstance. This in turn opens up and expands the range of criminological inquiry away from behavioural questions – Why did they do it? – and towards definitional issues – Why is that rule there? Who created it? In whose interests? How is it enforced? What are the consequences of this enforcement? (Cohen, 1973a, p.623). It implies that we will only come to understand why an action is regarded as criminal by examining *processes* of rule creation *and* law enforcement. We will not discover 'crime' simply by looking at behaviours, for there is nothing intrinsic to any behaviour which makes it criminal. We will not discover 'crime' simply by looking at violations of legal statutes, for they are only one element of rule-breaking, and in themselves are subject to social perception and interpretation. Similarly, asking the perennial question: What makes some people commit crime? is short-sighted because there cannot be specific kinds of motivation to engage in crime if there are no categories of activities which are inherently criminal (Sharrock, 1984, p.99). In this way the interactionist approach denies that criminality is driven by some peculiar motivation or that criminals are a species apart. Rather, criminality is *ordinary*, *natural* and *widespread* and thus requires no different explanation from that which might be attached to any everyday activity. However, what does require explanation is the complex process by which agencies of social control are able to realize the public identification of *certain* people as criminal; how social reaction and labelling are able to produce and reproduce a *recognizable* criminal population. A corollary of this, of course, is that the more such labels are applied and enforced, then the greater the chance that more 'crime' will be discovered.

2.4 Crime as ideological censure

Conflict-based analyses of the social order have developed the basic premise of interactionism (that crime only exists through the labelling of certain behaviours as such) by arguing that it is essential to ground such generalities in specific relations of power and domination. It is not simply a question of any number of interest groups acting in competition with each other (as in the interactionist version), but of the systematic and consistent empowerment of some groups to the detriment of others. Some Marxist conceptions would, for example, emphasize class divisions in which those who own and control the means of production are in a position to assert their economic and political power by using the law to protect their own interests. Some feminist conceptions would, in contrast, emphasize gender divisions and the discriminatory implications of a patriarchal monopoly of political, economic and legal power. Each stresses the political nature of crime. Law supplies to some people both the means *and the authority* to criminalize the behaviour of others.

political nature of crime

Crime can also be viewed as political in the sense that it involves and requires the deployment of the *power* to translate legal rules into action, to impose one's will on others and to enforce one's definition of another's behaviour as illegal. The Schwendingers' (1970) argument, that current practices of law creation and enforcement are selective and partial, is underlined by Cohen's insistence that: 'damage, victimisation, exploitation, theft and destruction when carried out by the powerful are not only not punished, but are not called "crime"' (Cohen, 1973a, p.624). Conflict-based conceptions of crime thus tend to question the consensus assumptions of legal, behavioural and state definitions because these latter act to confine the criminologist to the established order and to official versions of reality. Characteristically, the concept of 'crime' is viewed not as value free, but as a highly politicized state-constructed category. It has no 'objective' reality other than in the ways in which the state construes 'criminality' for its own ends. Rather, if the signifier of 'crime' is to be retained, it should be equally applied not only to 'ordinary crime' or behaviours that are not typically prosecuted (such as tax avoidance, environmental pollution and government corruption), but also to crimes of the state and mass political killings (such as the Holocaust, the genocide of the East Timorese and the 'ethnic cleansing' in Bosnia). Such an approach significantly opens up what have been long-neglected topics for criminological investigation (**Cohen, 1993**). By doing so, the *ideological* nature of what constitutes 'crime' can be revealed. For example, until relatively recently, the activities of the African National Congress (ANC) in South Africa or the Palestine Liberation Organization (PLO) in the Middle East were defined as criminal by many Western jurisdictions. Yet without such 'criminality' it is unlikely that the repressive (and equally 'criminal'?) policies of apartheid and armed occupation would have come to be internationally recognized. In both cases this broad criminological agenda would point out how the opposing terms 'terrorist' and 'freedom-fighter' illustrate how notions of 'crime' can also be politically informed and tied to particular political ideologies (this is discussed further in Chapter 7).

In developing a Marxist theory of crime and criminal law, **Chambliss (1975, p.152)** argues that acts are defined as criminal only when it is in the interest of the ruling class to define them as such; and that crime is a reality which exists only as it is created by those in society whose interests are served by its presence. In capitalist societies 'crime' performs the vital function of diverting the lower classes' attention away from the condition and source of their exploitation and allows the bourgeoisie to expand penal law in an effort to coerce the proletariat into submission. Behaviours are criminalized in order to maintain political control and to counter any perceived threat to the legitimacy of ruling-class rule (the clearest examples of such a process being public order offences and trade union legislation):

> Criminality is simply *not* something that people have or don't have; crime is not something some people do and others don't. Crime is a matter of who can pin the label on whom, and underlying this socio-political process is the structure of social relations determined by the political economy.

(Chambliss, 1975, p.165) [DEFINITION 7]

social censure

Sumner (1990) presents a development of this line of argument which continues to recognize how criminal law (and thus crime) can be a crucial instrument of class power, but also argues that it retains a relatively autonomous character which cannot be simply reduced to class relations and class conflict. He prefers to treat crime and deviance as matters of moral and political judgement – as *social censures* rooted in particular ideologies. The concept of crime, then, is neither a behavioural nor a legal category, but an expression of particular cultural and political configurations. Neither is 'crime' simply a label, but a generic term to describe a series of 'negative ideological categories with specific historical applications ... categories of denunciation or abuse lodged within very complex, historically loaded practical conflicts and moral debates ... these negative categories of moral ideology are social censures' (Sumner, 1990, pp.26, 28) **[DEFINITION 8]**.

2.5   Crime as historical invention

Troublesome behaviours have been defined as 'crimes' (whether or not they are recognized in law) for so long that the concept is routinely applied in condemnations of the 'unwanted' and the 'undesirable'. Yet crime is a fairly recent method of social disapproval. If 'crime' is intrinsically tied to 'criminal law', as various definitions assume, then we can only discover the origins of crime in the development of criminal law. Until the eighteenth century, the nation-states emerging in Europe lacked sufficient resources to invest in the wholesale formulation and enforcement of such law. Many behaviours that are now deemed criminal were dealt with by civil law and religion. In other words, there was less 'crime' and more 'sin', 'civil wrongs' and 'private disputes'. The terms in which crime might be construed as a problem had not yet been formed (Chapter 3 examines this further).

However, this is not to argue that the criminal law did not exist. Rather, it was in a slow process of development until its acceleration in the eighteenth century, as particular groups sought to protect their own interests and property. As Hall (1952, p.34) notes, it was not until then that such crimes as receiving stolen property, obtaining goods by false pretences and embezzlement were first legally recognized. For example, in 1799 a bank teller received a £100 deposit, credited it to the customer's account, but then put the money in his own pocket. However, he could not be found guilty of any crime, because he had not stolen the money from the bank (they had never possessed it) and he had not stolen from the customer (because the money was handed over freely). As a result of this case the British parliament passed the first embezzlement statute.

Many explanations of the origins of criminal law have illustrated such a relationship between economic power and the forging of new legislation suited to protect the unique interests of dominant groups. For example,

Chambliss (1964) has demonstrated how vagrancy laws owe their origins to economic circumstance and class power. Originating from 1349, these laws stipulated that it was a crime to give alms to the unemployed. Such a measure was instigated because of a chronic shortage of labour experienced by landowners following the Black Death of 1348. The common custom of migratory and free labour was criminalized in order to ensure an abundant supply of cheap labour. Agricultural labourers could no longer move from county to county to seek higher wages. These laws fell into disuse once the labour market was full, but were revived in 1530 to protect the interests of a new mercantile class. The emphasis shifted to controlling the movement of 'rogues' and 'vagabonds' in order to reduce the risk of robberies of commercial goods whilst in transit. In 1743, the type of person liable for prosecution was extended to all those 'not giving good account of themselves'. At this time, such legislation was designed to serve the interests of powerful interest groups who needed a stable and static workforce to fill the fields and the emergent factories.

Hall's (1952) study of the 1473 Theft Act again demonstrated the role of economic power in the criminalization of customary or common-law practices. Prior to the Act a necessary element of theft was trespass. Thus persons hired to transport goods who subsequently absconded with such goods could not be legally charged. The protection of property by trust seemed to have been satisfactory during the Middle Ages when the economy was dominated by feudalism and commercial exchange through barter. With the development of merchant trading companies in the fifteenth century and the break-up of feudal estates by a mercantile and commercial complex, the emerging institutions required a new rule. The self-interest of an economically empowered minority was thus able to dictate the rewriting of theft law.

Galliher's (1989, p.151) examination of the history of American colonies also supports the contention that powerful groups create law to protect their own interests. He notes how, originally, the concept of crime was closely associated with a Puritan concept of sin. Thus court records up to the 1800s reveal that 'crime', if used at all, referred to personal depravity and that most prosecutions were for fornication, violation of the Sabbath and adultery. Offenders were found in all social classes. However, by the nineteenth century concern shifted from the preservation of morality to the protection of property which necessitated the formulation of precise criminal laws. New forms of private land ownership, economic depression and unemployment accelerated the rate of convictions for property offences. Predictably, criminal records began to show that offenders were clustered amongst the urban poor (as do records today). The function of law in these instances appears to be the protection of the interests of property owners and the criminalization of non-owners. Criminal law is dictated by particular economic and political interests.

From such analyses 'crime' has been defined as: 'human conduct that is created by authorised agents in a politically organised society' and used to describe: 'behaviours that conflict with the interests of the segments of the society that have the power to shape public policy' (Quinney, 1970, pp.15–16) **[DEFINITION 9]**. The identification and delineation of 'crime' is thus an inherently political process. Law (and thus crime) is created and applied by those who have the power to translate their interests into public

criminalization

17

policy. Criminal law is coercive and partial, its political neutrality a myth. Developing this line of argument, De Haan is able to claim that 'crime' is an ideological concept which 'serves to maintain political power relations; justifies inequality and serves to distract public attention from more serious problems and injustices' (**De Haan, 1991, p.207**) **[DEFINITION 10]**. In a similar vein, the professional historian, E.P. Thompson (1975, p.194), has claimed that 'crime' is a disabling and moralistic category. To accept the definitions of those who own property and control the state can only hinder accurate historical research and produce pre-given moral interpretations.

ACTIVITY 1.2

The preceding text has highlighted ten definitions of 'crime'. Some of these share the same assumptions about the inseparability of crime and law. Others place more emphasis on social categories such as deviance, or move beyond behavioural issues to focus almost entirely on questions of definition. Go back through section 2, identify what these are and make some notes on each. The key questions to keep in mind are:

1   Does the definition assume a particular model of society? Is that society deemed consensual, pluralist or conflictual?
2   Can 'crime' be delineated through some value-free means and measures? Is it forever relative to social and historical circumstance?
3   What is the relationship between what can be considered as 'crime' and criminal law?
4   What is the relationship between criminal law and social orders?
5   What are the advantages and limitations of viewing 'crime' as (a) a legal concept; (b) a behavioural concept; or (c) a socio-politically constructed concept?

COMMENT

Definitions of crime are neither right nor wrong: they do, however, point out the elusive and the essentially contested nature of our subject matter. Definitions based on criminal law prescriptions appear to have some advantages in that they are able to provide some objective criteria by which 'crime' can be reliably recognized. 'Crime' is whatever the law deems to be illegal at particular times and in particular jurisdictions. Such a definition does, however, tie us to state-generated notions of law-breaking. It narrows our attention to those formulations enshrined in legal statutes. It assumes a greater objectivity but overlooks the fact that 'the law' itself is deeply problematic: as a site of struggle, dispute, construction and contestation in its own right. It systematically excludes notions of deviance, anti-social conduct, injustices and rule-breaking. We lose sight of how and why it is only *certain* behaviours that come to be considered deviant and how and why it is only *some* deviant practices that are ultimately subject to criminal sanction. In short, we lose sight of 'crime' as a forever-shifting concept, as a morally and politically loaded term, or as something constructed through social processes and social censures.

social order   Importantly, the various conceptions of crime appear to be generated from competing accounts of the **social order**. If that order is consensual, 'crime' can be defined as the infraction of legal, moral or conduct norms. When the social order is considered pluralist or conflict-based, 'crime' refers not to particular behaviours, but to the social and political processes whereby those actions are subjected to criminalization. Accordingly, it can be argued that whatever we consider 'crime' to be will rest on how we consider 'order' to be conceived and achieved. Indeed, this has led some to argue that crime only comes to be a problem when order is a problem. Our key problematic then may not be 'crime', but the 'struggle around order and the products it produces among which are crime and criminal justice' (Shearing, 1989, p.178).

Given the inability to define 'crime' in any consistent or objective fashion, other authors have gone further and argued that the concept should be abandoned once and for all. Crimes should be recognized as 'moral–political judgements' and as 'social censures rooted in ideological formations' (Sumner, 1990, p.25). Given the vast diversity of behaviours or acts that have been (or can be) considered 'criminal', Hulsman is also in favour of rejecting the concept. He argues that: 'crime has no ontological reality. Crime is not the *object* but the *product* of criminal policy' (**Hulsman, 1986, p.71**). Thus for De Haan what is required is not a better definition, but a more powerful critique of crime: 'this is not to deny that there are all sorts of unfortunate events, more or less serious troubles or conflicts which can result in suffering, harm or damage ... these troubles are to be taken seriously but not as "crimes" and ... not to be dealt with by means of criminal law' (**De Haan, 1991, p.208**). In these formulations the signifiers of 'crime' and 'criminal law' are retained only to raise a much broader set of issues concerned with the nature of the social order and the role that law plays in processes of criminalization, power, control, domination and resistance.

3 How much crime?: statistical measures

The most widely used and commonly accepted measures of the extent of crime are the rates recorded by police, prison and court statistics. Collectively, they paint the following picture:

- The overall crime rate in England and Wales, with the exception of small decreases in the early 1950s and mid 1990s, has increased every year since elementary records were first kept in the mid nineteenth century (see Figure 1.1).

- The greatest increase occurred in the 1980s. In 1979 notifiable offences recorded by the police (excluding some minor offences) stood at 2.4 million, whereas by 1992 the figure was 5.4 million.

- Half of all offences are for theft and handling stolen goods. Crimes against property make up the vast majority of offences. Crimes against the person account for some 5 per cent of all offences (see Figure 1.2).

- In 1989, 83 per cent of known offenders were male, a figure virtually unchanged from a decade earlier. Crime is predominantly a male activity.

- In England the peak age for offending is 18 for males and 15 for females. In Scotland the peak age for both sexes is 18; in Northern Ireland 19 and 20 respectively.

- A third of all men born in the early 1950s had a conviction by the age of 31.

- In 1971 the police clear-up rate in England was 45 per cent. By 1980 it had fallen to 36 per cent and to 25 per cent in 1992. Clear-up rates for 1992 in Scotland and Northern Ireland were over 30 per cent.

- Young men, people from minority ethnic backgrounds and those from unskilled occupations are the most likely to make up the prison population. Women account for some 4 per cent of the total average daily prison population; people from minority ethnic groups account for some 18 per cent.

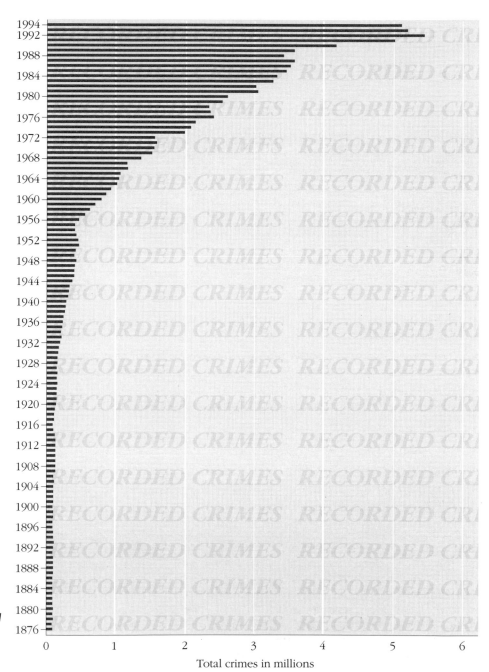

Figure 1.1 Crimes recorded by the police, England and Wales, 1876–1994. (Excludes criminal damage of £20 and under) (Source: based on Home Office, 1993, p.8; 1995)

Total crimes in millions

- Afro-Caribbeans make up some 1 per cent of the national population, but some 11 per cent of the prison population.

- The UK has the highest rate of imprisonment in Europe. On the basis of numbers of prisoners per 100,000 population, in 1991 Northern Ireland recorded 105.7, Scotland 95.2, England 91.3, Germany 78.8 and Holland 44.4. Over 70 per cent of the Northern Ireland rate was believed attributable to politically inspired offences.

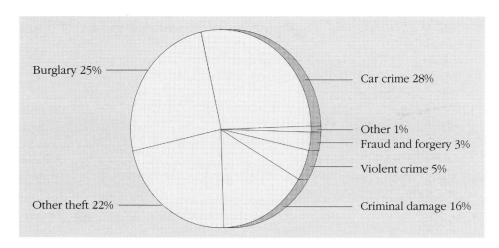

Figure 1.2 Crime breakdown, April 1993 to March 1994 (Source: Guardian Education, 11 October 1994, p.11)

Raw figures such as these (derived from Home Office, 1991, 1992, 1993; Council of Europe, 1992; Northern Ireland Office, 1993) are often used to make the following assumptions:

- Crime is soaring out of control. Moreover, it is a recent (that is, a post-1960) phenomenon.

- The present can be contrasted with a relatively trouble-free past (for example, the 1950s, 1930s, Victorian/Edwardian England).

- Crime is the preserve of young and working-class men in which those from minority ethnic backgrounds are over-represented.

- Their crimes are mainly those of theft and burglary.

- Law-enforcement agencies are losing the fight against crime.

- Falling clear-up rates suggest police inability to stem the tide.

- Rising crime rates, despite high rates of imprisonment, suggest a failure of prison to rehabilitate or deter.

Such conclusions, however, represent only one possible reading of the crime data. Quinney and Wildeman (1977, p.97) suggest at least three interpretations. First, an orthodox approach to statistical measures would contend that the data reflect a growing wilful and conscious choice of individuals to violate the legal or moral consensus. Official statistics are thus more or less actual measures of the level of offending. The concentration of crime amongst minority ethnic groups and the lower classes reflects their weaker and more tenuous commitment to the social order. Second, an interactionist approach, on the other hand, would argue that, as not all the crimes occurring in a population are reported or recorded, then what is counted as crime merely reflects what, where and when the law-enforcement agencies decide to target. In this respect, crime rates are accurate measures, but only of the activities, priorities and labelling processes of official agencies. Third, a structural conflict approach would present a somewhat different argument: that official statistics do not measure crime as such, but the ability of dominant groups to achieve their rule through the consent or coercion of the 'subordinate'. Escalating crime rates are thus a reflection of a failure to achieve consensus; of increasing social division and inequality; and of an increased willingness on the part of the state to achieve its dominance through criminalization, coercion, oppression, persecution and authoritarianism.

As we shall see below, the official criminal statistics do not provide any straightforward answers to the questions of: How much crime? How many criminals? How many victims? The 'true facts' of crime are probably unknowable. They depend not only on what we define as crime, but also on the *validity* of statistical measures and the range of *interpretations* that can be legitimately made of any figures, no matter how they are produced.

3.1   Criminal statistics as social products

reported and recorded crime

Even if we adopt an orthodox position on statistics, the best that can be said of the official crime statistics for England and Wales, as gathered by the Home Office, is that they do not measure the true extent of crime in society, but rather the extent of *reported and recorded* crime. Although most academic analysts, the media, politicians and the public rely on official statistics as 'hard facts', the first and most paramount 'fact' is that they are both partial and subjectively constructed. There are a number of reasons for this:

1   Crime statistics are based on those crimes reported to and subsequently recorded by the police. However, whilst the police detect some crime themselves, in the main they depend on the general public or victims to bring crime to their notice. But some offences may not be reported because of ignorance that a crime has been committed (for example, tax evasion, computer fraud); there appears to be no victim (for example, certain drugs offences, prostitution, sexual offences between consenting adults, illegal abortion); the victim is powerless (for example, child abuse); ambivalence towards or distrust of the police (for example, certain youth cultures); the offence may be considered trivial (for example, thefts from work, vandalism, minor shoplifting, brawls); the victim may be concerned that the offence will not be taken seriously (for example, some cases of rape); or the victim has no faith that the police will act to protect his or her interests (for example, racial intimidation and harassment). Victim surveys, such as the five British Crime Surveys (BCS) carried out between 1982 and 1994, have suggested that only about a half of known crime is reported. Theft of vehicles and burglaries with loss were generally reported; vandalism, theft from the person and attempted motor vehicle theft were less so. The main reasons given were that victims felt they were not serious enough or that the police would be unable to take any effective action. However, not all unreported crime is trivial. Some involves substantial loss or injury. Comparing survey and police statistics in 1992, it was found that only 48 per cent of violent

incidents and only 40 per cent of robbery and theft from the person were reported (Mayhew and Maung, 1992, p.6). Burglary with loss and auto theft, on the other hand, had an almost 100 per cent rate of reportage.

2   A wide range of personal and social factors are likely to affect both whether an incident is perceived as criminal, and whether the observer then decides to report such an incident to the police. For example, there may be a higher possibility that some acts of vandalism will be viewed as symptomatic of 'high spirits', if carried out by university students (in rag week or at May Balls, for instance), than if a group of working-class youths is involved. Box concludes that: 'an offence was more likely to be reported to the police if the suspect apprehended by the complainant ... was a member of the less privileged section of society; the closer the psychological and social identification of the complainant and the suspect, the less likely the former was to report the offence' (Box, 1981, p.176). Similarly, Stevens and Willis (1979) and Shah and Pease (1992) note that ethnic factors help to determine both the victim's decision to report a crime and the police decision to record it. In particular, they suggest that, in assaults when no injury is afflicted, the incident is more likely to be reported if it was committed by a non-white rather than a white suspect. Such discrepancies once more underline the proposition that measurements of crime rest initially and critically on the extent to which the public perceives and interprets behaviour as 'criminal' (Walker, 1983, p.292).

3   An 'increase in crime' may be due to more crime being reported, rather than to more crime being committed. The 1992 BCS, for instance, explains an increase in the reporting of certain offences (for example, car theft and burglary with loss) from 1981 to 1991 with reference to increases in telephone ownership and wider ownership of house contents and car insurance policies. Discrepancies between survey and police statistics can indeed radically alter our perception of the 'crime problem'. In Bottomley and Pease's (1986, pp.22–3) attempt to account for a nationwide burglary prevention campaign mounted in 1982, they note that, whilst the number of *recorded* burglaries increased by 50 per cent between 1971 and 1981, data from General Household Surveys concluded that there was almost no change. They contend that one reason for this discrepancy may be the increased availability of 'new for old' insurance policies at this time which increased the amounts claimed and also the incentive for fraudulent claiming. Since 1981, burglary, as reported by BCS respondents, has risen broadly in line with recorded crime figures, but similar recorded increases in violent crime and vandalism are not confirmed by the survey data. This may be because the police choose to record some offences as vandalism which the BCS classifies as attempted burglary, or, where there is an option for classification — between, say, wounding and common assault — the police may choose the more serious.

4   Not all offences reported are recorded as such by the police. The amount of resources available to the police and courts is limited and thus subjective and/or administrative decisions are made concerning which crimes to act against. It is only recorded crime which enters the official statistics. As Walker (1983, p.286) notes, although the police have a statutory obligation to record crimes, considerable discretion remains about whether it is considered sufficiently serious to warrant their

attention. Violent disputes between neighbours or members of a family may, for example, be classified as 'domestic – advice given' and the alleged 'offence' not recorded. Similarly, how a recorded offence is classified by the police – as 'theft from a person' or 'robbery', for example – will affect the rate at which certain crimes appear to be committed. Problems inherent in recording, and variations due to local police 'targeting', will also colour our understanding of the extent of particular crimes. Williams (1994, p.49) cites a clear example of these effects. In 1932 London's commissioner of police ruled that cases classified as 'suspected stolen' should be redesignated as either lost property or actually stolen. The result was that recorded thefts increased by over 300 per cent in a year! Similarly, Lea and Young recall how a 108-fold increase in the figures for homosexual importunity in Manchester between 1958 and 1963 had 'a great deal to do with the predilections of the Chief Constable and very little to do with the changing desires of gay men' (Lea and Young, 1984, pp.15–16). The *Criminal Statistics* also provide an inaccurate picture because many crimes such as tax evasion (recorded by the Inland Revenue) and VAT evasion (recorded by Customs and Excise) will only appear in official criminal records if they are subsequently brought to court. As **Box (1983, p.13)** argues, such offences may be more personally and economically damaging than those which make up official depictions of crime, but are generally rendered invisible as the number of eventual prosecutions is low.

5   Changes in law enforcement and in what the law counts as crime also preclude much meaningful discussion over the extent of historical increases and decreases in crime. Legislative changes may mean that existing categories are redefined, thus rendering historical comparison meaningless. Pearson (1983, p.216), for example, notes how successive pieces of legislation governing the treatment of young people in the early twentieth century (for instance, the formation of specific juvenile courts by the 1908 Children Act and the incorporation of welfare-based principles in the 1933 Children and Young Persons Act) encouraged law-enforcement agencies to proceed with a significant number of cases which previously might have been dealt with informally. Increasing the likelihood of bringing young people before the courts, however, also produces a sharp increase in committals, creating the *impression* of successive 'crime waves' and 'crime explosions'. More recently, the use of formal cautions in the 1970s, rather than unregistered cautioning, did not simply divert:

> work away from the courts – as was its intention – but added substantially to the volume of recorded crime and recorded police activity. Among boys under 14 years of age, the increased use of the formal caution is enough to account for the whole of the increase in recorded crime for this age-group during the 1970s.
>
> (Pearson, 1983, p.217)

Similarly, Rohrer notes how some increases in crime can be artificially constructed solely by economic and administrative circumstance:

> Inflation provides a perfect example of one distortion of crime trends. The law is not index linked and so acts of criminal damage, officially defined as damage

exceeding £20 in value, have shot up from 17,000 in 1969 to 124,000 in 1977. Inflation has shifted many thousands of previously trivial incidents of damage into the more serious crime bracket.

(Rohrer, 1982, p.6)

Pearson further elaborates on this process by recording how, after 1977, the distinction between minor and major criminal damage was abandoned in favour of a classification of all as 'known crimes'. This resulted in an apparent doubling of vandalism in one year: 'adding at a single stroke a sixth of a million indictable offences to the criminal records ... or four times the *total* number of criminal convictions in 1900' (Pearson, 1983, pp.217–8).

6   The implications of such analysis are far-reaching. As well as exposing the fallacy of historical comparison, it also undermines any definitive (though widely held) notion that 'things are getting progressively worse' and that 'if we could only recover the past our troubles would be over'. Indeed, in a series of backward glances through English social history, Pearson illustrates how images of a more peaceful and orderly past (against which the present can be unfavourably compared) fail to stand up to close scrutiny. Drawing on the popular idioms of '20 years ago' and 'in my day', he shows how, 20 years before the moral outrage surrounding the 1981 riots, similar fears centred on the lawlessness of the Teddy Boys; in the inter-war years the 'folk devils' were football rowdyism and the demoralizing influence of the American cinema. At the turn of the century the term 'hooligan' emerged as a media description of street gangs in south London, only later to be generically applied to similar gangs such as the Peaky Blinders in Birmingham, the Scuttlers in Manchester and the Redskins in Glasgow. Victorian England, meanwhile, was 'plagued' by the garrotters of the 1860s and the street urchins of the 1840s, as well as numerous instances of riot. All these phenomena attracted the (now familiar) official responses of historical decline, excessive leniency of the law and moral degeneracy, yet each illustrates how understandings of the present are coloured by an idealistic historical romanticism (see Extract 1.1)

7   The deeper we delve into the processes of criminal justice and the more we rely on court and prison statistics, the more we reduce our chances of saying anything straightforward about the nature and extent of crime. Self-evidently, changes in the number of arrests, trials and sentences may not represent actual changes in the amount of crime, but rather changes in the *capacity* of the criminal justice system to process individual cases. Increases or decreases in the number of police, judges, courtrooms and prison places will inevitably affect these statistics: 'There is no doubt about it: more police, more judges and more prisons appear to have a nearly infinite capacity to increase the amount of officially recorded crime' (Galliher, 1989, p.119). This is partly because there is a forever-present unlimited well of unrecorded criminal behaviour which can be tapped when and if the political will and the resources for law enforcement are sufficiently activated. It is also because there exists a huge potential to perceive and redefine actions as 'crimes' as the technological ability to implement forms of mass surveillance increases.

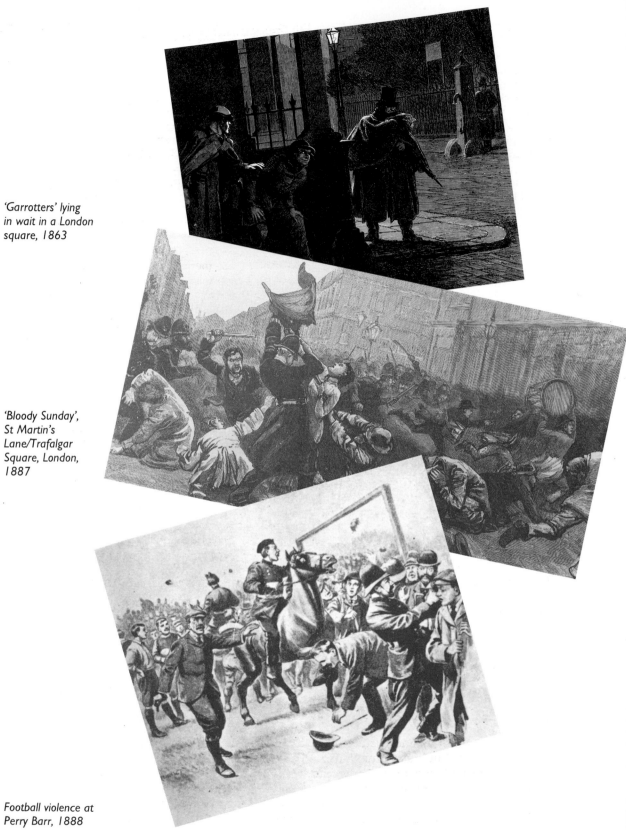

'Garrotters' lying
in wait in a London
square, 1863

'Bloody Sunday',
St Martin's
Lane/Trafalgar
Square, London,
1887

Football violence at
Perry Barr, 1888

Extract 1.1   Pearson: 'Painting by numbers'

Criminal statistics are notoriously unreliable as measures of the actual extent of criminal activity, to such a degree that it is not unknown for historians to discount them altogether [Tobias, 1972]. The reason for their notoriety is that they are complicated by a number of factors other than real changes in levels of crime. The growing size of the police force and its supporting apparatus is the most obvious and general factor. Changes in the routines of law enforcement, the increased mobility of the police, changes in what the law counts as crime, fluctuations in the vigour with which the law is applied, and shifts in public attitudes and tolerance – these must all be counted within the hidden dimensions of the manufacture of crime figures.

To take just one example of where a naive reading of official crime statistics will lead us, Chief Constable James Anderton in his 'Crime Top Growth Industry' speech of 1978 pointed to the apparently disturbing fact that 'crimes recorded in England and Wales in 1900 stood at 77,934; by 1976 that figure had reached 2,135,713'. 'In the same period', he added for good measure, 'convictions rose from 45,259 to 415,471' [*The Guardian, The Daily Telegraph*, 26 April 1978]. It is all too obvious what conclusion Mr Anderton would like us to arrive at. But having spent a little time among the disorderly streets of the early 1900s – the home of the original Hooligans – what sense can we possibly make of these numbers?

…

… What is usually known as the 'dark figure' of crime – illegalities that go unnoticed, or ignored, or unreported, or unrecorded – is such an imponderable that all statements about movements in the levels of crime (whether up or down) are largely a matter of guesswork. We neither know with any useful degree of certainty what proportion of the 'dark figure' is reflected in the crime statistics, nor how this proportion might fluctuate across time. The only certainty is

that the crime statistics are but a pale shadow of the total volume of illegalities. Estimates of the size of the 'black economy', for example, suggest that it dwarfs conventional theft; and more generally some informed guesses put the proportion of crime revealed by official sources as low as 15 per cent [Radzinowicz and King, 1977, p.49]. But there is no way of reliably counting on the size of this 'dark figure' and hence no way of making sure-footed judgements about whether movements in recorded crime reflect actual alterations in criminal activity; or shifts in public tolerance; or changes in policing; or some messy permutation of any of these factors. Statements about rising crime (or about falling crime) can neither be regarded as true nor false in this strict sense. Instead, we must regard them as logically *undecidable*. That is, unless we totally disregard these long-standing and deep-rooted controversies about the interpretation of crime statistics and accept a naive view of them as straightforward reflections of criminal activities.

If we reject these myths of numerical certainty, as I think we must, then the strictly regulated operations of rational thought can only supply us with a quicksand of indecision when we attempt to strike comparisons of the state of lawlessness in different historical times. The only guarantee is that the continually mounting crime figure cannot be used to lend some objective status to feelings of historical decline. Computer-assisted quantum-leaps in the crime rate, while they certainly reflect massive changes in the scope and organization of policing, tell us nothing much worth knowing about the historical realities of crime and violence.

References

Radzinowicz, L. and King, J. (1977) *The Growth of Crime*, Hamilton.

Tobias, J.J. (1972) *Crime and Industrial Society in the Nineteenth Century*, Penguin.

(Pearson, 1983, pp.213, 218–9)

As Christie argues: 'this new situation, with an unlimited reservoir of acts which can be defined as crimes, also creates unlimited possibilities for warfare against all sorts of unwanted acts' (Christie, 1993, p.22). As such, increases in police resources and staffing will almost inevitably lead to a statistical rise in crime, just as the expansion of prison-building programmes will create more prisoners, or the creation of new legislation will criminalize ever wider sections of the population (for example, the powers of the 1994 Criminal Justice Act which criminalized squatting, New Age Travellers, hunt saboteurs, 'rave' parties and 'mass trespass').

The least reliable statistics to depend upon in attempts to answer the questions: Who is likely to be criminal? and: What offences are the most prevalent?, are statistics of known offenders: those collected by the courts and the prisons. These statistics can be revealing about trends in sentencing practices, but are meaningless in understanding trends in crime. The history of a crime – from the time it becomes known to the police through to it being taken seriously, recorded and proceeded with (arrest, prosecution, conviction and sentence) – reflects a myriad of public perceptions, professional judgements, judicial discretions and sentencing policies (see *The Guardian*, 10 June 1993 and 27 November 1993, reproduced below and opposite).

Judge's comments echo 'silly' remarks

Injudicious pronouncements have raised public hackles before. Clare Dyer reports

Judge Ian Starforth Hill's comment that an eight-year-old victim of a sexual attack was 'not entirely an angel' raises echoes of the notorious remark by Judge Bertie Richards in 1982 that a teenage hitch-hiker who was raped after thumbing a lift late at night was 'guilty of a great deal of contributory negligence'.

The judge, who was banned from trying sex cases as a result, caused an uproar when he let the rapist, a businessman, off with a £2,000 fine.

Judge Starforth Hill's words also recall the comment of Mr Justice Owen, a High Court judge, that a 12-year-old rape victim had been 'asking for trouble' by going to a 19-year-old man's room.

Such pronouncements regularly provoke accusations that the judiciary is soft on sex offenders and prone to belittle victims' ordeals.

In February Judge John Prosser let a 15-year-old rapist go free, ordering him to pay his teenage victim £500 'for a good holiday'.

The Court of Appeal later increased the penalty to a two-year custodial sentence.

In 1984, Lord Hailsham, then Lord Chancellor, complained that judges say 'particularly silly things which are then widely publicised in the media.'

In 1988 Judge Sir Harold Cassel, QC, refused to jail an ex-policeman for indecently assaulting his 12-year-old mentally retarded step-daughter.

He said the man was driven to assault the girl because his wife's pregnancy had dimmed her sexual appetite, causing 'considerable problems for a healthy young husband'.

Judge Cassel was strongly rebuked by Lord Mackay, the Lord Chancellor, and retired early on medical grounds.

Most of the injudicious remarks have come from circuit judges, like Starforth Hill, Cassel, Richards, and Prosser.

But High Court judges are not immune: Mr Justice Leonard, the judge in the Ealing Vicarage rape trial, provoked a furore when he commented that the victim's trauma was 'not so great,' and gave the burglar who organised the raid a much harsher sentence than the two rapists.

Other sufferers from judicial foot-in-mouth disease include Judge Brian Gibbens, who told a 35-year-old builder who had sex with a neighbour's seven-year-old daughter while drunk: 'It strikes me, without belittling the offence, as one of the accidents which happen in life to almost everyone, although of a wholly different kind.'

Judge Gibbens has since retired, as has Judge Gabriel Hutton.

He pronounced, when jailing a lorry driver briefly for attempted rape: 'I hope you'll be able to keep your well-paid job and that the couple of weeks you spend in prison will be treated by your employers as part of your holidays'.

(*The Guardian*, 10 June 1993, p.3)

Such processes have recently been well documented in relation to race. In England and Wales, Afro-Caribbeans are significantly more likely than whites to be stopped by the police, even when factors such as age and employment are controlled; their arrest rate is higher; in court they are more likely to be remanded in custody before conviction; and average sentence length is higher despite fewer previous convictions (Hood, 1993; Skogan, 1990; Hudson, 1989; Walker, 1987) (see the CRE poster reproduced on page 30).

As Chambliss has remarked, this is the end result of the concentration of law enforcement on *particular* offences and within *particular* sections of the population:

> Persons are arrested, tried and sentenced who can offer the fewest rewards for nonenforcement of the laws and who can be processed without creating any undue strain for the organisations which comprise the legal system ... The lower class person is (i) more likely to be scrutinised and therefore to be observed in any violation of the law, (ii) more likely to be arrested if discovered under suspicious circumstances, (iii) more likely to spend the time between arrest and trial in jail, (iv) more likely to come to trial, (v) more likely to be found guilty, and (vi) if found guilty, more likely to receive harsh punishment than his middle or upper class counterpart.

(Chambliss, 1969, p.84)

Levittating the laws

ITEM: According to Home Office research, 40 per cent of people found guilty of theft of under £200 are sent to prison by the Crown Courts.

ITEM: A pregnant mother was this week sentenced to five days imprisonment for failing to come up with a £55 penalty for not paying her television licence. She was only saved from jail when two solicitors had a whip-round to pay the fine.

ITEM: Yesterday Roger Levitt, founder of the Levitt Group, which crashed in 1990 owing £34 million and who ploughed nearly £900,000 belonging to Frederick Forsyth, the author, into his doomed business instead of buying bonds, walked free. Mr Levitt, who admitted lying to the City watchdog body to keep his debt-ridden company afloat, was ordered to serve 180 hours community service – though whether anyone would want this discredited fraudster anywhere near them, even on community service, remains to be seen.

There are, of course, as there always are on these occasions, Excuses. Earlier this week Mr Levitt and his former managing director and right-hand man, Mark Reed, unexpectedly pleaded guilty to fraudulent trading. This undoubtedly saved a lot of public money in a trial which was expected to last at least four months. And, of course, the authorities weighed the chances of securing a conviction – never certain in complicated City cases tried before juries – against the public resources which would inevitably be devoured. Mr Justice Laws, a highly regarded judge, described Levitt's acts as 'thoroughly and markedly dishonest'. He said: 'Actions of this kind must tend to subvert the efficacy of the regulatory bodies which have so important a role to play in keeping up standards in the financial services industry. The court has no option but to take a serious view of these offences.' He added that he felt a community service order was 'most suitable' punishment and 'commensurate' with what he had done. What Mr Levitt had admitted was extremely serious. In a failed bid to keep trading, bogus documentation was handed to Fimbra, the City's financial regulator, when it began investigating the Levitt Group shortly before it crashed in December 1990 with debts of £34 million. But, apart from anything else Mr Levitt may or may not have done, if lying on this scale to the City regulator only carries a penalty of community service (plus loss of directorships for seven years) then what message is this sending to everyone else in the City?

If the worst that can befall you for hood-winking the regulator is working in the community (which enlightened City folk surely ought to be doing anyway) then maybe the Serious Fraud Office should pack up shop or be merged with some of the community action programmes. What the pregnant woman sentenced to prison for failing to pay her television licence makes of all this can only be guessed at. But to the average person, unversed in the niceties of plea bargaining, the sight of Mr Levitt walking free (as long as he remembers to pay his TV licence) is further proof that there is one law for the rich and one for the poor. The whole episode stinks, stinks, stinks.

(*The Guardian*, 27 November 1993, p.24)

CRIMINAL ISN'T IT?

A 1992 survey of Midlands crown courts revealed that some ethnic minorities are receiving longer prison sentences. On average, up to 9 months longer than white people for the same crimes. If this is typical, it leads to one simple and rather alarming conclusion.

The criminal justice system is heavily weighted against some ethnic minorities.

Sadly other similar investigations seem to bear this out.

Blacks and Asians are more likely to be charged than cautioned.

They are more likely to be refused bail.

Ethnic minorities are also more likely to be stopped by the police than whites.

(In one London borough Black people are four times more likely to be stopped by the police than whites.)

Mark a British born Afro-Caribbean is a case in point.

"I had never been involved or in trouble with the police before.

"They said – "I'm talking to you jungle bunnie." I felt like it went on for hours and hours. I knew what he was trying to do, he was trying to coax me into causing trouble, start a fight, so he could have an excuse to arrest me.'

Contrary to what some people might think, minorities are more often the victims of crime than the perpetrators.

Black and Asian people are more likely than whites to be the victims of violence against the person and property.

And yet the stereotypical image of Black people is as aggressors.

It's a terrible slur on the vast majority of ethnic minorities in Britain who are law abiding contributors to society.

Moreover when Blacks and Asians are charged with a criminal offence, the courtroom ritual is quite daunting.

They are likely to be faced with a predominantly white institution.

From white judges and lawyers to white clerks of the courtroom.

(Out of 2,887 judges in England and Wales, only 32 are from ethnic minorities.)

The chances are they might not see a black face on the jury either.

They have to endure uncomfortable and humiliating displays of ignorance about their culture and lives.

It's a small wonder they find it difficult to co-operate with the system.

This then confirms the stereotypes of people who are alienated, hostile and aggressive to authority.

At the Commission for Racial Equality we believe there is hope.

We were set up in 1976 by the Race Relations Act to eliminate every kind of racial discrimination.

The CRE is an independent body funded by an annual Home Office grant.

The 1976 Race Relations Act quite simply states that people should not be discriminated against on the ground of colour, race or national origin.

It makes discrimination unlawful in jobs, training, housing and education.

The irony is it doesn't cover certain areas of the criminal justice process.

This basically means if you have been discriminated against in the justice process it is not possible to bring a complaint against a police officer or a judge under the Race Relations Act.

Clearly the Act should apply to these and many other similar institutions.

But the CRE are working to put an end to discrimination on how people are treated by the police force and other organisations and are working with the Association of Chief Police Officers to this end.

Secondly, we are influencing the judicial process to eliminate any kind of discrimination within their own system.

The judiciary is now undertaking training courses on racial equality issues and are planning to monitor sentencing trends to eradicate racial bias.

But what can you do?

If you feel you have been racially abused or harassed by a police officer, or if you feel you have been denied your rights and treated harshly because of your race or colour, complain.

Write to the superintendent at the station where the offending officer works.

Or, if you think you may have been unfairly discriminated against by the court system, complain.

Write to the Lord Chancellor's office.

You may be entitled to legal aid.

You could also apply to the CRE or contact your local Racial Equality Council for assistance and guidance.

We're not advocating special treatment for Britain's ethnic minorities.

(That would be positive discrimination, which is not allowed under our legislation.)

White or Black, if a person is found guilty of a criminal offence it's only right they should be justly punished.

Our criminal justice system is seen as being one of the best in the world.

It's something we can all be proud of.

But growing evidence suggests a more even handed approach is needed.

The sooner we can address these fundamental imbalances, the fairer the system will be for everyone.

If you're concerned about race issues, write to your MP and say so, or if you'd like a copy of the CRE report this advert was based on, write to the address below.

Prejudice and bigotry are passed from one generation to the next.

We have a simple choice, either take this opportunity to set an example, or ignore the problem altogether.

But that truly would be criminal.

COMMISSION FOR RACIAL EQUALITY
CRE Communication Section, Elliot House, 10-12 Allington Street, London SW1E 5EH.

Car theft 1½ y

eft 9 months.

ACTIVITY 1.3

The process whereby an incident or behaviour may or may not be registered as an official statistic is illustrated in Table 1.1. This uses the example of illegal drug use to show how 'official data are social products' (Box, 1981, p.208). How well do you think it would apply to other incidents that are liable to criminalization? Are there any crimes to which the 'social construction of official statistics' argument is more difficult to apply? Make some notes to record your responses to such questions.

Table 1.1 Factors affecting the criminal processing of an incident

Event	Factors
Incident occurs	Marijuana smoking at a student party
Reported	1 Country where incident takes place 2 Visibility: public or private space? 3 Ignorance or support for sub-cultural norms 4 Notions of seriousness in eyes of observer 5 Social status of offenders
Taken seriously by police	1 Social status of reporter 2 Seriousness as defined by police 3 Presence of 'law and order' campaigns 4 Chief constable directives
Individual detected and apprehended	1 Police resources and available time 2 Nature of evidence 3 Possibility of successful arrest
Station arrest	1 Inter-organization obligations 2 Typifications of criminals 3 Behaviour and attributes of suspect 4 Dramaturgical skills of suspect
Charge; court	1 Past record of suspect 2 'Normal' or 'abnormal' crime?
Trial verdict	1 Quality of legal representation 2 Personal appearance in court 3 Nature of plea
Sentence	1 Previous sentences 2 Notions of habituality 3 Closeness of status of judge to that of offender

Collectively, such processes of data collection inevitably mean that notions of crime waves and of perpetual increases in offending have to be interpreted with extreme caution. Nevertheless, the picture they create of crime, criminals and offending remain some of the key means through which academic, political, media and public knowledge is gained. The statistics cannot be dismissed as simply meaningless. They can provide valuable insights into police and court definitions of crime and the operation of social, legal and organizational constraints and priorities. They cannot, however, be expected to aid our understanding of the 'independent entity of crime' for, as Lea and Young acknowledge: 'by its nature no such fact exists' (Lea and Young, 1984, p.15). Consequently, statistics remain ripe ingredients for media interpretation and political manipulation. It is only through being employed within a variety of discourses that they come to have meaning. Here are some examples:

- The 1982 British Crime Survey revealed a rate of 250 burglaries per 10,000 households in England and Wales in 1981. This rate, though, can be expressed in a variety of ways depending on the intended message the user wishes to put across:

  (a) a burglary every minute throughout the country;

  (b) a one-in-forty likelihood of being burgled in a year;

  (c) the likelihood of being burgled once in every 40 years.

- In March 1982 the Metropolitan Police released the annual crime figures for the London area. The occasion was chosen to issue a press release which concentrated on the smallest category of crime: the 3 per cent of offences constituting 'robbery and other violent theft'. These had risen by 34 per cent from 13,984 in 1980 to 18,763 in 1981. The figure included 5,889 cases which were described as 'street robbery of personal property'. Although these amounted to only 0.9 per cent of all recorded offences, they attracted extensive media interest because 'street robbery of personal property' is what is popularly known as 'mugging'. These particular statistics were also for the first time officially classified according to the race of the offender and suggested that some 55 per cent of offenders were black. No such descriptions of the other 97 per cent of offences were offered. Thus the *Daily Mail* of 11 March 1982 could latch on to the headline: 'Black Crime: The Alarming Figures'.

- Statistical sources can be used in quite contradictory ways to support or disclaim the view that the UK is on an ever-increasing crime spiral. Following the release of crime figures for the London Metropolitan area in February 1980, the London *Evening News* (28 February) could claim on its *front* page: 'London Violence Growing', whilst the *Evening Standard* of the same day declared on its *page 5*: 'London Is Winning the Crime War'. Both papers were 'right', although they provided totally opposing impressions of the 'crime problem'. Serious crime as a whole (as recorded by the police) decreased by 2 per cent, whilst various categories within this, for example assaults, rose by 12 per cent.

- Crime statistics can be selectively used or summarily dismissed by politicians, depending on their ability to confirm or deny ideological preferences. In 1993 the Home Secretary chose the occasion of the release of Home Office statistics which revealed a marked *fall* in the number of juvenile convictions and cautions between 1981 and 1991, to claim that the figures were 'next to useless'. Rather, he maintained that juvenile offending was on the rise, but that much was going unrecorded because of a rise in the 1980s of informal police cautioning (*The Independent*, 25 February 1993, p.3). Responding to the prevailing image of a hard core of young persistent offenders, the Home Secretary was simultaneously planning to expand the secure accommodation network for offenders aged under 15.

- At the end of September 1994, crime figures showed the biggest fall in recorded crime in England and Wales for 40 years. This might make it appear that the Home Secretary, who had announced a 27-point plan for tackling crime in the previous year, had been successful. However, police and statistical analysts suggested that the decrease was a myth, created by the non-recording and re-classification of certain offences (see *The Sunday Times*, 16 October 1994, reproduced below).

Fall in crime a myth as police chiefs massage the figures

by Ian Burrell and David Leppard

The government's much heralded fall in crime is a myth. Hundreds of thousands of serious crimes have been quietly dropped from police records as senior officers massage their statistics to meet new Home Office efficiency targets.

Crime experts say at least 220,000 crimes, including burglary, assault, theft and car crimes, vanished from official statistics last year as a result of police manipulation of the figures.

The disclosure undermines claims by Michael Howard, the home secretary, that the government's controversial law and order policies are finally winning the war on crime. Last month Howard announced a 5.5% fall in recorded crime – the biggest drop for 40 years.

However, police and crime experts revealed that most of last year's fall of 311,000 crimes could be accounted for by officers 'cooking the books'. They said the dishonest practice of not recording crimes – known in police circles as 'cuffing' – was becoming increasingly common.

Their views are backed by the British Crime Survey, which recently reported that actual crime rose faster over the past two years than during the 1980s.

This weekend chief constables revealed a range of 'Spanish practices' which allowed them to conceal the full extent of crime. These included cases where:

- Victims of violent attacks, previously classed as actual bodily harm, are having the crimes described by police as common assault, a civil offence which does not feature in official crime statistics.
- Attempted burglaries are logged as criminal damage to windows and doors and not put down as crimes.
- Thieves caught breaking into cars are being charged with tampering – which is not a recordable offence – rather than theft.
- A whole category of offences such as malicious telephone calls, assaults, deception and minor criminal damage are not classified as crimes because police say they are too trivial to record.

The growing practice has outraged crime victims, who say it undermines their confidence in the criminal justice system.

Celia, 30, from Lambeth, south London, was left severely injured last month after she was attacked by another woman and sustained a cut mouth and neck injury. She identified the assailant to police but officers refused to record the incident as a crime.

'I was advised by the police to take out a private prosecution. I was absolutely furious,' she said.

Home Office figures released last month reveal that only 57% of the nearly 10m reported crimes in England and Wales were recorded in official statistics. A spokesman said the government could not explain why the proportion of recorded crime was falling. Police chiefs and experts, however, said the practice is the inevitable result of recent Whitehall pressure on police to improve crime statistics. When the Police and Magistrates' Courts Act comes into effect next April, all 43 forces in England and Wales will for the first time be judged on their detection rates.

Professor John Benyon, director of the Centre for the Study of Public Order, which carries out research for the Home Office, said the manipulation of figures by senior officers had become prevalent in the past nine months, since the government announced the new efficiency measures.

'These are real crimes with real victims, yet 43% of them are not being logged by police. We ought to be very sceptical of this so-called fall in crime,' Benyon said.

Malcolm Hibberd, of the Police Foundation, an independent think tank, said police were deliberately failing to record crimes if they appeared difficult to solve: 'Police forces are cynically going through their crime books doing their reclassification to reduce their burglary figures.

'If police get the impression that a crime is unlikely to be cleared up then it is to their advantage, in terms of their performance, that it does not go down as a crime.'

Chief constables say plans to introduce performance-related pay and short-term contracts will put financial pressure on senior officers to fiddle the figures. Richard Wells, chief constable of South Yorkshire police, said crime had increased in his area compared to most other forces after he instructed all his officers to be totally honest about recording crime. Wells said that while he had refused to allow his officers to distort crime figures, efficiency league tables 'would inevitably result in a number of officers misusing or manipulating the figures'.

Charles Pollard, chief constable of Thames Valley police, who is leading police negotiations with the Home Office over the new efficiency targets, said they encouraged dishonest or unscrupulous officers to use 'Spanish practices' to manipulate crime figures.

(*The Sunday Times*, 16 October 1994, pp.1, 5)

3.2 Hidden crime

hidden crime

As criminologists began to acknowledge that there is no reliable statistical measure of the extent of crime, they were led to admit the widespread existence of hidden crime. Radzinowicz and King (1977), for example, suggested that only about 15 per cent of all crimes committed in England and Wales were officially recorded. Given the inadequacies of official statistics, criminologists have turned to other methods. For example, the extent of crime can be assessed by self report studies (where people are asked to list crimes they have committed) and is now (as we noted in section 3.1) regularly 'measured' by victim surveys such as the BCS (where victims recall crimes committed against them). Whilst both of these sources may also be flawed because of the unwillingness of respondents to admit their criminality or to accept a victim status, both provide useful points of comparison with Home Office statistics, in particular via their ability to reveal the wide extent of a 'dark figure' of crime which has no official record. Thus the first BCS concluded that, for every offence recorded, four were committed (Hough and Mayhew, 1983). The fifth survey (Mayhew *et al.*, 1994) indicated that 59 per cent of crime was not *reported* and that only 27 per cent of comparable BCS crimes were *recorded* by the police (see Figure 1.3).

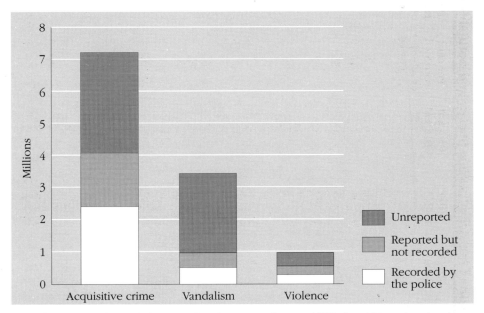

Figure 1.3 *Levels of recorded, reported and unreported crime, 1993. Acquisitive crime: burglary; all vehicle and bicycle theft and thefts from the person. Vandalism: against household property and vehicles. Violence: wounding and robbery (Source: Mayhew et al., 1994, p.2)*

Table 1.2 also shows that, between 1981 and 1993, according to police records the crime rate rose by 111 per cent, whilst the BCS data suggest a rise of 77 per cent.

Table 1.2 A comparison of the British Crime Survey and notifiable offences recorded by the police, 1981–1993

Figures in thousands	1993 police	1993 BCS	Per cent reported	Per cent recorded of number reported	Per cent recorded of all BCS crimes	Per cent change 1991–93		Per cent change 1981–93	
						police	BCS	police	BCS
Comparable with recorded offences									
ACQUISITIVE CRIME	2,410	7,259	56	59	33	6	17	107	130
VANDALISM	459	3,378	27	51	14	11	23	129	24
VIOLENCE	221	929	52	46	24	12	14	115	39
TOTAL	**3,090**	**11,567**	**47**	**57**	**27**	**7**	**18**	**111**	**77**
Vehicle vandalism	—	1,787	22	—	—	—	7	—	15
Vandalism to other property	—	1,591	32	—	—	—	49	—	38
Burglary	727	1,754	69	60	41	16	28	108	134
Attempts and no loss	185	948	53	37	20	28	43	152	152
Burglary with loss	542	806	87	77	67	13	14	96	116
All vehicle thefts	1,424	4,312	53	63	33	3	13	118	146
Theft from motor vehicles	785	2,546	50	61	31	1	6	132	98
Theft of motor vehicles	497	541	97	95	92	2	4	74	89
Attempted thefts of and from vehicles	143	1,225	40	29	12	16	37	407	582
Bicycle theft	208	595	72	49	35	-10	5	65	175
Wounding	169	692	54	45	24	7	10	100	36
Robbery and theft from person	102	835	32	38	12	27	34	92	40
Other BCS offences									
Other household theft	—	2,341	33	—	—	—	27	—	54
Common assault	—	2,210	25	—	—	—	25	—	58
Other personal theft	—	1,903	30	—	—	—	9	—	20
All BCS offences	**—**	**18,021**	**41**	**—**	**—**	**—**	**19**	**—**	**63**

Notes:

1 Acquisitive crimes: burglary, thefts of and from vehicles (including attempts), bicycle thefts, theft from the person. Vandalism: household property and vehicles. Violence: wounding and robbery.

2 Police figures have been adjusted to improve comparability with the BCS. The main adjustments needed are: to exclude offences against victims aged under 16, and vandalism against public property; and to add offences recorded only by the British Transport Police (which are excluded from police figures). Police figures for burglary comprise burglary in a dwelling only. Police figures of thefts of and from motor vehicles exclude nil value incidents; these are shown as 'attempted thefts of and from vehicles'. Some adjustment is also made to exclude incidents involving commercial vehicles.

3 Totals do not sum to sub-totals because of rounding. Percentage changes based on unrounded numbers.

Source: Mayhew *et al.*, 1994, p.6

Surveys of victimization in particular localities (for example, Islington in London) have tended to uncover even higher rates than those reported to the BCS, particularly incidents of burglary and vandalism. In addition, local surveys have attempted to bring to light the extent of offences which are generally omitted from BCS data, such as sexual abuse, threats and assaults (Crawford *et al.*, 1990). Nevertheless, corporate victims, such as businesses, shops and public services, remain infrequent objects of all forms of study.

Most self report studies have been directed at young people. Likewise, they have revealed that offending is more common than official statistics suggest and that in all probability law-breaking is a widespread phenomenon, practised by most, if not all, of the population at some time in their lives. A survey for *Crime Concern* in 1993, for example, revealed that nearly two-thirds of teenagers knew someone in their age group who had committed an offence: shoplifting, truancy, drug use and under-age drinking being the most common (*The Guardian*, 15 September 1993). Similarly, Rutter and Giller's (1983, p.27) summary of delinquency self report research found that, *inter alia*, 82 per cent admitted breaking windows of empty houses, 70 per cent had stolen from a shop and that almost no-one admitted no offences at all. Risk of prosecution ranged from 8 per cent (shoplifting) to 60 per cent (breaking and entering). Significantly, and in contrast to dominant statistical and public perceptions, middle-class children were just as likely to be involved in crime as working-class – a conclusion also reached through interviews with 4,000 11- to 15-year-olds in Edinburgh in the early 1990s (Anderson *et al.*, 1994). This latter study also noted how young people face serious problems as *victims* of crime, but again this was underreported either to parents or the police.

Indeed, the widespread nature of offending is fairly easy to establish. Taking stationery or other goods from office/work, using a firm's telephone for personal calls, taking souvenirs from pubs/hotels, overestimating expenses and keeping money found in the street, for example, all constitute theft, capable of attracting up to a £5,000 fine and/or 6 months imprisonment, in a magistrates court (as of 1994).

ACTIVITY 1.4

Consider the ten incidents shown in the self report questionnaire opposite. If you have at any time committed such an offence, tick the appropriate box. Finally, add up the maximum penalties which you could have received, if dealt with summarily in a magistrates court in October 1994.

Incident	Offence	√/X	Maximum penalty
1 Have you ever bought goods knowing or believing they may have been stolen?	Handling stolen property		£5,000 and/or 6 months imprisonment
2 Have you taken stationery or anything else from your office/work?	Theft		£5,000 and/or 6 months imprisonment
3 Have you ever used the firm's telephone for personal calls?	Dishonestly abstracting electricity		£5,000 and/or 6 months imprisonment
4 Have you ever kept money if you received too much in change?	Theft		£5,000 and/or 6 months imprisonment
5 Have you kept money found in the street?	Theft		£5,000 and/or 6 months imprisonment
6 Have you taken 'souvenirs' from a pub/hotel?	Theft		£5,000 and/or 6 months imprisonment
7 Have you ever left a shop without paying in full for your purchases?	Making off without payment		£5,000 and/or 6 months imprisonment
8 Have you used a television without buying a licence?	Using a television without a licence		£1,000 fine
9 Have you ever fiddled your expenses?	Theft		£5,000 and/or 6 months imprisonment
10 Have you ever been in possession of cannabis?	Misuse of drugs		£2,500 and/or 3 months imprisonment
Total			Fine = Prison sentence =

Source: based on *Daily Mail*, 31 May 1972; final column updated from Archbold, 1994

COMMENT

Such offending (yours and mine?) is not automatically synonymous with being criminal. A majority of us presumably lack criminal status, but only because our offences have remained excused, undetected, ignored or not reported. Indeed, we may justify our actions as insignificant, but collectively the economic and social ramifications of such behaviour may be far from trivial. For example, in 1972 it was estimated that £225–£300 million worth of goods would 'disappear' that year from shops, offices and factories. Similarly, the Grosvenor House Hotel in London wanted to trace the disappearance of 10,000 teaspoons and 40,000 napkins! (*Daily Mail*, 31 May 1972). In 1992–93 the report *Retail Crime Costs* estimated that employees were responsible for a quarter of thefts from shops and stores, amounting to £554 million, whilst a National Audit Office report reckoned that, overall, the hidden economy – activities not made known to the tax authorities – was running at between £36 billion and £48 billion a year (*The Guardian*, 19 January 1994; *The Independent*, 3 December 1993) (see also Chapter 6). The issue is effectively one of where do we draw the line? Where does 'respectability' end and 'criminality' begin?

3.3 Institutionalized crime

Research into 'crime at work' has largely been directed at employees in particular occupations, such as catering, bread sales and milk delivery. Each study has concluded that fiddling of stocks and sales returns is not only an established part of such jobs – a 'legitimate commerce' – but that it is also necessary for the smooth running of the companies involved, being a supplement to low wages and often allowed for in wage negotiations. The 'basic structural and normative similarity' between fiddling and legitimate business practice means that the fiddler, far from being vilified, is likely to attract an 'ambiguous (but generally) benevolent societal reaction' (Ditton, 1977, p.173). Crime in this context is an institutionalized practice. A 'hidden' economy co-exists with the 'legitimate' economy, each dependent on the other for goods and resources. Fiddling in the provision of professional services by doctors, surgeons, pharmacists, lawyers and business executives has also been shown to be widespread and 'normative' (Henry, 1978). Here 'offences' include charging for unnecessary work, use of fictitious or overvalued collateral and tax violations.

hidden economy

Indeed, white-collar crimes are probably far more numerous and more costly than recorded crime, but seldom come to the attention of law-enforcement agencies. Sutherland's pioneering work in the 1930s effectively destroyed the notion of criminality as an exclusively lower-class phenomenon. Using records of administrative commissions, he showed that the senior executives of the 70 largest industrial corporations in the USA had consistently violated the law with regard to trade restraint, misrepresentation in advertising, infringement of patent rights and unfair labour practices (Sutherland, 1949). Such 'legitimate rackets' are likely to be more economically significant than all the robberies, thefts and acts of larceny put together. In the USA in 1965, for example, the Federal Bureau of Investigation (FBI) estimated that some $284 million were lost in burglaries. This, however, paled into insignificance when compared to the estimated $9 *billion* of which the wealthiest one per cent of the American population defrauded their tax department in the same year (Pearce, 1976, pp.77–8). Similarly, Snider (1993) estimates the annual cost of street crime in the USA to be $4 billion or 'much less than 5 per cent of the take from corporate crime'. In the deregulated markets of the 1980s, corporate crime has come to be described as the 'fastest growing in Britain' (see *The Guardian 2*, 1 July 1993, reproduced opposite).

Crime in the City

Alex Brummer

Three decades ago, on August 8, 1963, an audacious group of British gangsters etched their names into folklore when they stole £2.5 million – the equivalent of £25 million at today's prices – from the Glasgow–London mail train and received 30-year jail sentences for their trouble. But by the standards of the late 20th century, when the most daring crimes are of a more cerebral kind and the proceeds start in the tens-of-millions and can reach the billions, the Great Train Robbery looks modest.

Clearly, men in grey suits with grand jobs in public companies – from whose ranks Britain's biggest criminals are often drawn today – do not conjure up the Wild West images which endowed the train robbers. Yet the sums looted from company coffers, pension funds and bank accounts in recent years, by executives with all the trappings of power, have been enormous by the standards of regular criminality. Robert Maxwell, arguably the biggest crook ever to sit at the top of a group of public companies, robbed his workers of some £500 millions of their life savings and could still look them in the eye.

Asil Nadir, whose case has become a political *cause célèbre* this summer, took investors on an astonishing roller-coaster ride. In a decade at the head of Polly Peck, where the riches were founded in the unglamorous trade of fruit packaging, Nadir took the company's shares from 8p each to £35 at their peak in 1983. In the process he made millionaires of investors who had put just £1,000 into his company. But the growth in the business and the huge profits were a chimera.

At the last count the administrators, charged with making as much recovery as possible for shareholders and creditors, found that £450 million had gone walkabout through a series of complex offshore banking arrangements with a complexity that made Hampton Court Maze look linear.

At the Bank of Commerce & Credit International, described by the Governor of the Bank of England, Robin Leigh-Pemberton, as the most fraudulent bank in the history of finance, directors siphoned off billions of pounds. They left a hole which has been estimated by some experts as being in the region of $10 billion. Such a sum would be all but impossible to stash away in a farm house.

But contemporary fraud is not just about men such as Peter Clowes, now serving a jail term, who made away with almost £100 million of elderly people's money, or the more complex financial shenanigans which earned the Guinness defendants Ernest Saunders, Gerald Ronson and Anthony Parnes a stretch at Ford Open Prison. It is a burgeoning business, which is growing so fast that it is almost impossible for the lumbering criminal justice system to keep up with it.

New figures produced this week by the management consultants KPMG show that in the first four months of this year alone some £571 million of new financial fraud was reported. This compares with £671 million in the whole of 1992. The new wave of financial fraudsters are not the modest or grubby clerks of the kind portrayed in Arthur Hailey's novels which sold so well in the 1970s. Most of them are right at the very top of their professions – company directors or chief executives – and drawn from the high achievement age group of 41–50 years old. They are the glitzy figures of Oliver Stone's film Wall Street. None of these fraudsters is content with fiddling his expenses.

(The Guardian 2, 1 July 1993, p.2)

The crimes of the powerful are not simply crimes against property. In 1978 four people died following a hoist accident at a power-station in Kent. The Health and Safety Commission subsequently identified the cause as the company's neglect of safety equipment. In the late 1970s the Chemie Grunenthal company of Germany had criminal charges brought against it for deliberately falsifying the test data on the drug thalidomide. Eight thousand pregnant women around the Western world had, in the meantime, given birth to deformed babies (**Box, 1983**). During the 1970s, 106 fatalities occurred in the North Sea Oil Industry, of which many were due to the operation of lower safety standards offshore when the rush for oil, with the blessing of successive British governments, placed profit before safety (Carson, 1981). Box (1983, p.28) estimates a ratio of 7:1 regarding deaths from occupational accidents and diseases, and deaths recorded as homicide.

Given the nature of much corporate crime, these cases stand only as examples of what is arguably a widespread practice. Corporate crime is relatively invisible and thus infrequently reported to, or detected by, the legal authorities. It is rarely the subject of a major public 'moral outrage' despite the economic costs. Box attributes the relative impunity of corporate crime not just to invisibility, but to various ideological mechanisms whereby the pursuit of profit is supported irrespective of its human costs:

Executives are able to violate the law without feeling guilt or denting their respectable self image ... corporate officials are both mystified as to their own crime and misdirected as to the distribution of crime in general. Both mystification and misdirection preserve the appearance of corporate respectability and help keep invisible to themselves and others the underlying ugly reality of corporate crime.

(Box, 1983, p.57)

These demonstrations of the extensiveness of crime may suggest and encourage such populisms as 'everyone is at it', but such a view tends to disregard the different opportunities for 'crime' available in different workplaces. A hidden economy analysis tends to cut across the issues of opportunity for crime, and type and extent of crime, by collapsing *all* crimes at or involving work into a homogeneous category. Not only does this deny the quantitative differences in out-of-market dealing, but it fails to recognize the qualitative differences in the work context which allow such opportunities. What is also disguised by this position is the existence of a hierarchy of acceptability within the full range of property crime. While tax avoidance (as opposed to evasion), for example, is defined as a legitimate business activity, social security fiddling is defined as a form of social malaise (Cook, 1989).

Chambliss goes further and argues that the state itself is frequently implicated in the organization and committal of criminal acts. By this, he refers not simply to questions of dubious morality or the denial of human rights, but to historical and current institutionalized state practices involving 'complicity in piracy, smuggling, assassinations, criminal conspiracies ... and diverting funds in ways prohibited by law (e.g. illegal campaign contributions, selling arms to countries prohibited by law and supporting terrorist activities)' (Chambliss, 1989, p.184). Some of the more infamous examples would include the Watergate scandals of 1973 in USA; the bombing of a Greenpeace ship by the French secret service in New Zealand in 1985; and the 1993 'arms for Iraq' allegations in England (Chapter 7 examines this further).

However, it is precisely these forms of 'respectable' crime that rarely feature in either the official statistics or victimization surveys. Despite the seriousness of some instances of white-collar, corporate and state crime, involving enormous sums of money and resulting in widespread human suffering, the subject has rarely been at the head of the 'problem of crime' agenda. Since the late 1960s, the growth of multinationals operating beyond the limits of national control, the rise of consumer protection movements, and the threat of more dangerous forms of pollution have, however, increased its public visibility (discussed further in Chapter 6). Nevertheless, the assumption that property crime (theft, robbery) is mainly a lower-class phenomenon retains its potency.

Property crimes – as Sutherland suggested in 1949 – are rooted in the very structure of society. However, only a small and specific section of the population is consistently singled out as a matter of social concern. Similarly, it is only from the analysis of such 'specific sections' that the vast majority of criminological theories, purporting to uncover the causes of crime, have been constructed. As mentioned earlier, most academic and public 'theories' about the causes of crime depend on the picture painted by official statistics. Because such statistics consistently report strong correlations between offending and young, male and low income sections of the population, it is to these particular groups that most academic research and public outrage is directed. For example, **Braithwaite's (1989)** list of 'thirteen powerful associations' (which he argues every criminological theory is bound to address), whilst undoubtedly having some validity, also allows statistical indices to set the research agenda (see Table 1.3).

Table 1.3   Thirteen powerful associations
1   Crime is committed disproportionately by males
2   Crime is committed disproportionately by 15- to 25-year-olds
3   Crime is committed disproportionately by unmarried people
4   Crime is committed disproportionately by people living in large cities
5   Crime is committed disproportionately by people who have experienced high residential mobility and who live in areas characterized by high residential mobility
6   Young people who are strongly attached to their school are less likely to engage in crime
7   Young people who have high educational and occupational aspirations are less likely to engage in crime
8   Young people who do poorly at school are more likely to engage in crime
9   Young people who are strongly attached to their parents are less likely to engage in crime
10   Young people who have friendships with criminals are more likely to engage in crime themselves
11   People who believe strongly in the importance of complying with the law are less likely to violate the law
12   Being at the bottom of the class structure increases rates of offending for all types of crime apart from white collar crime
13   Crime rates have been increasing in most countries since the Second World War

Source: based on **Braithwaite, 1989, pp.44–50**

In the process, street crime tends to be elevated as a more serious cause for concern than corporate crime; street violence more than domestic violence; and welfare benefit fraud more than income tax evasion. Common-sense 'theories' which single out poor parenting, low IQ, educational underachievement, lone-parent families, youth peer-group pressure, and so on, as key determinants of crime are readily applied to the former, but rarely (if ever) to the latter. Most criminological theory, then, tends to exacerbate the partial and distorted view of crime, first constructed by the statistical measures.

4   How serious is crime?: media representations and public perceptions

Popular attitudes to crime tend to be constructed around a number of stereotypes of a 'criminal other': the armed robber, the terrorist, the pervert, the murderer, the extremist, the scrounger, the rapist, the juvenile delinquent (rarely the corporate executive, the politician, the married man and so on). Such stereotyping is reinforced by the fact that a majority of people believe that they have little or no direct experience or expert knowledge of crime. Public awareness of crime is very largely dependent on such secondary sources as hearsay, newspapers, radio, novels, educational institutions, film and television. Indeed, the sources of crime imagery are wide and varied. Crime fiction and television police series are arguably a key element in the construction of public ideologies of crime, law and order. Here the vilification of the abnormal and censoring of the unusual provide a ready assumption that criminals live in a world apart, as aberrations on the map of social relationships. It is plain for all to see what and who is wrong and what is needed to return to 'normality' (Chapter 2 discusses this in greater detail with reference to the detective story).

4.1   News values and institutional sources

Much of our information about the nature and incidence of crime is provided by the secondary source of the media (newspapers and television, for example). Indeed, a main characteristic of living within large urban societies is that we rely on the media to learn, not only of global events, but also of those happening within our own localities. We should expect, then, the media to play a major role in our very perception and *construction* of the social world. Despite the powerful 'common-sense' view that the media merely provide the *facts* of a process in which crime occurs – police apprehend criminals, and courts punish them – the relationship between crime and media reportage is far from simple.

Crime stories have long been a core element of everyday media news reports (see Figure 1.4). Williams' and Dickinson's research of the national press in June 1989 found that, on average, 12.7 per cent of event-oriented news reports were about crime. The proportion was significantly higher in the tabloid press (see Table 1.4). Moreover, newspapers regularly devoted over 60 per cent of the space given to crime reporting to stories dealing with cases of personal violence (compared to the statistical occurrence of these as 5 per cent of all crimes recorded by the police) (Williams and Dickinson, 1993, p.40).

Figure 1.4 A staple diet?: headlines in one edition of a provincial newspaper (Source: Leicester Mercury, 21 January 1994)

Table 1.4 Proportion of newspaper newsholes devoted to crime, June to July 1989

Newspaper	Mean newshole area (cm²)	Mean crime area (cm²)	Crime area newshole area (%)	Rank
Times	11,777	748	6.4	(3)
Independent	10,251	591	5.8	(2)
Guardian	10,583	543	5.1	(1)
Telegraph	10,392	942	9.1	(4)
Mail	5,286	1,024	19.4	(7)
Express	4,465	775	17.4	(6)
Today	5,725	803	14.0	(5)
Mirror	4,346	1,151	26.5	(8)
Sun	4,284	1,304	30.4	(10)
Star	4,015	1,129	28.1	(9)
			Mean = 12.7	

Source: Williams and Dickinson, 1993, p.41, Table 1

Studies of the provincial press by Ditton and Duffy in Strathclyde and Smith in Birmingham also revealed that newspapers distort the 'official' picture of crimes known to the police. Most prominently, the amount of space devoted to crime news does not correspond to the recorded occurrence of certain crimes. In Strathclyde, an over-reporting of crimes involving violence and sex was noted to the degree that during March 1981, such crimes constituted 2.4 per cent of reported incidence, yet occupied 45.8 per cent of newspaper coverage (Ditton and Duffy, 1983, p.164). In Birmingham, offences against the person, including robbery and assault, accounted for less than 6 per cent of known crimes but occupied 52.7 per cent of the space devoted to crime stories (Smith, 1984, p.290). Smith also reported biases in the media's identification of key criminal areas of a city, although these did not have the highest reported crime rate, and a tendency to link issues of race with crime. Similarly, Young (1974) noted how the type of information which the mass media select and disseminate to the public is coloured throughout by the notion of newsworthiness. He argued that, rather than providing a pure reflection of the social world, 'newspapers select events which are *atypical*, present them in a *stereotypical* fashion and contrast them against a backcloth of normality which is *overtypical*' (Young, 1974, p.241). Box contends that: '90 per cent of media space devoted to the reportage of crimes, concentrates on serious crimes such as wilful homicide, forcible rape, aggravated assault, robbery, burglary and larceny and crimes currently fanning social hysteria such as trafficking and drug abuse' (Box, 1981, p.39). Such crimes, which even statistically are atypical, are consistently over-reported and presented as stereotypical of a perceived criminal fraternity. The criminal is, then, usually depicted as violent, immoral and a threat to the social order. Crime is presented in a way in which it continually breaches our 'normal' expectations about the world.

The media appear to be involved in a continual search for the 'new', unusual and dramatic. This is what makes the 'news'. Chibnall (1977, p.77) has noted five sets of informal rules of relevancy which govern the professional imperatives of popular journalism. These are:

1   visible and spectacular acts
2   sexual or political connotations
3   graphic presentation
4   individual pathology
5   deterrence and repression.

It is around such themes that *news values* are structured. According to Chibnall, press reports cannot simply be a reflection of real events because two key processes always intervene: *selection* – which aspects of events to report, which to omit; and *presentation* – choosing what sort of headline, language, imagery, photograph and typography to use.

news values

For example, the violence most likely to receive coverage in the press is that which involves sudden injury to 'innocent' others, especially in public places. Concern with such violence is a recurring feature of newspaper accounts, frequently bolstered by the media labels of 'cosh boys', 'bullyboy skinheads', 'vandals', 'muggers', 'hooligans', 'blood-crazed mobs' and 'rampaging thugs'. Other forms of violence are systematically neglected. Domestic violence, unsafe working conditions and pollution of the environment are cited by Chibnall as phenomena that have caused equal, if not more, suffering, but have received less press consideration because they do not conform to the criteria of spectacular newsworthiness (Chibnall, 1977, p.78).

One particular case stands out as worthy of critical reflection. Female criminality is almost always depicted and described in different terms to that of male. Partly because of women's under-representation in statistical measures and partly because of stereotypes regarding 'proper' gender roles, the female criminal is widely regarded as transgressing not only the law, but also sex-role norms. In short, she is likely to be considered as doubly deviant. As Hutter and Williams (1981, p.23) argue, female deviancy is characteristically portrayed as 'unnatural' or 'abnormal' behaviour to which the stereotypes of 'mad' or 'sad' are more readily applied than that of 'bad'. Female behaviour tends to attract a restricted range of media typifications, revolving around the sexually based dichotomies of chaste/unchaste, virgin/whore and Madonna/Magdalene (see *The Sun*, 7 July 1992, and *Daily Star*, 10 December 1994, reproduced overleaf).

Heidensohn notes how the image of the witch remains at the top of a 'pyramid of related images of deviant women as especially evil, depraved and monstrous' (Heidensohn, 1985, p.92). For example, whilst prostitutes are depicted as *sexual* deviants, as *fallen* women, their male clients are at worst viewed as misguided (or as propelled into their actions through unloving wives and/or mothers). Men and male sexuality is not seen to be the problem. Since 'true femininity' is assumed to preclude 'improper' behaviour, another recurring image is the denigration of deviant women as 'masculine'. Above all, there is no male equivalent for notions of 'the slag', 'the whore' or 'the witch'. Conversely, media reports of violence against women tend to reproduce a woman-blaming ideology – 'she asked for it'; 'she made me do it'. The celebration of famous murderers, such as Jack the Ripper, also reveals the media's voyeuristic pose and 'failure to take femicide seriously' (Radford and Russell, 1992, p.353).

THE 'KILLER' MISTRESS WHO WAS AT LOVER'S WEDDING

Hatred made her stab bride Alison 54 times, court told

By James Lewthwaite

It was bride Alison Shaughnessy's day of joy.

But standing among her wedding guests was her bridegroom's secret lover who was to murder her in a knife frenzy, the Old Bailey heard yesterday.

Michelle Taylor, 21, ... stabbed Alison 54 times, a jury was told.

WAIT

She hatched a murder plot with her sister Lisa, 18, because she was 'completely infatuated' with Alison's husband, prosecutor John Nutting said.

The pair had been making love at least twice a week before the wedding and continued even after it, he said.

Pretty bank clerk Alison, suspected nothing, even when husband John, 29, invited Michelle to their wedding in Ireland and paid for her fare and hotel bill.

But 11 months later Michelle used a knife five inches long and an inch wide to kill her love rival in her home in Battersea, South West London, Mr Nutting said.

(*The Sun*, 7 July 1992, p.1)

Convicted of murder in July 1992 and sentenced to life imprisonment, Michelle and Lisa Taylor were subsequently acquitted on appeal in June 1993. The appeal judge ruled that press publicity had prejudiced their chances of a fair trial. In December 1994 the sisters won the right to a review of their case to bring contempt proceedings against the tabloid press, including The Sun. Their appeal to the House of Lords was subsequently refused in August 1995

The abductor of Abbie Humphries in 1994 was placed on probation with the condition that she receive treatment at a psychiatric hospital, on the grounds that the kidnap was 'deliberate but not premeditated'

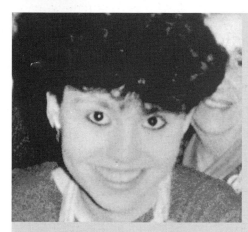

FRANK CURRAN

Baby snatcher Julie Kelley, who put newborn Abbie Humphries' parents through a 15-day nightmare, walked free yesterday.

The abductor smiled as she left the dock after a judge put her on probation, telling her she was 'more mad rather than bad.'

He ruled that Kelley should receive treatment at a mental hospital after her own baby is born in three weeks.

There were gasps of amazement when the verdict was returned at Nottingham Crown Court where Mr Justice Laws told Kelley she had put Abbie's parents through 'dreadful torture.'

But Abbie's forgiving mother Karen said yesterday she felt no malice towards her kidnapper.

Dream

Karen, 33, added at home in Sherwood, Nottingham: 'I don't blame Julie – we've put it all behind us like it was a bad dream.'

Kelley, her head bowed, had been told by the judge: 'It is hard to imagine the extent of the agony of Abbie Humphries' parents during that fortnight.

'They did not know if they would ever see her again.

'You were not completely mentally ill and you were under no delusions as to the nature of your act.'

Mr Laws said the kidnap was 'deliberate but not premeditated – although the consequences were horrific'.

The court heard that dental nurse Kelley faked a pregnancy after boyfriend Leigh Gilbert

YOU'RE MAD NOT BAD

Abbie snatch nurse is freed

dumped her.

The 23-year-old car mechanic took her back when she told him he was the father.

William Everard, QC, prosecuting, said Kelley kept up the elaborate hoax in a bid to save her relationship with Gilbert.

She moved into his home where a bedroom was turned into a nursery.

Kelley padded her abdomen, feigned morning sickness and pretended to make trips to her GP and an ante-natal clinic.

(*Daily Star*, 10 December 1994, p.1)

The ready application of stereotypes is a characteristic feature of most crime reporting. Crime tends to be depicted in terms of a basic confrontation between the symbolic forces of good and evil. Complex social events are collapsed into simplistic questions of right and wrong. The intricate history and consequences of an event necessary to provide a fuller and more complex picture are rarely provided, or only at a later date when the terms of debate have already been firmly set. Hall *et al.* (1975) conclude that crime reports tend to undo the complexities of crime by constructing a number of easy categories into which each type of crime can be placed (see Extract 1.2).

It is important to remember, too, that the news media have little direct access to crime as such. The majority of crime stories come to them via the police, the courts and the Home Office. These agencies of crime control are the primary definers and sources of crime news. As such they are in a position to provide initial definitions of crime and locate them within the context of a continuing crime problem. The credibility of their definitions is

primary definers

Extract 1.2   Hall et al.: 'The complexities of crime'

Though criminology has long aspired to the condition of a science, the fact is that explanations of crime are powerfully and massively overlaid by lay ideologies. These ideological frameworks set whole *chains* of explanations in motion; whole families of criminal types and categories are set going, which knit together, while appearing to unravel, the enigma of crime and its causation. Here one often finds the *complexities* of crime … 'classified out' into the genetic, or the psychopathic, or the environmental, or the sociological, or the psychiatric – or the socially disorganized and undersocialized 'explanations'. To each cluster of explanations is attached an appropriate typology of criminal: the under-chromosomed, the unregenerated evil, the criminally insane, the deprived, the sick, the weak, the mother-deprived, criminal type. To each is often also attached its chain of motivations: the irrational, the driven, the neurotic, the search for kicks, the congenitally wicked, motive. To each, often also belongs the appropriate social setting or scene: the back street, or multiply deprived working-class area; the bomb site; the high-rise block and the unused telephone kiosk; the football end; the drug scene or hippie pad … No doubt something of the truth lurks and hovers within and between these stereotyped and clustered maps of meaning. But they are rarely pressed through in depth and detail to the difficult and complex but necessary social connections which they index. Sometimes, after a parade of 'explorations and explanations', the argument is dissolved ideologically: into one of the great Public Images – Inner City Slum, Family whose Mother went out to work, etc. – which bring the

account conveniently to 'an end', if not to a resolution. …

The media provide the bridge or link between crime and the public anxiety or concern about crime. There is, of course, a widespread and growing anxiety about crime and its upward movement. But, over and above what we know of rising crime either from reported crime, or from the offered interpretations of the criminal statistics, there has been also the closely related phenomenon of a public 'moral panic' about rising crime: on the one hand panics about *certain specific* crimes which connect with troubling public issues (for example, race, drugs, pornography, youth) or, on the other hand, panics about the highly generalized but nameless unspecified 'tide' or 'epidemic' of crime itself. These 'panics' have grown in intensity and number through the post-war years; they clearly reflect very deep-seated public anxieties and uncertainties; but they are distinguished, above all, by four things: (1) the *discrepancy* between the scale of the known facts and the depth, intensity and escalation of the public perception and response; (2) the focusing of these 'panics' around key social themes and social groups (for example, black people) or social categories (for example, drugs offenders); (3) the way each 'panic' feeds off and spirals with *other* concerns which are mapped into it, or in some other way, identified with it; (4) the way in which 'moral panics' issue into control crusades and 'law and order' campaigns.

(Hall *et al.*, 1975, pp.13–15)

in turn enhanced by their 'official' and 'institutional' standing. The regular access of control institutions to media reportage is both open and 'acceptable'. They are the institutions in the front line of crime control; they have an everyday knowledge of the 'fight against crime'. It thus appears quite 'natural' that they should be the main source of news about crime: 'Law is among the dominant institutions entwined with the mass media. The people and organisations in the institution of law join with mass media operatives in constituting a deviance-defining elite that perpetually articulates morality and justice in all other social institutions' (Ericson, 1991, p.223).

As Chibnall (1977, p.49) argues, crime stories have historically been the bread and butter of popular journalism. From the nineteenth century onwards a tradition has developed of sensational crime reporting in the Sunday newspapers, the *Police Gazette* and the *Illustrated Police News*. These were initially dependent on court cases, but as popular journalism expanded in the twentieth century, information about the earlier, and potentially more sensational, aspects of criminal proceedings became highly sought after. Thus the press came to rely increasingly on one major institutional source – the police. Reporters' increased contact with the police gradually became more informal and their role more secure and autonomous. In 1945 these specialist journalists formed the Crime Reporters' Association in order to improve press–police relations. From the 1970s the police have also had considerable success in elevating themselves as authoritative political advisers, not only on the implementation of crime control, but also on matters of criminal justice policy and reform. Under the

Police remove a box, supposedly containing the remains of the victims of alleged serial killer Frederick West, from 25 Cromwell Street in 1994. Several newspapers carried the picture on their front pages. However, there were no human remains in the box at all. The police agreed to stage the scene after pressure from a section of the press corps

guidance of Sir Robert Mark, former Commissioner of the Metropolitan Police, a new and more 'open' press relations policy was instituted, in which press conferences and direct communication between editors and senior police officers have become commonplace.

This shift from a defensive to a proactive posture is such that 'the police now view the news media as part of the policing apparatus of society': a role underlined since the mid 1980s by the advent of such television programmes as *Crimestoppers* (ITV), *Crime Monthly* (LWT) and *Crimewatch UK* (BBC), where viewers are mobilized to help the police through dramatic reconstructions of various incidents (Schlesinger and Tumber, 1994, p.107). Murder, armed robbery with violence and sexual crime are the staple items of coverage, with fraud and corporate crime notable absences. In such 'documentary reconstructions', Schlesinger and Tumber note that the police have 'complete control over access to evidence and a determining voice over the possible uses to which this might be put' (Schlesinger and Tumber, 1994, p.268). *Crimewatch UK* regularly attracts 11 million viewers, many more than that of the national nightly news.

This is not to argue that journalists and broadcasters are incapable of presenting views that are controversial or unacceptable to established politicians or the control agencies, but that in the vast majority of cases their accounts are grounded in the agendas set, and interpretations provided, by these primary sources. These interpretations are in turn dependent largely on the rate of reported crime, the focused and organized police response to certain crimes, and the reports of Home Office statisticians reliant on eventual rates of conviction. Thus media and official definitions of crime are likely to be both partial and reflective of institutional constraints and demands.

They do not simply reflect social reality, but define it in a particular way, subsequently affecting the quality of public or lay opinions. In analysing this effect Hall *et al.* (1975) proposed replacing the 'everyday' assumption that: crime → apprehension → crime report, with the more complex model shown in Figure 1.5.

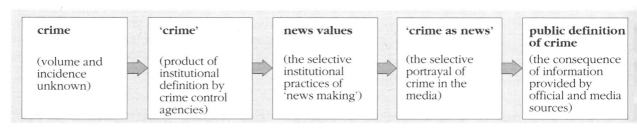

crime	'crime'	news values	'crime as news'	public definition of crime
(volume and incidence unknown)	(product of institutional definition by crime control agencies)	(the selective institutional practices of 'news making')	(the selective portrayal of crime in the media)	(the consequence of information provided by official and media sources)

Figure 1.5 (Source: Hall et al., *1975, p.2)*

In this way it can be argued that popular images about crime are 'popular' only in so far as they are consequences of information provided by official sources with a vested interest in crime control, and by media sources with a vested interest in maintaining news values. Such observations are not unique to the British media. Marsh's (1991) comparative analysis found a striking similarity amongst newspapers worldwide, in types of crime reported, lack of discussion of crime causation and the presentation of false images of the effectiveness of the police and courts in detecting and punishing criminals.

Roshier (1973, p.39), however, warns of accepting a simple, deterministic relationship between media reportage and public attitudes. He argues that we should also remain alive to the ability of the public to differentiate and interpret the information they receive. Notwithstanding the weight of available evidence concerning media partiality and distortion, it cannot by any means be assumed that media representations are always received uncritically.

4.2   The sociology of moral panics

moral panic

In the past three decades the concept of 'moral panic' has been used to describe public reactions (or, perhaps more pertinently, *media* and *political* reactions) to mugging, soccer violence, social security 'scroungers', child abuse, vandalism, drug use, student militancy, 'spectacular' youth sub-cultures, street crime, permissiveness, 'bail bandits' and lone parents.

The first systematic empirical study of a moral panic in the UK was Stanley Cohen's research on the social reaction to the Mods and Rockers disturbances of 1964 (Cohen, 1973b). Groups of working-class youths arrived in the seaside resort of Clacton over the Easter bank holiday, Clacton being traditionally the meeting place for holidaying youths from the East End of London. Easter 1964 was cold and wet and the facilities and amusements for young people were strictly limited. Shopkeepers were irritated by the lack of business, and the young people had their own boredom fanned by rumours of café owners refusing to serve some of them. Eventually, scuffles between groups of youths broke out, windows were broken, beach huts vandalized, and those on scooters and bikes roared up and down the promenade.

Such events were by no means new. Pearson's (1983) study of hooliganism in British history, as we saw in section 3.1, noted comparable disturbances in the 'lawlessness' of the Teddy Boys in the 1950s and in a series of clashes between police and East End youths (the first 'hooligans') during the August bank holiday celebrations in London in 1898.

However, the events of Easter 1964 were to receive front-page outrage in the national press. The media spoke of a 'day of terror'; of youngsters who beat up an entire town; of a town being invaded by a mob 'hell-bent on destruction'. Youths were presented as being engaged in a confrontation between two easily recognizable rival gangs. They were described as affluent young people who deliberately caused trouble by acting aggressively towards local residents and by destroying a great deal of public property.

Cohen's research, however, found no evidence of any structured gangs. He argued that the groups were not even at the time polarized within a Mod–Rocker distinction. Rivalries were more likely to have been built around regional identities. Motorbike or scooter owners were a minority. The young were not particularly affluent – in the main being unskilled or semi-skilled manual workers. Above all, Cohen argues, the total amount of serious violence and vandalism was not great. The typical offence throughout was not assault or malicious damage, but threatening behaviour. A few days after the event a journalist was forced to admit that the affair had been 'a little over-reported' (Cohen, 1973b, p.31).

By then, though, the media outrage had set in train a series of interrelated responses. First, it initiated a wider public concern which obliged the police to step up their surveillance. The result was more frequent arrests

Crowd scene: Margate, Whit Monday, 1964

which appeared to confirm the validity of the initial media reaction. Second, by emphasizing the antagonism between two groups, and their stylistic differences, the youths were encouraged to place themselves in one of the opposing camps. This polarization cemented the original image and produced more clashes in several other seaside resorts on subsequent bank holidays. Third, the continuing disturbances attracted more news coverage, increased police activity and furthered public concern.

Thus was a *deviancy amplification spiral* set in motion (see Figure 1.6). The media's distortion of the initial events in 1964 resulted in an amplification of youthful deviance both in perceived *and* real terms. Youths began to

deviancy amplification spiral

51

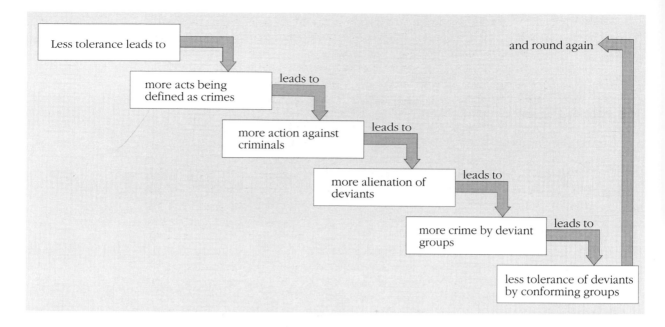

Less tolerance leads to				and round again
more acts being defined as crimes	leads to			
	more action against criminals	leads to		
		more alienation of deviants	leads to	
			more crime by deviant groups	leads to
				less tolerance of deviants by conforming groups

Figure 1.6 Wilkins' deviancy amplification feedback loop (Source: Wilkins, 1964, p.90)

identify with the label attached to them and thus believed themselves to be *more* deviant and separate from the rest of society. They had been singled out as society's 'folk devils' and acted out that role accordingly in subsequent years.

The moral panic thesis not only helps us to identify instances of media exaggeration and distortion, but also maintains that selective reporting and police targeting can *create* crime waves and social problems. The media can stir up public indignation and engineer concern about certain types of behaviour even when there is nothing new about that behaviour or when its real threat is minimal. Young (1974) went further and argued that there is an *institutionalized* need in the media to create moral panics in order to make 'good copy'.

Cohen (1973b) also addressed the question of why this process should have occurred at all in the 1960s. He argued that we need to place such reactions in their socio-historical context. The mid-sixties was the time of a supposedly new permissiveness, the beginnings of a Swinging London, a rise in working-class youth spending power, the onslaught of a new consumerism, and the decline of traditional working-class communities. It was, above all, a time of rapid social change. For Cohen, the ensuing public anxiety and uncertainty was resolved by identifying certain social groups as scapegoats or 'folk devils'. They became the visual symbols of what was wrong with society. In the meantime, the more intractable and structural problems to do with relative deprivation and a restricted opportunity structure could be overlooked and passed by. The public gaze was fixed on the symptoms rather than on the causes of social unrest.

During the 1970s youth was to play a central part in this scapegoating and diversionary process. Hall *et al.* (1978) reused the concept of moral panic in identifying a series of 'major social problems' to do with permissiveness, vandals, student radicals and so on, culminating in 1972–73 with the moral panic of 'mugging'. Hall *et al.* show how the news media, working with images from the New York ghetto, defined the incidence of street robberies by youth in Britain's inner cities as an outbreak of a new and dangerous kind of violent crime. What was previously known as 'snatching' or 'getting rolled' was now redefined as 'mugging'. Hall *et al.* trace the way this definition was employed to justify, not only a new category of crime, but also punitive sentencing and an image of a generalized breakdown of law and order in society. Also, as the panic developed, mugging became defined almost exclusively as a problem with black youth – they became the primary folk devils. As Cohen had previously concluded, Hall *et al.* noted how such problems were publicly defined as lawlessness, rather than the results of poverty, social deprivation or class and racial inequality.

The notion of moral panic is central to both studies in explaining how particular sections of youth (working-class/black) become identified as worthy of police and judicial attention. However, by adopting a conflict-based definition of criminalization, the implications of such identification are extended by Hall *et al.* For them a moral panic is the first link in a spiral of events leading to the maintenance of law in society by a legitimized rule through coercion and the general exercise of authority. Whilst interactionism talks of a 'society' that creates rules, Hall *et al.* locate moral panic in terms of a 'state' that has the power to criminalize. The sudden defining of the historically recurring event of street crime as a mugging created the impression of a crime wave and provided government with the justification to introduce repressive legislation which ultimately came to affect the quality of life of the vast majority (see Figure 1.7).

Discrete moral panics (1955–65)

1950s Teddy Boys
early 1960s Mods and Rockers

More diffuse moral panics (1966–70)

permissiveness; drugs; pornography; student radicalism
youth violence; skinheads; football hooligans
'radical' trade unionism

Generalized climate of hostility to 'marginal' groups and racial minorities (1971–)

street crime (e.g. mugging, early 1970s; joyriders, early 1990s)
political violence (e.g. IRA, 1970s, 1980s and 1990s)
trade union militancy (e.g. red scare, 1974; miners' strikes, 1974, 1985)
welfare liberalism (e.g. social security scroungers, 1974; teenage pregnancies, 1993)
drugs (e.g. glue sniffing, 1982; heroin, 1985; crack, 1992)
family morality (e.g. abortion, 1980; homosexuality, 1986; child abuse, 1974, 1987; satanic abuse, 1990; video nasties, 1993; single parenting, 1993)
black youth (e.g. inner city disturbances, 1980, 1981, 1985)
sub-cultures (e.g. punk, 1976; football hooligans, 1970s, 1980s; acid house and rave parties, late 1980s; hunt saboteurs, 1990s; New Age Travellers, 1990s; 'yob' culture, 1994)
feminism (e.g. Greenham Common protests, 1980)

Figure 1.7 A chronology of moral panics (Source: based on Muncie, 1987, p.45)

Extract 1.3 Scraton and Chadwick: 'The politics of criminalization'

Criminalization, the application of the criminal label to an identifiable social category, is dependent on *how* certain acts are labelled and on *who* has the power to label, and is directly limited to the political economy of marginalization. The power to criminalize is not derived necessarily in consensus politics but it carries with it the ideologies associated with marginalization and it is within these portrayals that certain actions are named, contained and regulated. This is a powerful process because it mobilizes popular approval and legitimacy in support of powerful interests within the state. As Hillyard's (1987) discussion of Northern Ireland illustrates clearly, public support is more likely to be achieved for state intervention against 'criminal' acts than for the repression or suppression of a 'political' cause. Further, even where no purposeful political intention is involved, the process of criminalization can divert attention from the social or political dynamics of a movement and specify its 'criminal' potential. If black youth is portrayed exclusively as 'muggers' (Hall *et al.*, 1978) there will be less tolerance of organized campaigns which emphasize that they have legitimate political and economic grievances (Gilroy, 1987). The marginalization of women who campaign for rights or for peace and the questioning of their sexuality is a further example of the process by which meaningful and informed political action can be undermined, de-legitimized and criminalized (Chadwick and Little, 1987; Young, 1990). Fundamental to the criminalization thesis is the proposition that while political motives are downplayed, the degree of *violence* involved is emphasized. In industrial relations, for example, it is the violence of the pickets which is pinpointed (Scraton and Thomas, 1985; Fine and Millar, 1985; Beynon, 1985), rather than the importance, for the success of a strike, of preventing supplies getting through to a factory. The preoccupation with the 'violence' of political opposition makes it easier to mobilize popular support for measures of containment.

In many of these examples, 'criminalization' is a process which has been employed to underpin the repressive or control functions of the state. ... Married to the process of marginalization, through which identifiable groups systematically and structurally become peripheral to the core relations of the political economy, criminalization offers a strong analytical construct. Taken together these theses provide the foundations to critical analyses of the state, the rule of law and social conflict in advanced capitalist society.

References

Beynon, H. (1985) *Digging Deeper: Issues in the Miners' Strike*, London, Verso.

Chadwick, K. and Little, C. (1987) 'The criminalisation of women', in Scraton (1987).

Fine, B. and Millar, R. (eds) (1985) *Policing the Miners' Strike*, London, Lawrence and Wishart.

Gilroy, P. (1987) *There Ain't No Black in the Union Jack*, London, Hutchinson.

Hall, S. *et al.* (1978) *Policing the Crisis*, London, Macmillan.

Hillyard, P. (1987) 'The normalization of special powers: from Northern Ireland to Britain', in Scraton (1987).

Scraton, P. (ed.) (1987) *Law, Order and the Authoritarian State*, Milton Keynes, Open University Press.

Scraton, P. and Thomas, P. (1985) *The State v The People: Lessons from the Coal Dispute* (*Journal of Law and Society*, special issue), Oxford, Blackwell.

Young, A. (1990) *Femininity in Dissent*, London, Routledge.

(Scraton and Chadwick, 1991, pp.172–3)

For example, as was evident by the late 1970s, the enunciation of authoritarian policies, if repeated often enough, comes to form the terrain of any debate concerned with issues of law and order. As Hall succinctly put it in writing about football hooliganism: 'the tendency is increased to deal with any problem, first by simplifying its causes, second by stigmatising those involved, third by whipping up public feeling and fourth by stamping hard on it from above' (Hall, 1978, p.34). Moral panics thus form part of a sensitizing and legitimizing process for solidifying moral boundaries, identifying 'enemies within', strengthening the powers of state control and enabling law and order to be promoted without cognisance of the social divisions and conflicts which produce deviance and political dissent.

For Sim *et al.* (1987, p.60) this process reached its apogee in the Thatcher administration of the 1980s with new forms of surveillance, regulation and control in all areas of social policy, welfare and criminal justice. Industrial conflicts, feminist activism, the peace movement and all manner of social protest and alternative life-styles became subject to a process of criminalization. In many respects political dissent was 'marginalized' and redefined as 'criminal' activity (see Extract 1.3).

Significantly too, major social problems such as urban decay, erosion of communities, poverty, unemployment, homelessness and drug addiction continue to be given less sustained attention, unless, and until, they are defined within a discourse of 'crime'.

The most telling critical evaluation of the moral panic thesis to date has come from a *left-realist* perspective in understanding crime and deviance. left realism
This maintains that it is both unrealistic and naively idealist to suggest that the problem of, say, youth disorder or street crime is merely a problem of miscategorization and concomitant moral panics (**Young, 1986**). However exaggerated and distorted the images of crime are in the media, the *reality* of crime can be, and often is, one of human suffering and disaster. As such, it needs to be 'taken seriously' and not simply dismissed as a media construction. So, whilst the left-realist position might sympathize with Cohen's notion of crime being a metaphor for wider social change, it maintains that it is a metaphor rooted in reality. That 'reality' is taken to be a growing public fear of crime, a recognition that crime is a problem, and an acknowledgement of the damaging effects of crime, particularly within inner city and other working-class communities. To this extent left realism moves away from notions of social construction and back to definitions of crime as violations of legal codes. Lea and Young (1984) maintain that certain crimes, such as the high rate of burglaries, sexual and racial attacks in working-class neighbourhoods, *are* part of the 'real problems' facing the population. It is thus myopic and politically naive to dismiss crime as a ruling-class mystification, or as something which is simply 'created' by the state and its agencies. However, as a result, left realism necessarily shifts the focus away from developing analyses of law, the state and corporate crime and towards establishing an accurate working-class victimology.

The problem, of course, is in charting a path which neither adopts a romanticist and idealist position (which might argue that crime is illusory and that the 'real' victim is the offender) nor falls into a position which celebrates moral panic and sees violence as ubiquitous. Left realism has indeed been accused of 'accepting' state-generated definitions of crime (particularly in relation to the question of race – see Gilroy, 1987) and official pictures of extent and seriousness, and, by doing so, of implicitly providing more armour for a conservative law-and-order position (Sim *et al.*, 1987, pp.39–46). A key issue remains, though, that whilst it may be morally acceptable (for some) to cite concern about marijuana smoking and youthful rowdyism as instances of moral panic, can the same be said of racial violence, rape and domestic violence? (This is discussed further in Chapter 5.)

4.3   Fear of crime in the risk society

The 1982 British Crime Survey was the first in the UK to suggest that fear of crime was as great a problem as crime itself. The survey asked: 'What sorts of crime do you worry about most?'. The percentages of 'worried' respondents mentioning particular types of crime were: vehicle theft 1 per cent, vandalism 4 per cent, assault 16 per cent, sexual attacks 25 per cent, mugging 34 per cent and burglary 44 per cent. Fear of crime appears to have an inverse relationship with statistical occurrence. In other words, according to the BCS, people are concerned most about those crimes which they are least likely to experience. Those who felt least safe were notably women, older people and those living in the inner cities. People in manual occupations were consistently more fearful than those in non-manual, and those living alone more than those living with others (Hough and Mayhew, 1983, p.23). The BCS data showed that, frequently, it was those who felt most unsafe who were the least likely to become victims. Conversely, young men expressed the least fear, yet young, working-class inner-city males were the most likely fear and risk   to be victimized. The discrepancy was marked for fear and actual risk of 'street crime' (see Table 1.5).

Table 1.5 Fear and risk of street crime		
	Percentage feeling very 'unsafe'	Percentage of victims of 'street crime'
Men		
16–30	1	7.7
31–60	4	1.6
61+	7	0.6
Women		
16–30	16	2.8
31–60	35	1.4
61+	37	1.2

Note: percentages represent responses to the question: 'How safe do you feel walking alone in this area after dark?'. Weighted data; unweighted n = 10,905.

Source: Hough and Mayhew, 1983, p.25, Table 5

The 1984 BCS similarly concluded that people tend to hold exaggerated estimates of the risks of such crimes as burglary, mugging and rape. One in nine women under 30, for instance, thought it likely or fairly likely that they would be raped in the next year; one in six people thought it likely they would be mugged; 53 per cent believed burglary to be the most prevalent crime in their area (Hough and Mayhew, 1985, p.38). However, most people were found to have an accurate idea of the *relative* risks of some crime. For example, whilst concern consistently outweighed occurrence, those most at risk of burglary, living in multiracial areas and poor council estates, also reported the highest levels of anxiety. Agricultural and high-income areas had both the lowest occurrence and lowest fear of property crime.

Such data raise the issue of irrational/rational fears and the degree to which public concern and policy should be analysed as panic or as reasonable responses to actual problems. The left-realist position has maintained that public experience of crime, particularly in the inner city, has generated a rational and well-founded fear. Young, for example, argued that: 'ascribing irrationality to women is based on ignoring that much crime against women, such as domestic violence, is concealed in the official figures, that women are less tolerant of violence and that they experience harassment on a level unknown to most men' (Young, 1992, p.50). Such analysis is, in the main, based on data gathered from local crime surveys. Whilst the first BCS reported only one attempted rape, the locally based Islington Crime Survey found that 20 per cent of women knew someone who had been sexually assaulted in the previous 12 months (Jones *et al.*, 1986). This has been confirmed by much sexual violence victimization research. A study in Leeds revealed that 59 per cent of women had experienced some form of sexual violence in the previous year; whilst a study in Wandsworth, London, found the rate to be as high as 76 per cent (Hanmer and Saunders, 1984; Radford, 1987). In this respect the BCS findings – that a third of women admitted not going out at night due to fear of crime – cannot simply be explained away as 'irrational'. Similarly, the fear expressed by older people may well be rational in reflecting their relative physical disadvantage and vulnerability. The lack of fear expressed by young males may, in any event, simply reflect a 'fearless' masculine bravado that is prevalent in a male-defined society. Crawford *et al.* (1990) maintain that fear *does* accord to people's real life circumstances.

Fear cannot, however, be simply accounted for with reference to likelihood of actual victimization. Rather, it may be generated by any number of personal and environmental factors. Box *et al.* (1988), for example, argue that 'incivilities' such as loud parties, 'street corner' rowdyism, boarded-up houses, subway graffiti, and broken windows may all signify a neighbourhood that is disorderly and threatening. They conclude that fear depends on an interactive complex of vulnerability, environmental conditions, personal knowledge of crime, confidence in the police, perceptions of personal risk and offence seriousness. Fear, it is argued, is extraneous, generated by factors other than risk of crime *per se*. Not least of these is the symbolic purchase of certain spaces and places as inherently dangerous (this is examined further in Chapter 4).

Attempts to measure the impact of the mass media in promoting fear have generally found that readers of those newspapers that report crime in the most dramatic and salient fashion also have the highest levels of fear of crime. Moreover, the majority of people attribute their knowledge of the risk of crime to information received from television and press reports (Williams and Dickinson, 1993). However, a *causal* link cannot be unequivocally established. Low socio-economic status remains a key predictor not only of tabloid readership and high levels of fear, but also of higher levels of actual victimization. Lea and Young (1984) note that being male, young and working class does enhance the likelihood of being both a criminal *and* a victim. Street crime, in particular, tends to be *intra*-class and *intra*-racial, committed by the relatively deprived on like-situated victims. Crawford *et al.* thus maintain that: 'in inner city areas mass media coverage of crime tends to reinforce what people already know', and that: 'crime is a product of inner city reality and government policy, not a figment of some editor's imagination' (Crawford *et al.*, 1990, pp.76–7) (see Extract 1.4).

Extract 1.4 Young: 'Crime really is a problem'

Crime is not an activity of latter day Robin Hoods – the vast majority of working-class crime is directed within the working class. It is intra-class *not* inter-class in its nature. Similarly, despite the mass media predilection for focusing on inter-racial crime, it is overwhelmingly intra-racial. Crimes of violence, for example, are by and large one poor person hitting another poor person – and in almost half of these instances it is a man hitting his wife or lover.

This is not to deny the impact of crimes of the powerful or indeed of the social problems created by capitalism which are perfectly legal. Rather, left realism notes that the working class is a victim of crime from all directions. It notes that the more vulnerable a person is economically and socially the more likely it is that *both* working-class and white-collar crime will occur against them; that one sort of crime tends to compound another, as does one social problem another. Furthermore, it notes that crime is a potent symbol of the anti-social nature of capitalism and is the most immediate way in which people experience other problems, such as unemployment or competitive individualism.

Realism starts from problems as people experience them. It takes seriously the complaints of women with regards the dangers of being in public places at night, it takes note of the fears of the elderly with regard to burglary, it acknowledges the widespread occurrence of domestic violence and racist attacks. It does not ignore the fears of the vulnerable nor recontextualize them out of existence by putting them into a perspective which abounds with abstractions such as the 'average citizen' bereft of class or gender. It is only too aware of the systematic concealment and ignorance of crimes against the least powerful. Yet it does not take these fears at face value – it pinpoints their rational kernel but it is also aware of the forces towards irrationality.

Realism is not empiricism. Crime and deviance are prime sites of moral anxiety and tension in a society which is fraught with real inequalities and injustices. Criminals can quite easily become folk devils onto which are projected such feelings of unfairness. But there is a rational core to the fear of crime just as there is a rational core to the anxieties which distort it. Realism argues with popular consciousness in its attempts to separate out reality from fantasy. But it does not deny that crime is a problem. Indeed, if there were no rational core the media would have no power of leverage to the public consciousness. Crime becomes a metaphor but it is a metaphor rooted in reality.

(Young, 1986, pp.23–4)

Nevertheless, the questions of how fear is constituted, experienced and constructed remain controversial. Sparks (1992), for example, questions the left-realist assertion that fear of crime, no matter the circumstances, is always *rational* and should be taken seriously. The ability of survey respondents to estimate risk, he argues, is more likely to be governed by 'uncertainty' than any 'known probabilities'. The measurements of risk and fear via surveys are likely to be complex and uneven given the 'inherent scope for discrepancy between what criminal events mean at the moment of their commission and what they stand for once they have entered the widening circles of punishment, retribution, reporting, rhetoric and rebuttal, election platforms and the multitude of communicative exchanges which compose the public sphere' (Sparks, 1992, pp.13–14). Fear of crime, as a mode of perception, then, may not necessarily be either rational or irrational, but reflective of a range of diffuse anxieties about one's position and identity in the world. In other words, the issue of fear always involves the problems of representation, interpretation and meaning. While victims of crime may be more fearful as a result of direct experience, the vast majority of the public's contact with crime is indirect and 'learnt' through a variety of 'readings' of neighbourhood conditions, media information and personal conversations. Moreover, the issue is characteristically clouded through being construed in a partial and limiting fashion. Downes (1988, p.182) usefully reminds us that the 'fear of crime thesis' remains most developed in relation to certain forms of street crime. It concentrates more on unpredictable violence than on those forms which are normalized as accidental, or where victimization is indirect and dispersed, as with corporate crime.

The key issue thus may not be whether 'fear of crime' has any rational basis, but rather how far its emotiveness as a topic, and the general fascination the public holds for 'all things criminal', can be (or is) used for ulterior, ideological and political motives.

ACTIVITY 1.5

Using the preceding discussion in sections 3 and 4 and referring to Extracts 1.3 and 1.4, draw up a list of the relative merits and weaknesses of the competing accounts of crime, offered by the moral panic and the left-realist positions. In particular, note how each holds a different definition of crime and focuses its analysis on (or ignores) different aspects of the 'crime problem' (for example, social construction, rational fear, property crime, conflict and dissent, victims, corporate crime, criminalization, marginalization, the role of the law, and so on).

5 Conclusion: crime as a problem and the problem of 'crime'

This chapter has been designed to reveal the complexities involved not only in what can be considered as crime, but also in measurements and assessments of its extent and seriousness. There are no easy answers to be gained. We may be tempted to conclude that, given the high profile of crime, as news and as drama, all we are dealing with is a never-ending and self-fulfilling series of social constructions. Yet few who have been the victims of abuse, personal loss or violent attack are likely to be reassured by such an argument. Whilst some advocates of a moral panic position might campaign for limitations in recourse to the law in dealing with certain social harms, others argue for an extension of the law's reach to afford some protection to systematically oppressed populations. Arguments for decriminalization stand uneasily against those which advocate a broadening of definitions of crime. For the former, 'crime' acts to simplify and mystify complex social conflicts, for the latter the delineation of certain practices as 'crime' remains one of the few ways in which otherwise ignored social problems can achieve social visibility and public acknowledgement.

Part of the problem in establishing the reality of crime does seem to lie in the concept of 'crime' itself. It implies a unity to what are a vast array of diverse behaviours, events and legal sanctions. Rather, this chapter has shown how the elusive nature of our subject matter can only begin to be captured by subjecting it to a series of *deconstructions* – revealing how the concept becomes active only through the variable meanings attached to it in specific political and socio-historical contexts and through the diverse 'voices' of the media, statisticians, the public, the police, politicians, victims and so on. 'Crime' clearly takes on different meanings to different social audiences. It is frequently depicted as a 'problem', yet it is also one of the most enduring and 'normalized' aspects of modern society. Its 'reality' is assumed, but its existence depends upon the prior formulation of criminal law. As a result it might also be tempting to abandon use of the concept altogether. It is of such emotional charge and historical variance to have little analytical validity. Yet such a position would leave us peculiarly stranded and unable to enter into what remains, whether we are aware of it or not, a recurrent and contested issue in our everyday lives. Nevertheless, as a governing principle we should refer not to '*the* crime problem' singular, but to a diverse and complex array of 'crimes'. As De Haan argues:

> disputes about the proper use of the concept of crime will be endless precisely because contending positions can be sustained by perfectly respectable arguments and evidence. This does not mean falling into a total and undiscriminating relativism, as good reasons can always be given for the claim that one interpretation of the concept enables one to see further and deeper than another.

(De Haan, 1990, p.154)

Accordingly, what this chapter advocates is a critical *reconstruction* of crime – by revealing how 'crime' is not as simple a concept as might be first presumed; that it has numerous contexts and consequences; and that it remains a site of legal, political and moral contestation. By exploring these ideas in more detail we might be better placed to make some measured judgement, not only of 'the problem of crime', but of the nature of a social order which, whilst consistently producing and reproducing that problem, remains selective and partial in delineating which social harms are to be deemed 'criminal' and which are not.

Further reading

There are lamentably few texts which begin by problematizing the concept of 'crime' itself. The American textbooks by Quinney and Wildeman (1977) and Beirne and Messerschmidt (1991) do, however, provide a critical introduction, as do Lacey *et al.* (1990) on the concept of 'criminal law'. The competing definitions offered by Tappan (1947), **Becker (1963)** and **Chambliss (1975)** continue to offer some valuable insights. A thorough account of the production and interpretation of crime data is provided by Bottomley and Pease (1986); a similar job is done on crime and media reporting by Schlesinger and Tumber (1994). A comparison of Hall *et al.* (1978) and Lea and Young (1984) will reveal why, even within criminology, the subject of crime remains contested and controversial. An introduction to issues surrounding women and crime can be found in Heidensohn (1985) and to gender and crime in Walklate (1995). **Box (1983)** and Pearson (1983) provide accessible means through which many of our taken-for-granted images of crime can be jolted out of their 'common-sense' and nostalgic complacency.

References

Anderson, S., Kinsey, R., Loader, I. and Smith, C. (1994) *Cautionary Tales: Young People, Crime and Policing in Edinburgh*, Aldershot, Avebury.

Archbold (1994) *Criminal Pleading, Evidence and Practice*, London, Sweet and Maxwell.

Becker, H. (1963) *Outsiders: Studies in the Sociology of Deviance*, New York, Free Press. (Extract reprinted as 'Outsiders' in Muncie *et al.*, 1996.)

Beirne, P. and Messerschmidt, J. (1991) *Criminology*, Fort Worth, TX, Harcourt, Brace College Publishers.

Bottomley, K. and Pease, K. (1986) *Crime and Punishment: Interpreting the Data*, Milton Keynes, Open University Press.

Box, S. (1981) *Deviance, Reality and Society* (2nd edn), London, Holt, Rinehart and Winston.

Box, S. (1983) *Power, Crime and Mystification*, London, Tavistock. (Extract reprinted as 'Crime, power and ideological mystification' in Muncie *et al.*, 1996.)

Box, S., Hale, C. and Andrews, G. (1988) 'Explaining fear of crime', *British Journal of Criminology*, vol.28, no.3, pp.340–56.

Braithwaite, J. (1989) *Crime, Shame and Reintegration*, Cambridge and New York, Cambridge University Press. (Extract reprinted as 'Reintegrative shaming' in Muncie *et al.*, 1996.)

Carson, W.G. (1981) *The Other Price of British Oil*, Oxford, Martin Robertson.

Chambliss, W.J. (1964) 'A sociological analysis of the law of vagrancy', *Social Problems*, no.12, pp.67–77.

Chambliss, W.J. (1969) *Crime and the Legal Process*, New York, McGraw-Hill.

Chambliss, W.J. (1975) 'Toward a political economy of crime', *Theory and Society*, vol.2, pp.149–70. (Extract reprinted in Muncie *et al.*, 1996.)

Chambliss, W.J. (1989) 'State organised crime', *Criminology* vol.27, no.2, pp.183–208.

Chibnall, S. (1977) *Law and Order News*, London, Tavistock.

Christie, N. (1993) *Crime Control as Industry*, London, Routledge.

Cohen, S. (1973a) 'The failures of criminology', *The Listener*, 8 November.

Cohen, S. (1973b) *Folk Devils and Moral Panics: The Creation of the Mods and Rockers*, London, Paladin.

Cohen, S. (1993) 'Human rights and crimes of the state: the culture of denial', *Australian and New Zealand Journal of Criminology*, vol.26, no.1, pp.98–114. (Extract reprinted in Muncie *et al.*, 1996.)

Cook, D. (1989) *Rich Law; Poor Law*, Buckingham, Open University Press.

Council of Europe (1992) *Penological Information Bulletin*, No.17, Strasbourg, Council of Europe.

Crawford, A., Jones, T., Woodhouse, T. and Young, J. (1990) *Second Islington Crime Survey*, Middlesex Polytechnic.

De Haan, W. (1990) *The Politics of Redress*, London, Unwin Hyman.

De Haan, W. (1991) 'Abolitionism and crime control: a contradiction in terms', in Stenson and Cowell (1991). (Extract reprinted as 'Abolitionism and crime control' in Muncie *et al.*, 1996.)

Ditton, J. (1977) *Part-Time Crime*, London, Macmillan.

Ditton, J. (1979) *Contrology: Beyond the New Criminology*, London, Macmillan.

Ditton, J. and Duffy, J. (1983) 'Bias in the newspaper reporting of crime news', *British Journal of Criminology*, vol.23, no.2, pp.159–65.

Downes, D. (1988) 'Crime and social control in Britain', *British Journal of Criminology*, vol.28, no.2, pp.45–57.

Ericson, R.V. (1991) 'Mass media, crime, law and justice', *British Journal of Criminology*, vol.31, no.3, pp.219–49.

Galliher, J.F. (1989) *Criminology: Human Rights, Criminal Law and Crime*, Englewood Cliffs, NJ, Prentice-Hall.

Gilroy, P. (1987) *There Ain't No Black in the Union Jack*, London, Hutchinson.

Guardian Education (1994) 'Cracking down on crime', 11 October, p.11.

Hagan, J. (1985) *Modern Criminology*, New York, McGraw-Hill.

Hall, J. (1952) *Theft, Law and Society*, Indianapolis, IN, Bobs-Merrill.

Hall, S. (1978) 'The treatment of football hooliganism in the press', in Ingham, R. (ed.) *Football Hooliganism*, London, Inter-Action.

Hall, S., Clarke, J., Critcher, C., Jefferson, T. and Roberts, B. (1975) *Newsmaking and Crime*, Paper presented to NACRO Conference on Crime and the Media, Birmingham, Centre for Contemporary Cultural Studies, University of Birmingham.

Hall, S., Critcher, C., Jefferson, T., Clarke, J. and Roberts, B. (1978) *Policing the Crisis*, London, Macmillan.

Hanmer, J. and Saunders, S. (1984) *Well-Founded Fears*, London, Macmillan.

Hartjen, C.A. (1978) *Crime and Criminalisation* (2nd edn), New York, Praeger.

Heidensohn, F. (1985) *Women and Crime*, London, Macmillan.

Henry, S. (1978) *The Hidden Economy*, Oxford, Martin Robertson.

Hester, S. and Eglin, P. (1992) *A Sociology of Crime*, London, Routledge.

Home Office (1991) *Digest of Information on the Criminal Justice System*, Home Office Research and Statistics Department, London, HMSO.

Home Office (1992) *Race and the Criminal Justice System*, London, HMSO.

Home Office (1993) *Digest 2: Information on the Criminal Justice System in England and Wales*, Home Office Research and Statistics Department, London, HMSO.

Home Office (1995) *Digest 3: Information on the Criminal Justice System in England and Wales*, Home Office Research and Statistics Department, London, HMSO.

Hood, R. (1993) *Race and Sentencing*, Oxford, Oxford University Press.

Hough, M. and Mayhew, P. (1983) *The British Crime Survey: First Report*, Home Office Research Study No.16, London, HMSO.

Hough, M. and Mayhew, P. (1985) *Taking Account of Crime: Findings from the Second British Crime Survey*, Home Office Research Study No.85, London, HMSO.

Hudson, B. (1989) 'Discrimination and disparity', *New Community*, vol.16, no.1, pp.23–34.

Hulsman, L. (1986) 'Critical criminology and the concept of crime', *Contemporary Crises*, vol.10, no.1, pp.63–80. (Extract reprinted in Muncie *et al.*, 1996.)

Hutter, B. and Williams, G. (1981) *Controlling Women: The Normal and the Deviant*, London, Croom Helm.

Jones, T., Maclean, B. and Young, J. (1986) *The Islington Crime Survey*, Aldershot, Gower.

Lacey, N., Wells, C. and Meure, D. (1990) *Reconstructing Criminal Law*, London, Weidenfeld and Nicolson.

Lea, J. and Young, J. (1984) *What Is To Be Done About Law and Order?* Harmondsworth, Penguin.

Marsh, H.L. (1991) 'A comparative analysis of crime coverage in newspapers in the United States and other countries from 1960 to 1989', *Journal of Criminal Justice*, vol.19, no.1, pp. 67–79.

Mayhew, P. and Maung, N.A. (1992) *Surveying Crime: Findings from the 1992 British Crime Survey*, Home Office Research and Statistics Department, Research Findings No.2, London, HMSO.

Mayhew, P., Elliott, D. and Dowds, L. (1989) *The 1988 British Crime Survey*, Home Office Research Study No.111, London, HMSO.

Mayhew, P., Mirrlees-Black, C. and Maung, N.A. (1994) *Trends in Crime: Findings from the 1994 British Crime Survey*, Home Office Research and Statistics Department, Research Findings No.14, London, HMSO.

Michael, J. and Adler, M. (1933) *Crime, Law and Social Science*, New York, Harcourt, Brace Jovanovich.

Muncie, J. (1987) 'Much ado about nothing? The sociology of moral panics', *Social Studies Review*, vol.3, no.2, pp.42–7

Muncie, J., McLaughlin, E. and Langan, M. (eds) (1996) *Criminological Perspectives: A Reader*, London, Sage in association with The Open University.

Northern Ireland Office (1993) *Crime and the Community*, Belfast, HMSO.

Pearce, F. (1976) *Crimes of the Powerful*, London, Pluto.

Pearson, G. (1983) *Hooligan: A History of Respectable Fears*, London, Macmillan.

Quinney, R. (1970) *The Social Reality of Crime*, Boston, MA, Little Brown.

Quinney, R. and Wildeman, J. (1977) *The Problem of Crime* (2nd edn), New York, Harper and Row.

Radford, J. (1987) 'Policing male violence', in Hanmer, J. and Maynard, M. (eds) *Women, Violence and Social Control*, London, Macmillan.

Radford, J. and Russell, D. (eds) (1992) *Femicide*, Buckingham, Open University Press.

Radzinowicz, I. and King, J. (1977) *The Growth of Crime*, London, Hamish Hamilton.

Rohrer, R. (1982) 'Lost in the myths of crime', *New Statesman*, 22 January.

Roshier, B. (1973) 'The selection of crime news by the press', in Cohen, S. and Young, J. (eds) *The Manufacture of News*, London, Constable.

Rutter, M. and Giller, H. (1983) *Juvenile Delinquency: Trends and Perspectives*, New York, Guilford.

Schlesinger, P. and Tumber, H. (1994) *Reporting Crime: The Media Politics of Criminal Justice*, Oxford, Clarendon Press.

Schwendinger, H. and Schwendinger, J. (1970) 'Defenders of order or guardians of human rights?', *Issues in Criminology*, vol.5, no.2, pp.123–57.

Scraton, P. and Chadwick, K. (1991) 'The theoretical and political priorities of critical criminology', in Stenson and Cowell (1991). (Extract reprinted in Muncie *et al.*, 1996.)

Sellin, T. (1938) *Culture, Conflict and Crime*, New York, Social Science Research Council.

Shah, R. and Pease, K. (1992) 'Crime, race and reporting to the police', *Howard Journal*, vol.31, no.3, pp.192–9.

Sharrock, W. (1984) 'The social realities of deviance', in Anderson, R.J. and Sharrock, W. (eds) *Applied Sociological Perspectives*, London, Allen and Unwin.

Shearing, C. (1989) 'Decriminalising criminology' *Canadian Journal of Criminology*, vol.31, no.2, pp.169–78.

Sim, J., Scraton, P. and Gordon, P. (1987) 'Crime, the state and critical analysis', in Scraton, P. (ed.) *Law, Order and the Authoritarian State*, Milton Keynes, Open University Press.

Simmons, J.L. (1969) *Deviants*, Berkeley, CA, Glendessary Press.

Skogan, W. (1990) *Police and Public in England and Wales*, Home Office Research Study No.117, London, HMSO.

Smith, S.J. (1984) 'Crime in the news', *British Journal of Criminology*, vol.24, no.3, pp.289–95.

Snider, L. (1993) 'The politics of corporate crime control', in Pearce, F. and Woodwiss, M. (eds) *Global Crime Connections*, London, Macmillan.

Sparks, R. (1992) *Television and the Drama of Crime*, Buckingham, Open University Press.

Stenson, K. and Cowell, D. (eds) (1991) *The Politics of Crime Control*, London, Sage.

Stevens, P. and Willis, C. (1979) *Race, Crime and Arrests*, Home Office Research Study No.58, London, HMSO.

Sumner, C. (ed.) (1990) *Censure, Politics and Criminal Justice*, Buckingham, Open University Press.

Sutherland, E. (1949) *White Collar Crime*, New York, Dryden Press.

Sutherland, E. and Cressey, D. (1970) *Criminology* (8th edn), Philadelphia, PA, Lippincott.

Tappan, P.W. (1947) 'Who is the criminal?', *American Sociological Review*, vol.12, pp.96–102.

Thompson, E.P. (1975) *Whigs and Hunters*, London, Allen Lane.

Walker, M.A. (1983) 'Some problems in interpreting statistics relating to crime', *Journal of the Royal Statistical Society, Series A*, no.146, part 3, pp.282–93.

Walker, M.A. (1987) 'Interpreting race and crime statistics', *Journal of the Royal Statistical Society, Series A*, no.150, part 1, pp.39–56.

Walklate, S. (1995) *Gender and Crime: An Introduction*, Hemel Hempstead, Prentice Hall/Harvester Wheatsheaf.

Wilkins, L. (1964) *Social Deviance*, London, Tavistock.

Williams, K.S. (1994) *Textbook on Criminology* (2nd edn), London, Blackstone.

Williams, P. and Dickinson, J. (1993) 'Fear of crime: read all about it?', *British Journal of Criminology*, vol.33, no.1, pp.33–56.

Young, J. (1974) 'Mass media, drugs and deviance', in Rock, P. and McKintosh, M. (eds) *Deviance and Social Control*, London, Tavistock.

Young, J. (1986) 'The failure of criminology: the need for a radical realism', in Matthews, R. and Young, J. (eds) *Confronting Crime*, London, Sage. (Extract reprinted in Muncie *et al.*, 1996.)

Young, J. (1992) 'Ten points of realism', in Young, J. and Matthews, R. (eds) *Rethinking Criminology: The Realist Debate*, London, Sage.

Chapter 2
Crime and Social Order: Interrogating the Detective Story

by John Clarke

Contents

1 Introduction

The issues of defining and making sense of crime are not simply the 'business' of official agencies or the social sciences. Definitions, interpretations and images of crime circulate widely in our society in both the news media and fictional entertainments. Both contribute to the complex ways in which we go about making sense of crime and its relationship to social order. This chapter explores how one type of fictional **representations** – those of the detective novel – deal with this relationship between crime and order.

This may seem an odd choice, but the detective story reveals different ways of looking at some of the issues raised in the previous chapter. In spite of being obviously about crime, detective novels also address the problems of how crime is defined, interpreted and responded to. Classic examples might be the apparent suicide or accidental death which can only be revealed as a murder by the efforts of the detective. Alternatively, many 'private' detectives find themselves in employment precisely because the legal authorities refuse to believe that a 'crime' has taken place or because the authorities themselves cannot be trusted.

Detective stories offer accounts of who commits crimes and who the victims are, as well as explaining why crimes take place. Perhaps more importantly, they tell stories about the relationship between types of crime and types of social order – ranging from familial murders in English country houses to the corruption of the American underworld. The social orders imagined and represented in the detective story provide us with different ways of seeing crime and the social relationships in which it is enmeshed.

There is a variety of ways in which studying such popular fictions can be approached. They can be the focus of psychological analyses of their popular appeal; sociological studies of their readerships; literary analysis of the form or narrative style of the genre; biographical or social analyses of their authors; and more (see 'Further Reading' at the end of the chapter). However, in this chapter the main focus will be on how they represent crime, its relationship to social order and the social place of the detective. Different versions of the detective story represent these elements in divergent ways, and examining them helps to illuminate issues about the definition and interpretation of crime.

Studies of the detective story as a literary genre have tended to stress the way in which it is structured around the question of order. Crime (usually a murder) disrupts order – it is an unwelcome and unexpected intrusion. The process of detection is a process of dealing with this disruption and it ends with the restoration of order (the solution). This view, though, tends to treat order as unproblematic – as if it was both clearly understood and unchanging. Considering different varieties of the detective story allows us to see that the social order is neither unproblematic nor unchanging – nor is it clearly understood. Like crime itself, it is the subject of divergent definitions and representations.

This chapter, then, will explore a range of questions about the who and why of crime – about the representations of who commits crimes, and their motivations, as well as who is the victim of crime. It will look at who solves crime problems and how. Most attention, however, will be focused on the relationship between crime and the social order – and more particularly on what sort of social order provides the framework within which crime and detection take place.

All these points of reference – the criminal, the victim, the detective and the social order – are subject to historical and cultural change as the novelist strives to make the novel meaningful, accessible or readable by audiences who are themselves members of a particular society in a specific historical period. How authors represent the social order, and the place of crime and detection within it, is the predominant concern of this chapter. The chapter is organized around the following questions about the changing representation of crime and social order in the detective story:

- What is the place of crime? (In what sort of social milieux or locations does it take place?)

  social milieux

- What are the social relationships of crime and detection? (Who are the victims, perpetrators and detectives?)

  social relationships

- What is the social order in which crime takes place?

  social order

What follows is an attempt neither to tell the history of the detective story nor to provide a reader's guide. Rather, it aims to distinguish different types of detective story in order to reveal the divergent perspectives they offer about crime and social order. It is necessarily selective and is concerned with tendencies rather than absolutes (that is, it will always be possible to imagine exceptions). Finally, the examination of the detective story presented here is based on novels rather than films or television programmes, despite the fact that more people are likely to encounter these fictional representations through film or television. The main reason for this choice is that the *diversity* of representations of crime and social order is still considerably wider in the written forms than on film or television.

2   It happens in the best of families: the classic English mystery

In an English village, a murder is discovered, probably in a large country house in which are assembled a variety of relatives, friends and business partners of the deceased. Within the next 200 pages we will have discovered that almost everyone present had either the opportunity or the motive to do away with the victim. In the final chapters, our detective will review the conditions, characters and clues and reveal that only one combination of these can point to the identity of the murderer – the one 'whodunnit'.

Although this 'mystery' format – the puzzling through of the clues – is the organizing principle of the classic detective story, the puzzle still needs to take on a human and social shape. It needs to be played out in a social context which is peopled with characters – however thinly drawn some of these may be. There are three common threads which run through and delineate this context: the social order within which the crime takes place; the milieu, or the location, of the crime; and the position of the detective. In each of these, the murder mystery sketches a particular view of crime and its relationship to the social order.

In the murder mystery, most associated with the inter-war 'Golden Age' of the English 'whodunnit', crime is an event which takes place in the upper reaches of an English class structure. To be more accurate, *the crime that matters* takes place in this milieu. Other crimes may be going on elsewhere and may distract the attention of the police, but the crime which is intended to

class structure

hold our attention – the central murder which provides the impetus of the plot – takes place here. The 'mystery' rests on an implicit hierarchy of crime in which murder is the most serious. This hierarchy intersects with the social ranking of the class structure, so that the primary victim is usually of high social status. It is one of the members of this social set who dies and the other members of the set who fall under suspicion. Lest there be any doubt, crime writers are at pains to rule out the possibility of the 'mysterious stranger'. As soon as any suspect raises the possibility of this red herring, an authoritative voice (usually the principal detective) demonstrates the impossibility of such a random or unauthorized intrusion and turns attention inwards to the intimate circle of suspects.

Of course, such limitations are functional for the purposes of plotting: they constrain attention and direct us and the author to concentrate on the minutiae of the clues and characters. But they also establish a distinctive social world – grand houses, the trappings of wealth and social demeanour – to which we are admitted as spectators. This world is founded on the complex imagery of social class and status distinctions. Crime centres in its upper reaches, among the country aristocrats, stockbrokers, old families clustered alongside *nouveau riche* businessmen and entrepreneurs. This stratum of wealth is supported by two other distinctive social groups. One is the old professional class: doctors (whether country GPs or Harley Street specialists) and solicitors (a vital role given the centrality of the laws of inheritance). The other group is composed of those in domestic service – butlers, maids and gardeners, for example. These loyal retainers people the world of the murder mystery, but mainly as props whose very presence demonstrates the social wealth and standing of the principal characters.

This is, of course, an imaginary England. It obscures about three-quarters of the real inter-war population – the mass of the working and lower middle classes leading their lives in urban settings. They are not part of the charmed world of the mystery, although they may occasionally be glimpsed going about their business in the margins of the story (through the window of a train or taxi). This imaginary nature of the country – what Watson (1979) calls 'Mayhem Parva' – can also be glimpsed geographically. The England of the Golden Age detective story is a strange composite of London and the rural counties. The counties may be identified by name ('Poirot took the train to Essex …') or be invented ('Loamshire'), but once the protagonists descend from the train or step out of the car they find themselves in the all-purpose English village, dominated physically and socially by the 'big house':

> At a window overlooking a garden in Kent, Brian Page sat amid a clutter of open books at a writing table, and felt a strong distaste for work. Through both windows the late July sunlight turned the floor of the room to gold. The somnolent heat brought out the odour of old wood and old books … .

> Beyond his garden wall, past the inn of the Bull and Butcher, the road wound for some quarter of a mile between orchards. It passed the gates of Farnleigh Court, whose thin clusters of chimneys Page could see above rifts in the trees, and then ascended past the wood poetically known as Hanging Chart … .

> There was, Brian Page thought lazily, almost too much excitement in Mallingford village.

> (From the opening of J.D. Carr, *The Crooked Hinge*, 1964)

Before long, of course, there will be still more excitement and it will centre on the 'big house' – Farnleigh Court. As in this introduction, certain features of the local physical geography may be worth a mention and diverse rural accents may be deployed in the bit-part players (here a touch of Somerset wisdom, there a hint of Cornish taciturnity), but for the upper classes any part of England is all of England.

Even London is a city partially imagined. Somehow the London of the Golden Age detective story finds its limits in the combination of the grand houses, clubs and hotels of the West End with occasional glimpses of respectable suburbia. The East End hovers in the background – providing a sense of 'otherness' which occasionally surfaces in the form of cheery cockneys or troublesome roughs. But, like the rest of urbanized and proletarianized Britain, it cannot play a central part in this imaginary social order. The distance between the late nineteenth-century detective story (such as Conan Doyle's Sherlock Holmes novels) and its inter-war counterpart can in some ways be measured by this changing place of the East End. In the late nineteenth century, it was the imagined haunt of crime – a dangerous place, filled by swirling fogs and nameless threats, an uneasy mixture of social groups (its indigenous working class, its mobile seafaring population) and vibrant with exotic promise (music halls, drugs, prostitution). By the 1920s and 1930s, the detective story has become respectable and the London of the detective story rarely ventures further east than the stockbrokers' and bankers' offices of the City.

This is an imaginary social order which is self-confidently imperial. It registers the place of the 'best of British' – the upper classes – and is at pains to delineate their world, their accomplishments, their property, their accommodation and their eating habits. It is hardly possible to ignore the intense round of breakfast, luncheon, tea, dinner and occasional cold supper which punctuates the solving of the mystery and provides a rhythm to the investigation – as well as providing convenient meeting points for all suspects, who are forced to stomach multiple courses while worrying about which of the others is the murderer. The hierarchies of status, demeanour and appropriate deference are lovingly observed: everyone knowing their place and behaving accordingly. This order is intermittently and marginally disrupted by someone who reveals a lack of social graces: a *nouveau riche* 'upstart' or a 'foreigner'. Such foreigners, for the most part, provide a foundation for demonstrating the unselfconscious superiority of the British race – whether they be 'brash' Americans, 'mysterious' middle-Europeans or 'excitable' Latins (Watson, 1979, chapters 9 and 10). They are not often the villians but they will certainly behave badly.

This non-central role of the 'foreigner' brings us to the paradox of this imaginary social order in the English mystery. On the one hand, it is self-confident, powerful and respected. On the other, its members keep killing one another – and when one of them is murdered, there is a long queue of likely candidates for the role of the chief suspect. They may maintain an equable veneer of self-confidence in public, but in private, it seems, they hate one another with considerable intensity. Crime is not a product of the dangerous world 'out there', but the effect of intimate relationships going wrong.

Pause for a moment and ask yourself what the main features of the social order of the mystery are.

2.1 Familiar motives: the why of the whodunnit

The setting of crime in the murder mystery is the family – or at least the familial milieu inhabited by the relatives and friends of the victim. What the murder and its investigation reveal is a tangled web of motivation in which all or most of the cast of characters are implicated in patterns of hostility towards the victim. It is this pattern of relationships which the detective brings to the surface and holds up to view. However much any particular detective may lean towards the 'scientific method' of detection and be concerned with physical evidence, the investigation nevertheless comes to focus on the characters, feelings and patterns of relationship between victim and suspects. What is drawn out for us is the shape of familiar motives – love, money, revenge – which are the elementary stuff of these family lives. Who hated or feared whom, and why, are the focus of the classic English mystery and these patterns are to be found at their most intense in the familial world. Even money, the most apparently impersonal of the 'classic' motives, is a focus for family feelings since the laws of inheritance bind people in complex and conflictual relationships. Many an apparently 'marginal' character has been revealed as the murderer through the disentangling of elaborate and forgotten blood relationships or complex patterns of inheritance.

As a consequence, much of the narrative involves the detective teasing out how people *really* felt about the victim from beneath the conventional poses and attitudes which they originally strike: the 'tear-stained widow' looking forward to a new relationship, the 'devastated son' anticipating release from a tyrannical father, or the 'meek governess' preparing to use her new inheritance to lead a full and active life. In this familial milieu, there is a sharp contrast between the surface appearances of convention and normality – wifely devotion, filial piety and genteel servitude – and the real passions which burn underneath. The family in the mystery story is a profoundly unhealthy place and the detective performs the role of psychological analyst bringing the repressed feelings and tensions out into the open. At one level, the classic English whodunnit is the fictional equivalent of psychoanalysis (even though English respectability requires scorn to be poured on such dubious and 'foreign' ideas). Nevertheless, what takes place is a 'talking cure'. Through recurring conversations with the main characters the detective manages to reveal that which up to now has been concealed. The problem for the detective is not in performing this role – all of them seem to possess the analyst's skill to get people talking about themselves – but in accomplishing the act of distinguishing those emotions and relationships which are merely dysfunctional from those which are dangerous and have led to the murderous impulse.

In the closing chapters of Agatha Christie's *Five Little Pigs* (1959), Hercule Poirot picks over a 16-year-old murder, demonstrating how things said at the time have been misinterpreted because they are not being heard in the context of the real characters and motives of those who said them:

> Poirot did not allow himself to be angered. He said 'You say we all know what happened. You speak without reflection. The accepted version of the facts is not necessarily the true one. On the face of it, for instance, you, Mr Blake, disliked Caroline Crale. That is the accepted version of your attitude. But any one with the least flair for psychology can perceive at once that the exact opposite was the truth. You were always violently attracted towards Caroline Crale. You resented the fact, and tried to conquer it by steadfastly telling yourself her defects and reiterating your dislike …'.

... 'There is always a danger of accepting facts as proved which are nothing of the kind. Let us take the situation at Alderbury. A very old situation. Two women and one man. We have taken it for granted that Amyas Crale intended to leave his wife for the other woman. But I suggest to you now that he never intended to do anything of the kind ...'.

(Agatha Christie, *Five Little Pigs*, 1959, pp.173, 183)

Poirot (David Suchet): the extraordinary detective?

In the course of this exposition, we are confronted by the possibility of several plausible murderers. As is usual in the mystery, almost anyone could have done it but only one did.

It is in this context that we discover something else about the upper classes who inhabit the world of the whodunnit. With few exceptions, they are all social performers – actors who maintain a social mask and play their roles. They are skilled performers who are continually engaged in the activity described by Erving Goffman (1959) as 'the presentation of self'. The detective must struggle to remove the masks being worn to reveal the *real* person behind. This performance – this acting of roles – seems to be a class-specific form of behaviour. It is as though the upper-class concern with manners and demeanour has produced an instinctive self-concealment, a preoccupation with how the self is managed and presented. The stability of this social order is maintained through the management of appearances. Agatha Christie's *At Bertram's Hotel* (1968) both exemplifies and uses this concern with maintaining a public face (see Extract 2.1).

presentation of self

The fact that these appearances are too good to be true is one of the central features of the story. It is, in fact, a hotel run by villains who find its 'respectable façade' a great help in carrying out their real business. But it is *not* the motive for murder. Once again, this is to be found in tangled family relationships.

By comparison, other social groups are much less good at this sort of self-presentation. It is true that domestic servants maintain a façade of deference, and getting access to below-stairs gossip and information may occasionally be helpful to the detective, but this is not a matter of getting to know who the servants really are. Similarly, the representatives of the lower middle classes may be seen presenting a veneer of respectability, but there is rarely little of interest behind the veneer – and the fact that they can be *seen* doing it suggests that they are not skilled in the art of self-presentation exhibited by the upper classes. Finally, we might note that the occasional member of the lower orders who enters such stories may display a degree of natural cunning. If they do, however, it tends to lead them into trouble – for

Extract 2.1   Christie: 'The problem of appearances'

In the heart of the West End, there are many quiet pockets, unknown to almost all but taxi drivers who traverse them with expert knowledge, and arrive triumphantly thereby at Park Lane, Berkeley Square or South Audley Street.

If you turn off on an unpretentious street from the Park, and turn left and right once or twice, you will find yourself in a quiet street with Bertram's Hotel on the right hand side. Bertram's Hotel has been there a long time. During the war, houses were demolished on the right of it, and a little farther down on the left of it, but Bertram's itself remained unscathed. Naturally it could not escape being, as house agents would say, scratched, bruised and marked, but by the expenditure of only a reasonable amount of money it was restored to its original condition. By 1955 it looked precisely as it had looked in 1939 – dignified, unostentatious, and quietly expensive.

Such was Bertram's, patronized over a long stretch of years by the higher *échelons* of the clergy, dowager ladies of the aristocracy up from the country, girls on their way home for the holidays from expensive finishing schools. ('So few places where a girl can stay alone in London but of course it is *quite* all right at Bertram's. We have stayed there for *years*.')

There had, of course, been many other hotels on the model of Bertram's. Some still existed, but nearly all had felt the wind of change. They had had necessarily to modernize themselves, to cater for a different clientele. Bertram's, too, had had to change, but it had been done so cleverly that it was not at all apparent at the first casual glance.

Outside the steps that led up to the big swing doors stood what at first sight appeared to be no less than a Field-Marshal. Gold braid and medal ribbons adorned a broad and manly chest. His deportment was perfect. He received you with tender concern as you emerged with rheumatic difficulty from a taxi or a car, guided you carefully up the steps and piloted you through the silently swinging doorway.

Inside, if this was the first time you had visited Bertram's, you felt, almost with alarm, that you had re-entered a vanished world. Time had gone back. You were in Edwardian England once more.

There was, of course, central heating, but it was not apparent. As there had always been, in the big central lounge, there were two magnificent coal fires; beside them big brass coal scuttles shone in the way they used to shine when Edwardian housemaids polished them, and they were filled with exactly the right sized lumps of coal. There was a general appearance of rich red velvet and plushy cosiness. The arm-chairs were

example, making them think they can blackmail the murderer. The inevitable consequences of setting 'natural cunning' against the performance skills of the upper classes are a testimony to social superiority being as marked in criminal ability as it is in the distribution of wealth (natural cunning loses). Otherwise, the lower orders are simply transparent: beacons of goodheartedness (the salt of the earth) in a murky world. They are, for the most part, 'below suspicion'.

      However, if no-one else can do it very well, there is no doubt that the family and friends of the deceased will be performing with consummate skill.

familial setting   And it is this peculiar combination of class position, familial setting and skills of self-presentation in the English mystery that necessitates the presence of some very peculiar detectives. This milieu means that the 'ordinary policeman' is doomed to fail from the outset. He (it normally is 'he') possesses neither the social standing necessary to gain access to, nor the social graces to move easily in, the intimate setting. Above all, he is not attuned to the arts of performance practised by this social group and is thus unable to accomplish the task of unmasking the murderer. Baffled, intimidated, patronized and ignored, the ordinary policeman can only stand by – more or less helpfully – while the 'extraordinary detective' solves the case.

not of this time and age. They were well above the level of the floor, so that rheumatic old ladies had not to struggle in an undignified manner in order to get to their feet. The seats of the chairs did not, as in so many modern high-priced arm-chairs, stop half-way between the thigh and the knee, thereby inflicting agony on those suffering from arthritis and sciatica; and they were not all of a pattern. There were straight backs and reclining backs, different widths to accommodate the slender and the obese. People of almost any dimension could find a comfortable chair at Bertram's.

Since it was now the tea hour, the lounge hall was full. Not that the lounge hall was the only place where you could have tea. There was a drawing-room (chintz), a smoking-room (by some hidden influence reserved for gentlemen only), where the vast chairs were of fine leather, two writing-rooms, where you could take a special friend and have a cosy little gossip in a quiet corner – and even write a letter as well if you wanted to. Besides these amenities of the Edwardian age, there were other retreats, not in any way publicized, but known to those who wanted them. There was a double bar, with two bar attendants, an American barman to make the Americans feel at home and to provide them with bourbon, rye, and every kind of cocktail, and an English one to deal with sherries and Pimm's No. 1, and to talk knowledgeably about the runners at Ascot and Newbury to the middle-aged men who stayed at Bertram's for the more serious race meetings. There was also, tucked down a passage, in a secretive way, a television-room for those who asked for it.

But the big entrance lounge was the favourite place for the afternoon tea drinking. The elderly ladies enjoyed seeing who came in and out, recognizing old friends, and commenting unfavourably on how these had aged. There were also American visitors fascinated by seeing the titled English really getting down to their traditional afternoon tea. For afternoon tea was quite a feature of Bertram's.

It was nothing less than splendid. Presiding over the ritual was Henry, a large and magnificent figure, a ripe fifty, avuncular, sympathetic, and with the courtly manners of that long vanished species: the perfect butler. Slim youths performed the actual work under Henry's austere direction. There were large crested silver trays, and Georgian silver teapots. The china, if not actually Rockingham and Davenport, looked like it. The Blind Earl services were particular favourites. The tea was the best Indian, Ceylon, Darjeeling, Lapsang, etc. As for eatables, you could ask for anything you liked – and get it!

(Agatha Christie, *At Bertram's Hotel*, 1968, pp.7–9)

In what sense are the place and the motives of crime in the mystery familial as well as familiar?

2.2 'Mon pauvre Japp': the problem of the detective

Given that the ordinary policeman cannot work effectively in this social milieu, the stage is set for someone who can bridge the world of the upper classes and the world of justice. The detective is thus an ambiguous figure – inside, but with a certain distance from, the social setting of crime. Predominantly, this role is one occupied by an amateur – or at least, someone who is not a member of the police force. Within this there are differences between those who are mainly bystanders (Agatha Christie's Miss Marple) and those who seek out crime (Christie's Poirot, Dorothy Sayer's Lord Peter Wimsey). The occasional extraordinary detective who is also an ordinary policeman is also different from the rest of the police – as in the case of Ngaio Marsh's Inspector Roderick Alleyn, who is enabled to move in the social milieu of the murder he investigates by virtue of his birth and breeding.

It is their access to the *manners* of the murder milieu that gives such detectives their edge over the ordinary police. Most of the murder mysteries play upon the tension between the dogged, decent but ultimately wrong police investigation and the triumph of their extraordinary detective. Each of these has his or her own particular idiosyncracy or characteristics. Poirot, while possessed of the social graces, is nevertheless a 'foreigner' and liable to be underestimated by English suspects. He also possesses a gift for encouraging people to talk. Miss Marple, meanwhile, is such an apparently familiar figure of this landscape – the elderly lady with a lot of time on her hands – that she is, like Poirot, underestimated, if not ignored. She has also developed the art of social observation to a high level through extensive practice on the inhabitants of St Mary Mead. As Mary Weinkaupf describes her: 'She is a fine actress, and she pretends to be dithery, fluffy and gossipy to disarm people. Though some might call her an "old scandalmonger", she is a fact finder, knitting and talking but mostly listening. People tend to overlook her ...' (Weinkaupf, 1980, pp.37–8).

It is also worth noting that the revelation of 'whodunnit' by the detective marks the closure of these narratives. The murder mystery usually ends with the solution to the puzzle rather than with the processes of criminal justice – arrest, trial and sentencing. More attention is paid to the removal of the 'problem' and the restoration of the social order of this world than to the wider social and legal processes. Indeed, the nature of this resolution means that there is scope for some flexibility in the detective's enactment of justice. So, in addition to the conventional 'seize him, Japp' of the moment of arrest when the murderer is finally revealed, there are deviations: the murderer killed while trying to escape; the opportunity for suicide (reflecting either the impossibility of proving the case in court or the fundamental decency of the murderer); or even the contrived escape for a particularly sympathetic murderer. The detective is not only the puzzle-solver but also the arbiter of human conduct. If murder happens in 'the best of families' it is also solved and sorted out within that world – the rest of us can only stand by and watch.

Why is it necessary for the detective to be an insider in the social order of the mystery story?

3 The rank smell of corruption: the arrival of the private eye

Meanwhile, on the other side of the Atlantic, a different type of detective and a different type of detective story were being created – most famously in the person of Raymond Chandler's Philip Marlowe. The 'private eye' novel offers a very different milieu of crime, a very different view of crime and a different role for the detective. The 'hard-boiled' detective story lays claim to a sense of social realism in its murky urban settings, its engagement with 'low life', and its use of everyday language to heighten the feel of reality. Wealth, power and status are still elements – indeed central elements – of these stories, but they function in a different way. They are bound up in a very different imaginary social order – a representation of society in which the rich, no matter how hard they may try to insulate themselves in a closed world, nevertheless find that their fortunes (financial and social) are inextricably linked to the wider world of the USA.

In this America, the city is a setting in which money links a variety of social groups – the old rich, businessmen, gangsters, hustlers and con men. Money – and its flows – binds these people together in symbiotic and unstable patterns of relationships. The city is ripe with the possibility and reality of corruption and moral decay. The gap which the English mystery establishes between the public surface and private disorder is closed in the American private investigator (PI) novel. The disorder is either close to the surface or, in some cases like Dashiell Hammett's novels, *is* the surface. The city is a tangled web of strands connecting apparently separate individuals in a network of power, money, corruption and crime. The challenge for the detective is to work his (and, until recently, the PI has been 'he') way through these tangles and save something or someone from perishing – physically or morally – in this urban swamp:

private investigator

> The strike lasted eight months. Both sides bled plenty. The wobblies had to do their own bleeding. Old Elihu hired gunmen, strike-breakers, national guardsmen, and even parts of the regular army, to do his. When the last skull had been cracked, the last rib kicked in, organized labour in Personville was a used firecracker.
>
> But, said Bill Quint, old Elihu didn't know his Italian history. He won the strike, but he lost his hold on the city and the state. To beat the miners he had to let his hired thugs run wild. When the fight was over he couldn't get rid of them. He had given his city to them and he wasn't strong enough to take it away from them. Personville looked good to them and they took it over.

(Dashiell Hammett, *Red Harvest*, 1975, p.11)

Personville (pronounced 'Poisonville') is probably the most extreme example of the corruption of the social order in the PI story, but its premise – the interlocking of 'respectable' wealth and crime – is one which is repeated consistently. This amoral order represents a different role or task for the detective. It is not a matter of solving the problem posed by a specific crime (the murder). Rather, it is a moral obligation to rescue someone or something in peril in a social order which is itself disordered. The 'crime' in these novels is not a one-off event which disrupts social stability (as is the English murder) and brings dangerous relationships to light. Instead, 'crime' is inherent in the social order, it is all around – illegal gambling, drug use, prohibition-breaking, corrupt business dealing, blackmail and prostitution, as well as murder. Murders certainly happen and may even be the focus of the plot, but the detective is likely to be drawn into the action by a variety of criminal or other 'problems' such as missing persons, kidnapping and blackmail.

Private – or familial – relationships reflect the disordered social order They, too, are likely to be tangled, corrupt and dangerous – morally unstable. For example, in Raymond Chandler's *The Big Sleep* (1988a) General Sternwood's daughters are embroiled in a web of relationships which involve murder, blackmail, disturbed sexuality, drug use and theft. Their social connections include gangsters, narcotics peddlers and killers. The boundary between public and private crime collapses while the General himself struggles to maintain 'traditional virtues' at the same time as colluding with the corrupt world at his door to protect his daughters and his family name.

disordered social order

In most PI novels, this sense of decay and corruption extends to the police as well. They are an integral part of the moral collapse of urban America. At best, they are hamstrung by local politics (and local politics are intimately woven into the web of corruption). Beyond that, they may be brutally incompetent, with a constant hostility towards the 'interfering' private investigator who is likely to be as much at risk from their attentions as he is from the criminals. In the worst cases, they may be intrinsically corrupt – tied directly into the local economy of business and crime. In any of these forms, there is clearly the investigative space for someone who is not beholden to any of these established interests – though they may be forced to deal with them along the way. Equally importantly, the PI is not bound by the legal and bureaucratic rules of law-enforcement agencies – he must make moral, rather than legal, choices in pursuit of his goal.

Why do you think the PI novel is likely to focus on the world of those with money?

3.1   Reluctant heroes: the PI's code of conduct

The PI is neither a gifted amateur nor a professional policeman. He is available for hire, but is unlikely to be restrained by the simple contractual framework of 'twenty-five dollars a day and expenses'. Once set to work, he creates his own trajectory through webs of relationships – identifying his own commitments, which may or may not be to the client who has paid his fee. In some cases, he may decide that someone else is more worthy of, or more in need of, his loyalty – even if that person is now dead. It is this sense of commitment – or obligation – rather than the contract which motivates his actions and informs his choices. Hammett's 'Continental Op' is both an exception to this description (because he is employed by the Continental Agency) and demonstrates the problem of the PI:

> It is into this bottomlessly equivocal, endlessly fraudulent, and brutally acquisitive world that Hammett precipitates the Op. There is nothing glamourous about him. Short, thick-set, balding, between thirty five and forty, he has no name, no home, no personal existence apart from his work. He is, and he regards himself as, 'the hired man' of official and respectable society, who is paid so much per day to clean it up and rescue it from the crooks and thieves who are perpetually threatening to take it over. Yet what he – and the reader – just as perpetually learn is that the respectable society that employs him is itself inveterately vicious, deceitful, culpable, crooked, and degraded.
>
> (Marcus, 1977, p.21)

The PI is necessarily a loner – someone not bound by pre-existing ties of loyalty but available for new attachments and commitments. Nor, given the corrupt social order in which he must work, are there many safe points of anchorage – the occasional journalist or decent policeman who may provide information and assistance – and there is no structural framework of order to which he is attached. Rather, if there is to be any order or any justice in the social milieu in which he works, the detective must create it for himself, by himself. He must impose a moral solution on an amoral world.

This detachment is a precondition for the work of the PI. It allows him to see clearly in a world which is complex and where moral judgements have collapsed. He is both cynical and idealistic. His cynicism is a world-weariness, underpinning the laconic, wisecracking and corrosive humour of his conventional style. It underscores his detachment from those he encounters, indicating his distance from conventional evaluations of wealth, power and status. He inhabits a world in which he suspects everyone and trusts no-one. If someone offers him money, it will have strings attached. If a woman makes advances, it will be because she intends to use him. In these ways, the PI is dislocated, alienated from the world in which he lives. But at the same time, he holds on to the possibility of making things right, of rescuing something of value from this corrupt order. This is the romance of the private eye: in spite of everything, he can, and will, make a difference. He will impose his order on disorder. But in setting the world – or this particular microcosm of it – to rights, he will not overcome his own alienation. He may rescue the innocent (or at least, the not so guilty) or may avenge the wronged, but he will return to the office, the bottle of bourbon and the neon sign through the window, knowing that the social order continues to be disordered (Grella, 1980).

For these men, attachments are dangerous. They threaten the PI's capacity to remain detached and cynical observers. This places women in the classic PI story in a profoundly ambiguous role. Women, especially attractive women, are a problem for the PI. He cannot but succumb to a code of chivalry which suggests that women are inherently more vulnerable than men in this corrupt world and thus in need of a defender or champion. The PI novel is rich in reworked 'knightly' metaphors, often with reference to rusting or tarnished armour. Other things being equal, women are more likely to engage the detective's loyalty and commitment than men. At the same time, women are a threat to detachment, undermining the hard-won capacity for independent thought and action. Worse still, attachment creates the capacity for betrayal and many a PI suffers from the discovery that he has been set up and exploited by a woman. The effect of this view of women in the PI novel is a situation in which the detective moves between the poles of attraction and repulsion, torn between the allurement and the threats of attachment.

The classic PI novel works through this tension between the amoral and corrupt world and the isolated moral sense or code of the detective. The detective must be mobile enough to work in a whole variety of urban milieux without becoming contaminated. He will be as at ease (and as cynically distanced) in the homes of the wealthy as he is in the low dives and bars; he will handle gangsters as disrespectfully as he does the police. He will kill, fix evidence, cheat and break and enter – all reluctantly, and all framed by a set of moral obligations which stand above and beyond the categories of the law. He is the moral conscience of America – the 'everyman' figure summoned up by Raymond Chandler's analysis of the detective:

> But down these streets a man must go, a man who is himself not mean, who is neither tarnished nor afraid ... He is the hero, he is everything. He must be a complete man and a common man and yet an unusual man. He must be, to use a rather weathered phrase, a man of honor – by instinct, by inevitability, without thought of it, and without saying it ... .

> He is a relatively poor man or he would not be a detective at all. He is a common man or he could not go among people. He has a sense of character or he would not know his job. He will take no man's money dishonestly and no man's insolence without a due and dispassionate revenge. He is a lonely man and his pride is that you will treat him as a proud man or be very sorry you ever saw him. He talks as the man of his age talks – that is, with rude wit, a lively sense of the grotesque, a distrust of sham and a contempt of pettiness.

> (Raymond Chandler, *The Simple Art of Murder*, 1988b, p.18)

A reluctant hero? Humphrey Bogart as Chandler's Philip Marlowe

However bruised, battered, drunk or in contravention of the law, the PI embodies the belief that there is still something beyond the swamp of corruption – some values, ethics and commitments: a not very well articulated vision that there can be something better than that which exists. In the absence of any other source of order, the PI must represent a *popular* commitment to decency and justice. He must stand for all the 'little people' who are not part of the centres of power and influence, but whose lives are threatened by their corruption. It is this that makes him Chandler's 'common man' and it is his resilient capacity for making a difference that makes him 'an unusual man'.

Why is the PI an outsider? What does he represent?

4 The policeman's lot is not a happy one

Since the 1960s, the police have been making a comeback in the world of the detective story. Clearly, this involves a different type of fictional realism – representing the fact that crime is the daily *business* of the police. The imaginary social order in which gifted amateurs could carry out investigations under the noses or over the heads of humble policemen could hardly be sustained (except as a pastiche) in the post-war context. In their place, the detective story moved its social milieu to the occupational world of the police procedural where stories are based in police settings, and detection becomes 'professionalized'.

In some variants, the 'mystery' novel does not change much in being scene-shifted to the world of the police. It remains a matter of the detective managing to penetrate masks and motives in order to arrive at a solution, but now the detective is (more or less) supported by the apparatus of organized investigation. However, the focus is still on the detective's capacity to uncover the truth beneath the surface appearances (Colin Dexter's Morse, June Thompson's Finch, P.D. James' Dalgleish). Each detective is likely to have his distinguishing quirks and idiosyncracies – he may even have a personal life more or less rich in problems, but the core is the ability to 'get to the bottom' of a mysterious murder. Other variants explore the tensions between the 'good cop' and the occupational world in which he is obliged to function. Here we are closer to the PI form, with the 'loner' having been institutionalized in a police department – and rather unhappily so. The solutions are accomplished as much in spite of, as because of, the police organization and procedure. Such stories transpose the classic tension between the 'extraordinary detective' and the 'ordinary policeman' to a new setting, this time inside the police itself.

An alternative view from the police procedural represents a growing tension between the 'interior' world of the police and social change in the world beyond it. This might be best described as the 'thin blue line' view of policing as an activity which stands between civilization and anarchy. The police embody and personify order but feel themselves increasingly isolated from the world beyond the station doors. What is represented here is a growing 'siege mentality' on the part of the police and the density of mutual support and affirmation provided by the occupational culture (see **McLaughlin, 1996**).

Other police procedurals go further to examine the flawed nature of policing itself. The Swedish series by Maj Sjöwall and Per Wahlöö presents a critique of the role of policing in sustaining a particular type of social order – Swedish social democracy. Their central characters (Martin Beck and Lennart Kollberg, in particular) exist in a state of permanent disenchantment, recognizing the interrelationship between crime and wider social problems, but increasingly frustrated by the nationalized, bureaucratized and paramilitary style of policing in which they are enmeshed. Crimes do take place and do get solved, sometimes even to the detectives' satisfaction. But, more often, the outcomes merely serve to underscore their deepening frustration and alienation. The novels provide a commentary on Swedish 'modernization' in both policing and wider social terms which is rare in the detective story. Extract 2.2 here, from *Cop Killer*, deals with the culmination of Kollberg's disaffection from the task of policing.

Extract 2.2   Sjöwall and Wahlöö: 'The detective who can't go on'

Stockholm
November 27, 1973
To: National Police Administration
Subject: Resignation

…

Lennart Kollberg typed slowly, with two fingers. He knew that this letter, which he had thought about for such a long time, had to be considered a formal document, but he didn't want to make it too long-winded. And as far as possible, he tried to keep the tone of it informal.

After long and careful consideration, I have decided to leave the police force. My reasons are of a personal nature, and yet I would like to try and explain them briefly. Right at the outset, I feel compelled to point out that my decision is in no way a political action, even though many people will see it in that light. To be sure, the police establishment has been increasingly politicized over the last few years, and the police force itself has been exploited for political purposes more and more often. I have observed these developments with considerable alarm, even though I, personally, have managed to avoid coming into contact with this aspect of police activity almost completely.

Nevertheless, during the twenty-seven years that I have served on the force, its activities, structure, and organization have altered in a manner that has convinced me that I am no longer suited to being a policeman – assuming that I ever was. Above all, I find that I cannot feel any sense of solidarity with the kind of organization the police department has become. Consequently, it seems to me that my own best interests and those of the department would be best served by my resignation.

The question of whether or not the individual policeman should be armed has long struck me as an especially important one. For many years, I have held to the opinion that, under normal circumstances, policemen should not be armed. This applies to uniformed patrolmen as well as to plainclothesmen.

The great increase in the number of violent crimes over the last decade is, in my opinion, largely due to the fact that policemen invariably carry firearms. It is a known fact, and can be demonstrated with statistics from many other countries, that the incidence of violent crime immediately increases when the police force sets, as it were, a bad example. The events of recent months make it seem more obvious than ever that we can expect our situation to deteriorate even further with regard to violence. This is especially true of Stockholm and other large cities.

The Police Academy devotes far too little time to providing instruction in psychology. As a result, policemen lack what is perhaps the most important prerequisite for success in their profession.

Some novels have begun to explore other dimensions of the occupational culture of policing, treating its mutual support and social density as problems. For some, this is posed in terms of the way police culture, in becoming alienated from mainstream or 'straight' society, finds itself more at home and having more in common with the 'underworld' or criminal sub-cultures:

The fact that we nevertheless have so-called police psychologists, who are sent out in difficult situations to try and bring the criminal to reason, seems to me to be nothing but an admission of defeat. For psychology cannot be used to camouflage violence. To my way of thinking, this must be one of the simplest and most obvious tenets of the science of psychology.

I would like to emphasize in this connection that for many years I myself have never carried a gun. This has often been a direct violation of orders, but I have never had the feeling that it hampered me in the execution of my duties. On the contrary, being forced to carry arms might have had a strong inhibiting effect, it could have caused accidents, and it could well have led to even poorer contact with persons outside the police force.

What I am trying to say, essentially, is that I cannot continue to be a policeman. It is possible that every society has the police force it deserves, but that is not a thesis I intend to try and develop, at least not here and now.

I find myself confronted with a *fait accompli*. When I joined the police department, I could not have imagined that this profession would undergo the transformation or take on the direction that it has.

After twenty-seven years of service, I find that I am so ashamed of my profession that my conscience will no longer permit me to practice it.

Kollberg rolled the paper up an inch or two and read what he had written. Once he had started, he had the feeling he could have gone on indefinitely.

But this would have to do.

He added two more lines:

I therefore request that this resignation be accepted effective immediately.

Sten Lennart Kollberg.

He folded the sheets of paper and stuffed them into an official plain brown envelope.

Wrote the address.

Threw the letter into his Out basket.

Then he stood up and looked around the room.

Closed the door behind him and went.

Home.

(Maj Sjöwall and Per Wahlöö, *Cop Killer*, 1978, pp.294–7)

'Thieves and killers,' said Cunningham, his face flushed with anger, 'not cops. Don't put me in the same category with them. It's bad enough I have to work for the same department.' He reached into his pocket for his cigarettes. After offering one to the other man, he stuck one in his mouth, but didn't light it, letting it dangle there as he spoke. 'First we got these animals in LA beating some guy to bloody pulp on videotape for the whole world to see, and now we have our own guys blowing dope dealers away and pocketing the drug money.'

(N.T. Rosenberg, *Mitigating Circumstances*, 1993, p.118)

Others have picked up the potential for corruption in the impact of other organizations on policing (Masonic lodges or local politics, for example). Yet others have explored the tensions posed for those who do not fit the conventional social specification of the police – black people, gay men, women and lesbians. Each of these social identities (to be discussed in more detail in section 6) reveals something of the social closure and social biases of policing which threaten both individual careers and the practice of investigation in a complexly patterned society.

Even within the confines of the police procedural, it is possible to trace a shift from a simple, firmly structured social order in which all that is required is the clarity of purpose and competence of the investigator, to a more complex, fluid and multi-faceted social order in which conventional wisdoms and moral judgements are not only problematic, but represent problems. In such novels, the police do not stand apart from the more complex social order – rather, their power is implicated in such complexities. For instance, the South Yorkshire-set procedurals of Reginald Hill (for example, *Underworld*, 1989) have engaged the problems of policing in the aftermath of the 1984–85 miners' strike, the attraction of a gay sergeant to a young Asian constable, and the impact of local women's groups (often involving Ellie Pascoe, whose husband is one of the main police officers).

We will come back to this question of the complex social order in section 6, but first we need to make a detour via a different vision – the nightmare of the collapse of social order and the rise of the serial killer.

Before reading on, consider why being a representative of the social order might be seen as increasingly problematic for the fictional detective.

5 Women and children first: the threat of the irrational

The traditional detective story, whether in its English mystery or American private eye forms, had little time for the *irrational* crime. Crimes in such novels were motivated: their causes could be traced somewhere in the nexus of love, greed or revenge. Indeed, the investigators go out of their way to pour scorn on the 'random killing' or 'mysterious stranger'. Although it is true that some of their murderers turn out to be multiple murderers, this is usually in the course of covering their tracks and stopping the mouths of potential witnesses or eliminating others in the line of inheritance. When an apparently random 'serial killer' *does* appear – as in Agatha Christie's *The ABC Murders* (1993) – this is revealed to be a ploy to hide the motivated murder (and its motive) in an apparently motiveless sequence.

serial killer

The serial killer is a significant new development in the detective story, since such a murderer changes the character of, and relations between, the imaginary social order, crime and detection. Where, in earlier forms of the detective story, victims are implicated in the commission of crime and crime is motivated against them as individuals, the serial killer creates the innocent, or, more accurately, the non-implicated victim. Randomized crimes of violence evoke a social order in which crime is not intrinsically or socially meaningful. They appear, as it were, out of nowhere. Whatever other features this imaginary social order might possess, it is distinguished by one overarching element – it includes those whose violence is unpredictable and symbolically much more dangerous than those whose violence can be comprehended. In this imaginary order, 'normality' co-exists with 'abnormality', as demonstrated by Dr Kay Scarpetta, medical examiner in Patricia Cornwell's *All That Remains*:

> Their murders were meticulously calculated, methodically planned. Bruce Phillips and Judy Roberts disappeared in June. Their bodies were found in mid-August, when hunting season opened.
>
> Jim Freeman and Bonnie Smyth disappeared in July, their bodies found the opening day of quail and pheasant season.
>
> Susan Wilcox and Carolyn Bennett disappeared in March, their bodies discovered in mid-May, during spring gobbler season.
>
> Deborah Harvey and Fred Cheney vanished Labor Day weekend and were not found until months later when the woods were crowded with hunters after rabbit, squirrel, fox, pheasant and raccoon.
>
> I had not assumed that the pattern meant anything because most of the badly decomposed and skeletonized bodies that end up in my office are found by hunters. When someone drops dead or is dumped in the woods, a hunter is the most likely person to stumble upon the remains. But when and where the couples' bodies were discovered could have been planned.
>
> The killer wanted his victims found, but not right away, so he killed them off season, knowing it was probable his victims would not be discovered until hunters were out in the woods again. By then the bodies were decomposed … . Most trace evidence would be dislodged by wind and washed by rain. It may even be that it was important to him that the bodies be found by hunters because in his fantasies he, too, was a hunter.
>
> (Patricia Cornwell, *All That Remains*, 1992, pp.218–19)

This interrelationship between normality and abnormality is fundamental to the fictional world of the serial murderer. The normality of social life must be underscored for us to appreciate the full horror of the random killings to come. The juxtaposition of normality and abnormality needs to be intense. For such reasons, the serial killer story will emphasize the absolute *ordinariness* of the victims. Investigations of their lives reveal nothing that would mark them out as potential victims, by contrast with the traditional victim who could be placed in a chain of motivation. They are also likely to be women and children – the most *symbolically* innocent and vulnerable.

The connection between normality and abnormality is also implicated in the problems of detecting the serial killer. The conventional wisdom of the detective story on this issue is that the 'sociopath' is capable of 'passing for normal'. Indeed, he (it normally is 'he') may be ultra-conventional, except when engaged in the process of killing. He will not stand out as a deranged and visible individual – on the contrary, he will blend invisibly into social life. Most alarmingly, he may, like Hannibal Lecter, be *'impenetrable'*: 'A pure sociopath, that's obviously what he is. But he's impenetrable, much too sophisticated for the standard tests. And, my, does he hate us' (Dr Chilton's description in *The Silence of the Lambs*, Harris, 1990, p.10). It is this ambiguity which makes the imaginary social order at once comfortable and familiar and unstable and threatening. The conventional 'clues' about dangerousness are not available.

This complexity of normality and abnormality poses a problem for detection. It makes it impossible for the classic individualist methods to work effectively, since they rely on the combination of suspects and victims which allows the investigator either to 'unmask' the real murderer or to disentangle the relationships which connect victim and killer. 'Motiveless' crimes offer little purchase to such approaches. In their place, we see the rise of scientific investigation which can assemble, from multiple sources, the physical, social and psychological profile of the killer. As a consequence, detection has become a more collective enterprise, involving collaboration between different types of expertise: forensic specialists, medical examiners, the police, the Federal Bureau of Investigation (FBI), psychologists and profilers. Such collaborations are not easy or comfortable processes – proving rich in interpersonal tensions and interprofessional rivalries and conflicts based on different sorts of expertise ('real' police work versus psychological speculation, for example). Despite this, and the focus on one particular investigator for the story line, there is a shift towards a more collective and scientific mode of investigation in the serial killer story. This produces a strange inversion of the traditional pattern of crime and its detection.

In the conventional detective story, the murderer is, in many senses, 'normal' – part of a particular type of social order with predictable motives which fit with the logic of that social order (killing for wealth, love, revenge, etc.). The detective is 'extraordinary', marked out by qualities which allow him or her to achieve a solution where others fail. In the case of the serial killer, this pattern is inverted – it is the murderer who is 'extraordinary' (while *appearing* normal) while the detective is part of a collective enterprise, increasingly dependent on the abilities and achievement of others to arrive at a solution.

Above all, the serial killer story relies on the capacity of the investigating team to make sense of the senseless – and this marks the rise of the importance of psychological approaches as offering a route to grasping the hidden logic of an abnormal mind. For all that the murders may appear 'senseless', 'motiveless', 'random', they are, in fact, organized by a logic – but not a conventionally recognizable one. The murderer had a rationale (even if he is not rational) and the problem for the detective is to discern this rationale, to uncover the hidden pattern. In the serial killer story, it is the murderer who is imposing his meaning (his twisted moral code) on the world through his acts. The difficulty is that conventional understanding cannot see the meaning behind the meaninglessness. This places specialist expertise at a premium – whether this be the forensic evidence of regularity, the uncovering of hidden patterns which link the victims, or the discovery of the symbolic significance of the victims and their deaths for the murderer.

How is the serial killer distinctively disruptive of social order?

6 Back on the mean streets: the 'deviant' detective

The imaginary social orders of the detective story have tended to be thoroughly *conventional* ones, even when the detective has been uncovering its 'underside' – the familial tensions of the English mystery or the corruption of power and wealth in the American PI novel. Nevertheless, the place of particular types of people in these social orders is taken for granted: the finely ordered gradations of class in which everyone knows their place; the gendered divisions of social roles, character and behaviour; the familial structures of age, gender and sexuality; the social architecture of 'race' and ethnicity – ranging from the English novel's suspect 'foreigners' to the subterranean world of black America in the PI story, whose members appear in service roles or as the indicators of another 'way of life' (clubs, gangs, petty crime, etc.) which lurks in the background of white America. Where the PI was quintessentially 'everyman' in his white, male heterosexuality, the development of the detective story through the 1970s and 1980s saw the 'eye' change social roles and places with disturbing implications for representations of social order. The detective has changed gender, 'race' and sexuality and each of these changes has had the effect of revealing different dimensions and assumptions about crime, the social order and detection. Different types of realism are evoked through these 'deviant' detectives – they lay claim to alternative 'realities'. More accurately, they demonstrate that the 'reality' of the social order looks different depending on the social position from which one views it.

gender, sexuality
'race'/ethnicity

heterosexuality

6.1 'But I was expecting a man'

With occasional exceptions, the detective has been predominantly male. In this, the detective story has reproduced wider social assumptions about the gendered distribution of capabilities and capacities – that men are the natural repositories of 'rational analysis' (as opposed to intuition) and physical action (as opposed to emotional energy). Since most detective stories have relied on one or other of these principles as the basis for resolving problems, the occasional woman detective tends to prove the rule. Jane Marple does not possess Hercule Poirot's 'little grey cells'; rather, she is an 'old biddy' who spends too much time watching people and speculating (if not actually gossiping) about them. Her counterparts appear in minor roles as witnesses in many detective stories – peering out from behind their curtains and keeping tabs on what the neighbours are up to.

In this respect, the existence of a woman detective (whether private or police) is itself a challenge to the conventional social order of the detective story – she is 'out of place' and is likely to experience troubles because of it. In particular, this is likely to mean negotiating a whole structure of male assumptions about the world, crime and the division between the sexes, from villains, cops, friends and relatives. Anna Lee's experiences with prospective clients at the Brierly Detective Agency in Liza Cody's *Dupe* are typical:

> The tea was poured and Beryl left with heavy-footed discretion. Mr Jackson seemed to take note of Anna for the first time.
>
> 'And who's this?' he said. 'You assured me over the phone that this business would be confidential.'

'Biscuit?' offered Brierly. 'No?, Ah, yes, forgive me. Mr and Mrs Jackson, this is Miss Lee. Let me assure you again that your affair will be treated in the strictest confidence. All my employees are hand-picked …'.

'That's as may be.' Jackson was unappeased. 'But this is just a slip of a girl. And it doesn't look to me as if you're taking this too seriously, Mr Brierly.'

'We take all our cases with the utmost seriousness,' Brierly said weightily.

'Miss Lee has spent five years in the police force prior to her employment here, and has subsequently undergone the special training needed for the unique requirements of this organization.'

'Well, she looks a bit young to me,' said Jackson, unwilling to give up his objection.

(Liza Cody, *Dupe*, 1982, p.14)

In many of these novels, the woman detective has to struggle for the 'right to detect' in the face of individual and institutional prejudice, but the rise of the woman detective is only superficially a demonstration of the fact that 'women can do it, too'. More substantially, it is an exploration of what is *in the way of* women doing it – the blocks and barriers that are placed in the way by a social order which systematically structures and legitimates sexual inequalities. As a consequence, the woman detective is likely to be attentive to particular patterns and relationships – gendered ones, especially – that may be ignored or simply dismissed as 'normal' by her male counterparts. Sara Paretsky's Warshawski, like others, has to struggle to explain why this 'normality' might be problematic:

I hunched a shoulder impatiently. 'The trouble is, Michael, you belong to a crowd where the girls sit on a blanket waiting for the boys to finish talking business and bring them drinks. I like LeAnn and Clara, but they'll never be good friends of mine – it's not the way I act or think or live or – or anything. I think that style – the segregated way you and Ernie and Ron work – it's too much part of you.'

(Sara Paretsky, *Burn Marks*, 1990a, p.48)

Such observations are *mundane* points in these detective stories – they are about the gendered patterning of everyday life. They underscore the sense of a different point of view – one that recognizes the socially constructed character of the apparently natural gender dimensions of social order. It is not that crime has changed – although the woman-centred detective story is likely to illuminate issues of physical, emotional and sexual abuse which are absent from the earlier generations of the crime novel (for example, Barbara Wilson's *Sisters of the Road*, 1986). Blackmail, corporate corruption and murder continue to be staple crimes. What does get changed are the ways in which those crimes are approached and understood – framed by an understanding of the gendered nature of the social order, and the roles and relationships within it.

Such women detectives are also inclined to be resourceful in unfamiliar as well as familiar ways. In addition to being physically tough and resilient (though with rather more attention to the physical and emotional costs of violence), as well as possessing investigatory skills, the woman detective tends to be 'networked' in different ways from the male detective. Thus, while Paretsky's Warshawski has two of the classic 'contacts' – a friendly detective and a reliable investigative journalist – she has other resources: women friends in business and financial circles who can access information, and her friend and mentor Doctor Lotty Herschel who runs a medical centre. Warshawski, like others, also has a distinctively gendered edge when it comes to investigating – whether it be forms of 'sisterly solidarity' as a means of gaining information (from women secretaries, for example) or the fact that men consistently underestimate the woman detective.

A woman in a 'man's' world? Detective Inspector Tennyson (Helen Mirren) in ITV's Prime Suspect

Whether alone and independent or involved and independent, the woman detective also has a more visible life alongside the job which requires attention, compromises and negotiation. Such lives may involve sexual relationships and the problems which they present (Johnson, 1994); they may involve friendships and the tensions they bring with them; or they may involve families and the difficulties which they create. These ongoing real lives interrupt the work rather than being marginal humanizing additions, and they require mundane maintenance if they are not to go wrong. Of course, what we might call the 'post-feminist' male detective is also rather self-consciously discovering some of these issues (for example, Robert Parker's Spenser's struggles to negotiate masculine codes in the face of female challenges: see *Looking for Rachel Wallace*, 1987, in particular). Nevertheless, the realism of the woman-centred detective story has tended to be achieved by reference to both a wider social order which is gendered and a more mundane conception of daily life as being more than the job.

Why does a difference in the gender of the detective reveal a different social order?

6.2 'Beyond the pale': detection and ethnicity

Where the rise of the woman detective has turned the assumptions about gender in the social order of the detective story on their head – examining and exposing the assumptions of the male-centred detective story – the black detective poses rather different issues. There have been black detectives, but with the exception of Chester Himes' novels (for example, *The Heat's On*, 1992), such figures have tended to be peripheral rather than central: supporting faces in the cast of the police procedural. Even Arthur Brown, the black member of Ed McBain's 'melting pot' of a detective team in the *89th Precinct* series, somehow never quite gets the front-line roles allocated to the other characters.

One might suggest that this is because the black detective threatens the conventional imaginary social order in a rather different way from the woman detective. In the conventional detective story, especially those set in the USA, we are aware of black people but as a potentially dangerous or exotic 'other' – an almost separate world and one which it is difficult or dangerous for the white detective to penetrate, even though it may need to be controlled or contained. In this conventional order, black people exist to be policed rather than to do the policing. As a consequence, a detective story which starts from and has its point of view within that 'other' world makes the social order look very different.

So what happens when the point of view shifts to within that other world? What one sees from the other side is not separateness, but profoundly unequal interdependence. These worlds interlock, although almost always to the advantage, and on the terms of, white America. Viewed from the other side, black people are seen to provide a vital, though forgotten or invisible, sub-structure for the white society. Dolores Komo's black woman investigator, Clio Browne, observes this social order from below, deliberately taking advantage of her 'racialized' invisibility by taking employment as a domestic servant:

> After flashing her Bi-State bus pass she seated herself near the front door, plunged her hand into the black recesses of her shoulder bag, and searched out a packet of business cards she'd collected over the years. Flipping through them, she selected one that read Maid-4-U domestics, a company that was now defunct. She'd used the ruse before and each time had been successful in gaining entrance to places that would have been off limits to anyone other than a dayworker.... . It always amazed Clio how invisible the maid became as secrets were openly discussed or classified materials were left carelessly about.
>
> (Dolores Komo, *Clio Browne Private Investigator*, 1988, p.9)

From this position as an invisible insider she is able to gain access to dimensions of the private or familial world which a conventional detective would struggle to discover. Nevertheless, her racialized identity is simultaneously a source of social vulnerability in terms of how power is socially distributed. These experiences are shared by Walter Mosley's Easy Rawlins – a solver of problems within the black community of 1950s Watts in Los Angeles, who is forced by circumstances also to solve crimes:

> In my time I had done work for the numbers runners, churchgoers, businessmen, and even the police. Somewhere along the line I had slipped into the role of a confidential agent who represented people when the law broke down. And the law broke down often enough to keep me busy. It even broke down for the cops sometimes.
>
> (Walter Mosley, *White Butterfly*, 1993, p.17)

Rawlins stands uncomfortably on those borderlines where the worlds of black and white America intersect, and is used by the police as a potential informant in settings to which they cannot gain access. In the process, Rawlins has to juggle conflicting demands – of friendships, community loyalty, self-preservation and pressures from white officialdom. As Extract 2.3 from *White Butterfly* indicates, this milieu is ambiguous and contradictory, as official and unofficial detectives work around and across the 'colour line' of 1950s Watts.

Extract 2.3   Mosley: 'Walking the line'

Quinten got his promotion because the cops thought that he had his thumb on the pulse of the black community. But all he really had was me. Me and a few other Negroes who didn't mind playing dice with their lives.

But I had stopped taking those kind of chances after I got married. I wasn't a stool for the cops anymore.

'I don't know nuthin' 'bout no dead girls, man. Don't you think I'd come tell ya if I did? Don't you think I'd wanna stop somebody killin' Negro women? Why, I got me a pretty young wife at home right now ...'

'She's all right.'

'How do you know?' I felt the pulse in my temples.

'This man is killing good-time girls. He's not after a nurse.'

'Regina works. She comes home from the hospital, sometimes at night. He could be stalkin' her.'

'That's why I need your help, Easy.'

I shook my head. 'Uh-uh, man, I cain't help you. What could I do?'

My question threw Naylor. 'Help us,' he said feebly.

He was lost. He wanted me to tell him what to do because the police didn't know how to catch some murderer who didn't make sense to them. They knew what to do when a man killed his wife or when a loan shark took out a bad debt. They knew how to question witnesses, white witnesses. Even though Quinten Naylor was black he didn't have sympathy among the rough crowd in the Watts community; a crowd commonly called *the element*.

'What you got so far?' I asked, mostly because I felt sorry for him.

'Nothing. You know everything I know.'

'You got some special unit workin' it?'

'No. Just me.'

The cars passing on the distant streets buzzed in my ears like hungry mosquitoes.

'Three girls dead,' I said. 'An' you is all they could muster?'

'Hobbes is on it with me.'

I shook my head, wishing I could shake the ground under my feet.

'I cain't help you, man,' I said.

'Somebody's got to help. If they don't, who knows how many girls will die?'

'Maybe you' man'll just get tired, Quinten.'

'You've got to help us, Easy.'

'No I don't. You livin' in a fool's nightmare, Mr. Policeman. I can't help you. If I knew this man's name or I knew somethin', anything. But it's the cops gotta gather up evidence. One man cain't do all that.'

I could see the rage gathering in his arms and shoulders. But instead of hitting me Quinten Naylor turned away and stalked off toward the car. I ambled on behind, not wanting to walk with him. Quinten had the weight of the whole community on his shoulders. The black people didn't like him because he talked like a white man and he had a white man's job. The other policemen kept at a distance too. Some maniac was killing Negro women and Quinten was all alone. Nobody wanted to help him and the women continued to die.

'You with us, Easy?' Roland Hobbes said. He put his hand on my shoulder as Naylor stepped on the gas.

I kept my silence and Hobbes took his friendly hand back. I was in a hurry to get to my house. I felt bad about turning down the policeman. I felt miserable that young women would die. But there was nothing I could do. I had my own life to attend to – didn't I?

(Walter Mosley, *White Butterfly*, 1993, pp.18–20)

Rawlins both belongs to the black community and has to negotiate its interactions with white America. In *A Red Death* (1992), his investigations (forced on him by the threat of prosecution for his tax evasion) result in him being alienated from friends and sections of the community. Despite this, his identity – the basis from which he views the world – cannot be separated from his position in America's racialized social structure. Being pressured to take on working with the police again in *White Butterfly*, he responds to the demands of the (white) Captain Violette:

> 'What the hell are you trying to do, Rawlins?' Violette yelled.
>
> 'Man, I'm in my own house right? I ain't ask you over. Here you come crowdin' up my livin' room an' talkin' t'me like you got a blackjack in your pocket' – I was getting hot – 'an' then you cryin' 'bout some dead girl an' I know they's been three before this one but you didn't give one good goddam! Because they was black girls and this one was white!' If I had been on television every colored man and woman would have stood from their chairs and cheered.
>
> Violette was up from his chair, but not to applaud. His face had turned bright red. That's when I remembered him. He was only a detective when he dragged Alvin Lewis out of his house on Sutter Place ... I remembered how red his face got while he beat Alvin with a police stick. I remembered how cowardly I felt while three other white policemen stood around with their hands on their pistols and grim satisfaction on their faces. It wasn't the satisfaction that a bad man had paid for his crime; those men were tickled to have power like that.
>
> (Walter Mosley, *White Butterfly*, 1993, p.50)

Like the classic PI, Rawlins is an 'outsider', not part of the power structures and relationships that dominate the social order. But he is not just an outsider – he is also located somewhere else, in another conventionally unacknowledged part of the social order. And because he is based there, he has the advantage of seeing how these different elements of the social order interlock – and the problems of negotiating them.

The 'colour line' – or its equivalent of 'racial' structuring – is a necessary part of the detective story which features detectives who are not part of the dominant ethnic group, whether the Native Americans in Tony Hillerman's Leaphorn and Chee series or the positions of Kramer and Zondi in James McClure's South African-set novels. What they construct as imaginary social orders – and what is most explicit in Mosley's novels – are patterns of order which are not simple or uni-dimensional but complex, multiple and contradictory.

How is the 'outsider' role of the black detective different from the classic PI?

What difference does it make that they are 'insiders' in a different part of the social order?

6.3 'Off the straight and narrow': gay and lesbian detectives

The last disruption of the conventional social order of the detective story is associated with novels whose investigators do not conform to the heterosexual assumptions of that order. Gay men and lesbians have not played major roles in the conventional detective story, except as 'bizarre' exceptions that demonstrate by their deviance the overwhelming 'normality' of everyone else. However, when they move to the centre of the detective story as investigators, this 'normality' comes to look rather different. Joseph Hansen's Dave Brandsetter stories centre on a gay insurance investigator whose employment is protected by family wealth in the face of organizational prejudice.

A rather more troubled existence is led by Milo Sturgis in Jonathan Kellerman's Alex Delaware novels. Delaware, the principal figure, is a child psychologist (and is actively heterosexual) and has formed a complex friendship with Sturgis, a Los Angeles Police Department detective. Sturgis, in other respects a classic 'good cop' of the genre, is given constant grief by the department for his homosexuality. In *Over the Edge*, his career is threatened by a new superior, Cyril Trapp:

> Used to be the biggest booze-hound, pillhead and whore freak in Ramparts Division. Then he found Jesus and become one of those scrotes who think everyone who doesn't agree with him deserves the gas chamber. He's opined in public that faggots are moral sinners, so needless to say, he adores me.' ...

> 'It wouldn't be that bad if he were blatant about it – good old honest hostility. I could quietly put in for a transfer on the basis of personality conflict and maybe squeak through. I like working West LA, and it wouldn't do wonders for my personnel file, but I could handle it. But a transfer wouldn't satisfy Trapp. He wants me off the force, period. So he takes the subtle approach – psychological warfare. Puts on the polite act and uses the duty roster to make my life miserable.'

> 'Bad cases?'

> '*Faggot* cases!' He raised his big fist and put it down hard on the table. The Black couple looked over. I smiled and they returned to their headphones.

> 'For the last two months,' he went on in a low voice, starting to slur, 'I've had nothing but gay cuttings, gay shootings, gay stompings, gay rapes. Faggot DOA, call Sturgis, captain's orders. It didn't take long to see the pattern, and I protested right away. Trapp put down his Bible and said he understood how I felt but that my experience was too valuable to waste. That I was a specialist. End of discussion.'

> (Jonathan Kellerman, *Over the Edge*, 1988, p.181)

This uncomfortable relationship between the gay or lesbian detective and the heterosexual culture of the police department is also a strong thread in the novels by Katherine V. Forrest, featuring detective Kate Delafield. In *Murder at the Nightwood Bar* (1987) and *Murder by Tradition* (1993), in particular, her own sexual identity is an integral element of the narrative. In the former, she is trapped between the official culture in which she works and the lesbian community focused around the bar at which the murder of a young lesbian has taken place. Like Easy Rawlins, Delafield is located 'elsewhere' in the social order, increasingly identifying herself with the gay and lesbian community. She is both an insider and an outsider, able to use her social location to see the conventional norms of the official social order. As a consequence, her role as a detective is both informed and made uncomfortable by her lesbian identity. Extract 2.4 from *Murder by Tradition* represents a moment when these tensions come to a head in a case involving the killing of a gay man.

Extract 2.4   Forrest: 'Challenging convention'

Kyle Jensen, his confession signed, had been officially arrested, and incident to that arrest had been booked, strip-searched and incarcerated, had had samples drawn of his blood and urine, as well as hair follicles taken from his head and crotch – all of this to his profane displeasure. On Monday he would be arraigned and assigned a public defender. And he would remain in jail, Kate was reasonably sure, until the disposition of his case; bail of any amount appeared beyond his resources.

She walked into the Detectives Squad Room, Taylor at her side, and dropped into her desk chair, feeling as if her bones had turned into quick-melting plastic.

Taylor propped a hip on the edge of her desk, crossed his arms, and gazed down at her. 'That's the best goddamn interrogation I've ever seen you do, maybe the best I've ever seen, period. Nobody else in the department could have pulled that confession out of him. We had diddley shit and you nailed him, trussed him up like a Thanksgiving turkey. Partner, you were great.'

Smiling her thanks, warmed by his appreciation, she felt – knew – that she had been like an athlete in peak performance, she had extended herself fully, used every ounce of her training, experience, instincts, knowledge, courage. She felt expended, spent.

'I figure a plea bargain, involuntary manslaughter,' Taylor said.

'You're not serious,' she said, gaping at him, realizing that she did have something left in her; astonishment.

'I hope we *get* involuntary. He draws a public defender that takes it to trial, he could even get off. Hey,' he said as she stared at him, 'figure it out for yourself. Teddie Crawford made a pass at another guy, backed up his cock with a knife. A jury's looking at this red-blooded normal guy, they'll figure Jensen freaked out and just lost it, that's all.'

'*Just lost it?* With effort she lowered her voice. 'Look Ed, I know juries are capable of anything. But we throw in the towel and take manslaughter? This red-blooded normal guy let himself get picked up by a gay man, he robbed him, he hacked and *mutilated* him to death.'

'Hey, I'm on your side – sure the guy should do time,' Taylor said, spreading his hands. 'And maybe a jury's gonna buy it. But I say Jensen's story hangs together just enough. I say a jury's gonna look at Kyle Jensen and see a regular guy who got freaked out by a cock-sucking fag.'

'Let me ask you something, Ed.' She was amazed by the calmness of her voice, the coherency of her words. '*Why* do men freak out over gay men? *Why is calling another man homosexual the ultimate insult? Why* are gay men so completely disgusting to other men?'

He pinched the crease in his brown pants between his thumb and forefinger, pulled at

Although Delafield is an official investigator, other lesbian detectives have tended to be 'unofficials', tied to investigations either by mischance or familial obligation (Sarah Dreher's trouble-prone Stoner MacTavish), or networks of solidarity (Barbara Wilson's Pam Nilsen), or by being in other investigatory trades (Val McDermid's Lindsay Gordon). What these stories have in common is a complex view of a social order which is hostile and oppressive but where there is an interlocking of 'straight' and 'alternative' worlds. There may be gay and lesbian 'sub-cultures', but, like the black America of Easy Rawlins, these are not separate from or outside the social order – they are integral elements of it.

What conventional assumptions are likely to be challenged by a gay or lesbian detective story?

it. 'Come on, Kate. The shit they do to each other is so up-chucking putrid you can't even think about it.'

She could see his tension and discomfort. She pushed on. 'Why not? Please do your best to tell me, Ed,' she said. 'I really want to know.'

'Jesus, Kate.' He looked at a spot somewhere over her head. 'What's to tell? They aren't men. They're faggots.' He raised a hand, waved it limply. 'Mincy little faggoty fake-men.'

'That doesn't answer it. And not all of them are effeminate. Look at Rock Hudson,' she argued, wishing she could name other virile but closeted movie stars made known to her by gay friends Joe and Salvatore. 'Some of them are really masculine.'

'Rock Hudson was a pervert, not a faggot. All those masculine-type guys are perverts. They use the faggoty men like some guys use sheep or a piece of liver.'

She could hardly wait to pass on this piece of wisdom to Joe and Salvatore. 'Ed, so what if somebody's a mincy little fake-man? Some people grow to be over seven feet tall. Some people –'

'Some people are freakish, but they're still men or women. Faggots, they want to be fucked, so they turn themselves into women. If you're a real man, then you aren't a woman.'

She chose her words. 'Ed, what you just said – do you realize, do you have any idea how much it shows utter contempt for women?'

His face acquiring a florid cast, he got up from her desk. 'Hey, Kate. With all due respect – don't tell me how men feel about women. I'm a normal guy. I been married twenty-three years to a woman who's very happy about it. You don't understand. I don't expect you to. Just drop it.'

Here it was again, his unspoken judgment that being a lesbian rendered her invalid – an outsider, a misfit. 'Ed –'

'Do me a huge favor, Kate. Drop it. You're a great detective, a terrific partner. Let's not get into this other crap with each other, okay?'

Cold fury gathered within her. 'Then you do me a favour too, Ed. I intend to put together the best possible case for Kyle Jensen spending the rest of his unnatural life in the cage where he belongs. What he did was not manslaughter. It was murder.'

She watched in escalating rage as Taylor stood with his arms crossed and his legs spread , his face closed. 'Monday I'm in court so I need you at the autopsy.' She snapped off the words. 'The favor is, do only what you need to do on this case. Let me do the rest, and stay the hell out of my way.'

'It'll be a pleasure, not a favor.' He made a tiny, ironic bow, and turned his back on her. 'With your approval, I'll leave you to sweep up and I'll just take myself on home to Marie.'

(Katherine V. Forrest, *Murder By Tradition*, 1993, pp.66–8)

6.4   Absences and presences: the 'deviant' detective story

What these new variations on the detective story create is a more complex and conflictual sense of a social order composed of multiple social differences and divisions. Crime and its solution become intrinsically more problematic because they are bound up in these social complexities and antagonisms. For these 'deviant' detectives to act – to bring about a resolution – not only must they solve the problem, but they must do so while negotiating the social minefield of divisions, inequalities and hostilities. Victims, villains, suspects, witnesses and the investigators are all placed in this complex of social relations and the social judgements or evaluations with which they are associated.

In the process, they overturn the assumptions associated with the conventional nature of social order in the detective story. In the past, the imaginary social orders of the detective story have been self-consciously concerned with class and status (the social distribution of power and wealth), and the allocation of other social roles, places and identities has been treated as unproblematic. They have 'naturalized' gendered, racialized and sexual identities. The rise of the 'deviant detective' makes these assumptions visible and renders them problematic. In the process, the nature of the imaginary social order changes, revealing different experiences, different structures of inequality and power and different sorts of crime – as well as placing familiar types of crime in new perspectives.

deviant detective

They do this by changing the characteristic structure of absences and presences in the detective story. In writing about the place of black people in the social sciences, Ann Phoenix (1990) has referred to the way in which they are defined by 'normalized absence' and 'pathologized presence'. When studying 'normal' patterns of social life in the UK and USA, social scientists tend to draw their evidence from the majority white population and identify its patterns as the 'norm'. In doing so, black people are invisible to such research and theorizing – they exist only as a 'normalized absence'. Contexts in which they have been actively researched tend to be associated with 'deviant' behaviours, so that when they become visible they do so as a 'pathologized presence'. Although developed in relation to social science research, this framework also offers a way of understanding the changing social order of the detective story.

absences and
presences

This is perhaps least obvious in the case of gender – in the English mystery, the PI story and the police procedural, women characters abound. But such women rarely escape a conventional repertoire of roles, ranging from the fragile flower to the *femme fatale*. They may well commit murders ('poison … a woman's weapon'), but they will do so from within a thoroughly conventional set of motives (greed, love, jealousy, revenge). In this sense, women have a 'conventionalized presence', in which the gendered differentiation of roles, character traits, motives and psychology are naturalized. It is in the gender of the detective that we see the pattern of 'normalized absence', solving the problem of crime tends to be a masculine prerogative, whether it is accomplished by rational thought or dynamic action.

Looking at racialized characterization in the detective story reveals more clearly the structure of normalized absence and pathologized presence. The world of the detective story is predominantly a white one – minority ethnic groups are not a feature of this world and do not provide central protagonists: they are a 'normalized absence'. Occasionally, they may appear peripherally in service roles, a 'conventionalized presence'. But if they do step out of the background, they are likely to do so as a 'pathologized presence': exotic, mysterious, suspicious and dangerous.

Similar observations can be made about the place of gay and lesbian characters. The interpersonal and sexual relationships of the conventional detective story are almost exclusively heterosexual ones – gay men and lesbians are a 'normalized absence'. Occasionally, they may gain a marginal appearance in stereotypical forms as an outrageously camp theatrical or hairdresser. If they move beyond this 'conventionalized presence', they represent the 'unnatural' and are suspect or dangerous because of it, a 'pathologized presence'.

It should be clear that the 'deviant' detective cannot be contained by these *naturalizing* assumptions. Indeed, the very presence of a woman, black or gay or lesbian detective at the centre of the story creates a different social order because we are viewing the world through what is, in the conventional story, an impossible perspective. We are seeing the world of conventional assumptions from outside rather than from inside and, as a result, we see different things. However, this metaphor of inside and outside is not really adequate or accurate – what we are seeing is the social order viewed from somewhere else within it. Such positions are usually 'looked at' rather than 'looking'. Seeing the social order from these 'elsewheres' changes the structure of normalized absences and pathologized presences – the 'deviant' becomes a normalized presence in a more complex social order.

In the process, some of the concerns of the conventional detective story take on different inflections. Like the traditional private eye, the deviant detective is a disenchanted observer of the social order and its corruption. For the woman detective, her disenchantment is not simply a state of mind but the product of her

Television's first lesbian detective? Detective Sergeant Maureen Connell (Siobhan Redmond) from BBC1's **Between the Lines**

place and experiences – she will see the patterns of power and wealth in both corporate crime and the gendered structure of relationships. Like the traditional solver of mysteries, she may be attentive to the 'familial' settings of crime, but her view of these settings will include an understanding of the gendered structuring and dynamics of power and its abuse. Like all the 'classic' detectives, she may understand the distinction between the Law and Justice, but she is likely to find it more complicated because neither individual justice nor social justice is easy to define. Perhaps most importantly, she must live with the problem that 'solving the problem' and restoring order at the end of the narrative is simultaneously restoring an order which is inequitable and oppressive.

Where analyses of the classic detective story have been able to assume that 'solving the problem' is equivalent to 'restoring order' in that it is crime which disrupts normality, no such easy assumption can be made in the context of the deviant detective story. *Crime is not a disruption of a stable social order, rather it is an expression of an order which is intrinsically unjust and dangerous.* Crime involves both 'crimes of the powerful' and the 'crimes of the powerless' – and is not separable from questions of power. Thus, there will always be a tension between 'solving the problem' and the wider context in which the conflict- and tension-ridden order continues. Even Warshawski's accomplishments in closing down a polluting chemical plant (Paretsky, 1990b), or stopping murderously corrupt corporate medicine (Paretsky, 1988), leave the structures which facilitate corporate crime untouched.

7 I have asked you all here ...

By now you must be wondering what the conclusion to all this is. Unfortunately, this is not a detective story in which all is revealed in the final section – no dramatic discovery of 'whodunnit'. The reality is rather more dull. While there may be many reasons for enjoying detective stories, the concern here is with what is interesting about them in terms of a popular imagery of crime. We might simply note that they are not very 'realistic' in that they are predominantly concerned with the rarest of crimes – murder – rather than the commonplace. But that would be to miss the point that murder – perhaps more than anything else – is implicitly understood to be the most serious of crimes, the point at which the social relations of the social order are dramatically torn apart. Murder is so frequently the starting point or the focus for the detective story because it shows up the social relations of crime and order in stark relief. The extraordinary event, so to speak, casts a new light on the ordinary world, revealing things which might otherwise remain invisible.

Poirot (Peter Ustinov) reveals all in Evil Under the Sun

Detective stories, are, of course, 'only entertainment'. They do not claim to be factual analyses of crime and society or to offer profound theoretical investigations of crime and policing. Nevertheless, there are two ways in which paying these popular entertainments some attention is justified. The first of these concerns the conventional distinction between factual (or informational) reportage of crime and crime control and the fictional representation of these issues. Factual reportage – of crimes, policing, court cases and official statements about crime and criminality – aims to command our attention by telling us about something serious. In brief, such information tells us about the 'war against crime'. In such settings, 'crime' is the object of fear, anxiety and hostility on the part of society: it is something to be controlled and overcome.

Popular entertainments such as the detective story do not fit this conventional assumption about the opposition between crime and society. Rather than crime being an object of 'repulsion', detective stories suggest that crime is simultaneously an object of fascination and attraction – an issue from which we can gain pleasure. **Jack Katz (1988)** has discussed this double relationship to crime in terms of its 'seductions and repulsions'. Certainly, the detective story demonstrates this ambiguity. Its popularity as a form of entertainment is a telling reminder about the seductions and attractions of crime as a social issue.

Second, we need to think of the detective story as one of the strands contributing to our collective stock of images about crime and social order – one of the ways in which societies 'talk about crime'. Alongside official statements, reporting of criminal cases and documentary reconstructions, detective stories both *draw on and contribute to* the social imagery of crime. They draw on social imagery in the ways in which they construct and present themselves as being realistic, plausible or even simply 'fun'. Like the classic mystery, they may lay claim to a nostalgically invented past of a stable aristocratic England, or, like the classic private eye stories, their 'realism' may be associated with everyday speech and the promise to reveal the 'seamy side' of life. But all of them have to make connections between their specific story and the wider stock of imagery about pasts, presents and futures of social order.

In the telling of their stories, though, they also add to the collective imagery of crime and social order. They contribute to the ways in which we can understand and imagine the relationships between order and disorder. They provide other 'ways of seeing' crime – whether it be about tortuous family relationships, corporate corruption or how the social order looks when viewed from unfamiliar places. Like social science analyses, the detective story cannot escape making connections between crimes and their social settings, simply in order to be able to tell stories. In doing so, though, it may reinforce, reimagine or challenge conventional assumptions about both crime and the social order. The history of the detective story presents us not merely with changes in the sorts of crime that are the object of attention, and changes in who can be the detective, but also reveals shifting social perspectives on the societies in which crimes take place. In the course of this chapter, it has been possible to see the move away from a social order which was represented as stable and static (the mystery) to one which was flawed, disordered and corrupt (the PI). The rise of the 'deviant detective', however, has been accompanied by new representations of order as complex, unequal and *socially constructed*: no longer stable and 'natural' but tense and conflictual.

These different perspectives on crime and society are also central to social science approaches – even though they may be expressed differently or be more explicitly theorized. Nevertheless, distinctions are drawn between views of crime and order which reflect those we have seen in the detective story. Some theories identify the social order as a *stable context* which is disrupted by crime. Others identify it as *disorganized and corrupting*. Still others treat it as a *complex and constructed matrix of inequalities and power relationships*. The detective story, then, provides one setting in which these differences are dramatized and demonstrated.

Further reading

Studies of detective and crime fiction

The detective story has been subjected to very different types of analysis. Symon's *Bloody Murder* (1992) offers a literary history of the development of the detective novel, while Mandel's *Delightful Murder* (1984) presents a Marxist social history of the crime novel. Watson's *Snobbery With Violence* (1979) is an amusing and thoughtful discussion of the social order represented in the English 'murder mystery' novel. Palmer's *Potboilers* (1991) is a more analytical approach to the methods of studying popular fiction, including crime novels. Munt's *Murder By the Book* (1994) explores the relationships between gender, crime and detection in crime fiction.

Detective novels

Each of the novels which are the source of the extracts in this chapter bears reading. Of particular interest to those concerned with the intersection between crime fiction and theories of criminality is Philip Kerr's futuristic novel *A Philosophical Investigation* (1992) which also raises issues about the relationships between gender, social order and policing.

References

Carr, J.D. (1964) *The Crooked Hinge*, New York, Collier Books. (First published in 1938.)

Chandler, R. (1988a) *The Big Sleep*, Harmondsworth, Penguin. (First published in 1939.)

Chandler, R. (1988b) *The Simple Art of Murder*, New York, Vintage Books. (First published in 1934.)

Christie, A. (1959) *Five Little Pigs*, Glasgow, Fontana Collins. (First published in 1943.)

Christie, A. (1968) *At Bertram's Hotel*, London, Fontana. (First published in 1965.)

Christie, A. (1993) *The ABC Murders*, London, HarperCollins. (First published in 1936.)

Cody, L. (1982) *Dupe*, London, Pan.

Cornwell, P. (1992) *All That Remains*, London, Warner Books.

Forrest, K.V. (1987) *Murder at the Nightwood Bar*, London, Pandora.

Forrest, K.V. (1993) *Murder by Tradition*, London, Grafton. (First published in 1991.)

Goffman, E. (1959) *The Presentation of Self in Everyday Life,* New York, Doubleday Anchor.

Grella, G. (1980) 'The hard-boiled detective novel', in Winks, R.W. (ed.) *Detective Fiction*, New York, Prentice-Hall.

Hammett, D. (1975) *Red Harvest*, London, Pan. (First published in 1950.)

Harris, R. (1990) *The Silence of the Lambs*, London, Mandarin.

Hill, R. (1989) *Underworld*, London, Grafton.

Himes, C. (1992) *The Heat's On*, London, Allison and Busby. (First published in 1961.)

Johnson, P.E. (1994) 'Sex and betrayal in the detective fiction of Sue Grafton and Sara Paretsky', *Journal of Popular Culture*, vol.27, no.4, pp.97–106.

Katz, J. (1988) *Seductions of Crime: Moral and Sensual Attractions in Doing Evil*, New York, Basic Books. (Extract reprinted as 'Seductions and repulsions of crime' in Muncie, J., McLaughlin, E. and Langan, M., eds, 1996, *Criminological Perspectives: A Reader*, London, Sage in association with The Open University.)

Kellerman, J. (1988) *Over the Edge*, London, Futura.

Kerr, P. (1992) *A Philosophical Investigation*, London, Arrow.

Komo, D. (1988) *Clio Browne Private Investigator*, Freedom, CA, The Crossing Press.

Mandel, E. (1984) *Delightful Murder: A Social History of the Crime Novel*, London, Pluto.

Marcus, S. (1977) Introduction to Hammett, D. *The Continental Op*, London, Pan.

McLaughlin, E. (1996) 'Police, policing and police work', in McLaughlin, E. and Muncie, J. (eds) *Controlling Crime*, London, Sage in association with The Open University.

Mosley, W. (1992) *A Red Death*, London, Pan.

Mosley, W. (1993) *White Butterfly*, London, Serpent's Tail. (First published in 1992.)

Munt, S. (1994) *Murder by the Book: Crime Fiction and Feminism*, London, Routledge.

Palmer, J. (1991) *Potboilers: Methods, Concepts and Case Studies in Popular Fiction*, London, Routledge.

Paretsky, S. (1988) *Bitter Medicine*, Harmondsworth, Penguin.

Paretsky, S. (1990a) *Burn Marks*, London, Chatto and Windus.

Paretsky, S. (1990b) *Toxic Shock*, Harmondsworth, Penguin.

Parker, R. (1987) *Looking for Rachel Wallace*, Harmondsworth, Penguin.

Phoenix, A. (1990) 'Theories of gender and black families', in Lovell, T. (ed.) *British Feminist Thought: A Reader*, Oxford, Blackwell.

Rosenberg, N.T. (1993) *Mitigating Circumstances*, London, Orion Books.

Sjöwall, M. and Wahlöö, P. (1978) *Cop Killer: The Story of a Crime*, New York, Vintage Books. (First published in Swedish in 1974, in English in 1975.)

Symons, J. (1992) *Bloody Murder: From the Detective Novel to the Crime Novel – A History* (3rd edn), Harmondsworth, Penguin.

Watson, C. (1979) *Snobbery With Violence*, London, Eyre Methuen.

Weinkaupf, M.S. (1980) 'Miss Jane Marple and aging in literature', *Clues: A Journal of Detection*, vol.1, no.1, pp.32–40.

Wilson, B. (1986) *Sisters of the Road*, London, Virago.

Chapter 3
Crime, Order and Historical Change

by Jim Sharpe

Contents

1 Introduction

*I*n this chapter we shall be examining a number of ways in which studying 'crime' as a historical phenomenon not only creates a number of points of contrast with current approaches to crime and criminals, but also suggests some long-term continuities. Although some reference will be made to earlier and later periods, our main concern will be with eighteenth-century England. (Regrettably, current levels of writing on crime and punishment in Scotland and Wales before the nineteenth century preclude these countries being treated with the same depth as England, while the study of crime in Ireland in the eighteenth and earlier centuries is impeded by the loss of records caused by fire in the Dublin Public Record Office earlier this century.) It was the first two thirds of the nineteenth century that were crucial in shaping 'modern' conventional thinking about crime and punishment (see also Chapter 4). For this reason, studying the very different law enforcement system of the eighteenth century and the attitudes that underpinned it forces us to focus on a number of issues: definitional problems, including those arising from a conflation of sin and crime, from conflicting notions about property rights, and from the friction between customary practices and statute law; the peculiarities of a system of law enforcement dependent upon local, amateur officers; the peculiar logic of the ideology of punishment during this period; and the importance of the community in law enforcement. These and other factors combined to produce distinctive attitudes to crime and its control. Some of these seem very distant to the citizen of the modern, bureaucratized state.

This distance has not deterred intensive work on the history of crime over the last twenty-five years, and research on periods between the fourteenth and twentieth centuries has revealed a great deal about criminal behaviour in the past. There is no unified 'historical approach' to the study of crime in the past: historians, like criminologists, disagree about how best to gather, conceptualize and analyse their data. However, there is a substantial body of published work available which both presents research findings and discusses approaches to the subject (see Cockburn, 1977; Brewer and Styles, 1980; and Innes and Styles, 1986).

The need to have some historical background can be justified by two main lines of argument. The first is the frequency with which the current debate about crime and punishment all too easily slides into contrasting our present situation with some supposed earlier state, in which the problems we experience are presumed either to have been absent or to have been present in a much less serious form. Studying the history of crime and punishment does at least facilitate informed comment on this type of discussion. Second, and more relevant for the immediate purposes of this chapter, studying the history of crime (like studying the history of anything) forces us to forget the assumptions of our own culture and to confront those of another. In so doing, we have to accept the sometimes uncomfortable notion, equally present in anthropology, that other people act on other assumptions, and organize their ways of doing things differently from those in a declining post-industrial state at the end of the twentieth century. Attempting to grasp these differences, to understand how they were rational in their own cultural context, can inform our understanding of the complexities we face. If nothing else, studying the history of crime and punishment reminds us that our current ways of thinking about and dealing with these problems are not the only ones that human beings have found appropriate.

2 Crime in eighteenth-century England: the problem of definition

Throughout this chapter we will be looking at how conceptions of crime have changed through time, and how this was often reflected in how crime was punished. This section discusses the problem of defining crime, and focuses on the eighteenth and early nineteenth centuries. Any attempt to range more widely would be confusing in the space available. However, it is important to grasp that by the beginning of the eighteenth century competing definitions of crime were already well established in two areas. The first was constituted by what could be described as competing notions of 'state' and 'community' perspectives on crime and law enforcement. The second was created by the problems which many contemporary observers had in distinguishing between 'crime' and 'sin'. To these might be added, at the risk of dipping too deeply into the complexities of legal history, a third complication: the distinction between civil and criminal law was not as clear in earlier periods as it is today. This could be especially relevant to the treatment of, and the formation of attitudes towards, certain types of property offences in a period that witnessed increasing commercialization and in which the law relating to property and to related matters of debt, credit and fraud was still developing (see Chapter 1, section 2.5).

As will be discussed later in this chapter, neither 'state' nor 'community' were unproblematic concepts in the eighteenth century. However, between the Middle Ages and the eighteenth century, in England as in much of western and central Europe, there was a general tendency for state law to impinge increasingly on the region or the community, and on the plural legal systems which these enjoyed. There are enormous problems in defining exactly what state law was, not least in a political system like eighteenth-century England where the state was at a curious stage of its development, showing both 'modern' and pre-modern tendencies. Broadly, state law could be regarded as the law being supported by central government, created, extended or redefined by parliamentary statute, and, arguably, representing either the ideology and objectives of England's ruling elites or of sections of those elites or of interest groups within them. Thus, over the seventeenth and eighteenth centuries, the criminal law, constantly extended by parliamentary statute, was becoming increasingly important in the wider repertoire of social control.

The locus of law-making and legal thinking represented by parliament and central government contrasted with the situation in the localities. Although the common law, enforced in the monarch's courts, had long been, in theory at least, the decisive element in most legal matters, before the seventeenth century most villages and small towns were very much self-policing communities. Law enforcement officers were local, and the law, although in England essentially the common law of the realm, was often modified by local custom, local laws, and local opinion on what might be the best way of dealing with specific offenders and offences. This situation was

state law

always at its most marked when petty offences were under consideration: the more serious offences, such as murder, theft, burglary, robbery and rape, were increasingly left to royal judges. But over the period 1500 to 1700 it is possible to trace a slow process by which petty offenders would be more likely to be tried before the local manorial courts in 1500, before the ecclesiastical courts (still in many respects locally based) in 1600, and before justices of the peace (local men, but essentially royal officials) at petty sessions in 1700. The law in eighteenth-century England was still not the preserve of a centralized sovereign state, but a transition towards something like this situation took place over the seventeenth and eighteenth centuries. This transition involved changing emphases on what was considered deviant.

The Bench, *an engraving by William Hogarth (1758)*

2.1 Sin and crime

Most local communities without doubt desired order, and the fact that the state legal system was able to make such an advance was largely due to a growing awareness in communities that it offered an effective way of dealing with local troublemakers and settling local disputes. Sometimes the range of deviant behaviour reported by local law enforcement could be very wide, and might seem very odd to the modern observer. The archives of the ecclesiastical courts give a good indication of this. During the seventeenth century (and possibly later in some areas) the ecclesiastical courts were responsible for disciplining the clergy, maintaining the fabric of church buildings, and ensuring attendance at church and conformity to the rites of the Church of England, but they were also responsible for controlling sexual morality and matrimonial disputes. The occasional prosecution for working on the sabbath or for usury involved the courts in economic regulation, while their role in testamentary business rendered them important in property transactions. Thus the function of the church courts in disciplining society demonstrates that studying the criminal law and its operation alone in the early modern period would lead us to miss a number of important points.

The importance of the ecclesiastical courts in maintaining social discipline is well illustrated from a contemporary document. The following presentment, the ecclesiastical courts' equivalent of a formal criminal charge, was made by the churchwardens of Banbury in Oxfordshire to the local archdeacon's court in 1610:

> wee present Anthony Hall upon a fame and suspition of incontinencie [sexual immorality] with Sarah Band. Wee present Wm Cooke for sicking in the church yeard the 1st of October. Wee present James West and John Greene for working on St Micaels Day. Wee present Thomas Tymber upon a suspition of incontinencie with Sarah Band. Wee present Sarah Band upon a fame of suspition of incontinencie with Anthony Hall & with Thomas Tymber. Wee present Humfray Devis for sicking in the church the 5 of November. Wee present Mary Smith for fornication. Wee present Robart, servant with the myller for fornication with a woman's daughter of Broughton. Wee present Epiphan Bird for unseemly speeches to Bartholomewe Naler Churchwarden. Wee present Henry Glover for making water in the church.

> (cited in Hair, 1972, p. 80)

This indicates the dimensions of control at which the authorities might aim in this period, and the range of behaviour that might be prosecuted once those dimensions were accepted. The presentment reminds us that in the seventeenth century, notions about the suppression of crime were very closely connected with ideas about the need to combat sin: indeed, before the eighteenth century it is very difficult to find much by way of discussion of 'crime' in the modern sense. It has been argued that over the eighteenth century a conventional wisdom about crime control which sprang from religion was replaced by one which saw the need to control crime as an important aspect of that most secular of concerns, the defence of property (Hay, 1975).

sin

Despite the beginnings of a more secular attitude to crime, the religious input into thinking about crime in the eighteenth and early nineteenth centuries was considerable. The start of the eighteenth century witnessed a moral crusade against prostitutes, drunkards, the keepers of disorderly alehouses, swearers and sabbath-breakers in the form of the Societies for the Reformation of Manners, locally based and religiously driven organizations which sprang up in London and a number of provincial centres. This development originated from a grassroots concern among respectable householders on what were then the fringes of London that these offences, many of them within the jurisdiction of the ecclesiastical courts, whose criminal business was probably fading in the metropolitan and other urban areas, were being allowed to flourish. The great drive towards prison reform in the later eighteenth century, symbolized by John Howard and Elizabeth Fry, similarly owed much to the religious values of its proponents. Throughout the century, the sermons preached at assizes, the accounts of the careers and executions of criminals written by the Ordinary of Newgate, and a continual output of moral tracts served to remind public opinion of the close connection between criminality and sinfulness.

2.2 Social crime

Despite these provisos, the eighteenth century and, perhaps less equivocally, the first half of the nineteenth century did witness the development of what we would consider to be 'modern' attitudes to crime and what ought to be done about it. Crime was increasingly seen as a phenomenon devoid of overtones of sin, which was best dealt with through legislation, trial before royal judges, and punishment in officially sanctioned methods by the state. Moreover, the eighteenth century, as we have hinted, was also the period which saw the emergence of crime or, perhaps more accurately, of law and order in general, as matters of public debate. By the middle of the century a number of writers, of whom the brothers John and Henry Fielding were the best known, were alerting the public to the menace posed by crime, and were suggesting methods of dealing with it. At the same time the respectable could read in their newspapers of sensational crimes, of the rewards that were being offered for stolen goods, or of the penalties awarded to run-of-the-mill offenders at the local county assizes. The media in earlier periods were just as likely as their modern counterparts to sensationalize the more newsworthy aspects of crime. Most important, perhaps, 'crime' was beginning to take on something like the modern layperson's definition: murder, rape, the more serious property offences like theft, robbery and burglary, and the host of lesser offences which served as precursors to them.

Yet, as historians have argued, even as the eighteenth-century elites were slipping into accepting this set of 'modern' attitudes towards crime, their social inferiors were holding alternative views. The key concept here is that of social crime. According to the classic definition of this concept, crime can be regarded as 'social' when it represents 'a conscious, almost a political challenge to the prevailing social and political order and its values'. It occurs when there exist conflicting sets of official and unofficial interpretations of the legal system, when acts of law-breaking manifest distinct elements of social protest, or when such acts are clearly connected to social or political unrest (Hobsbawm, 1975, pp.5–6).

The concept is a somewhat slippery one. It was developed largely by a group of Marxist historians who were anxious to interpret certain forms of law-breaking as what might be termed 'pre-class, class conflict'. Thus a number of offences which could be portrayed as reflecting popular or community values, such as rioting, poaching, smuggling and wrecking, were singled out for special attention. The concept is of less use, as the group of historians in question accepted, in explaining the actions of 'those who commit crime without qualification: thieves, robbers, highwaymen, forgers, arsonists and murderers' (Hay *et al.*, 1975, p.14). It has, however, proved important in demonstrating how various forms of popular action and popular customs in this period, although criminalized by officialdom, were not regarded as blameworthy either by those committing them or by the communities from which they came.

Perhaps the clearest, and certainly best documented, area where these differing attitudes can be seen in operation was constituted by rioting and other forms of popular disturbances (Stevenson, 1979). Close examination reveals that many eighteenth-century 'riots' were in fact what modern terminology would describe as demonstrations, and had rational ends rather than being the product of gin-sodden desperation. The historian E.P. Thompson has argued that those participating in riot often held legitimizing

social crime

popular custom

notions, 'legitimation' to Thompson meaning that 'the men and women in the crowd were defending traditional rights and customs; and, in general, that they were supported by the wider consensus of the community' (Thompson, 1975).

Other offences, less dramatic than the riot, allow us to reconstruct how the conflict between elite law and popular custom might work itself out in the local context. The game laws, which might have led to an agricultural labourer suffering severe legal penalties for stealing a rabbit or two for the pot, are an obvious example. Less well known, but equally important at the time, were disputes over 'gleaning' and the collection of firewood, which was redefined by landlords as a form of theft on many estates (Bushaway, 1982). Gleaning was the poor's customary right of picking over the fields for ears of loose corn at harvest time. As agriculture became more capitalist and more market-oriented, landowners and farmers, increasingly anxious to maximize profits, became impatient of what they considered to be encroachment on their property.

Detailed study sometimes casts doubt on this 'custom into crime' paradigm. Gleaning provides an interesting example. The poor's notion that they had a right to glean was apparently quashed following a decision in a civil case, *Steel* v. *Houghton* (1788), in which the Court of Common Pleas decided that there was no right to glean under common law, and that persons gleaning fields without the permission of the landowner were trespassing. As might be imagined, this intensified confrontations between gleaners and farmers. It also prompted a minor social debate, in which a number of contributors argued in favour of gleaning on moral grounds (biblical texts could be found to justify it) and on the more pragmatic basis that denying the poor this access to gleaning would increase demands on the poor rates. The poor themselves pleaded that although they might have no common law right to glean, they had customary rights, and a number of legal decisions, sidestepping *Steel* v. *Houghton*, upheld this point of view. The upshot was that, despite the 1788 ruling, many of the rural poor in Eastern England continued to feel that they had a traditional right to glean. As *The Farmer's Lawyer* of 1819 put it, the poor had no common law right to glean, but should be permitted to do so, subject to local practices, if there was 'an immemorial custom or usage in the parish' (King, 1989).

The definition of crime in rural areas was thus being complicated by popular ideas on custom, ideas which could hold such a consistent traditional view of social norms and obligations, and of the proper nature of economic relations between different social strata, as to constitute a moral economy Meanwhile, the continuing economic development of the eighteenth and early nineteenth centuries was creating further complexities. Modern criminologists are now familiar with the concept of 'white-collar' crime – that is, crime committed by ostensibly 'respectable' people in the everyday course of their professional or business life. So far historians have paid little attention to the historical antecedents of white-collar crime, yet it is obvious that something very like it was emerging with fraud and forgery cases in the eighteenth century. The subject awaits further investigation. Yet it is clear that forgery was regarded as a serious offence. In the middle of the eighteenth century the celebrated legalist Sir William Blackstone claimed that the growth of statutory capital sanctions against forgery was the outcome of a perceived need to protect financial and banking interests which were seeking

moral
economy

legal defences for paper credit and exchange in a period of rapid commercial growth. In the period 1812–15, 84 people were capitally convicted for forgery in London and Middlesex, and 47 executed. In the same period, and in the same area, 26 people were executed for murder, 18 for burglary, and 17 for highway robbery. Clearly the courts were treating forgery, essentially an offence created in the eighteenth century, with considerable severity (Emsley, 1987, p.212).

ACTIVITY 3.1

Historians studying early modern England have commented on the problems of distinguishing between sin, crime and social crime. To what extent can you sympathize with their comments? And how far, in a modern society, can thinking about crime be separated from wider concerns about morality? Make some notes of your own on why it might be difficult to reach an incontrovertible definition of crime.

COMMENT

When considering 'crime' in eighteenth- and nineteenth-century England we are, as now, confronted by a wide range of behaviour and definitions. Then, again as now, 'crime' was essentially a blanket term that enfolded a number of acts, from murder to illicit wood-taking. Obviously people at the time had some notion of the relative seriousness of these acts, although different people might rank them differently, while, as we have seen, a number of different perspectives might add coherence to these rankings. Religious individuals, imbued with a strong sense of humankind's sinfulness, would have one set of ideas on crime. Rural labourers and their families performing acts which they thought were defended by custom but which were now declared illegal, and hence criminalized, might have another. Further complications lay in the right which many industrial and craft workers felt they had to the benefits of fiddles and of the right to 'waste' materials (a category which workers might interpret generously), generically known as 'perquisites', at the workplace. Men of property, whether country gentry concerned about the burglary of their houses or the theft of their horses, or merchants concerned over forgery, might have another. Thus even a brief review of the problems of defining crime in just one historical period helps remind us of how definitions might shift and how, at any given point, there might not be an absolute, or indeed any, consensus as to what constituted a 'criminal' act.

3 The system of crime control

It is perhaps a little misleading to describe the apparatus for detecting, trying, punishing and deterring crime in eighteenth-century England as a 'system'. It was, rather, a complex of institutions, officers and practices which interacted, usually more or less in unison, to punish offenders. Yet understanding at least something of this complex is a logical next step, now that we have considered some of the definitional problems of crime. Unfortunately, the documentation of the period rarely provides us with more than scattered evidence of how those involved in enforcing the law felt about what they were doing. But, arguably, the attitudes of such people are crucial to our understanding of conceptions of crime. Similarly, a study of penal practices, not least of forms of punishment, gives us, if only by inference, insights into how crime was regarded. Here, as elsewhere, the interplay between crime, law and control agencies is of importance. And, once again, consideration of these issues in a historical context provides us with a number of points of contrast and comparison with the current situation.

3.1 Capital punishment: the Bloody Code

The aspect of this complex that has perhaps attracted most attention from historians was the heavy dependence on capital punishment. Most contemporary European states exercised capital punishment, of course, while some regularly adopted aggravated forms of judicial killing, such as breaking on the wheel, which many English observers felt to be repugnant.

In eighteenth-century England aggravated capital punishment was largely reserved for those convicted of treason: males thus convicted might be subjected to the barbarities of hanging, drawing and quartering, while women convicted of treason (which included wives murdering their husbands) might be burnt at the stake. For persons convicted of felony, the punishment was generally hanging. At the end of every county assize, and eight times a year at Tyburn, murderers, burglars, thieves, rapists, sodomites, highway robbers, forgers and infanticidal mothers were hanged, sometimes in large numbers (Linebaugh, 1991). The frequency with which different types of offenders were hanged, and fluctuations in the use of this punishment, will be discussed in the next sub-section. The emphasis here is on the importance of the public execution of criminals as a symbolic expression of the majesty of the law.

As the eighteenth century progressed, the number of offences that could incur the death penalty increased steadily. Indeed, in 1688, the year of the glorious Revolution which the eighteenth-century English were to regard as the salvation of the English constitution and the English way of political life, about 50 offences already carried the death penalty. By 1800 this total had risen to about 200, all of the additions being imposed by parliamentary statutes, and most of these being concerned with the defence of property (see the appendix to the report from the Select Committee on Criminal Laws, 1819, reproduced overleaf).

	1776.			1777.			1778.			1779.		
	Convicted of.	Committed for.	Executed.	Convicted of.	Committed for.	Executed.	Convicted of.	Committed for.	Executed	Convicted of.	Committed for.	Executed
Arson - - - - -	–	–	–	–	–	–	–	–	–	–	–	–
Burglary - - - - -	19	13; Simple Larceny 5, Robbery, 1	9	19	13; Simple Larceny, 3 Highway Robbery, 3	12	29	28; Simple Larceny, 1	24	16	15; Highway Robbery, 1	7
Cattle Stealing - - - -	–	–	–	1	1	–	–	–	–	–	–	–
Coin, counterfeit putting off at a lower rate, &c. having before been allowed the benefit of Clergy - - -	–	–	–	–	–	–	–	–	–	–	–	–
Customs, assembling with others, being armed, in order to rescue uncustomed Goods after seizure, and molesting the Officers in securing the Goods after seizure - - - - -	–	–	–	–	–	–	–	–	–	–	–	–
Dwelling-house, entering and destroying Silk in a loom - - - -	–	–	–	–	–	–	–	–	–	–	–	–
Forgery - - - - -	2	2	1	3	3	1	2	2	–	2	1; Stealing a Bill of Exchange,1	2
Horse, wilfully and maliciously wounding	–	–	–	–	–	–	–	–	–	–	–	–
Horse Stealing - - - -	3	3	–	4	4	–	3	2; Robbery, 1	–	4	4	–
Housebreaking in the Day-time, and Larceny therein - - - -	–	–	–	4	Simple Larceny, 4	–	–	–	–	–	–	–
Larceny in a Dwelling-house to the value of 40 s. - - - -	7	Robbery, 1 Privately Person, 1 Simple Larceny 4 Burglary, 1	3	8	2; Simple Larceny, 6	5	8	2; Simple Larceny, 6	2	10	2; Burglary, 1 Privately in a Shop, 1 Robbery, 1 Simple Larceny, 4 Larceny on Person, 1	4
Larceny on a Navigable River, to the value of 40 s. - - - -	–	–	–	–	–	–	–	–	–	–	–	–
Larceny privily from a Person, to the value of 1 s. - - - -	1	Simple Larceny, 1	–	–	–	–	–	–	–	–	–	–
Larceny privily in a Coach-house, to the value of 5 s. - - - - -	–	–	–	–	–	–	–	–	–	–	–	–

Appendix to the report from the Select Committee on Criminal Laws, 1819: a statement of the number of people who were capitally convicted and of those who were executed in London and Middlesex

| | YEARS: | | | | | | | | | | | |
| | 1776. | | | 1777. | | | 1778. | | | 1779. | | |
(continued.)	Con-victd of.	Committed for.	Exe-cuted.	Con-victd of.	Committed for.	Exe-cuted.	Con-victd of.	Committed for.	Exe-cuted.	Con-victd of.	Committed for.	Exe-cuted.
Larceny privily in a Shop, to the value of 5 s.	4	1; Simple Larceny, 3	–	1	1	–	1	Simple Larceny, 1	–	2	1; Simple Larceny, 1	–
Larceny privily in a Stable, to the value of 5 s.	–	–	–	–	–	–	1	1	1	–	–	–
Larceny privily in a Warehouse, to the value of 5 s.	–	–	–	–	–	–	–	–	–	–	–	–
Letter, Threatening	–	–	–	–	–	–	1	1	–	1	1	–
Letter, Secreting, containing valuable Securities, being employed in the Post Office	–	–	–	–	–	–	–	–	–	1	1	1
Mail, Stealing Bags and Letters from	–	–	–	–	–	–	–	–	–	–	–	–
Maiming a Person maliciously, and lying in wait	–	–	–	–	–	–	–	–	–	–	–	–
Murder	6	6	6	2	2	2	1	1	1	1	1	1
Naval Stores, Stealing, to the value of 20s.	–	–	–	–	–	–	–	–	–	–	–	–
Oath, False, to receive a Seaman's Wages	–	–	–	–	–	–	–	–	–	–	–	–
Personating another, and obtaining a Transfer of Bank Annuities	–	–	–	–	–	–	–	–	–	–	–	–
Personating another, to receive a Seaman's Wages	–	–	–	–	–	–	–	–	–	–	–	–
Rack and Tenters, Cutting and Stealing Cloth from	–	–	–	–	–	–	–	–	–	–	–	–
Rape	–	–	–	1	1	1	1	1	1	1	1	1
Riot, and demolishing Dwelling-houses, &c.	–	–	–	–	–	–	–	–	–	–	–	–
Robbery	28	27; Simple Larceny, 1	10	16	12; Maliciously Shooting, 1 Larceny in Dw. Ho. 1 Burglary, 1 Larceny on Person, 1	9	31	26; Simple Larceny, 3 Defraud, 2	6	13	11; Simple Larceny, 2	5
Sheep Stealing	1	1	–	–	–	–	–	–	–	1	1	–
Shooting at another maliciously	–	–	–	1	1	–	3	2; Transports at large, 1	3	–	–	–
Sodomy	2	2	2	–	–	–	–	–	–	–	–	–
Stamps, denoting the Payment of Duties, forging them	–	–	–	–	–	–	–	–	–	–	–	–
Transport at large, without lawful cause	3	2; Simple Larceny, 1	–	1	1	–	–	–	–	1	Robbery, 1	–
Treason, High, compassing the King's Death	–	–	–	–	–	–	–	–	–	–	–	–
Treason, High, relating to Coin	10	10	7	1	1	1	1	1	–	4	4	3
	86	–	38	62	–	31	82	–	38	57	–	24

The statutes recommending capital punishment have commonly been referred to as the 'Bloody Code'. The reasons for this legislative process remain obscure, and research in progress suggests that they probably owed more to parliamentary processes and an extension of what were perceived as normal ways of dealing with crime than anything else. But established interpretation attributes the Bloody Code to an increased capitalist and commercial ethic among Britain's ruling class, who were therefore anxious to defend property through legislation. This has led a number of historians to consider the eighteenth-century Bloody Code as a straightforward example of the law as a form of class oppression, of the rule of the rich and propertied over the poor and propertyless (Hay, 1975; Linebaugh, 1991). The observations of some contemporaries lend support to such a view. For example, Adam Smith, the well-known proponent of capitalist economics, wrote:

> When ... some have great wealth and others nothing, it is necessary that the arm of authority should be constantly stretched forth, and permanent laws or regulations made which may protect the property of the rich from the inroads of the poor ... Laws and governments may be considered in this and in every case as a combination of the rich to oppress the poor, and preserve to themselves the inequality of the goods which would otherwise soon be destroyed by the attacks of the poor, who if not hindered by the government would soon reduce the others to an equality with themselves by open violence.

(cited in Emsley, 1987, p.8)

Both what can be recreated of the formulation of statutes in parliament, and research into the actual workings of the courts, demonstrate that a simple model of 'class law' does not provide a complete explanation for the English situation in the eighteenth century. Even so, the heavy dependence of eighteenth-century English criminal law on capital punishment, and the frequent execution of property offenders in England, are remarkable phenomena.

3.1.1 Public execution

As many historians have noted, these frequent executions of property offenders and others were carried out in public. Again, there are considerable dangers of oversimplification: it is all too easy for the modern historian to write off the public execution as a sign of the barbarity of past periods. But the comments of some eighteenth-century observers lend weight to such a view:

> Tho' before setting out, the prisoners took care to swallow what they could, to be drunk, and stifle their fear; yet the courage that strong liquors can give, wears off, and the way they have to go being considerable, they are in danger of recovering, and without repeating the dose, sobriety would often overtake them: for this reason they must drink as they go; and the cart stops for that purpose three or four, and sometimes half a dozen times or more, before they come to their journey's end ... At the very place of execution, the most remarkable scene is a vast multitude on foot, intermixed with many horsemen and hackney-coaches, all very dirty, or else cover'd with dust, that are either abusing one another, or else staring at the prisoners, among whom there is commonly very little devotion; and that, which is practis'd at dispatch'd there, of course, there is as little good sense as there is melody. It is possible that a man of extraordinary holiness, by anticipating the joys of heaven, might

embrace death in such raptures, as would dispose him to the singing of psalms: but to require this exercise, or expect it promiscuously of every wretch that comes to be hang'd, is as wild and extravagant as the performance of it is commonly frightful and impertinent: besides this, there is always at that place, such a mixture of oddnesses and hurry, that from what passes, the best dispos'd spectator seldom can pick out any thing that is edifying or moving.

(de Mandeville, 1725, pp.23, 24-5)

Yet this concentration on the bestial elements of public execution has tended to obscure a number of nuances. The public execution could be a complex cultural event (in fact, some have claimed that it marked a meeting point between elite and popular culture) in which a number of complex rituals might be observed.

The central performers (for the public execution was, on a number of levels, a piece of theatre) were the convicted felons. These were expected to 'die gamely'. Thus a highway robber, a category of offender which was already being mythologized as a popular hero, would be expected to die bravely, showing no signs of fear on the gallows. For other offenders remorse might be seen as a more appropriate emotion; from the early seventeenth century onwards, convicted murderers in particular were expected to make a speech along more or less conventional lines, in which offenders would confess their crimes, express the hope that their fate would serve as a deterrent to others, and link their presence on the gallows to a gradual slide into sinfulness which usually began with disobedience to parents and went on to include idleness, drunkenness, and consorting with prostitutes. If the offender behaved appropriately, the crowd responded accordingly, cheering the game highwayman, perhaps weeping with the penitent murderer, booing and perhaps pelting the offender who behaved inappropriately or who was thought to have committed an especially heinous crime. The hangman was also expected to behave

A mock invitation to the execution and burial of Jonathan Wild, 'thief-taker'

efficiently and with a proper regard for those suffering at his hands. Failure to do so on his part could lead to rioting by the crowd, who were also prone to attempt to rescue the bodies of hanged felons destined for dissection in anatomy classes (Linebaugh, 1975), or to save those 'half hanged' individuals who survived the initial attempt to strangle them at the rope's end.

In the eighteenth century (indeed, down to 1868) executions of criminals were normally carried out in public. What do you think were the objectives and outcome of this practice?

3.2 Courts and officers

This 'theatre of punishment' coexisted with a rather more mundane system of courts and law-enforcement officers (Sharpe, 1984). At the centre of the court system lay the assizes. Since the Middle Ages the assize system had been a vital component of England's law-enforcement machine. The country, with the exception of London, Middlesex and a few provincial palatinate jurisdictions (that is, areas which, since the Middle Ages, had enjoyed a degree of autonomy within the English administrative system), was divided into six circuits, each comprising a number of counties. Twice every year, in January and around midsummer, teams of two judges would be sent out from Westminster to hear civil disputes in the provinces and to try criminal cases. Serious offenders would be held in the county gaols until the assize judges came, and would then be tried before them. The assizes thus constituted an effective, and by the eighteenth century widely accepted, means of bringing royal justice to the localities.

3.2.1 The criminal courts

The county assizes, like so much else in the eighteenth century, consisted of a curious mixture of the august and the ramshackle. As with public execution, the assizes were surrounded by ceremony. The judges were met at the borders of each of the counties they were to visit by the sheriff and a retinue of gentlemen. They were wined and dined in style, the proceedings of the court were attended with due ritual, and prefaced by a sermon in which a local clergyman would be allowed to display his rhetorical powers. Yet descriptions of trials (alas, all too rare for the earlier eighteenth century) reveal a rather less decorous situation. The accused and their accusers might indulge in unseemly wrangles. Idiosyncratic judges, then as now, might make the law an ass. The growing attractions of the assizes as an occasion for general socializing meant that there was usually a large crowd of spectators present in court. Indeed, by the eighteenth century assize week was one of the main events in the social calendar for the county gentry and the elite of the town where the assize was held, the deliberations of the courts normally being accompanied by social gatherings, balls and horse races.

Although it was the assizes that most commonly dealt with serious crime, a number of other courts were still active. County quarter sessions, although by now concerned with local administration as much as crime control, still tried petty offences such as the less serious forms of larceny, assault and the breach of economic regulations. Many boroughs had the right to hold sessions, and tried a similar range of offenders. However, perhaps the most remarkable aspect of the English system was the use of petty sessions as a means of local regulation and crime control. The petty sessions, despite a number of earlier experiments, were essentially the result of an attempt to tighten local administration in 1631 after two years of economic crisis. One aspect of this push towards greater administrative efficiency was the practice of encouraging groups of local justices of the peace (in effect, normally three or four at a time) to meet every month to supervise various aspects of local government and law enforcement over a sub-unit of their counties known as a division. By the eighteenth century these monthly meetings of justices were known as petty sessions, and were an established part of local government.

3.2.2 Justices of the peace

The operation of the petty sessions, and indeed the functioning of law enforcement in general, depended heavily on the justices of the peace. The office of justice had its origins in the fourteenth century, but perhaps experienced its most important formative period during the Tudor and Stuart periods, when the justices had an ever expanding burden of administration and law enforcement placed on them by statute. That the justices were willing to co-operate with this imposition is evidence of changes in the nature of local elites in England. Again, we confront a peculiarity of the English system. Most aspects of local law enforcement were dependent not on state-appointed salaried officials, but rather on unpaid amateur gentlemen administrators, many of them with little formal legal training. By the eighteenth century it had long been established that becoming a justice of the peace was a sign that a gentleman had arrived socially and politically in his locality. The assize judges from Westminster might inject a professional judicial element into the trial of serious offenders, but the initial examination of those offenders and sending them to prison, as well as the punishment of petty offenders, was essentially the work of the justice of the peace.

Many justices kept notebooks in which they recorded their activities, and these can provide fascinating evidence into crime control in the period. Consider, for example, a series of entries from the notebook of William Hunt, a JP in Wiltshire:

11 May 1747. Granted a warrant at the complaint of Jane French of Earl Stoke against Mary Wise of the same parish, single woman, touching in particular the said Mary Wise's violent abusing of her the said Jane French so that she was actually in great fear of her life, as also her threatening to burn her house. She ran away so could not be apprehended whereby to be brought to justice.

13 May 1747. Granted by Thomas Phipps, esq, a warrant at the complaint of Mary the wife of Edward Tucker of Imber, carpenter, against Christopher Beaven of the same parish, thatcher, and Jane, his wife, for their violent assaulting and beating of the complainant in a barbarous manner and threatening to shoot her with a pistol. The parties agreed without a hearing.

15 May 1747. Granted a warrant at the complaint of Thomas Shipman or Sims of Allington, labourer, against Daniel Neat of the same parish, labourer, touching in particular the said Daniel Neat's unlawfully detaining and keeping in his custody divers household goods, the property of the said Thomas Shipman or Sims and for his refusing to deliver up the same on demand thereof. The parties agreed on hearing before me.

15 May 1747. Granted a warrant at the complaint of John Swain of the parish of Urchfont, labourer, against James Allexander of the parish of Tilshead, labourer, touching in particular the said James Allexander taking up a hat in the market place of Market Lavington and abusing it by pissing in it, the property of the said John Swain as he was about his lawful business as a sack-carrier. The defendant made the complainant satisfaction for the hat.

(Hunt, 1744–49, p.63)

One aspect of the justices' powers was that they enjoyed formidable powers of summary conviction. The country gentleman serving as justice of the peace might expect to enjoy considerable informal paternalistic powers over his neighbourhood, and frequently used his influence to settle disputes between neighbours without invoking the law. William Hunt's notebook, as the brief passage cited above makes clear, contains numerous references to this practice. When the law needed to be invoked, the justice possessed considerable authority by statute. Thus Gabriel Walters, a justice in Kent in the early eighteenth century, was involved in 304 cases between July 1708 and December 1710. Many of these involved purely formal action on the justice's part, signing 123 certificates that recently deceased persons had been buried in wool, for example. But 54 of these cases, heard in the parlour of his house, involved criminal matters (Landau, 1984, p.177). More generally, the justice was involved in such essential matters as binding over offenders, accusers or witnesses to appear at court, binding people over to keep the peace or to be of good behaviour, and taking pre-trial examinations of suspects in serious cases and committing them to prison. Whether one sees the justice of the peace as a benevolent paternalist or an agent of class oppression, it is clear that his role as a law enforcer was strengthened by his position in the local social hierarchy.

3.2.3 Parish constables

Considerable attention, much of it favourable, has been focused on the justice of the peace. Rather less has been devoted to the eighteenth-century parish constable. Most recent commentators have been content to accept the conventional wisdom that the parish constable was inefficient, lazy, and likely to employ a substitute. However, research into early seventeenth-century constables has created a rather different impression. The parish constable was, like the justice of the peace, an unpaid amateur, ideally a man of some wealth and ability chosen from his neighbours to serve his turn for a year. Work on the early Stuart periods has suggested that in some parishes at least, constables and other local officers worked reasonably efficiently within the limits of contemporary expectations about law enforcement. Like the county gentry from whom justices were recruited, the yeomen farmers, petty gentry and richer artisans and tradesman who served as constables now felt that they had a stake in upholding the status quo (Wrightson, 1980).

How far this situation obtained in the eighteenth century remains largely uninvestigated. What needs to be stressed is that most of our existing knowledge for that century comes from the London area, where, as might be imagined, a system originally designed for policing villages and parishes in small towns was being regarded as increasingly inadequate. Little is known for the eighteenth century about the situation outside the capital. Certainly men chosen as rural constables in that century chose and paid deputies, and some of these deputies enjoyed sufficient length of service to constitute virtual 'professional' police officers. Conversely the high constables, in charge of a subdivision of their counties, were men of social standing who occasionally involved themselves, as did some of the more active justices, in primitive detective work (Emsley, 1987, pp.172–6 and **Emsley, 1996**).

ACTIVITY 3.2

Make some notes on the defining characteristics of eighteenth-century law enforcement. One strand of thinking has stressed its paternalistic and localized nature. What did this amount to in practice? How did eighteenth-century criminal justice differ from its twentieth-century counterpart?

COMMENT

As this brief outline has suggested, the eighteenth-century law-enforcement machine worked on assumptions that were in many ways different from those obtaining in a modern industrial state. There was little by way of crime detection or prevention, only the first glimmerings of a 'professional' police force, and a heavy dependence on the death penalty, publicly inflicted, as a method of punishing and deterring criminals. Yet the system had its own logic, and, in many respects 'worked', perhaps more certainly at the beginning than at the end of the eighteenth century. Without doubt its functioning was partially dependent on the fear and deference which the lower orders felt towards their social superiors. Yet no system of authority can function without the co-operation, or at least acquiescence, of substantial sections of the ruled. The extent to which the eighteenth-century law-enforcement system worked was connected to the willingness of people to make it operate, for perhaps the main peculiarity of the system was its dependence on the participation of a large number of people: the county gentlemen who served as justices; the lesser gentlemen who served as chief constables or grand jurors; the farmers and artisans who still, in some areas, served as constables; the men who served as petty jurors; and the wide range of people who, in the last resort, made the system work through their willingness to take suspected criminals to court. Even the crowd at the public execution, cheering felons who died gamely, weeping with those felons with whom they sympathized, and booing incompetent hangmen, were participating in the suppression of crime. The catching, punishment and treatment of criminals was not yet the province of a professional specialist operating within the closed doors of police stations, local government offices or prisons.

4 Patterns of prosecution and punishment

4.1 Constructing criminal statistics

By the early nineteenth century, as now, arguments about crime were frequently couched in terms of whether levels of crime were rising or falling. Indeed, central government facilitated such arguments when in 1810 it published criminal statistics going back to 1805. Thereafter statistics were published annually. By the 1830s and 1840s discussing social problems on the basis of statistics, in England as in Europe as a whole, had become a standard method of social debate (see, for example, **Quetelet, 1842**). In 1834, as part of this general movement, the annual statistics in England, which thus far had appeared in elementary form, were published under six categories of offences, while from 1836 these figures were supplemented by an annual statistical digest of commitments to prison. This taste for collecting and publishing figures, totally appropriate to the period which saw the birth of social science in the modern sense, led to further developments in 1857 when, as a result of an appendage to the previous year's County and Borough Police Act, British criminal statistics were divided into three groupings: indictable offences reported to the police; commitments for trial, on both indictment and summary conviction; and the totals of those convicted and imprisonments (Emsley, 1987, p.19). Thus historians of crime in the nineteenth and twentieth centuries have easy access to quantified data in the form of statistics collected and published by central government.

Historians working on the periods before 1810 have a somewhat more difficult task in their attempts to quantify crime. As ever, the definitional problem arises. 'Crime', as we have argued, could include the felonies indicted at the assizes and the minor offences presented at the ecclesiastical courts or the local manorial leets, as well as those summary convictions before magistrates, records of which are largely missing before the late eighteenth century. Anybody attempting to amass global figures for prosecuted crime in the period before the publication of official criminal statistics needs to work systematically through the records of a multiplicity of courts. Records of all these courts survive very rarely for any given area, and hence it is difficult to construct 'crime rates' or to obtain an impression of the total dimensions of prosecuted crime.

For this reason, arguments about levels of crime over the eighteenth century have tended to concentrate on offences indicted before the assizes. Yet even here there are problems, since assize records have not survived for some areas (notably the Midlands), while for others they exist in only a broken series. Analysing assize records, even where they do survive in bulk, is a laborious business. Before the 1750s indictments were kept in Latin, and a skilled eye and a patient frame of mind is needed to unlock their secrets.

In addition to these particular problems, there are the more general ones inherent in attempting to interpret any set of criminal statistics. The early nineteenth-century positivists were convinced that social statistics, of which figures relating to crime were far from the least important, were facts which spoke for themselves. (Chapter 1 has already introduced some of the difficulties with this proposition, and they are equally marked for the period with which we are concerned.)

First, details of crime culled from eighteenth-century assize indictments, like those derived from nineteenth- or twentieth-century official criminal statistics, concern only a sample of crime: in the eighteenth century they relate to crimes that were formally prosecuted by indictment. The modern historian has no means of establishing what the relationship was between the total of crimes indicted and those actually committed. Nor is there any method by which it is possible to ascertain if the 'dark figure' of crimes which were committed but never brought to justice fluctuated. Second, levels of prosecuted crime can be affected by the intensity of official action. If twice as many offences of one type are prosecuted in one year than in the previous year, is this a reflection of rising levels of crime or simply of an increased propensity to prosecute? The modern mind is attuned to the idea of crime waves, but recent criminology has also alerted us to the effect on criminal statistics of control waves. This issue is probably more relevant to the regulatory offences tried so frequently in the seventeenth century, or to a state with a modern police force, than it is to an eighteenth-century assize. Clearly, however, it is one that must be considered.

crime waves and control waves

4.2   Patterns of indicted crime before the eighteenth century

The above problems notwithstanding, a number of historians have attempted to reconstruct the statistical pattern of crime in the eighteenth century, and our discussion here will focus on the research of John Beattie, who so far has produced the most detailed published work. However, let us first consider briefly the findings of historians who have worked on the earlier period. Their labours, dictated very much by record survival, have tended to concentrate on the south eastern assizes (notably the county of Essex), and the palatinate of Cheshire, whose Court of Great Session (the local equivalent of the assizes) enjoys the best surviving run of records of criminal prosecutions in early modern England. Analysis of the records of these courts demonstrates a pattern which is rather surprising, and certainly challenges any notion of a simple development showing steadily increasing levels of crime (Sharpe, 1984, pp.53–63).

Briefly, indictments rose steadily from about 1580 onwards. This increase was the outcome partly of population growth, but it reached a peak (according to area) in either the 1590s or the 1620s, both of these decades being periods of severe economic and social disruption. In all areas, as in twentieth-century Britain, it was crimes against property (larceny, burglary and robbery) that formed the largest category of serious offence. Thus between 1559 and 1625, 86 per cent of offences indicted at the Hertfordshire assizes were property offences, and 5 per cent homicide and infanticide. Levels of prosecution appeared to be dropping in the 1630s, while the disruptions of the 1640s, with the coming of the civil wars, meant that levels of indicted crime were low. Whatever the actual levels of lawlessness, courts were being held infrequently as the normal processes of law enforcement were disrupted. Levels of indicted crime stayed low both in the 1650s, when something like normal administrative processes were resumed, albeit without monarchical authority, and in the 1660s, when monarchical authority was restored.

4.3   Indicted crime over the 'long eighteenth century'

Thus in 1660, the year at which Beattie commences his research on the assizes of the southern counties of Surrey and Sussex, crime of all sorts, and especially property offences, were running at a lower level than they had been fifty years previously. The later chronological pattern of offences reconstructed by Beattie, pared to its essentials, is straightforward. Turning first to property offences, we find that these tended to fluctuate seriously on an annual basis (we shall turn to the causes of these fluctuations shortly) but that there was little by way of a sustained rise in the areas of his study until the middle of the eighteenth century. There was a sharp rise around 1750, then a fall, but from 1760 levels of prosecution of property crimes rose, with a real and sustained take-off in the 1780s and 1790s. In 1800 prosecuted property offences in urbanized areas of Surrey (notably Southwark) were roughly three times what they were in 1700, an increase that could not wholly be explained by population growth. Throughout the period studied by Beattie, 1660–1800, property offences formed the greater part of indicted felony in Surrey and Sussex. On the sample of cases studied by Beattie, 7,061 persons were accused of property offences in Surrey over that period, as opposed to 334 accused as principals and 81 as accessories in homicide cases. Other felonies were much fewer: for example, only 42 men were tried at the Surrey assizes for rape, with a further 86 for attempted rape (Beattie, 1986).

Although indicted homicides in the sample of material studied by Beattie were running at a lower level than property offences, they too showed a clear pattern. Prior to 1660, rates of homicide in England had been high: most samples studied show an annual rate of more than 10 per 100,000 of population in the Elizabethan and early Stuart periods (Stone, 1983). In Beattie's analysis this level had fallen to 2.5 per 100,000 of population by the post-Restoration period, 2.1 per 100,000 by the early eighteenth century, and less than 0.3 by the early nineteenth century (Beattie, 1986, p.112). Thus the homicide rate in England, on these figures, experienced a massive decrease in the three centuries following the death of Queen Elizabeth I. Obviously all of the strictures that apply to criminal statistics generally must operate here, but one major shift which historians of crime do seem to have established is that there was a major decline in felonious killing as England entered the modern world.

To these figures, however, must be added cases of infanticide, the killing of newborn children by their (usually unmarried) mothers. This offence was a fairly typical one in the early modern period, and one such killing was tried every eighteen months or so before the eighteenth-century Surrey assizes. Infanticide was unusual, of course, in being a predominantly female offence, and a number of studies (for example Malcolmson, 1977) have identified it as one of the characteristic female offences of the period, and one for which juries, in Scotland as well as England, became increasingly reluctant to convict as the eighteenth century progressed. Infanticide apart, most serious offenders tried before the courts were men, though to a lesser extent than now: only 24 per cent of those accused of property offences in Surrey between 1660 and 1800, and 13 per cent of those accused in the more rural county of Sussex, were women (Beattie, 1986, pp.239–40).

4.4   Short-term fluctuations

It is possible, then, to trace long-term trends in the prosecution of serious crime in early modern England. It should also be appreciated that the level of indicted crime, and especially of property offences, might be subject to violent short-term fluctuations. Two main factors (leaving control waves aside) were present here (Hay, 1982). The first was economic. From the 1590s, a bad harvest was usually followed by an upsurge in property offences, while a depression in local industrial activity, although somewhat harder to measure, seems to have had the same effect. As Figures 3.1 and 3.2 demonstrate, this connection between short-term fluctuations in prices and property offences was still marked in local assizes in the late eighteenth century.

Perhaps less obviously, historians of eighteenth-century crime have also detected a tendency for levels of indicted crime, and for official fears of crime, to increase when any of the wars of the era ended. Isolated soldiers returning from foreign wars had caused law and order problems from the late Middle Ages, but the emergence of large standing armies and large navies in the eighteenth century meant that at the end of every conflict large numbers of young men from the labouring classes (the people most likely to be

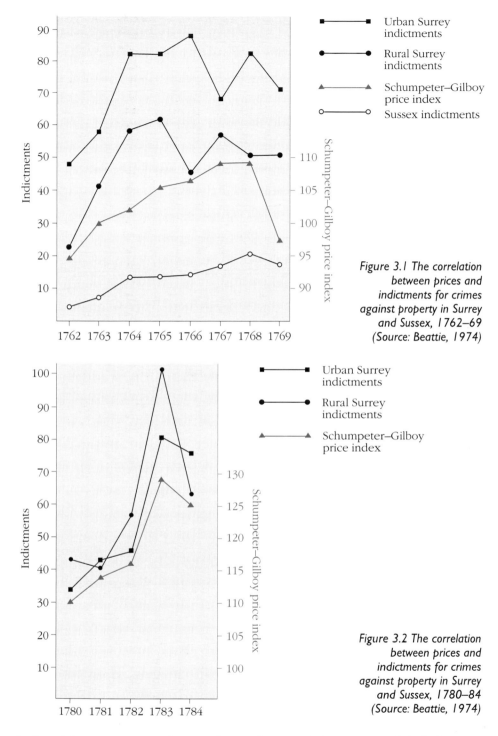

Figure 3.1 The correlation between prices and indictments for crimes against property in Surrey and Sussex, 1762–69 (Source: Beattie, 1974)

Figure 3.2 The correlation between prices and indictments for crimes against property in Surrey and Sussex, 1780–84 (Source: Beattie, 1974)

indicted for serious crime) were dumped on English society with little by way of means of support. It is therefore hardly surprising that in 1795 the *Leicester Journal* should note the paucity of criminals standing trial at the assizes in the eastern counties as one of the few benefits of the war against revolutionary France (Emsley, 1987, p.28).

Many historians working on the history of crime have seen counting offences as their initial task. What flaws does this exercise inevitably contain? To what extent can levels of reported or indicted crime that is prosecuted be regarded as an accurate indicator of the number or types of crimes actually committed?

4.5   Patterns of capital punishment

As we have noted, the relationship between criminal statistics and crime actually committed is, in any period, a questionable one. Arguably, statistics concerning punishment are on a surer foundation, and it is certainly possible to trace real changes over the eighteenth and early nineteenth centuries. Once again, although we shall focus on these later periods, it is important to grasp that some major developments had taken place before 1660.

Despite the emphasis placed on public execution in the eighteenth century, levels of execution were much higher in the Elizabethan and early Stuart periods. As with criminal statistics, what we know about punishment in these earlier periods has to be pieced together from scattered and sometimes fragmentary materials. Even so, the pattern is plain. If we return to the excellent Cheshire records, we find that the Court of Great Sessions was passing death sentences at a very high rate in the 1590s and 1620s, with over 160 such sentences being found in the latter decade (Sharpe, 1984, p.64). Even if not all these sentences were inflicted, the rate of execution must have been far higher than the eighteenth century, in the first decade of which only about ten death sentences were passed in the county. In general, it seems that death sentences in England in the period 1580–1630 were running at roughly ten times the level of the early eighteenth century. These death sentences were passed overwhelmingly for property offences rather than murder. At the Chester Court of Great Sessions between 1580 and 1619, some 337 death sentences were passed, 294 (87%) for property offences, 35 (10.5%) for homicide, and 8 (2.5%) for other felonies (see Figure 3.3). Compared to this, the eighteenth–century penal regime, so often characterized as harsh, seems positively humane (Sharpe, 1990, p.31).

Sufficient materials survive to allow us to chart the progress of capital punishment over the eighteenth century, although it should be emphasized that most analyses so far carried out have concentrated on London or the south east. Beattie's work on Surrey shows that an average of seven persons a year were being hanged by that county's assizes in the 1660s, a figure which rose to a peak of 13 or so in the 1720s, but which fell back to its 1660s levels, despite a tripling of the level of crime and a doubling of the county's population, by 1880 (Beattie, 1986, p.589). Even at that later date, most of those suffering execution had been convicted of property offences. Turning to the neighbouring courts of London and Middlesex, between 1795 and 1804 23 persons were hanged for burglary, 22 for highway robbery, 40 for forgery, and only 18 for murder. In the rural Western Assizes Circuit over the same ten years, 34 persons were executed for burglary, 11 for forgery, 25 for highway robbery and 25 for murder. The idea that the death penalty should only be inflicted for killing another human being was clearly not yet established in the early years of the nineteenth century (Emsley, 1987, pp.209–11).

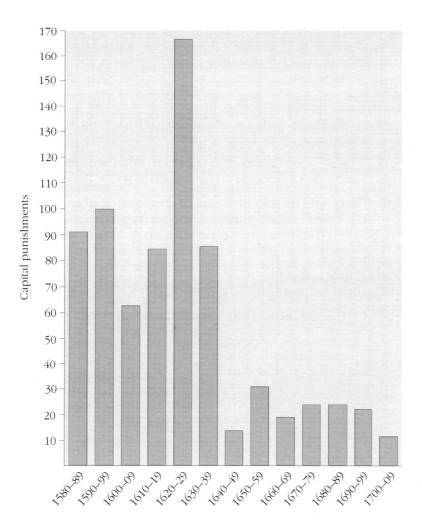

Figure 3.3 Capital convictions for felony, Court of Great Sessions, Chester, 1580–1709 (Source: Sharpe, 1984)

4.6 The logic of reprieve and execution

These figures for execution in the eighteenth century lead us into one of the great peculiarities of eighteenth-century capital punishment, a peculiarity which in turn helps us to understand the rationale of the system. Let us consider those sentenced to death in London and Middlesex between 1795 and 1804. True, 23 people were hanged for burglary, but this was from a total of 168 capitally convicted for the offence, while the 22 hanged highway robbers were drawn from 127 who had been capitally convicted. Although the practice of pardoning was not unknown in the seventeenth century, it seems that in the eighteenth century pardoning a high proportion of those capitally convicted was common, and, a few exceptional years notwithstanding, became more so as the century progressed.

pardoning

What detailed research has revealed is that the eighteenth-century Bloody Code, for all its theoretical ferocity, masked a system of penal practices in which those actually executed, especially for property offences, were only a small sample of those who might have been so treated. If law enforcement in the eighteenth century depended on terror, it was a selective terror. As defenders of the system pointed out when reformers began to criticize it in the later eighteenth century, its whole point was that it provided the capacity to bring stern retribution upon a minority of offenders: typically, those with a bad record or reputation, those who had committed unusually heinous offences, or those who were unfortunate enough to commit capital offences in a crisis period when it was thought necessary to make examples. Most of those capitally convicted of property offences would, under normal circumstances, be pardoned and escape the noose. In the eighteenth century, as in modern Britain, the courts operated a sentencing policy in which punishments were adjusted as far as possible to meet a variety of factors felt by the court to be relevant. But in the eighteenth century, it has been argued, clemency in sentencing strengthened the ideological authority of the law by demonstrating that it could be merciful as well as harsh. Moreover, given that most of those pardoned escaped through the intercession of their social superiors, anxious to extend and demonstrate the extent of their patronage or win the good opinion of their locality by helping a member of the poor to escape the noose, it helped strengthen the hegemony of the existing social hierarchy (Hay, 1975).

ACTIVITY 3.3

Read Extracts 3.1 and 3.2 opposite, which both reflect on the broader significance of the law in eighteenth-century England. The first, by the Canadian social historian Douglas Hay, is written from a Marxist viewpoint and comes at the end of an essay arguing that the criminal law's ability to mix terror and mercy made it a more effective agent for maintaining ruling-class hegemony. The second, by the United States legal historian John Langbein, is part of a critique of that essay. The two views suggest different ways of interpreting the criminal law in the eighteenth century. Which do you find the more convincing? Are they incompatible? Reflect on whether they have any bearing on current law and order problems.

4.7 Secondary punishments

Pardoning criminals so that they escaped execution made it necessary to find some other means of dealing with them, and one of the more interesting areas of recent research into eighteenth-century law enforcement has been the unearthing of changing patterns in secondary punishments. Clearly, by the early eighteenth century, escape through the old legal fiction of benefit of clergy was no longer felt to be appropriate. The first major innovation came in 1718 when, in the face of a crime wave created by demobilized servicemen at the end of the War of Spanish Succession, an Act was passed making it possible to transport convicted criminals as indentured servants (in effect, temporary slaves) to the American colonies. This practice was ended with the outbreak of the American War of Independence in 1776, by which time some 30,000 convicted criminals from England, 13,000 from Ireland and a few hundred from Scotland had crossed the Atlantic (Ekirch, 1987).

The other major innovation, apparently enmeshed in the practice of the courts rather than established by one sweeping statute, was the use of brief periods of imprisonment. Although the use of imprisonment, in the modern

Extract 3.1   Hay: 'Property, authority and the criminal law'

Many historians, confronted with the hegemony of the eighteenth-century ruling class, have described it in terms of absolute control and paternal benevolence ... It seems more likely that the relative insecurity of England's governors, their crucial dependence on the deference of the governed, compelled them to moderate [ruling-class] ferocity ... Benevolence, in short, was not a simple positive act: it contained within it the ever-present threat of malice. In economic relations a landlord keeping his rents low was benevolent because he could, with impunity, raise them. A justice giving charity to a wandering beggar was benevolent because he could whip him instead. Benevolence, all patronage, was given meaning by contingency. It was the obverse of coercion, terror's conspiracy of silence. When patronage failed, force could be invoked; but when coercion inflamed men's minds, at the crucial moment mercy could calm them.

A ruling class organizes power in the state. The sanction of the state is force, but it is force that is legitimized, however imperfectly, and therefore the state deals also in ideologies. Loyalties do not grow simply in complex societies: they are twisted, invoked and often consciously created. It was a society with a bloody penal code, an astute ruling class who manipulated it to their advantage, and a people schooled in the lessons of Justice, Terror and Mercy. The benevolence of rich men to poor, and all the ramifications of patronage, were upheld by the sanction of the gallows and the rhetoric of the death sentence.

(Hay, 1975, pp.61, 62–3)

Extract 3.2   Langbein: 'Albion's fatal flaws'

The criminal law is simply the wrong place to look for the active hand of the ruling classes. From the standpoint of the rulers, I would suggest, the criminal justice system occupies a place not much more central than the garbage collection system. True, if the garbage is not collected then society cannot operate and ruling-class goals will be frustrated, but that does not turn garbage collection into a ruling-class conspiracy. The Hay thesis, in a similar fashion, confuses necessary and sufficient conditions ...

I have been maintaining two themes about the administration of the criminal law in the eighteenth century. First, most of the discretion was exercised by people not fairly to be described as the ruling class, especially the prosecutors and the jurors. Secondly, the discretion that characterized this system was not arbitrary and self-interested, but rather turned on the good-faith consideration of factors with which ethical decision-makers ought to have been concerned. The historian does not need a conspiracy theory to explain the discretion, and the discretion does not fit the theory. I concede fully that when men of the social elite came into contact with the criminal justice system in any capacity, they were treated with special courtesy and regard, just as they were elsewhere in this stratified society. To seize upon that as a *raison d'être* of the criminal justice system is, however, to mistake the barnacles for the boat.

(Langbein, 1983, pp.119–20)

sense the standard punishment for serious crime, was essentially a nineteenth-century innovation, it is evident that from the 1730s onwards English assize judges and justices of the peace at quarter sessions were becoming increasingly used to sentencing offenders to a few months in prison, perhaps also with a whipping or hard labour added (Beattie, 1986, pp.520–618). Thus the eighteenth century, so often portrayed as the great era of the death penalty, in fact saw an increasing use of other punishments.

What can be learnt about the 'problem of crime' from studying patterns of crime and punishment in the eighteenth century?

Studying patterns of serious crime and its punishment in the eighteenth century allows us to move a step further from the impressionistic perceptions of contemporaries and the folklore constructed about crime and punishment in the past by later generations. We are able to trace trends in serious crime, to see how they fluctuated over the long term and also how they reacted to other social phenomena in the short term. The pattern leads us back to the notion that 'crime' is a term which covers a wide variety of behaviour: even if we restrict ourselves to the two most obvious categories of serious offence, we see two completely different patterns. Property offences fluctuated violently in the short term in response to economic and social stimuli, and began a pronounced and sustained upward movement at the end of the eighteenth century. Homicide, conversely, seems to have occurred at a decreasing rate over the period 1660–1800. With punishment, too, we see a system which at first sight, with its apparent dependence on the large-scale use of the death penalty for property offences, might seem very alien, but which was in fact regarded by contemporaries as flexible and one into which new elements could be incorporated.

5 Crime and the community

5.1 Defining 'community'

community

Whether used in the context of the debate over current law and order issues or in discussion of crime as a historical phenomenon, the term community is not an unproblematic one. Contrary to popular myth, the inhabitants of England before the Industrial Revolution did not live in idyllic village settlements. The early modern small town or village was as likely to be riven by problems, albeit of a different nature, as any modern city. Legal records, criminal and civil alike, contain ample evidence of social tensions and interpersonal malice. Indeed, by the eighteenth century most English villages, although capable of showing community spirit on occasion, were often so socially stratified as to make it possible to speak of a number of 'communities' within their boundaries. The most significant divergence was between the poorer inhabitants of the parish and a stratum of richer villagers: farmers, tradesmen and petty gentry who were doing well economically, whose education and literacy put them in contact with the cultural mainstream, who were regular churchgoers, and from whose ranks constables, churchwardens and parish Poor Law officials were drawn, and who formed the stable and respectable element in their communities.

At the other end of the local social system resided a stratum of agricultural labourers and rural industrial workers. Many of these were doubtless honest and respectable, but they all suffered from considerable economic hardship. Most of them might expect to be in receipt of poor relief at some point in their lives, while it was from the less respectable elements in this group that unmarried mothers, many of the fathers of their children, drunkards, swearers, petty thieves and potential vagrants were drawn. The notion of 'community' looks very shaky in a period when one section of the local population was involved in policing the other (Wrightson, 1980).

Thus if 'the community' is something which currently figures prominently in discussions of crime, law and order, it was also of vital importance to these subjects in the past. If nothing else, the community was a medium through which a large number of criminal accusations were filtered. In the absence of a professional police force, most criminal accusations were brought by private individuals, and hence community values might be involved when the decision to prosecute a specific offender was taken. As we have seen, in many villages and small towns such policing as existed was essentially carried out by local men (women were generally barred from holding office at any level) serving temporarily as law-enforcement officers. Once again, therefore, we return to community values, with decisions about the practicalities of law enforcement often being taken in the context of an awareness of local needs and conditions. Even the justice of the peace, although a member of the gentry, might well be a man of a paternalistic cast of mind, who would pride himself on his knowledge of his locality and the people living within it.

5.2 The mechanisms of local law enforcement

Policing the local community might take many forms, and one of the lessons to be derived from law enforcement at this level is that communities, however defined, had methods of combating crime other than formal prosecution before a court. For evidence on this point, let us turn to Richard Gough, who in 1700 wrote what was more or less a recent history of his parish, Myddle in Shropshire. Gough's work consists in large measure of reminiscences about his co-parishioners, among whom were the Wenlockes, one of the 'problem families' of the parish.

Two brothers, Reece and John Wenlocke, were descended from a man described by Gough as 'a bad husband, and a pilfering, thievish person'. The two sons were as bad as the father, typical rural petty criminals, who never stole any substantial goods, but 'stole hay when out of meadows, and corn when it was cut in the fields, and any small things that persons by carelessnesses had left out of doors'. Reece in particular had a reputation for wood theft, and the neighbourhood feared depredations on its hedges and fences when news spread that he had built a new oven and was planning to fire it. Richard Mercer, 'a very waggish fellow' and the servant to one of the parishioners, decided on a stratagem. As he walked by Reece's house, he saw a large dry stick which he took home, hollowed out, filled with gunpowder, and replaced in the hedge. Reece found the stick, and used it when he fired his oven, with the result that the oven was blown up and the end of his house set on fire. One suspects that this informal action gave the community as much satisfaction as having Reece Wenlocke prosecuted for theft would have done (Gough, 1700, p.46).

Such stories place us directly in the context of local law enforcement, a context where much depended on reputation, where a degree of petty crime was tolerated, if only because it was too much trouble to take to court, and informal sanctions where a range of informal sanctions might be mobilized against the wrongdoer. The nature of these sanctions might very much depend on the nature of the offence or offences in question, and the status, reputation or sex of the offender. Thus at one end of the scale there were such common practices as the dismissal of pregnant servant girls or thieving manservants, while at the other might come ritualized statements of communal disapproval.

A good example of an informal community sanction occurred at the Gloucestershire village of Westonbirt in 1716. When an unpopular estate bailiff had allegedly committed a homosexual act with another man, the villagers turned out to perform a 'groaning', in the course of which what was perceived as an unnatural sexual act was parodied, and a mock birth acted out (Rollinson, 1981). The more familiar aspects of 'police' action were therefore at one end of the spectrum whose other pole might include folkloric popular actions (Sharpe, 1980). Given the range of informal sanctions available, it seems that formal prosecution was often most readily employed against habitual local offenders who were thought to have gone too far, or against outsiders, especially vagrants who committed theft as they passed through the parish.

5.3   Local knowledge and the offender in court

These 'community' aspects of law enforcement – the adjustment to knowledge of local circumstances – also affected the legal process proper. As we have seen, the large number of pardons that followed capital conviction at the assizes were in large measure the result of offenders being reprieved in the light of their personal circumstances, or the result of a gentleman or some other notable interceding on their behalf. For the most part, assize judges and jurors seemed happy enough to go along with the perception of local circumstances and to adapt the law to the individual. John Aston, another deviant inhabitant of Myddle recorded by Richard Gough, provides a good example of how the courts might react. Aston, 'a sort of silly [simple] fellow much given to stealing of poultry and small things', was frequently 'caught in the act' and, as was probably typical of many such local delinquents, was 'sometimes well cajoled by those that would trouble themselves no further with him'. At length, however, 'he grew unsufferable', and was indicted at Shrewsbury assizes for stealing cocks and hens. The judge, 'seeing him a silly man', advised the jury that they had no alternative but to find him guilty, but dropped them a broad hint to undervalue the stolen goods, a common way of saving criminals from a charge of grand larceny. The jury followed this advice, 'at which the judge laughed heartily and said he was glad to hear that cocks and hens were so cheap in this country' (Gough, 1700, p.78). In the seventeenth century, then, we were still some way from the standards of a modern, bureaucratized law-enforcement system.

5.4 Towards new forms of policing

As the eighteenth century progressed it became evident that the old world of informal sanctions and adjustment to local perceptions of the individual offender was passing, even in many rural parishes. The professional police, as established in 1829, was still some way off, but attempts were made to inject a more businesslike element into the parish constable system, and a number of other expedients were tried. Perhaps the most significant of these were the Associations for the Prosecution of Felons which sprang up from about 1760. The dependence on the victim of crime to bring criminal charges had always begged the question of the victim's ability to find and apprehend the relevant offenders, and bear the cost of prosecuting them. Such costs could stretch to well over £10 by the later eighteenth century. The Associations for the Prosecution of Felons, numerous by the 1780s, were essentially private institutions which were usually composed of and formed by local property owners to organize and provide funding for the prosecution of offenders against their members or their property. The associations flourished in a period when concern about crime was increasing, and when the deficiencies of England's 'police' system and plans for reforming it were being eagerly debated. Some associations organized their own police, although many were content to work in conjunction with the established system of parish constables. What the associations demonstrate, for our immediate purposes, is how far the concept of community was fractured by the end of the eighteenth century, and how far it was felt on a local level that the traditional methods of dealing with crime were no longer operable.

Arguably, such a perception had long since informed ideas about crime and law enforcement in London. By 1750 the London area's population was probably about 675,000, which made it the largest city in Europe and, by a very wide margin, the biggest urban centre in England. By that date, crime in the metropolitan area was becoming a regular source of comment and debate. The size of the capital, the anonymity it was felt to offer the law-breakers, and the concentration of wealth which offered such a tempting target for thieves were all held to contribute to the capital's unique crime problem. It is hardly surprising therefore that the novelist and justice of the peace Henry Fielding should begin his *Enquiry into the Causes of the Late Increase of Robbers* of 1751 with the claim that 'the streets of this town, with the roads leading to it, will shortly be impassible without the utmost hazard; nor are we threatened with seeing less dangerous gangs of rogues among us, than those which the Italians call the Banditti' (Fielding, 1751, p.292).

Fielding, like so many of those who participated in the burgeoning law and order debate which commenced about the middle of the eighteenth century (and, indeed, like many subsequent commentators on law and order), was arguing a case, and we must be careful in treating as fact a rhetorical flourish from even so well informed an observer. More research needs to be done on the social life of the capital before the picture of social breakdown and a high crime rate can be accepted. There were certainly bad areas, some of them recognized from the Elizabethan period as places where criminals were likely to reside. Conversely, other London parishes were still run fairly effectively along traditional local government lines, and in these something like community values operated. Certainly, the occasional practice of mob action against thieves, which might include their being violently doused under the parish pump, would suggest this. Overall, however, the traditional notions of control, both formal and informal, seemed redundant in the London area. The paternalistic rule of justices aspired to in some rural areas was absent. By the eighteenth century gentlemen on the fringes of the capital were refusing to become justices because of the workload involved, while, in any case, the gap between the lives of the rich and poor in the capital ended even that partial understanding by the rich of the life of the poor upon which the old system to some extent depended. Fielding, describing conditions in cheap lodging houses around the capital in a tone which was to become common in Victorian social reportage, pointed out that 'this picture, which is taken from the life, will appear strange to many; for the evil here described is, I am confident, very little known, especially to those of the better sort' (Fielding, 1751, p.387). Given such a growing social gulf, it is little wonder that the 'better sort' should look to more efficient policing as the way of protecting their interests. (This theme is explored more fully by **Emsley, 1996**).

The dependence of the pre-nineteenth-century law-enforcement system on adjustment to individual circumstances and individual offenders seems to have had many advantages. What changes were taking place in society which prevented effective community-based social control and which led to increased support for moving to a more modern system?

5.5 Law and the sense of 'national community'

If crime and law enforcement were important issues on a local level, it is important to understand that a respect for the law was part of a national consciousness. The English common law had long been held up as a matter of national pride by legal writers, but it was the constitutional conflicts of the seventeenth century, and above all the Glorious Revolution of 1688–89, that placed the common law squarely in the consciousness of the 'free-born Englishman'. After the revolution, men of property were able to look back at the supposedly tyrannous actions of the Stuarts, or look across the Channel at the reported oppressive conditions suffered by the subjects of the French and other European monarchs, and count their blessings. The common law was held to be a fundamental of English political culture: the terms constitutional and unconstitutional were more or less equated with legal and illegal. This increased weight on the constitutional and ideological significance of the English common law coincided with, and was part of, that process by which what could (if a little simplistically) be characterized as 'central' or 'state' law was reaching a decisive stage in eroding the importance of other legal systems and custom. Hence even the informal aspects of justice and crime control were regarded as operating within a known constitutional framework, while other concepts of legality, notably those of the church and of customary law, while still present and occasionally important, were gradually losing their significance.

Surprisingly, it was not just men of great property, the men whose interests might be thought to have benefited most obviously from the provisions of the Bloody Code, who held this view. Even men of little or no property (the opinions of women on the matter are not much recorded) to a greater or lesser degree accepted the law as part of the constitution they lived under. The poor knew they lived in a land which manifested massive

common law

Gin Lane, Hogarth's famous portrayal of the degradation resulting from drinking gin (1754).
On an immediate level, Hogarth's message is obvious. It has been suggested, however, that he is
intending not just to show the degradation of the lower orders, but also to expose the lack of
responsibility on the part of the lay and secular authorities which allowed such conditions to
flourish. The year after this print appeared, effective licensing legislation was introduced which
curbed the worst excesses of the gin trade. Before this legislation it was reported that in some
parts of the capital one house in five was a gin-shop

variations in wealth and status, but, in so far as they had internalized ruling-
class ideology, they also 'knew' that they lived under the same law as the
rich. Consequently, they believed that their country was not an arbitrary
tyranny, but rather a land that was governed by a known and rational
constitution. The law was one of the ideological cements which held society
together.

The concentration on crime and punishment tends to obscure the degree to which the law was part of early modern culture. The two centuries before 1700 had seen an explosion of civil litigation in both the local courts and the central courts at Westminster. Indeed, it could be argued that litigation was one of the main social phenomena of the early modern period. By that date the great age of expansion in litigation had finished, but even in the eighteenth century people were much more used to settling disputes by going to law than is currently the case. One consequence of this was a continuing dislike of lawyers.

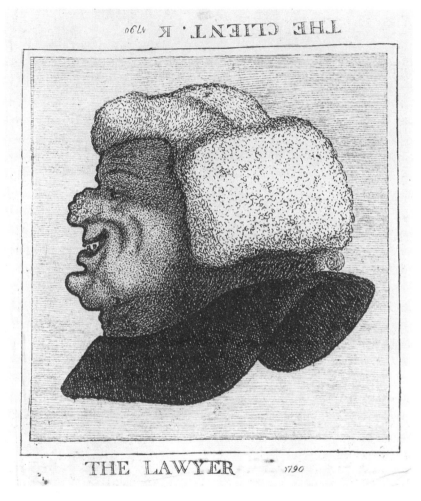

An anti-lawyer satire of 1790: inverting the image contrasts the happy lawyer with a distressed client

Another consequence was the tendency for people to interpret disputes in legal terms, which might involve a clash between an older, customary law, and law as it was being interpreted in the interests of eighteenth-century men of property. Until well into the nineteenth century it is possible to interpret clashes between the people and landlords in rural areas in terms of differing notions of common right usages, law and property rights. But what is obvious is that these clashes were conducted, to a sometimes surprising extent, in terms of legal rights. The point is perhaps most clearly made in E.P. Thompson's discussion of the rule of law in eighteenth-century England.

ACTIVITY 3.4

Read Extract 3.3, and then answer the following question: How does Thompson explain the relationship between law and class power? Was the law used against or to protect local community interests?

Extract 3.3 Thompson: 'The rule of law'

The law when considered as institution (the courts, with their class theatre and class procedures) or as personnel (the judges, lawyers, the Justices of the Peace) may very easily be assimilated to those of the ruling class. But all that is entailed in 'the law' is not subsumed in these institutions ...

What was often at issue was not property, supported by law, against no-property; it was alternative definitions of property: for the landowner, enclosure; for the cottager, common rights; for the forest officialdom, 'preserved grounds' for the deer; for the foresters, the right to take turfs. For as long as it remained possible, the ruled – if they could find a purse and a lawyer – would actually fight for their rights by means of law ...

Turn where you will, the rhetoric of eighteenth–century England is saturated with the notion of law. Royal absolutism was placed behind a high hedge of law; landed estates were tied together with entails and marriage settlements made up of elaborate tissues of law; authority and property punctuated their power by regular 'examples' made upon the public gallows. More than this, immense efforts were made ... to project the image of a ruling class which was itself subject to the rule of law, and whose legitimacy rested upon the equity and universality of those legal forms. And the rulers were, in serious senses, whether willingly or unwillingly, the prisoners of their own rhetoric; they played the games of power according to rules which suited them, but they could not break those rules or the whole game would be thrown away. And, finally, so far from the ruled shrugging off this rhetoric

as a hypocrisy, some part of it at least was taken over as part of the rhetoric of the plebeian crowd, of the 'free-born Englishman' with his inviolable privacy, his habeas corpus, his equality before the law ...

What had been devised by men of property as a defence against arbitrary power could be turned into service as an apologia for property in the face of the propertyless. And the apologia was serviceable up to a point: for these 'propertyless' ... comprised multitudes of men and women who themselves enjoyed, in fact, petty property rights or agrarian use-rights whose definition was inconceivable without the forms of law. Hence the ideology of the great struck root in a soil, however shallow, of actuality, and the courts gave substance to the ideology by the scrupulous care with which, on occasion, they adjudged petty rights, and, on all occasions, preserved proprieties and forms.

We reach, then, not a simple conclusion (law = class power) but a complex and contradictory one. On the one hand, it is true that the law did mediate existent class relations to the advantage of the rulers; not only is this so, but as the century advanced the law became a superb instrument by which these rulers were able to impose new definitions of property to their even greater advantage, as in the extinction by law of indefinite agrarian use-rights and in the furtherance of enclosure. On the other hand, the law mediated these class relations through legal forms, which imposed, again and again, inhibitions upon the actions of the rulers.

(Thompson, 1975, pp. 260–4)

COMMENT

Thompson's comments serve to remind us of the degree to which an acquaintance with law had penetrated into local English society, and arguably this penetration was of some consequence for local law enforcement. However, the use of the law as a mediator may be more applicable to what modern terminology would regard as civil disputes than the criminal law.

Discussing the law and the community introduces a complex set of problems. On one level, the law operated as one of the great constitutional glories of post-1688 England, and respect for the law was one of the great rhetorical commonplaces of political discourse. Conversely, its actual implementation against criminals often involved a pragmatic flexibility and, on a local level, considerable informality. What needs to be stressed is that the criminal law, like the civil law, was something that people *used*. One interpretation is that the law was obviously something which people of property (but not only large property) used to protect that property. Peers in the House of Lords and rich gentry in the Commons passed the law, country gentry administered it in the shires, and substantial farmers acting as parish constables administered it in their communities. But throughout the system the criminal law was subject to adjustments, to choices made by people administering or using it, and to the pressures of local knowledge and local circumstance. In most ways the law was created from above, but its actual implementation involved a spectrum of 'decision makers', frequently ordinary people, who were pulled into the legal process (King, 1984).

The statutes creating the Bloody Code are part of the history of crime in early modern England. So, too, are Reece Wenlocke's exploding oven in Myddle or the assize judge at Shrewsbury joking as the jury found John Aston guilty of a non-capital charge. Beneath such anecdotes there rest the recurring themes of shifting definitions, of choice, flexibility and the distinctiveness of a system of law enforcement which depended on a wide measure of public participation. Modern law-enforcement and crime control systems depend, to a far greater degree than is apparent on initial analysis, on the actions of decision-makers. Historical materials help illuminate this point, and suggest how it was equally true in very different contexts.

6 Towards modern thinking on crime

6.1 The nineteenth-century context

As has been stressed throughout the preceding sections, the eighteenth-century law-enforcement system was not static or unchanging. Nevertheless, it is true that the system developed very rapidly over the first two thirds of the nineteenth century, and, as was suggested at the beginning of this chapter, it was in this period that many of the main characteristics of 'modern' thinking on crime were established.

Crucial to this development was the context provided by the broader changes in government of the period. As ever, it is easy to caricature the situation before the nineteenth century. 'Government' in the broad sense of the word was developing, both in terms of the national state and in terms of local, and especially urban, government. Yet the period between the outbreak of the wars against revolutionary France in the late eighteenth century and the Great Exhibition of 1851 saw the emergence of a state in something like the modern sense. The exact forces behind this development are difficult to unravel: certainly, interpretations that attribute all such developments to the influence of Jeremy Bentham and utilitarianism are over-simplified. A broader set of elite objectives, a religious input, and the emergence of the state almost as an independent historical actor all had a bearing on what happened. The problems of socialization and conceptualizations of order on a more general level are also relevant. As we have suggested, early modern England was a society characterized by a plurality of legal orders. The nineteenth-century changes did not entirely alter this situation, and it is still possible to see differing attitudes to crime and punishment depending on class, religious sympathies, or political persuasions. Yet a marked relative shift occurred, whereby the state achieved at least a near monopoly over that arena where competing moral orders met: the criminal justice system. As important elements in this process there emerged professional police forces, a national prison system, and a clear notion of a 'criminal' or 'dangerous' class.

6.2 Industrial society and a rise in crime

These developments took place against a rising concern over crime. Those given to examining the newly available crime statistics found little that was encouraging. The peace of 1815 was followed by a massive increase in the number of people committed for trial in England and Wales, from 5,000 annually in the first decade of the nineteenth century to nearly 15,000 in 1820. After a brief decline, the upward trend continued in 1825. People who discussed the issue of crime and punishment, whether in parliament or at the middle-class dinner table, now thought they had hard evidence to go on (Emsley, 1987, p.30).

Such discussion, especially among the middle classes, would be heightened by a conflation of crime and revolution. In early nineteenth-century England older models of social hierarchy, based on notions of deference and paternalism, were replaced by a conceptualization of society based on class relations. To elite observers the industrialization and urbanization of the period meant the end of the old social ties, and they felt threatened by a two-pronged attack. The new industrial workforce could easily be characterized as disorderly and potentially criminal, impervious to the traditional controls. But this workforce was also seen as potentially revolutionary. To traumatic memories of the French Revolution were added the concerns generated by a number of domestic phenomena: the Luddites – craft workers who broke the new industrial machines in the Midlands and the north; the Swing Riots, those outbreaks of desperation among the depressed agricultural workers of the south; Chartism, that national political movement of artisans and industrial workers who saw gaining the vote and entry into parliament as the way forward; and early trade unionism. Here are the comments of Harriet Martineau, the daughter of a Norwich manufacturer, made in a year when revolution was about to recur on the continent and agitation over parliamentary reform seemed to be making it an issue in Britain:

class relations

The year 1830 opened gloomily. Those who believed that revolution was at hand, feared to wish one another a happy new year, the anxiety about revolution was by no means confined to anti-reformers. Society was already in a discontented and tumultuous state; its most ignorant portion being acted upon at once by hardship at home and example from abroad; and there was every reason to expect a deadly struggle before Parliamentary Reform could be carried. The ignorant and misled among the peasantry and artisans looked upon the French and other revolutions as showing that men had only to take affairs into their own hands.

(Martineau, 1850, p.24)

What Martineau would doubtless have described as the least ignorant portion of society could read in their newspapers during 1830 that getting on for 20,000 committals for criminal offences had been made in England and Wales that year. Among them were two men, John Morgan and James Lilburne, accused of theft at Dunstable, who claimed that they were in such distress that they stole in the hope of being 'taken up': prison was seen as preferable to starvation (Emsley, 1987, pp.30–3).

How was the 'problem of crime' constituted in the early nineteenth century? Was it simply a concern about crime, or was it broader concerns about economic hardship, foreign revolution and social protest that fired the Victorian imagination?

6.3 Victorian crime and the rhetoric of 'social problems'

dangerous classes

Whatever the reality of the threat of revolution or social breakdown, the mid-nineteenth-century willingness to conceptualize crime in terms of the activities of a 'criminal' or dangerous class is symptomatic of a wider development. The language of social debate, encouraged by early positivist social investigation, now increasingly operated in terms of identifying 'problems'. Thinking about crime and other social issues could be packaged, and people could deal with crime increasingly in terms of stereotypes. At the very least, thinking on crime led to concerns over other issues (see Extract 3.4 opposite and also Chapter 4).

To take one example, it is significant that the concept of the 'juvenile delinquent' was essentially an invention of the period 1820–50 (Margery, 1978). There had, of course, been earlier schemes aimed at saving the young criminal, for instance the Marine Society of 1756, founded on the perhaps unlikely premise that criminally inclined youths might be reformed by serving in the Royal Navy, and Robert Young's Philanthropic Society of 1788. But it was the first half of the nineteenth century, with its obsession with the classification of offenders and its concern over social reform, that created the category of young offenders, and established a body of institutions with the aim of reforming them (see **Muncie, 1996**).

Another aspect of crime that appears frequently in current social debate, domestic violence, was also widely commented on in the Victorian period (see Chapter 5 and Doggett, 1992). As so often, it is unclear whether the problem was new or merely talked about more: work on earlier periods suggests the latter (Beattie, 1986, pp.105–6). Certainly legal theory, at least until the eighteenth century, held that a husband's rights over his wife

Extract 3.4   Gatrell: 'Crime as a social problem'

Victorian observers would have been struck by their forefathers' relative indifference to crime as a 'problem', and by their relative satisfaction with the apparently arbitrary and capricious mechanisms which contained it. This was not because crime was infrequent then: it is not at all clear that there was less thieving and violence *per capita* in eighteenth-century cities than in nineteenth. But crime did not as yet appear to threaten hierarchy, and the terms in which crime might be debated as a 'problem' were not yet formed. Historians of early modern crime must realize not only that 'their subject was not known then by that name' but that as a subject it did not exist. The word 'crime' when used at all before the 1780s, usually referred to a personal depravity. It lacked the problematic and aggregative resonance it was soon to acquire. Despite occasional panics about the ubiquity of thieving, crime in aggregate was not yet thought to be increasing as a necessary and potentially uncontrollable effect of social change. Similarly, the 'criminal' was not yet discerned as a social archetype, symbolic of the nation's collective ill-health …

By the time Peel took up the challenge of penal, police and law reform in the 1820s, the political and cultural climate was quite transformed. Crime was fast becoming 'important'. In the post-war world, and on into the 1840s, the subject came to be cemented into an ideology about the Condition of England. Crime was becoming a vehicle for articulating mounting anxieties about issues which really had nothing to do with crime at all; social change and the stability of social hierarchy. These issues invested crime with new meanings, justified vastly accelerated action against it, and have determined attitudes to it ever since.

(Gatrell, 1990, pp.248–9)

included that of moderate physical chastisement. This practice was upheld in 1782 when Judge Buller summed up the legal position by declaring that a man was entitled to beat his wife with a stick, so long as it was no thicker than his thumb.

It is impossible to calculate how frequently wife-beating took place in the past, not least because the factors that inhibit the reporting of domestic violence today were even more prevalent in the eighteenth or nineteenth centuries. Indeed, given that divorce was not an option for most people, reporting a violent husband to the law would probably have been regarded as inherently counter-productive. But if the incidence of domestic assault cannot be traced accurately, changes in attitudes can. Legal commentators and social reformers alike became increasingly unhappy with the traditional right of chastisement. These feelings led, in 1853, to the passing of an Act for the Better Prevention and Punishment of Aggravated Assaults upon Women and Children. How effective the Act was in saving wives and children from the consequences of domestic violence remains uncertain, although its provision that complaints could be brought by third parties at least lessened the chances of a husband complained against taking revenge on his wife. It did, however, represent an important change in legal thinking.

6.4   The media and a moral panic: garrotting

By the 1850s, then, thinking about crime was changing, and was moving towards a set of attitudes with which we are currently familiar. To conclude, and perhaps confirm this point, it is instructive to look at one of the great moral panics of the nineteenth century, the 'garrotting panic' of 1862.

The background to this panic lay in a widespread, but not altogether justified, fear that crime was increasing and that respectable society was threatened by the core elements of the criminal class. Transportation to Australia had fallen off rapidly over the 1850s, so that what were categorized as 'habitual criminals' were discharged out of prison into England rather than being sent to the other side of the world. In theory such criminals were still under police supervision, but this proved difficult to enforce. Moreover, faith in the reformatory notions that had influenced early nineteenth-century thinking about dealing with criminals was fading. The occasion for the panic came on 17 July 1862 when the MP Hugh Pilkington was attacked and robbed on Pall Mall as he was walking from the Houses of Parliament to the Reform Club. Pilkington was attacked from behind and 'garrotted' – that is, temporarily incapacitated by choking. The robbery, and a few others of a similar nature, provoked a full-scale press campaign in which facts were rapidly left behind and opinions allowed to flourish unhindered. A comparison could be made with similar modern episodes, notably the concern prompted by 'mugging' in the 1970s (see Chapter 1). At the very least, it is noteworthy that the arguments put forward about the punishment of criminals are still familiar:

> Under the influence of our humanity-mongers, we have nursed and fostered a race of hardened villains ... well the public is now learning, in rather a startling fashion, what is the natural result of making pets of thieves and garrotters.
>
> (*Manchester Guardian*, 2 November 1862)

> Money should be spent on the real punishment of criminals, instead of squandering the hard earnings of honest mechanics and working men and making them objects of interest to idle spinsters and gaol chaplains of the maudlin class.
>
> (*The Observer*, 30 November 1862)

The immediate result of the garrotting panic was the passing of the Security from Violence Act, which, among other things, reversed the previous trend away from the use of corporal punishment for adult offenders (Davis, 1980). The harsher mood against criminals was reinforced by the passing of a severe Penal Servitude Act in 1865, and by the appointment in 1869 of Edmund Du Cane, a hardliner, as Chairman of the Directors of Convict Prisons (see **Muncie, 1996**).

Yet the significance of the garrotting panic is deeper than the harder line against criminals that it encouraged, this line itself being reversed by a swing to more liberal policies by the end of the nineteenth century. It serves to symbolize the emergence of modern ideas on crime and its treatment. With the panic we find ourselves firmly in the world of professional police forces, of national prison systems, of the widespread acceptance of criminal stereotypes, and of crime and punishment as issues that were debated by newspapers, usually in terms of straightforward appeals to the instinctive reactions of potential readers.

7 Conclusion

The first half of the nineteenth century thus constitutes a distinct watershed between current 'conventional thinking' about crime and punishment and those earlier attitudes and practices that we have examined in this chapter. It is to be hoped that discussing these earlier phenomena, through their very 'otherness', will help to understand and challenge both everyday and criminological debate about the criminal universe which we currently experience. Definitions of crime change, as do the agencies that are designed to control and eliminate it, and the means by which it is punished. Yet in all periods there is a natural tendency to regard the criminal justice and penal systems that are familiar to us as the only ones that are appropriate. The fact that these systems have changed in the past, sometimes radically, might encourage reflection on how our current thinking about and methods of dealing with crime might be subjected to constructive criticism. Studying the history of crime also serves to cast doubt on the cosy assumptions that there have never been crime waves or fears of social disintegration in the past. Crime has been a recurrent theme in social complaint, social debate, and social fears for a long time, even if those complaints, debates and fears have usually expressed themselves in rhetorics different from those currently in vogue. This knowledge is of some use, and possibly of some reassurance, as we attempt to understand, and defend ourselves against, crime as we know it today.

Further reading

Newcomers to the history of eighteenth-century crime should begin with three collections of essays: Hay *et al.* (1975), Cockburn (1977) and Brewer and Styles (1980). Innes and Styles (1986) summarize the first wave of writing on the subject and suggest directions for future research. Sharpe (1984) is an initial introduction to the subject, while Beattie (1986) is the most advanced and technically accomplished regional study. Although it appeared too late to be integrated into the text, Gatrell (1994) replaces all existing work on capital punishment in its period.

References

Beattie, J.M. (1974) 'The pattern of crime in England, 1660–1800', *Past and Present*, no.62, pp.42–95.

Beattie, J.M. (1986) *Crime and the Courts in England 1660–1800*, Oxford, Clarendon Press.

Brewer, J. and Styles, J. (eds) (1980) *An Ungovernable People*, London, Hutchinson.

Bushaway, B. (1982) *By Rite: Custom, Ceremony and Community in England 1700–1880*, London, Junction Books.

Cockburn, J.S. (ed.) (1977) *Crime in England 1550–1800*, London, Methuen.

Davis, J. (1980) 'The London garrotting panic of 1862: a moral panic and the creation of a criminal class in mid-Victorian London', in Gatrell *et al.* (1980).

de Mandeville, B. (1725) *An Enquiry into the Causes of the Frequent Executions at Tyburn*, London, J. Roberts.

Doggett, H.E. (1992) *Marriage, Wife-Beating and the Law in Victorian England*, London, Weidenfeld and Nicolson.

Ekirch, A.R. (1987) *Bound for America: The Transportation of British Convicts to the Colonies, 1718–1775*, Oxford, Oxford University Press.

Emsley, C. (1987) *Crime and Society in England 1750–1900*, London, Longman.

Emsley, C. (1996) 'The origins and development of the police', in McLaughlin and Muncie (1996).

Fielding, H. (1751) *An Enquiry into the Causes of the Late Increase of Robbers*, London, publisher unknown.

Gatrell, V.A.C. (1990) 'Crime, authority and the policeman state', in Thompson, F.M.L. (ed.) *The Cambridge Social History of Britain 1750–1950*, vol. 3, Cambridge, Cambridge University Press. (Extract reprinted in Muncie *et al.*, 1996.)

Gatrell, V.A.C. (1994) *The Hanging Tree: Execution and the English People 1770–1868*, Oxford, Clarendon Press.

Gatrell, V.A.C., Lenman, B and Parker, G. (eds) (1980) *Crime and the Law: The Social History of Crime in Western Europe since 1500*, London, Europa.

Gough, R. (1700) *The History of Myddle*, reprinted 1979, London, Caliban Books.

Hair, P. (1972) *Before the Bawdy Court*, London, Elek.

Hay, D. (1975) 'Property, authority, and the criminal law', in Hay *et al.* (1975).

Hay, D. (1982) 'War, dearth and theft in the eighteenth century: the record of the English courts', *Past and Present*, no.95, pp.117–60.

Hay, D., Linebaugh, P., Rule, J.G., Thompson, E.P. and Winslow, C. (eds) (1975) *Albion's Fatal Tree: Crime and Society in Eighteenth-Century England*, London, Allen Lane.

Hobsbawn, E. (1975) 'Distinctions between socio-political and other forms of crime', *Society for the Study of Labour History Bulletin*, no.25.

Hunt, W. (1744–49) *The Justicing Notebook of William Hunt 1744–1749*, ed. E. Crittall, Devizes, Wiltshire Record Society, 1982.

Innes, J. and Styles, J. (1986) 'The crime wave: recent writing on crime and criminal justice in eighteenth-century England', *Journal of British Studies*, vol.25, no.4, pp.380–435.

King, P. (1984) 'Decision-makers and decision-making in the English criminal law, 1750–1800', *The Historical Journal*, vol.27, no.1, pp.25–58.

King, P. (1989) 'Gleaners, farmers and the failure of legal sanctions in England 1750–1850', *Past and Present*, no.125, pp.116–50.

Landau, N. (1984) *The Justices of the Peace, 1679–1760*, Los Angeles and London, University of California Press.

Langbein, J. (1983) 'Albion's fatal flaws', *Past and Present*, no.98, pp.96–120.

Linebaugh, P. (1975) 'The Tyburn riots against the surgeons', in Hay *et al.* (1975).

Linebaugh, P. (1991) *The London Hanged: Crime and Civil Society in the Eighteenth Century*, London, Allen Lane.

Malcolmson, R.W. (1977) 'Infanticide in the eighteenth century', in Cockburn (1977).

Margery, S. (1978) 'The invention of juvenile delinquency in early nineteenth-century England', *Labour History*, no.34.

Martineau, H. (1850) *History of England during the Thirty Years Peace*, London, publisher unknown.

McLaughlin, E. and Muncie, J. (eds) (1996) *Controlling Crime*, London, Sage in association with The Open University.

Muncie, J. (1996) 'Prison histories', in McLaughlin and Muncie (1996).

Muncie, J., McLaughlin, E. and Langan, M. (eds) (1996) *Criminological Perspectives: A Reader*, London, Sage in association with The Open University.

Quetelet, M.A. (1842) *A Treatise on Man*, Edinburgh, Chambers. (Extract reprinted as 'Of the development of the propensity to crime', in Muncie *et al.*, 1996.)

Rollinson, D. (1981) 'Property, ideology, and popular culture in a Gloucestershire village 1660–1740', *Past and Present*, no.93, pp.70–97.

Sharpe, J.A. (1980) 'Enforcing the law in the seventeenth-century English village', in Gatrell *et al.* (1980).

Sharpe, J.A. (1984) *Crime in Early Modern England 1550–1750*, London, Longman.

Sharpe, J.A. (1990) *Judicial Punishment in England*, London, Faber and Faber.

Stevenson, J. (1979) *Popular Disturbances in England 1700–1817*, London, Longman.

Stone, L. (1983) 'Interpersonal violence in English society 1300–1980', *Past and Present*, no.100, pp.22–33.

Thompson, E.P. (1975) *Whigs and Hunters: The Origins of the Black Act*, London, Allen Lane.

Wrightson, K. (1980) 'Two concepts of order: justices, constables and jurymen in seventeenth-century England', in Brewer and Styles (1980).

Chapter 4
Dangerous Places: Crime and the City

by Peggotty Graham and John Clarke

Contents

1 Introduction

C hapter 3 discussed the emergence of specifically 'modern' conceptions of crime in the early nineteenth century (see also **Gatrell, 1990**). These modern conceptions are closely linked to the rise of the city and to processes of urbanization. From the mid nineteenth century onwards they became linked to ideas of the city as a 'dangerous place': a place where people become criminals and victims. The city is always the subject of a tension between two representations. On the one hand, it is seen as the embodiment of progress – the basis for the development of the 'good society' – and is constantly being reconstructed in search of that objective. On the other hand, the city is also seen as a place of danger – the urban nightmare of the underworld – and is constantly at risk of crime and disorderliness.

In reading this chapter it will be useful to keep in mind a few key themes and concepts. A central theme is that historically there has been a continuing association between notions of 'the city' and 'dangerousness'. Changing definitions of dangerousness have interacted with ideas of the city and crime. Although dangerousness and crime are related, it is important to remember that they are not the same (recall the discussion of differing definitions of crime in Chapter 1 of this volume). A second theme is that dangerousness (however defined) has become associated in the popular imagination with the concept of a 'class apart' or 'other'. The chapter examines the ways in which this notion of 'other' has at different times provided a metaphor for the city as a crime-ridden and dangerous place. It appears in different guises. The 'dangerous classes', the 'casual poor', the 'social residuum' and the 'underclass' are all terms that have been used to denote this idea of a class apart. Dangerousness evokes ideas of both the 'dangerous classes' and of 'dangerous places'.

It is important also to remember that any consideration of crime and the city brings certain kinds of crime to the fore and minimizes others. The focus tends to be on crimes of the street and the alleyway, such as mugging, assault, car theft and crime against personal property. Different types of urban crime, for instance financial fraud and other white-collar crimes, tend to go unremarked and are rarely associated with processes of urbanization (see Chapter 6). Similarly, domestic violence is a feature of city life but until recently was not designated a crime and was rendered invisible (see Chapter 5). In short, when considering crime and the city, what is usually being referred to is crime that is 'visible' and 'on the street'.

In this chapter our main focus is on changing representations of order and disorder in the city and the place of crime in these representations. We begin, in section 2, with the period in which this 'modern' conception of crime and the city was formed – the mid nineteenth century – since the basic elements established then have continued, in changing combinations, to dominate our understanding of how the city is a dangerous place. Section 3 provides a brief account of some of the practical attempts that were made

social order

between 1900 and 1970 to remake the social order of city life. This, we suggest, was a period of optimism, though we also find evidence for our contention that the city is constantly caught in a tension between the two representations of progress and danger. Section 4 focuses on the 1980s and

1990s and argues that these two decades saw the emergence of a new set of concerns about dangerousness which gave rise to renewed fears about crime and threats to social order. Woven throughout the chapter is the idea of struggle – struggle about the city as an arrangement of space and as a configuration of public and private places, and struggle over who has rights and over what. Our argument is that in the processes of urban reform, renewal and reconstruction that have gone on since the mid nineteenth century there have been struggles over the organization of urban space in which issues of crime, criminality and criminalization have always appeared central rather than peripheral. This is because each attempt to change the social and spatial organization of the city poses the question of social order – in particular, *what sort of social order* is being sought in the reorganization of the city. Finally, therefore, in section 5 we look into the future and ask what is the nature of the urban order that we might expect to find in the twenty-first century.

Before reading on, consider the following questions:

1   What are your feelings about the city?
2   Is it an exciting or a dangerous place?

2 Nineteenth-century nightmares: the city and the dangerous classes

The mid nineteenth century was the time when the city became firmly connected in the popular imagination with notions of dangerousness and crime. The city evoked powerful and disturbing images. In the city were to be found the 'teeming hordes' living in an unimaginable squalor. The city was the engine of progress, but it was also a turbulent and troubling nightmare of disorder: 'Here was a Dickensian city-scape of dirty, crowded and disorganized clusters of urban villages … where the "Great Unwashed" lived in chaotic alleys, courts and hovels just off the grand thoroughfares' (Walkowitz, 1992, p.19). London especially 'was regarded as the Mecca of the dissolute, the lazy, the mendicant, "the rough" and the spendthrift' (Jones, 1971, p.12).

The intimacy of order and disorder – the proximity of the 'great unwashed' to the 'great and the good' – was understood in terms of dangerousness. The threat was from the dangerous classes, the paupers and the criminals who made up the so-called 'casual poor', whose existence at the heart of the city represented a multiple threat to safety and order. The idea of the 'great unwashed' gives a clue to some of the ways in which this dangerousness was perceived.

dangerous classes

First, there was a threat to public health posed by insanitary and overcrowded living conditions and the constant threat of contagion to those leading more ordered lives. Second, there was the threat to public order posed by the perception of these groups as an 'unruly mob' – a different sort of contagion involving the risk of the respectable labouring classes becoming infected by the mob with dangerous political ideas and enthusiasms such as Chartism, socialism and the like. Third, by their difference and diversity the casual poor represented a threat to moral order – a contagion arising from ways of life not founded on the principles of thrift, sobriety and self-discipline that were being articulated as the essential Victorian values. Fourth, there was the threat to the legal order from those leading half-lives involving marginal patterns of employment, begging and outright criminality. Finally, in a period of economic development and imperialism there was the threat that all of these would undermine the very force of progress itself.

These multiple threats were wrapped together in an overarching perception of a dangerousness which lay in the heart of the city. Mayhew's description of the 'nomad' sums up some of the themes:

> The nomad ... is distinguished from the civilized man by his repugnance to regular and continuous labour – by his want of providence in laying up a store for the future – by his inability to perceive consequences ever so slightly removed from immediate apprehension – by his passion for stupefying herbs and roots ... and for intoxicating fermented liquors ... by an immoderate love of gaming ... by his love of libidinous dances ... by his delight in warfare and all perilous sports – by his desire for vengeance – by the looseness of his notions as to property – by the absence of chastity among his women, and his disregard for female honour.
>
> (Mayhew, 1851–62, vol.1, p.6)

social residuum

These notions of dangerousness were fed by stories, from those who went into the poverty-stricken areas of the city, of a strange and worrying underworld: a social residuum who were quite different from the respectable working class. The fevered imaginations of educated readers were fed with literary constructs of the metropolis as a 'dark, powerful and seductive labyrinth' (Walkowitz, 1992, p.17). As the century wore on and the liberal utopia seemed almost to be within grasp, there remained the nagging anxiety that all was vulnerable to the disorder of the street. The nightmare was that 'progress might be swamped by the corrupting features of urban life' and that, unless checked or reformed, the residuum would overrun the Victorians' 'newly built citadel of moral virtue and economic rationality' (Jones, 1971, p.16).

These feelings of danger and fear can be illustrated by examining three features of the nineteenth century which indicate some of the ways in which the inner city became a symbolic place of danger and associated fear.

2.1 Dangerous places

One way in which the urban poor became seen as dangerous was that the differences in the customs and habits of the poverty-stricken set them apart from the usual middle-class experience of life. The very degree of the difference – the 'strangeness' of working-class life – created for the respectable middle-class Victorians a sense of an 'alien people' in their midst. It was perhaps no coincidence that at the same time as missionaries and explorers were venturing into Africa, the same language of danger and adventure was adopted by the new breed of urban explorers who were venturing into the 'unknown' at home. 'Urban explorers never seemed to walk or ride into the slums but to "penetrate" inaccessible places where the poor lived in dark and noisy courts, thieves' "dens", foul smelling "swamps" and the black "abyss"' (Keating, 1973). Pearson argues that the description of these places combines their physical condition with the moral condition of their inhabitants:

Sewage and drains were guiding metaphors for those who depicted the deviants of this time. 'Foul wretches' and 'moral filth' lay heaped in 'stagnant pools' about the streets. When they moved they were seen to 'ooze' in a great 'tide'. The population was 'slime' which gathered in ghettos which were described as 'poisoned wells', 'canker-worms', 'sinks of iniquity' and 'plague-spots'. Their houses were described as 'cess-pits'; and their way of life was a 'moral miasma', for it was essentially a moral condition which was captured in these lurid images. The city 'reeked' of vice; the 'scum' and the 'dregs' of society was a 'moral debris' and 'residuum': the words 'pustule', 'fever', and 'wart' came readily to hand when describing the moral condition of the labouring and dangerous classes.

(Pearson, 1975, p.161)

The language reflected the tendency of moral reformers to see the urban poor as a 'race apart' from the national community. Jennifer Davis comments that the missionaries and reformers constructed the residuum as a group which had been 'left behind by the mid-Victorian march of moral and material progress' (Davis, 1989, p.11). Furthermore, the values and behaviour attributed to this residuum – violence, licentiousness, thriftlessness, criminality and political volatility – 'were those which many believed had now been spurned by the respectable majority of the English nation' (Davis, 1989, p.11).

Moss Street, Bankside, London, 1896. The inhabitants of the houses on Moss Street were classified as 'Lowest class. Vicious; semi-criminal' and 'Very poor, casual. Chronic want' by Charles Booth in his social survey, Life and Labour of the People in London *(1889–1902)*

147

2.2 Dangerous people

The language of exploration and the idea of anthropological reportage were products of, and deeply embedded within, the imperialism of the time. It was the domestic usage of this imperial framework that was in part responsible for the transformation of the unexplored territory of the inner-city poor into an 'alien place', since it provided both the language and the way of thinking of the 'other'. The context of imperial Victorian Britain therefore imparted a racialized overtone to the concept of an 'alien place'.

2.2.1 'Maintaining the race'

Victorian missionaries and reformers articulated a strong sense of the superiority of the (white) British race which emanated from Britain's role as a colonial power. Imperial Britain abroad was still engaged in 'taming the savage', and images of the 'uncivilized' (black) savage fused with the excitement of the exotic to provide a heady cocktail of 'racialized danger' in the colonial imagination.

The notion of white supremacy received additional impetus from the emergence in the 1880s of the new science of eugenics. Based on the theories of Social Darwinism, eugenics was the study of ways in which the mental and physical abilities of a people could be shaped and developed through breeding. White peoples – and the British in particular – were understood as representing the highest point of human evolution. Looked at from the imperial vantage point of the time, the evidence from the missionaries, explorers and administrators abroad of the lack of civilization of 'the African' simply confirmed the theories back home. Its domestic significance was manifested in fears about the 'degradation' of the British race being brought about by the overbreeding of the 'unfit' parts of society.

2.2.2 Losing control

spatial and social segregation

Victorian Britain witnessed spatial and social segregation between the prosperous and impoverished, between respectable and unrespectable people, and between secure and insecure places (Jones, 1971). This took on a particularly sharp focus in London, though it applied in differing degrees to all the major industrializing towns and cities of Britain. The segregation was arguably far more complete *symbolically* than it ever was in reality, though the stark difference in the living conditions of the prosperous middle classes and the poor was real enough. But it is the symbolic division that interests us here. Representations of East and West London in the mid nineteenth century suggested two distinct cities. For example, commentators of the time 'juxtaposed a West End of glittering leisure and consumption and national spectacle to an East End of obscure density, indigence, sinister foreign aliens and potential crime' (Dore and Jerold, 1872, cited in Walkowitz, 1992, p.20).

This was a contrast based on differences in both visible and imagined lifestyle. It is significant for its notion of a semi-submerged danger and the association of that danger with 'sinister foreign aliens'. Walkowitz (1992), in her study of late Victorian London, argues that by the end of the century the opposition of East and West London had taken on imperial as well as racial dimensions. She contrasts a West End in Queen Victoria's Golden Jubilee year (1887), with its national monuments, government and colonial offices, with an East End which by then had become an international entrepot and was receiving succeeding waves of migrants: 'Gravitating to the central districts, the declining inner industrial rim, the "foreign element" had to compete with the indigenous labouring poor for housing and resources' (Walkowitz, 1992, p.26).

The significance of these influxes of 'the foreign element' comes into particular focus in the match girls' strike of 1888. It was a time of crisis – severe depression as a result of poor trade, the structural decline of some of the older industries, a chronic shortage of working-class housing, and an emerging socialism and collectivism challenging traditional liberal ideology (Jones, 1971). This was the context in which the poor Jewish immigrants fleeing the pogroms of Eastern Europe in 1886–87 found themselves competing for jobs in the clothing and footwear industries and disturbing the precarious relations of East London trades by making visible the conditions of work in the sweat shops of the East End.

This led to the widespread publicity over wages and conditions, and there were large-scale strikes by match girls and by East End dockers. Walkowitz (1992, p.28) reports that 'Both strikes involved unskilled and impoverished labourers and were heavily dependent on public sympathy and financial support'. The match girls' strike in particular was a demonstration of mass solidarity and the power of unionization. More ominously for many members of the propertied class, 'The demonstrations confirmed their worst fears of Outcast London as a vast, unsupervised underclass that could be readily mobilized into the revolutionary ranks of the new socialist movement' (Walkowitz, 1992, p.29). Such fearful responses had been prefigured in reactions to an earlier demonstration and subsequent riot in February 1886, when a political rally of mainly unemployed dock and building workers traversed the fashionable streets of the West End attacking property and all signs of wealth and privilege. It is argued that the real significance of this riot was 'the strength of the middle-class reaction to it and the extent of the fear of the casual residuum that it revealed' (Jones, 1971, p.292).

In short, not only were middle-class fears of class conflict and social disintegration confirmed as the 'menacing presence of "King Mob" in their part of town threatened the imaginative boundaries erected to mark off and contain the poor' (Walkowitz, 1992, p.29), but both riot and strikes seemed to confirm much more general anxieties about urban pathology and the potential for an uprising of the casual poor (see Chapter 3).

2.3 Dangerous sexualities

Such fears of the mob were accompanied by other anxieties about the state of the nation as manifested in the urban centres: anxieties which focused on the Victorian obsession with sexuality. This obsession had three dimensions which are particularly significant here: unregulated sexuality and the future of the 'race'; the discovery of 'unnatural passions' in the form of homosexuality; and the public visibility of sexuality in the guise of prostitution.

unregulated sexuality

We have already touched on the first of these in terms of the eugenics movement and its arguments about the threat of racial decline. Such perspectives draw a sharp contrast between the increasingly planned and regulated family life of the middle classes (including a decline in middle-class family size) and the unregulated sexuality and breeding habits of the poor. According to the eugenicists, this discrepancy was likely to weaken the genetic stock of the British race as the weak and feckless overproduced while the sensible and provident middle classes underproduced.

At the same time, the Victorian enterprise of scientific classification was leading to the delineation of 'normal' and 'abnormal' sexualities. While the idea of 'unnatural passion' in the form of homosexuality was unadmitted within the average Victorian household, it was nonetheless an area of scientific enquiry and moral anxiety. One particular focus was provided by the celebrated trials of Oscar Wilde on grounds of homosexuality, followed by his imprisonment from 1895 to 1897. Throughout his life Wilde had challenged Victorian ideas and norms (especially the place of sexuality). He was spokesman for the late nineteenth-century Aesthetic movement which was the constant butt of antagonism for its 'unmasculine' devotion to art for art's sake. His novel *The Picture of Dorian Grey* attracted charges of immorality by its combination of the Gothic novel with the 'unspeakable sins of French decadent fiction'. His last plays were 'satirical epigrams' which on the surface may have seemed like 'trivial froth' but which mercilessly exposed Victorian hypocrisies. Wilde and his like-minded contemporaries therefore represented a very particular threat of moral danger and challenge to the social order, not least because of their place *within* the respectable classes.

A different challenge was posed by prostitution. Prostitutes, almost more than any other single group, became an overarching metaphor for the threat to social order. Walkowitz (1980, p.32) reports: 'An object of fascination and disgust, the prostitute was ingrained in public consciousness as a highly visible symbol of the social dislocation attendant upon the new industrial era. By the 1850s prostitution had become "the Great Social Evil"'.

Some of what Walkowitz calls 'fascination and disgust' in Victorian views of prostitution are visible in Henry Mayhew's descriptions of the classes of prostitutes in London (see Extract 4.1).

contagion The Victorian prostitute became constructed as a potent source of contagion. As the streetwalkers ventured into the fashionable thoroughfares, tempting middle-class sons (or so it seemed to the evangelical upholders of the patriarchal family), they appeared both literally and figuratively to be the conduit for all the immorality, pestilence, pollution and infection that emanated from the 'great unwashed': 'Like the slums from which she emanated, she carried with her ... "the heavy scents of the masses" with their "disturbing messages of intimate life". She evoked a sensory memory of all the "resigned female bodies" who serviced the physical needs of upper-class men in respectable quarters' (Walkowitz, 1980, p.22).

The imagery of the prostitute belied the reality of most prostitutes' lives and backgrounds. The majority were members of the casualized labouring poor, rural migrants forced to leave the countryside for economic reasons, or city 'natives' pushed into prostitution in response to local conditions in the labour market. In both cases poverty was the underlying cause for the move to prostitution, giving lie to the stereotypical vision of girls seduced, pregnant and abandoned and turning to prostitution. The majority of prostitutes catered for a working-class clientele, again refuting the claim that prostitutes were in the business of seducing middle-class men (Walkowitz, 1980).

Extract 4.1 Mayhew: 'London's underworld'

The second class of prostitutes, who walk the Haymarket – the third class in our classification – generally come from the lower orders of society. They consist of domestic servants of a plainer order, the daughters of labouring people, and some of a still lower class. Some of these girls are of a very tender age – from thirteen years and upwards. You see them wandering along Leicester Square, and about the Haymarket, Tichbourne Street, and Regent Street. Many of them are dressed in a light cotton or merino gown, and ill-suited crinoline, with light grey, or brown cloak, or mantle. Some with pork-pie hat, and waving feather – white, blue, or red; others with a slouched straw-hat. Some of them walk with a timid look, others with effrontery. Some have a look of artless innocence and ingenuousness, others very pert, callous, and artful. Some have good features and fine figures, others are coarse-looking and dumpy, their features and accent indicating that they are Irish cockneys. They prostitute themselves for a lower price, and haunt those disreputable coffee-shops in the neighbourhood of the Haymarket and Leicester Square, where you may see the blinds drawn down, and the lights burning dimly within, with notices over the door that 'beds are to be had within'.

Many of those young girls – some of them good-looking – cohabit with young pickpockets about Drury Lane, St. Giles's, Gray's Inn Lane, Holborn, and other localities – young lads from fourteen to eighteen, groups of whom may be seen loitering about the Haymarket, and often speaking to them. Numbers of these girls are artful and adroit thieves. They follow persons into the dark by-streets of these localities, and are apt to pick his pockets, or they rifle his person when in the bedroom with him in low

coffee-houses and brothels. Some of these girls come even from Pimlico, Waterloo Road, and distant parts of the metropolis, to share in the spoils of fast life in the Haymarket. They occasionally take watches, purses, pins, and handkerchiefs from their silly dupes who go with them into those disreputable places, and frequently are not easily traced, as many of them are migratory in their character.

The third and lowest class of prostitutes in the Haymarket – the fourth in our classification – are worn-out prostitutes or other degraded women, some of them married, yet equally degraded in character.

These faded and miserable wretches skulk about the Haymarket, Regent Street, Leicester Square, Coventry Street, Panton Street and Piccadilly, cadging from the fashionable people in the street and from the prostitutes passing along, and sometimes retire for prostitution into dirty low courts near St. James Street, Coventry Court, Long's Court, Earl's Court, and Cranbourne Passage, with shop boys, errand lads, petty thieves, and labouring men, for a few paltry coppers. Most of them steal when they get an opportunity. Occasionally a base coloured woman of this class may be seen in the Haymarket and its vicinity, cadging from the gay girls and gentlemen in the streets. Many of the poor girls are glad to pay her a sixpence occasionally to get rid of her company, as gentlemen are often scared away from them by the intrusion of this shameless hag, with her thick lips, sable black skin, leering countenance and obscene disgusting tongue, resembling a lewd spirit of darkness from the nether world.

(Mayhew, 1851–62, vol.4, pp.358–9)

2.3.1 Patriarchy threatened

If the reality was so far from the image, how is it that the prostitute and prostitution became so potent a symbol of danger? The real threat was arguably to patriarchal social relations and social order. Sexuality in the nineteenth century became the site for other struggles, especially around gender and class. Just as Wilde challenged Victorian norms about heterosexuality, so prostitutes challenged the gender norms of Victorian patriarchal society. They were women who had broken out of the stranglehold of 'normal' female socialization. Many prostitutes ran their own lives, organizing their trade, and often living together as part of an all-female sub-group. Prostitutes were still subject to many forms of male domination but they had wrested some control over their lives. Contrary to the prevalent ideological imagery of women in passive domesticity, here were women who were far from passive. Furthermore, when dressed up in fine clothes, patrolling the elegant shopping streets at the smart end of town, they were frequently indistinguishable from their 'respectable' sisters. For an ideology of womanhood which depended on clearly visible and identifiable differences between 'the fallen' and 'the virtuous', and of class divisions which depended on the working class being kept clearly segregated, such confusions were a potent signal that everything was far from in its rightful place and, worse, was getting out of control.

In the 1860s, attempts were made to address this issue of control, and prostitution was officially labelled a dangerous form of sexuality through the Contagious Diseases Acts of 1864, 1866 and 1869, introduced primarily to address the 'problem' of prostitution in garrison towns. This is not the place to examine the details of the Acts nor the subsequent successful campaign for their repeal, but it should be noted that the Acts inadvertently created a fulcrum around which new challenges to the existing social order could coalesce: 'The double standard of sexual morality, the participation of women in political activity, the control of women by male doctors, and the role of the state in enforcing sexual and social discipline among the poor were all subjected to public scrutiny' (Walkowitz, 1990, p.3). To the degree that the Acts aimed to control sexuality and via such control to reinforce class and gender domination, they failed. However, in this failure, the imagery of the subversive power of the prostitute (and the threat she posed to the social order) was confirmed.

In this way sex, like 'race', became a metaphor of danger. Unregulated sexualities threatened the reproductive capacity and moral order of the nation. This 'threat' combined with visions of illicit, extra-marital and unrepressed sexuality in the slums and ghettos of the working poor to raise the spectre of a multiplication of the 'great unwashed'. The eugenicists' concern with the purity of the race not only received validation from abroad, but it was deeply rooted also in fears at home. For the safety of the nation (the white, middle-class and *male* nation) homosexual men had to be imprisoned and prostitutes had to be labelled as deviant and dangerous, and treated as criminals.

2.4 Order and danger: the dynamics of the city and crime

The dangers represented by the 'dangerous classes' in the nineteenth century define the problem of social and political order in ways which have carried forward into perceptions of the modern city. The dangerous classes are both the 'other' and inextricably linked with the development of the city as a way of life. Their dangerousness is only partly a matter of crime. Their criminal deeds are invariably represented as the visible tip of an iceberg and hint at the multiple dangers below. Their symbolic existence at the heart of the city is the essential underpinning to the ways in which ideas about the city have subsequently developed and coalesced into a vision of urban areas as criminal places.

reform   The dangers embodied in the dangerous classes formed the targets of multiple attempts at reform, rescue, regulation, reconstruction and institution building. From sanitary improvements to the emergence of modern forms of policing, these attempts can be best understood through the language of social disorder and disorganization. In the twentieth century we tend to speak of social problems in the plural – referring to poverty, criminality, juvenile delinquency, mental illness, or deviant sexualities as more or less separate phenomena, each requiring particular types of analysis and intervention. In the mid nineteenth century, and notwithstanding the new forms of classification that were coming into vogue, many observers still tended to view 'the social problem' in the singular. For these, the obsession remained with the notion of the dangerous classes – in whom were condensed the multiple dangers and threats of the disordered lower orders.

These responses to 'danger' also helped to shape the modern city. A multi-faceted array of interventions were aimed at the city in order to reform and regulate the lower orders. It is beyond the scope of this chapter to go into detail, but they included the following:

- The physical destruction and reconstruction of areas of the city – combined with sanitary reform and other public health initiatives – opened up the 'dangerous places', establishing new forms of residential segregation which 'rescued' the respectable from too great a proximity to the dangerous and created places which could be more systematically subjected to surveillance, regulation and policing.

- 'Street life' – in the form of casual trades, begging, prostitution, petty crime or mere 'hanging about' – was subjected to greater legal control and policing, following on from the creation of 'professional' police forces.

- The provision of 'rational' forms of recreation and temperance movements offered a more 'ordered' use of free time among the poor, paralleled by greater legal and social restrictions on 'irrational' leisure pursuits (gambling, drinking, and so on).

ACTIVITY 4.1

What were the general aims of these interventions? What different kinds of 'dangerousness' were associated with mid-nineteenth-century fears of the inner city? Make a few notes and then consider in what ways any of these might be seen as continuing themes in fears about the city today.

COMMENT

The aim of these and other interventions was to impose a physical, social and cultural order on the city in the image of respectability by repressing the city's dangerousness and making it a place where the law-abiding could 'go about their normal business' in safety and comfort. In doing so, the interventions sowed the seeds for many of the responses to the 'problem' of the inner city which followed in the twentieth century. The use of planning laws to determine areas of development (or decline), slum clearance schemes which rehoused the poor in tower blocks or on the city periphery, public housing allocatory mechanisms which created 'respectable' or 'sink' estates, the routines of inner-city policing – all had their origins in this period.

3 Progress and the urban problem: twentieth-century dreams

The period between 1900 and the 1970s can be seen as the peak of the time when crime was almost exclusively understood and responded to as an urban phenomenon. Rural crime, like the countryside itself, was seen as a 'backwater', an innocent hangover from old ways, by contrast with both the dynamism and the danger of cities.

3.1 Grounds for optimism: mobility

The starting point for any discussion of this period must be the sheer scale of urbanization during the twentieth century – towns and cities became the dominant places of the British landscape. Between the start of the century and the late 1970s there was an unchecked population flow towards urban centres. In the process, the city grew, condensing work, leisure and home in a compressed and organized space. The city simultaneously expanded and became denser.

spatial and social mobility

The theme of growth is inseparable from the theme of mobility – both spatial and social. In spatial terms, the city is the place to which people moved – they gravitated there in search of work, in pursuit of leisure, in the quest for excitement. As the city expanded, it also became a more complex space for people to move within. It developed its own spatial dynamics. Some of these dynamics involved the increasing separation of home and paid employment. Others arose from the unceasing quest for better places to live within the city. For much of the twentieth century, the search for these better places pushed back the boundaries of the city, as social mobility, linked with spatial mobility and the imperatives of the economy, caused an upward and outward movement to the city's edge – a process described by Rex (1973, p.84) as the 'great urban game of leapfrog'. The spatial outcome of this economic and social mobility was suburbanization in the shape of new developments on the city edge. Suburbanization – the confluence of spatial and social mobility – represented progress towards a better life away from the hustle, dirt and 'messiness' of city life. In the direction of that progress, looking outwards not inwards, the older grand homes and respectable housing of the nineteenth-century city rim were left behind to run down and decay, to move 'downmarket' and become the resting place of those unable to afford access to the newer and better places at the edge of the expanding city.

3.2 Zones of transition: the Chicago School

This combination of expansion and mobility underpins what remains the most famous approach to urban sociology of this century, the work of the Chicago School, most notably that of Robert E. Park and Ernest W. Burgess (Park *et al.*, 1925). What is important for us in this context is Burgess's zonal theory of city development and its relation to both the dynamics of urban change and the problems of crime and social disorder. The theory is based on the idea that, as the city expands, so, outside the central business district, residential zones develop as a series of concentric rings of increasing affluence moving from centre to periphery (see Extract 4.2 and Figure 4.1).

Extract 4.2   Park et al.: 'The growth of the city'

In Europe and America the tendency of the great city to expand has been recognized in the term 'the metropolitan area of the city', which far overruns its political limits, and in the case of New York and Chicago, even state lines. The metropolitan area may be taken to include urban territory that is physically contiguous, but it is coming to be defined by that facility of transportation that enables a business man to live in a suburb of Chicago and to work in the loop, and his wife to shop at Marshall Field's and attend grand opera in the Auditorium …

No study of expansion as a process has yet been made, although the materials for such a study and intimations of different aspects of the process are contained in city planning, zoning, and regional surveys. The typical processes of the expansion of the city can best be illustrated, perhaps, by a series of concentric circles, which may be numbered to designate both the successive zones of urban extension and the types of areas differentiated in the process of expansion.

This chart [see Figure 4.1] represents an ideal construction of the tendencies of any town or city to expand radially from its central business district – on the map 'The Loop' (I). Encircling the downtown area there is normally an area in transition, which is being invaded by business and light manufacture (II). A third area (III) is inhabited by the workers in industries who have escaped from the area of deterioration (II) but who desire to live within easy access of their work. Beyond this zone is the 'residential area' (IV) of high-class apartment buildings or of exclusive 'restricted' districts of single family dwellings. Still farther, out beyond the city limits, is the commuters' zone – suburban areas, or satellite cities – within a thirty- to sixty-minute ride of the central business district.

This chart brings out clearly the main fact of expansion, namely, the tendency of each inner zone to extend its area by the invasion of the next outer zone. This aspect of expansion may be called *succession*, a process which has been studied in detail in plant ecology. If this chart is applied to Chicago, all four of these zones were in its early history included in the circumference of the inner zone, the present business district. The present boundaries of the area of deterioration were not many years ago those of the zone now inhabited by independent wage-earners, and within the memories of thousands of Chicagoans contained the residences of the 'best families'. It hardly needs to be added that neither Chicago nor any other city fits perfectly into this ideal scheme. Complications are introduced by the lake front, the Chicago River, railroad lines, historical factors in the location of industry, the relative degree of the resistance of communities to invasion, etc. …

In the expansion of the city a process of distribution takes place which sifts and sorts and relocates individuals and groups by residence and occupation. The resulting differentiation of the cosmopolitan American city into areas is typically all from one pattern, with only interesting minor modifications. Within the central business district or on an adjoining street is the 'main stem' of 'hobohemia', the teeming Rialto of the homeless migratory man of the Middle West. In the zone of deterioration encircling the central business section are always to be found the so-called 'slums' and 'bad lands', with their submerged regions of poverty, degradation, and disease, and their underworlds of crime and vice. Within a deteriorating area are rooming-house districts, the purgatory of 'lost souls'. Near by is the Latin Quarter, where creative and rebellious spirits resort. The slums are also crowded to overflowing with immigrant colonies – the Ghetto, Little Sicily, Greektown, Chinatown – fascinatingly combining old world heritages and American adaptations. Wedging out from here is the Black Belt, with its free and disorderly life. The area of deterioration, while essentially one of decay, of stationary or declining population, is also one of regeneration, as witness the mission, the settlement, the artists' colony, radical centres – all obsessed with the vision of a new and better world.

The next zone is also inhabited predominatingly by factory and shop workers, but skilled and thrifty. This is an area of second immigrant settlement, generally of the second generation. It is the region of escape from the slum, the *Deutschland* of the aspiring Ghetto family. For *Deutschland* (literally 'Germany') is the name given, half in envy, half in derision, to that region beyond the Ghetto where successful neighbours appear to be imitating German Jewish standards of living. But the inhabitant of this area in turn looks to the 'Promised Land' beyond, to its residential hotels, its apartment-house region, its 'satellite loops', and its 'bright light' areas.

This differentiation into natural economic and cultural groupings gives form and character to the city. For segregation offers the group, and thereby the individuals who compose the group, a place and a role in the total organization of city life. Segregation limits development in certain directions, but releases it in others. These areas tend to accentuate certain traits, to attract and develop their kind of individuals, and so to become further differentiated.

(Park *et al.*, 1925, pp.49–52, 54–6)

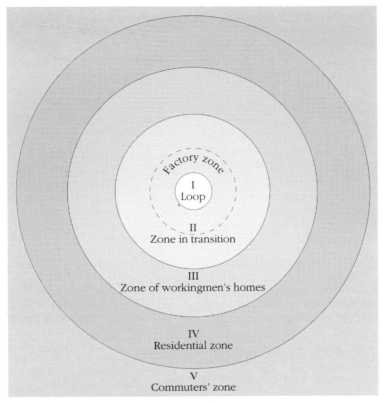

I
Loop

II
Zone in transition

III
Zone of workingmen's homes

IV
Residential zone

V
Commuters' zone

Figure 4.1 The growth of the city

zone of
transition

It was the zone of transition in Burgess's model – an area characterized by older, low-cost housing intermingling with factories and close to the centre of the city – that was identified with successive waves of migrants. In the context of the USA (and Chicago in particular) these were Irish, Italian and Eastern European, together with black families from the South who all sought the American Dream in the urban-industrial centres of the northern states. The point about the zone of transition in the model is precisely that it is *transitional*. New migrants would move into it because of its cheap housing and proximity to factories, but as they became economically established they would migrate onwards. These were people who were on their way to somewhere, moving outwards into more permanent and stable accommodation in the outer rings as they became assimilated to the 'American way of life' (Clarke, 1991, Chapter 3). It was thus a continuous process: as each successive generation of migrants became 'Americanized', each progressed and moved on. Mobility – social, spatial and cultural – underpinned the essential optimism of this model.

Within the zone of transition, life was hard and it was disorderly. It lacked the social, spatial and cultural stability of the outer rings. Instead, it was characterized by transitions, transience and turbulence and as such was both a zone of disorder and potential criminality – widely referred to by the Chicago School as an area of social disorganization. Indications of this potential were identified by another classic Chicago study – that of Shaw and

social
disorganization

McKay (1942). Basing their approach on Burgess's zonal theory, Shaw and McKay mapped where juvenile delinquents in Chicago (and other American cities) lived according to zone of residence. Their finding that juvenile delinquency was highest in the innermost ring and declined steadily outwards, *and* that this pattern appeared to remain stable over time, appeared to support the view that crime could be equated with the socio-spatial disorderliness of the zone of transition (Shaw and McKay discussed in Bottoms, 1994, p.590 and also in **Bottoms and Wiles, 1992**). In trying to explain this finding Shaw and McKay focused mainly on the constant population movement of the zone of transition. But they also noted its cultural heterogeneity, and equated this with an absence of cultural integration. They contrasted this heterogeneity with an assumed high level of cultural integration in the outer residential areas. They saw the zone as a place that was conducive to the development of a criminal subculture and to the cultural transmission of delinquent values (Bottoms, 1994, p.50). Both social disorganization and the idea of 'criminal sub-culture' have been important strands in subsequent explanations of crime. However, what is relevant here is the way in which cultural differences were represented as deviations from the norm and as a lack of culture, both 'creating' social disorganization. In this view, crimes of violence and crimes against property were the effect of the 'ecology' of the inner area – its inability to provide integrative mechanisms that could link inhabitants to the wider social order. Here was the downside of the optimism about urban growth and mobility.

The other feature which helped to dramatize the zone of transition as different and deviant was that it was transitional in another sense. It was regularly traversed or passed through by those making their way from work to home, from the outer residential areas to the central business district. What such commuters perceived was *difference* – neither the orderly commercial world of the business district nor the planned residential order of the outer suburbs. Instead, they confronted a microcosm of disorder – decaying properties, marginal businesses, a diverse population and a visibility of 'life on the streets'. The zone of transition almost necessarily involved forms of what Whyte (1959) called 'street corner society' because of the distribution of private and public space. Since the accommodation in the zone was dominated by forms of multi-occupancy – lodging houses, sub-divided properties, small-scale rented accommodation – the access to private space taken for granted in the suburbs was much less available. As a result, life in these areas of the city spilled out into the public spaces of the street. In the process it fed a spectre of disorder identified with inner-city life.

The Chicago School's model of the city captures two central themes. One is the predominant optimism of mid-twentieth-century views about the city, grounded in the ideas of mobility and transitions. The pattern of urban processes demonstrated an apparently infinite capacity of the city to absorb, assimilate and civilize its newest inhabitants, as most of its succeeding waves of migrants moved upwards and outwards on the escalator towards suburbia. Second, the model embodies the growing conception of a changing relationship between crime and the city in which crime and dangerousness become associated with specific places. The Chicago School's concept of a zone of transition prefigures what, in the 1960s and 1970s, comes to be the 'inner city' – a disorderly place which breeds disorderly behaviour.

3.3   Grounds for optimism: urban reconstruction

The growth of the city and the forms of mobility associated with that were not just the result of the workings of the market in land and housing, but also involved self-conscious attempts to plan the future through systematic urban reconstruction. The New Towns movement in Britain in the 1950s was one such example. Another was urban reform in the shape of slum clearance and rehousing programmes intended to reclaim the declining areas of the city. These were either on the fringes of the zone of transition (replacing older working-class/artisanal housing built in the mid to late nineteenth century) or on peripheral public housing estates developed by town and city councils. In these latter developments, working-class families found themselves made part of the 'great urban game of leapfrog'

Typical middle-class, low-density suburb laid out in gentle curving roads and cul-de-sacs. Note also the presence of gardens and trees, giving the whole a very different look to the stark bareness of the working-class suburb

Typical working-class suburb of a planned type with its virtually identical houses, laid out in straight lines with the occasional cul-de-sac. The wide straight roads and lack of trees, together with the sameness of the houses, gives the area a bare, uniform appearance

and rehoused beyond the old suburbia on the city's rim. Such shifts were rarely in the same direction as the new suburbia, creating different 'corridors' of housing type and social class radiating outwards from the city (Thorns, 1972).

Urban reform was a testament to the power of municipal politics and to the underlying belief in the transformative power of the built environment. Moving people from the slums to rational, well-planned and modern forms of housing was equated with changing them from the habits of 'slum culture' to being 'modern citizens'. The idea of housing as a way of promoting assimilation to the social order had underpinned urban reform from the beginning. The slum clearance programmes added to the earlier private/market escalator of suburbanization a municipal or public escalator to a better life in new council estates. Each testified to the city's capacity to absorb and assimilate as part of a continual programme of modernization and progress. As the photographs opposite show, the social character of private and public development differed markedly.

3.4 Lingering pessimism

The reform of the city in the late nineteenth and early twentieth centuries destroyed the 'wens and rookeries' that had seemed to be the natural habitat of the dangerous classes. The dangerous places had been levelled or opened up to public regulation and policing. The rehousing of the poor had promised both the spatial separation of the respectable and labouring classes from their dangerous neighbours and, at the same time, attacked the environment that bred dangerousness. In the process, the great fear of the 'social problem' had been dispersed, and the dangerous classes disappeared along with their dangerous places. For the most part, then, it seemed that order had triumphed over disorder. But worries remained.

Disorder persisted, although in apparently more mundane and manageable forms. Crime and disorderliness, rather than outright dangerousness, characterized the city in the first half of the twentieth century. These were certainly 'problems', but they were concentrated in some places rather than others – in the 'haunts of the habitual criminal'. They disturbed the peace rather than threatened the breakdown of the social order. They became simply matters of policing. There were only isolated fragments of the old social problem: here a few juvenile delinquents, there a few prostitutes; here the odd 'criminal family', there a few maladjusted 'problem families'.

These residual problems were associated with residual areas – the unreconstructed slums, the 'transitional' areas and, subsequently, the 'rough estates'. Each was identified – and identifiable – as different from the rest of the social order of the city. Each had its reputation – 'tough', 'rough', 'unrespectable', 'disreputable', the 'red light district'. There were occasional 'moral panics' about crime and disorderly behaviour, often centring on youth (mods and rockers, drugs, juvenile delinquency) and sometimes on more serious crime (the London gangland of the 1960s), but such concerns lacked the widespread social intensity that surrounded nineteenth century dangerousness. For the most part crime and disorder were to be explained by reference to 'slum culture', or the 'culture of poverty' or 'lower-class values' – explanations which marked a suitable distance between such problems and the respectable majority. Crime and disorder became the province of the expert rather than the focus of popular attention. The connection between the city and crime became 'routinized' – something to be left in the hands of professionals who were best able to secure progress and reform.

3.5 Emerging new concerns

This view of the *residual* nature of crime in the context of urban modernization and progress was undercut by a multiplicity of different processes in the 1960s and 1970s. At the risk of oversimplifying, we have identified three clusters of processes which were particularly significant in changing the perceived relationship between the city, crime and danger:

1 a crisis of 'progress' in the city;

2 the emergence of new spatial struggles over the social order of the city; and

3 new patterns and perceptions in the zones of transition.

In addition, from the mid 1970s cities faced financial crises. Global recession together with changing central government priorities acted to produce a fiscal crisis at local and municipal government level (Cochrane, 1993). There is not the space here to examine this in detail. The point to note for our purposes is that just as doubts about whether all the problems had been resolved were reappearing, so the ability of urban governments to finance new initiatives aimed at their resolution came under threat.

A crisis of 'progress'

We have argued that the promise of progress underpinned the view that disorderly behaviour in the twentieth-century city was simply a 'residual' matter, and that this promise rested on the idea that there were 'escalators' (new housing markets and urban reform) which moved people upwards and outwards. By the 1960s and 1970s there were growing doubts about the effectiveness of these 'escalators', as those left behind began to look more like structural features of the urban social order than groups who were merely waiting their turn. Two key factors seemed to be significant in solidifying the inner areas of the city. The first was age. The social composition of the inner areas was structured around the extremes of age – they contained young and old rather than working-age adults and families. The young were generally too poor to enter housing markets or council accommodation and, whether in education or early working careers, were looking for cheap rented accommodation. The elderly were simply too poor to move on and, often, too attached to old neighbourhoods to want to do so.

The second factor was the structuring effect of racialized divisions which resulted in a heavy concentration of black and other minority ethnic groups in the older, inner areas of the city – as individuals and as families. Barred from both the housing market and public housing by discrimination, accommodation in the zone of transition and the older areas of workingmen's housing became the focal points for minority ethnic groups. Although the density of these racialized divisions of British cities never approached that of the USA, the imagery of the ghetto did cross the Atlantic, as did the 'blaming the victim' ideologies of 'ghetto culture' and the 'culture of poverty' which sought to explain the immobility of such groups in terms of their own cultural patterns and choices.

The effect of these two changes was to create specific cultural patterns and tensions around life on the streets in the inner areas. These streets, more than anywhere else in the city, displayed the symbolic forms of a multi-ethnic society and the tensions associated with the non-integration of old white and new minority ethnic communities. The potential for disorder and danger was demonstrated by the riots of Nottingham and London's Notting Hill area in the 1950s. The tensions were further dramatized by the 'ghetto riots' of the USA in the 1960s.

Equally significant for the state of the inner areas was the population bifurcation between young and old and the lack of visible family life in the inner areas. Life on the streets increasingly became the province of the young – particularly in the male-dominated youth cultures of the 1960s and the 'bohemian' or counter-cultural patterns of the late 1960s and early 1970s. The effect was an increasingly disconcerting vision of the inner areas as socially and ethnically diverse, mixing complex cultural forms in highly public ways and making public places look and sound highly disorderly and potentially criminal. Parties, loud music, groups of young people, drug use and street crime emerged as the dominant imagery of the inner areas. In the early 1970s, these concerns came to focus on 'mugging' as an index of both the increasing fear about public safety in the city and the presence of black youth on the city's streets (Hall *et al.*, 1978).

The third element of the 'crisis of progress' related to what happened at the other end of one of the escalators – the new public housing estates. This crisis became focused most explicitly on the patterns of high-rise developments ('cities in the sky'). Disaffection among their populations about the physical and social environments was eventually reflected in professional and political disenchantment with these approaches to urban renewal. A particular focus was on their apparent lack of 'community' and the implied decline in informal social controls. Subsequently the project designs themselves came under criticism for not building in 'defensible space' against crime (Newman, 1973), and the question of a relationship between building design and crime more generally was considered (Coleman, 1990). Similarly, the role of city planners in deciding land use and thereby 'creating' (or eliminating) the potential for 'dangerous space' became the focus of some attempts to explain the apparent association of crime with particular areas of the city (Herbert, 1982).

Spatial struggles

The second cluster of processes marks the beginnings of attempts to reshape the spatial and social orders of the city. Historically, mobility had meant movement outwards – the trend of suburbanization. However, the 1970s saw a reverse trend, involving pressures to 'reclaim' the inner areas of the city. An expanding middle class, particularly those sections based in welfare state professions, began to identify older housing as an economic and cultural alternative to moving out to suburban estates, and embarked on the process known as 'gentrification' – the rescue of 'nice houses' in unrespectable areas. As a result the inner areas became the focus for new spatial and social struggles. As gentrification proceeded and more and more areas became identified as potentially desirable, the members of the economically and racially marginalized social residuum found themselves further displaced, with their housing rehabilitated and sold off or rented at prices far beyond their reach (Goldberg, 1993).

Following such changes in the housing market were wider cultural attempts to 'clean up' the area, architecturally, socially and culturally. Central to these were efforts to control and, if possible, remove the disorderliness of street life – disorderliness which was recognizable in the forms of prostitution, of young people 'hanging about', and of the homeless and transients (who became known pejoratively as 'street people'). These struggles exposed the complex cultures of the inner areas as 'problems' of public order.

New patterns and perceptions

Finally, all of these processes underpinned the changing imagery of the inner areas in the 1960s and 1970s. This is best captured in the language used to describe these areas: they become either ghettos or the 'inner city'. Both terms identify these places as solidified spaces (clearly identifiable and distinguishable from the rest of the city) and as problem areas. These terms are different from the Chicago School's concept of a zone of transition. They are no longer transitional, in that they are disconnected from processes of mobility. Rather they have become blocks to progress. They are sullen and resistant to change. They have become dangerous places once again, not safe for respectable people.

ACTIVITY 4.2

Before reading on, make a few notes on how you perceive the key characteristics of dangerousness in the city implied by the changes from the beginning of the twentieth century up to the 1970s.

COMMENT

As in the nineteenth century, the revival of dangerousness of the inner city was multi-dimensional. It was spatial, in that specific parts of the city were identified as dangerous, and the physical characteristics of these parts were linked to the social problems within them (decaying properties and disorganized households). It was also spatial in the way that attention was focused on the dangerousness of public places – the street in particular – as posing problems about the maintenance of both public order and the social order. It was also sexual: there were recurrent concerns with prostitution; with the sexual misdemeanours of the young; with the greater public visibility of gay and lesbian sexualities; and with the apparent fecundity of black and other minority ethnic families. It was potentially political, as the traditional right began to see municipal socialism as 'the enemy within'. It was profoundly racial, with the black 'other' seen as a social, cultural and criminal threat to a naturalized English social order or way of life. Above all, it was criminal: it was about crime, and crimes of the street in particular, but crime which exceeds the capacity of society to contain or manage it. It was crime seen as the basis of a crisis of law and order (see **Hall, 1980**).

4   The 1980s and 1990s: recurring nightmares

By the early 1980s the optimism outlined in section 3 appeared to be over. Recorded crime had been rising since the 1960s, and in the ten years 1975–85 there was an apparently startling increase of 63 per cent (Smith, 1989, p.270). Public concerns again turned to the city, and in the 1980s the inner cities came to stand for and represent the 'crime problem' just as they symbolized equally powerfully economic and social decay and the challenge of 'urban regeneration' (Deakin and Edwards, 1993; Robson, 1988).

4.1   Urban decline

One of the ways in which these concerns about the city were manifest was in a sharpening sense of urban decline. Cities up and down the country saw their remaining factories closing, manufacturing being replaced by service industries, and already run-down areas appearing ever more derelict. It seemed as if the old industrial-urban centres of Britain were in a terminal condition, and popular anxieties about this were given impetus by visions of an urban landscape of extreme decay in which the remaining public areas were covered in graffiti and vandalized. A more general feeling of street lawlessness crept into the public consciousness. Such feelings were further fuelled by an association of the city's 'twilight districts' and estates with a 'tangle of pathologies' (Robins, 1992, p.1). Truancy, crime, family and community breakdown were among the issues which made up this 'tangle' and which, along with the degradation of the physical environment, made people ever more fearful that the city and city life were disintegrating.

The complexity of the meanings embedded in the ideas of 'urban decline' means that any assessment of how far such fears are objectively justified is fraught with difficulties. However, what is relevant here is not the issue of whether decline (whatever that might mean) was occurring (however that might be measured) but the idea that there is a symbolic link between people's views about the health of the city and their feelings about security and *civilization* and, ultimately, the state of the nation. 'Urban decline' in the late twentieth century resonated with many of the same perceptions of threat that fear of 'the mob' had engendered a century earlier. The effect of the rhetoric about urban decline was to tap into a much wider set of feelings of social malaise at the heart of the city – including fears about crime – than simply worries about a declining urban landscape. As Beauregard (1993, p.192) puts it, 'Urban commentators cannot refer to urban decline without setting in motion subtle harmonics that cause many listeners and readers to reflect on the precariousness of their way of life'.

4.2   The enemy within?

These 'subtle harmonics' set the context for the re-emergence of other fears. The riots that took place in the inner cities of England in the early 1980s were regarded by many as 'without equal in this century' (Waddington *et al.*, 1989, p.142), and they revived long-standing fears relating to notions of an 'enemy within'. It seemed as if the sites of rioting could be pinpointed on a map simply by identifying those areas where there were concentrations of black or Asian people (Young, 1992). The spectre of the 'race riot' appeared to be once again reaching across the Atlantic to become resident in Britain.

To read these uprisings of black communities as race riots, however, is to misunderstand their background and also to misread the history of policing in working-class areas. The riots were the product of long-standing relations of conflict between the police and local black communities in the areas in which they occurred. These were places 'resonant with contested meanings' (Keith, 1993a, p.154). They were the symbolic 'front lines' in which the place of black people in Britain was being played out and redefined on a daily basis. The relationship with the police was the central element of these processes. This had 'deteriorated steadily for more than 30 years through the combined influences of racism, marginalization, labelling and criminalization' (Keith, 1993a, p.159). The 'front lines' marked the points of resistance to police oppression, where challenges to police authority had become a part of the daily routine. It is this notion of *routine* that is the key to understanding the riots. It was not that police/black relations were worse in the riot areas; rather, the riots were in locales where resentment of power relations had been transformed into routine resistance (see **Keith, 1993b**). The riots occurred when some 'trigger' event tipped this routine of daily resistance into collective disorder.

routine
resistance

Although the disorders of the 1980s were not race riots, they were of symbolic significance in that they appeared to forge a new link between 'race' and inner-city disorder. There was a new 'enemy within' and it was black (Gilroy, 1987). In this sense the 1980s riots marked a turning point in the public perception of the 'urban other' and a re-emergence of nineteenth-century fears about the 'alien'. The significant result of the racial dimension of the riots was that 'blackness' was coming to play 'a cautionary role similar to ... that once occupied by nineteenth-century fears of the crowd' (Cross and Keith, 1993, p.10).

4.3 Law and order

More specific fears also flourished concerning issues of law and order. At the same time as crime was rising, it seemed that the capacity of society and the police to cope with crime was diminishing. The clear-up rate for crimes *reported* to the police had fallen steadily from 45 per cent in 1970 to 31 per cent in 1986. Unreported crime was on the increase. The streets *felt* risky and unsafe. Low-level harassment, not in itself criminal, could nonetheless be at one end of a spectrum of activity at whose other end were criminal acts (for example from sexual harassment to rape). All these factors fuelled fears about urban crime such that, by the middle of the decade, 60 per cent of the public said they were worried that 'they or members of their household might become victims of crime'. The conditions were set for the politicization of law and order, and it was notable that by the late 1980s, 25 per cent of those surveyed said they regarded law and order as 'today's most important political issue' (Smith, 1989, p.272; see also Chapter 1).

Meanwhile, the police were also under pressure. In addition to the pressure from the public concern about escalating lawlessness, there was a chorus of criticism about the routine policing practices employed in the so-called 'notorious' inner-city areas. Historically, policing the working-class areas of the city had always been a politics of choice between enforcing law *or* maintaining order (Cohen, 1981). One result was that the police had come increasingly to rely on the use of discretionary powers with all that implied for undermining 'the official posture of the force as neutral arbiters of justice' (Cohen, 1981, p.126). As a result there was a strong likelihood that the targets of police action would feel unjustly treated.

Such feelings of injustice were given affirmation through the implementation of the 'sus' law (which permitted police to stop and search any individual on the grounds only that their behaviour was 'suspicious'). As applied by police in the inner city – overwhelmingly to black and Asian young men – it was highly discriminatory and conflicted with the citizenship rights of the black population as a whole. The effects of 'sus' were of wider significance, too, in that its use against *some* members of black and ethnic minority groups was read as 'providing validation of hostility towards *all* members of ethnic minorities as potential criminals' (Waddington *et al.*, 1989, p.146). In the context of a government committed to tougher measures, such validation of hostility aided the politicization of law and order by drawing more rigid boundaries between criminals and victims. The 'support for the fight against crime is best mobilized where there are clear symbolic distinctions between the deviant few and the law abiding majority' (Smith, 1989, p.274). The labelling of black inner-city residents as 'criminal' in the public mind thus served the purposes of those who wanted to push law and order up the political agenda. In the process, notions of *specific* dangerousness were also revived and redefined and associated once again with the 'alien other'.

4.4 Discovering young men

The themes of decline and dangerousness in the city were intensified in the 1990s. As the recession of 1990 persisted, there was an outburst of rage as gangs of youths (white and black) rioted and laid siege to some of the most depressed city estates in the country. From Ely on the edge of Cardiff and Blackbird Leys just outside Oxford to the Meadowell, Elswick and Scotswood estates on Tyneside, riots became 'routine' as 'incendiary young bucks confronted the Boys in Blue' (Campbell, 1993, p.2). The triggers were diverse, but arguably the underlying causes were the same. What appeared to unite those taking part in the 1990s riots was a common (class) experience of economic *extremis*.

The riots were only the tip of the iceberg. The estates on which they occurred were in many respects 'doomed': they were mostly in areas evacuated by business and industry, so there was little hope of employment for their poverty-stricken inhabitants. As a result, a large cohort of young men and women found themselves not only 'on the edge of politics but exiled from the social world' (Campbell, 1993, p.94). 'Exiled' from access to the social institutions and roles which might provide legitimate meaning to their lives, they turned violently on their own communities. What characterized the estate crime of the 1990s was that it took place 'at home' against friends and neighbours and even family. Young men (very few women) 'took over the streets', illegally riding motor-cross bikes across the estates' vacant grass, racing up and down in stolen cars, and terrorizing their communities with a criminal tidal wave of personal harassment, vandalism, burglary, car theft, drug dealing and riotous behaviour. The problem for the estates was not just crime against the individual, dangerous though the streets might feel; it was also the feeling of total impotence against the power of 'youths on the rampage'.

The riots marked a new phase in working-class relations with the police. As already noted, policing the city had never been an entirely neutral affair, especially as between different classes and groups. Moreover, since the emergence of the modern police force, policing has had an ideological as well as a repressive role in targeting those who were seen to be disturbing the social order (Cohen, 1981). Inevitably, given middle-class perceptions of the street culture of the working class, this involved targeting working-class youth. Such targeting established a pattern of antagonism between police and working-class youth, the result of which, along with contradictions within the police force itself, narrowed 'the scenario of law and order down to a battle between two rival gangs, both composed of young, single, working-class males, each seeking territorial control over the class habitat' (Cohen, 1981, p.131). This was the battle that, in part, was played out in the streets of the run-down estates in the 1990s.

These riots were significant because they indicated in dramatic form a new spatial patterning of dangerous places:

> The 'symbolic locations' shifted from the *frisson* of chaos and cosmopolitanism in the inner city – *the interior* of the celebrated metropolis – to the edge of the city, archipelago, out there, anywhere. These were places that were part of a mass landscape in Britain, estates were everywhere. But in the Nineties estates came to mean crime.

> (Campbell, 1993, p.317)

Rioting youth thus became constructed as part of the new dangerous classes, and the estates where they lived finally lost their status as the proud emblems of urban reform. Instead they became symbolic of a new 'disordered' class – home to the single mothers and 'disorganized families' who had failed to instil in their young men a proper respect for authority.

4.5 The old in the new: discovering the underclass

underclass

This 'disordered class' – the 'disorganized' families, 'single parents', the 'unruly' and 'criminal' (frequently black) youth of popular representation – has become the underclass. A twentieth-century incarnation of the dangerous classes of a century earlier, the underclass is a concept whose origins are American, although it has been exported from there to Britain. It overshadows contemporary discussions of 'urban problems' and 'social problems' (see **Murray, 1990**). It points to decay, disorganization, disorder and demoralization at the heart of the contemporary city. One of the earliest attempts to research and define the nature of this underclass was provided by Auletta, who saw it as composed of a range of threatening groups:

> I learned that for most of the 25 to 29 million Americans officially classified as poor, poverty is not a permanent condition. Like earlier immigrant groups, most of these people overcome poverty after a generation or two. There are no precise numbers for this but an estimated 9 million Americans do not assimilate. They are the underclass. Generally speaking, they can be grouped

into four distinct categories: (a) the *passive poor*, usually long-term welfare recipients; (b) the *hostile* street criminals who terrorize most cities and who are often school drop outs and drug addicts; (c) the *hustlers* who, like street criminals, may not be poor and who earn their livelihood in an underground economy, but rarely commit violent crimes; (d) the *traumatized* drunks, drifters, homeless shopping-bag ladies and released mental patients who frequently roam or collapse on city streets.

(Auletta, 1983, p.xvi)

This description and others like it evoke the 'otherness' of the underclass as a disorderly and unassimilated presence in the city. They are, as one American magazine made clear, to be feared: 'Behind [the ghetto's] crumbling walls lives a group of people who are more intractable, more socially alien and more hostile than almost anyone had imagined. They are the unreachables: the American underclass' (*Time*, 19 August 1977).

The underclass has come to carry exactly the mixture of 'horrible fascination' that characterized nineteenth-century investigations into, and reportage of, the dangerous classes. They are in, but not of, the city, representing an exotic and unregulated other way of life. As in the nineteenth century, the underclass plays across our concerns and fears about class, 'race' and gender. The very idea of the under*class*, especially in supposedly 'classless' societies, solidifies the identity attributed to this group. It confirms their difference from the majority and deflects attention from differences between the groups who make up this supposed class. For example, the groups identified above by Auletta would seem to have little in common except their undesirability. Just as the idea of the dangerous classes in the nineteenth century condensed a variety of groups and behaviours into one entity that could be distinguished from the respectable, so the underclass condenses a variety of 'dangers' in order to separate 'us' from 'them'.

Partly because of its American origins, the idea of the underclass comes loaded with racialized meanings. In the USA, poverty, welfare dependence, street crime, disorganized families and inner-city ghettos are all understood to refer to the experience of black people. Despite the fact that there are more white Americans living in poverty than black, the underclass – the 'unassimilated' in Auletta's terms – are presumed to be mainly black (Clarke, 1991, Chapter 6).

The concern with the family and moral order brings us to the role of gender in the underclass. Above all, this underclass is both marked by, and seen as, the product of households headed by lone mothers. It is claimed that liberal welfare provisions for child support have made it possible for lone mothers to live without their children's fathers. Although some moral outrage has been directed at the 'absent father', this has been much less significant than the condemnation of the lone mother, who is viewed as being encouraged by social policies to make bad choices. In the process such women have become identified as 'failures'. They 'fail' to keep their men in stable and monogamous family relationships. As a result, they fail to 'civilize' men, allowing them instead to break free of the ties of responsibility to maintain and provide for their family. Underpinning this view of failure is a conception of gender differences which presumes that men are essentially 'wild spirits' who need, for the sake of society, to be 'tamed'. Women, 'proper women', are essentially oriented to domestication and civilization and have a responsibility to rein in undisciplined masculinity. This is one reason why prostitution was seen in the past as such a potent threat to the social order. The final failure of the underclass mother is in respect of the next generation. Denied by their mother's failure, these children grow up without access to male role models and paternal discipline, thus producing the next generation of the underclass – feckless mothers-to-be and uncontrolled males. Just like their nineteenth-century predecessors, they breed too much.

The underclass has been the subject of extensive debate. There have been arguments about whether such a group exists or whether it is an ideological fiction which lumps together different groups and different behaviours in an unwarranted way. There are also arguments about the causes of poverty, marginalization and disorganization (see for example Katz, 1989, and Morris, 1993). For the purposes of this chapter, however, the significance of the underclass lies in the way that the idea has revived older themes about dangerousness and the city. Fears about the underclass bear a remarkable similarity to the nineteenth-century anxieties about the dangerous classes that we discussed earlier. Once again it is claimed that the city contains a virulent threat to the social order, and one that is a volatile cocktail of immorality, criminality and political instability.

4.6 The menace of drugs

This image of the city as a volatile cocktail of danger is further reinforced by the 'menacing' presence of drugs. From the 1960s there have been intermittent anxieties about the availability and increasing use of illegal drugs. Associated with youth cultures such as the mods and the 'counter-culture' of the hippy, illicit drug use has been a recurring theme in adult anxieties about the 'youth problem'. In particular, there has been a concern that users of 'soft' drugs such as marijuana or cannabis would inevitably graduate to 'hard' drugs such as cocaine and heroin.

While research suggests that such fears are largely ungrounded, this has not stopped them remaining part of the general set of drug-related concerns. Indeed, during the 1970s and 1980s there was an increase in the overall numbers involved in drug dealing, together with an increasing penetration of the drugs industry by professional criminals. The result in the 1990s is a billion-dollar drugs industry operating in an international market. Alongside the professionals are numerous small-time drug traffickers. Many of these operate largely on their own and participate in a wide variety of petty crimes as well as dealing in drugs. Others, 'the retail specialists', operate as illegal enterprises alongside legitimate businesses. There are also those for whom the drug industry, as compared with the petty humiliations and harassment of a secondary sector job, offers a hope of self-determination and economic independence (Hagan, 1994). These groups present in different degrees a 'publicly visible spectacle ... threatening the public's sense of tranquillity and safety' (Dorn *et al.*, 1992, p.42), with the result that through the 1980s and into the 1990s drugs and drugs-related crime have occupied centre stage in the litany of fears about the city.

The new concerns over drugs have operated to undermine feelings of social safety at several different levels. First, there is undoubtedly a general disapproval of the buying and selling of drugs. However, in a study of the Kings Cross area of London, Lee (1995) argues that anxieties in the local community went far 'beyond disapproval of the buying and selling of drugs *per se*. Rather, people were anxious about the general degradation of street life that was associated with the drug culture and the prostitutes, pimps and kerb-crawlers that coexisted with it. It was these corollaries rather than the presence of drugs as such which meant that the population studied lived in a state of increasing fear 'as every corner and doorway became a haven for dealers and prostitutes and the streets and open spaces were littered with syringes, condoms and the general detritus of the criminal activity' (Camden Council, cited in Lee, 1995).

Second, although the visible presence of drugs on the streets is a largely urban phenomenon, drug dealing and addiction are far from confined to the derelict areas of the inner city. Rather, the problem of drugs appears to have the ability to reach out and touch all sections of society: upper-class sons and daughters have been exposed to 'designer' drugs at all-night raves and clubs, while the acid house rave scene attracted City 'whiz-kids'. Neither can heroin addicts simply be dismissed as the 'detritus' of society when they prove to come from every background and class.

Once again, therefore, there is a multiplicity of fears at work in which the concern surrounding drugs echoes the multiple anxieties that constitute the general feelings of malaise about the city. Like the other fears, these too have a racial dimension. The drug consumers may come from every walk of life, but the shadowy world of big-time drug dealing is represented as involving any number of 'sinister aliens' – the Italian Mafia, Colombian drug barons and Chinese Triads. All evoke varying images of 'racial' menace and evoke fears of potential 'takeover'. This threat gained a more domestically racialized emphasis in the late 1980s when the so-called Jamaican 'Yardie' became represented by the media as a particularly erratic and violence-prone example of the dangerous drug dealer (Dorn *et al.*, 1992). All of this, along with an increasing competitiveness, violence and instability in the illegal drugs industry, especially when crack came along (Hagan, 1994), helped to give credence to the Yardie demonology.

It is worth noting that the observation of low-level participation in the drugs economy by increasing numbers of individuals is explained by some commentators as 'cultural adaptation' in the absence of better sources of employment. This may, in turn, explain any apparently high black and ethnic minority involvement in drug dealing, since such groups are within an unequal structural position *vis-à-vis* the formal labour market. Other explanations focus on police methods of drug law enforcement, pointing out that at the level of the small-time inner-city street dealer, the focus will inevitably be on black rather than white populations because of the demographic characteristics of inner-city areas. In the case of the Kings Cross area study the author concluded that 'focused' drug enforcement inevitably brought more Black than White people into the receiving end of technological targeting and surveillance operations (Lee, 1995).

While explanations are important, they are less relevant here than the imagery of drug use. In this case the image is of the menace of drugs striking at the heart of society, 'contaminating children' and perpetuated by people outside of and 'foreign' to that society. The existence of drug dealing adds to our fears, and where that drug dealing appears to be associated with the alien, those fears become multiplied.

4.7 Fears confirmed?

Finally, in the 1980s latent feelings of malaise took on a specific form as victimization research appeared to show that people's fears about the risks of crime and the dangers of the city were founded in the day-to-day reality of many city residents.

It should be noted that there are a number of problems with 'victim surveys' and the measurement of fear. For example, it is not clear what *exactly* such surveys are measuring (fears and worries are influenced by much broader factors than just crime, as we indicated earlier). There are also problems with the process of *labelling* people as victims (since labelling involves a statement of values and different people give different meanings to being victimized). Furthermore, surveys which only use legal definitions of crime are intrinsically flawed. Indeed, the British Crime Surveys, first conducted in 1982, were criticized for *setting out* to show that the city was dangerous. This focus on crime in the inner city simply confirmed a political point: urban is dangerous and therefore 'something must be done' (see Chapter 1 for a discussion of the shortcomings of victim surveys).

In the light of these problems the results of such surveys must be treated with caution. Nevertheless, the reports in the popular press of the findings of the British Crime Surveys succeeded in turning into a 'moral panic' the mix of fears about crime, danger and the inner city that had been brought to the fore by the apparent collapse of law and order. In other words, the surveys appeared to confirm everybody's worst fears.

Further research (some of it based on secondary analysis of the survey data) also appeared to ground some of the fears in firm evidence. The city could be a dangerous place, for some people (but not always those who were most fearful) at some times of the day. Certain 'routine practices of an urban lifestyle' did seem to increase the likelihood of becoming the subject of criminal action (Smith, 1989). Those residing in high-status, non-family and multi-ethnic areas of the inner city had been experiencing increased rates of crime. In addition, evidence from the USA suggested the existence of 'hot spots' of crime where people going about their daily business were especially vulnerable (Sherman *et al.*, 1989).

However, in contradiction to what had been supposed, it was the young, not elderly people, who were more at risk from personal and property crimes. Furthermore, with the important exceptions of rape and domestic violence, it was men who were more at risk than women from violent attack on the street (Smith, 1989). In addition, the vision of black and Asian ethnic communities as perpetrators of crime was counterbalanced by evidence of a higher risk of (racial) attack among those groups as compared with whites. These findings need qualification and illustrate the shortcomings of the surveys. Women walking the streets face a range of 'non-criminal' offensive behaviour (often directed at their sexuality) which profoundly shapes their experience of danger in a way that is very different from that of men (Painter, 1992). Similarly, low-level racial harassment often does not get counted in the crime statistics (since it remains largely unreported) but together with the experience of 'multiple stop and search' creates a very different street reality for blacks than for whites. In other words, by focusing on *legal* definitions of crime, the crime surveys glossed over key differences in how the 'dangers' of inner-city street life are experienced.

It became clear that it was not just the inner city that was suffering high rates of victimization. Many of the poorest council estates on the city rim were experiencing high and increasing rates of victimization and crime. The deprived were becoming the multiply victimized as evidence indicated that 'areas with the highest rates of criminal victimization also had the highest rates of multiple victimization' (Bottoms, 1994, p.616). The spatial dispersion of crime was undermining the assumed connection between the inner city and dangerousness.

4.8 The problem of the crime problem

Although the 'crime problem' is the constant subject of public and political attention, the evidence suggests that there is no such thing as the 'crime problem'. Rather, there exists a variety of different and occasionally overlapping crime problems which rarely focus on the same issues and concerns (see Chapter 1). These crime problems will tend to move into or out of focus partly in response to media interest, partly in response to what and who the police choose to target. So when rioting youth in the 1990s drew police attention to the outer-city estates, these became the new 'criminal places', just as the 'ghettos' of the inner city were so labelled in the 1980s. What is striking in this process of crime definition and the connections between crime and the city is that it never includes white-collar or corporate crime. The 'City', with its crimes of fraud, corruption, illegal trading and misuse of funds (such as pension funds) is never included as a 'criminal place', even though the personal consequences of the crimes can be devastating and are intimately bound with urbanism as a way of life (see Chapter 6).

the 'problem of crime'

To the extent that there is overlap between the different crime problems, it is that they relate to 'traditional' or 'conventional' concerns about crimes against the person and property. But within this frame of reference there are different interests and priorities about types of crime: sexual violence, racial violence, burglary, street theft, vandalism, and so on. Around each focal concern clusters a range of fears and anxieties which are only partly about crime in its legal sense. We have noted the kinds of questions raised by women in relation to the gamut of potentially threatening but non-criminal behaviour that they face. Anti-racist groups have demanded that racially motivated violence should be a distinct and specific criminal offence. They, too, have pointed to a range of behaviour which runs from direct assaults to harassment and intimidation. People living in the inner city or on council estates have long complained about vandalism, but this covers a wide range of environmental defacement and destruction only some of which is perpetrated by 'yobs'; other aspects may result from neglectful councils or landlords. All, however, contribute to a perception of a decaying or disorderly environment. Car-driving commuters may identify the crime problem as one of personal safety or car theft, but may themselves be perceived as a problem by parents concerned about the vulnerability of children to the dangers of drivers passing through at excessive speeds, or kerb-crawling on their way home to suburban respectability.

There are, then, different crime problems. But the issue is made still more complex because controlling crime (or perceived danger) has also involved criminalizing particular social groups – targeting them as 'suspicious persons'. Young people – and young black people especially – face the presumption that they are 'suspect', with all the resulting surveillance, intrusion and harassment that this entails. Young women in public spaces (especially after dark) have the prospect of being viewed as likely prostitutes – both by the police and by would-be clients – as a result of the assumption that 'respectable' women are not out on the streets alone. Youngsters roaming unsupervised and 'street people' loitering in shopping centre precincts are moved on in order to keep the place safe and clean for the 'real' customers. In such ways, the control of public space has increasingly come to involve a binary distinction between the 'respectable' and the 'suspicious', or between the 'acceptable' and the 'excluded'.

What different forms did dangerousness take in the 1980s and 1990s, and how did these link with those of earlier periods?

What is meant by 'the crime problem'?

5   Signs of the future: towards a new urban order?

Throughout this chapter we have tried to draw attention to the dynamics of urban change and the ways in which the question of crime is linked to changing social orders in the city. In this final section we want to concentrate on new trends in the remaking of the social order of the city that are visible in the 1990s and their connections to issues of crime and disorder.

ACTIVITY 4.3

In looking to the future, the question implicitly posed is: Can the city be a safe place to live, and if so for whom?

We suggest you take a little time before reading on to consider and make notes on your own views about this question.

5.1   New urban spaces

The 1980s and 1990s have seen a multiplication of urban spaces. In Britain, attempts at city centre redevelopment, inner-city regeneration and new developments on the outer edges of the city have reshaped the urban environment. Inner areas have been rejuvenated both by individuals, as 'gentrification' heralded by the ubiquitous 'skip' reclaimed previously run-down inner-city streets, and collectively, through the attempt to reconstruct whole city centres in order to 'rescue' the city from its decline and make it attractive to inward investment and population movement. Competing with the attempt to rejuvenate the centre has been the development of out-of-town hypermarkets and new superstores – 'monuments to consumption' built to cater for the car-owning residents of the private housing estates on the city rim. In many areas the shopping mall has taken over from the high street as the place to go for consumer goods.

Across the Atlantic new developments can also be found, some of which hint at possible futures. 'Edge city' is the term that has been used to describe a new genre of urban area which contains all the functions of a city but in a spread-out form tied together by 'jetways, freeways, and rooftop satellite dishes' (Garreau, 1991, p.4). Its hallmarks are jogging trails, single-family detached dwellings and glass atria 'reaching for the sun and shielding trees perpetually in leaf at the cores of corporate headquarters, fitness centres, and shopping plazas' (Garreau, 1991, p.4). 'Edge city', it is claimed, is the logical next step from suburbanization and the growth of the out-of-town mall, developing when the strains of commuting and disillusion with the old inner city mean that the jobs begin to locate where most people now live and shop.

Spatially and socially the result in both Britain and the USA is a 'disconnection' between the environment and its geographical location (Harvey, 1989) and between the concept of 'urbanism as a way of life' and the places where the routine activities that make up that way of life take place. There is so little sense of grounding in a specific place or locale or culture in many of the new developments that they could 'almost be anywhere in the world' (Savage and Warde, 1993, p.140). The shopping mall epitomizes this new trend – a self-contained and enclosed environment of exotic greenery, international muzak, marbled floors and subtle lighting. Once inside, 'The visitor is wrenched … away from the culture of the specific city in which it is located, into a new imaginary realm' (Savage and Warde, 1993, p.141).

5.1.1   Exclusion and the 'model' citizen

The development of these urban spaces has been accompanied by forms of social exclusion. Many of the new housing developments are unaffordable to the inhabitants of the regenerated areas. Waterfront schemes (popular in both Britain and North America as mechanisms of cultural and urban regeneration) typify the case. An illustration is the London Docklands, where it was middle-class 'yuppies' from the City who moved into the converted river-front warehouses and bijou terraces of the in-filled docks. 'Edge city' has been hailed as the next step in the search for the American Dream, but past history suggests that it will not be available to all Americans. Some will get left behind, just as many of the poor, blacks and dispossessed were unable to get on the escalator and out of the zone of transition.

In Britain other forms of exclusion have arisen as a result of cash-strapped municipal authorities going into partnership with private developers. All too frequently in the process of negotiation, public amenities such as a library, or a community centre, or shops selling basic foodstuffs lose out to the commercial pressure to achieve a 'profitable' rate of return. Shareholders gain but the town centre as a civic or collective amenity is devalued. Here is an example of another trend – that of an increasing demarcation between public and private space. The case of the shopping malls illustrates the point. When built by local authorities, malls were designed to be thoroughfares and public spaces in addition to providing shops, restaurants, community areas, and so on. But across Britain they have been sold off in a process which has been described as 'the privatization of the public realm' (John Punter, Professor of Planning at Strathclyde University, on BBC Radio 4's 'File on 4', 1 March 1994). Once privatized, they become subject to new exclusions ranging from the closing of the centre after shopping hours because it is 'too expensive' in terms of security to keep open, to controlling anything and everything that is seen as a potential threat to the task of maximizing returns. That this can take some curious forms was illustrated in the same 'File on 4', which documented the banning of

social exclusion

preaching by the Salvation Army (too 'political'), the advertising by a women's institute of home-made jam (a threat to established businesses), and primary school children with clipboards (too intrusive). Even sitting was discouraged by making the seats less comfortable, and in one case was justified by reference to market research which purported to demonstrate that the general public was 'particularly distressed' by the sight of old people sitting down. The underpinning purpose was that nothing should hinder people's willingness to part with their money. As one centre manager put it, he didn't want people disturbed by contentious issues, so 'we don't allow people to come in in an uncontrolled manner'.

Such dynamics of change and processes of exclusion have at their heart an imagery of the 'model' citizen whose needs the new urban spaces and places are intended to serve. These model citizens wish to live somewhere 'interesting' (whether in privatized family spaces at the edge of the city or in renovated places within the city). They expect, and are expected, to be 'consumers', exercising 'lifestyle choices' in the boutiques and malls. They are 'affluent', possessing the financial basis for exercising consumer choice. Perhaps most important, they are mobile, having the means to move between spatially distributed sites of home, work, shopping and entertainment. The dynamics of urban development in the 1990s reflect this model of what it means to live in the city.

5.2 Crime control or criminalization? The regulation of public and private space

The new urban geography impinges on crime in a number of ways, some of which can be seen if we examine how crime control, as well as urban space, is being remapped. Alongside the process of privatization there has been the development of a new set of relationships between the individual and private action against crime, and the role of the police.

Throughout the 1980s and 1990s individuals and communities have been exhorted to take more responsibility for their own crime protection, which at times has engendered a fortress mentality. This ranges from taking care to lock doors and windows, installing household security systems or fitting anti-car theft devices, to community schemes like Neighbourhood Watch or the emergence of privately financed 'street patrol' officers and other forms of 'community force'. Some of these are funded by local councils who see the 'real' police as being overworked and understaffed and 'are prepared to operate their own streetwise forces' despite their 'strictly limited legal powers' (*The Guardian*, 16 April 1994), but others are run by private security firms called in to police affluent suburban neighbourhoods. By the mid 1990s it has been estimated that in Britain there were already more people employed in *private* security firms than in the *public* police force. Meanwhile, official Conservative government policy was to seek a new 'partnership between police and community', including a force of 'special constables' (unpaid part-timers, under police control).

What effect this will all have against crime is hard to assess. More surveillance (such as Neighbourhood Watch) may result in crime displacement to other areas (see also **Walklate, 1996**). The issue of where crimes take place is complex and involves not only 'suitable targets in the absence of direct social control' but also the 'cognitive spatial awareness of

fortress mentality

offenders' (Bottoms, 1994, p.621); that is, not only opportunity but perception of that opportunity are needed for the crime to occur. More significant, perhaps, suspicious neighbours and community patrols may create less tolerance of 'unusual' behaviour. The tougher line on trespass embodied in the 1994 Criminal Justice and Public Order Act is likely to be felt most keenly by those on the margins of society – squatters, gypsies and new age travellers. Securing the city by enlisting respectable citizens to 'clean it up' may result in anything that seems exciting, 'exotic', 'dangerous' or that is simply different being seen as a threat to that cleansing operation.

Private policing and the more elaborate neighbourhood security strategies are in their infancy in the UK, although it is clear that this is a direction in which the government wishes to go. Some indication of their possible implications for the future can again be gleaned from the USA. Davis has termed Los Angeles 'Fortress LA', and he describes how new luxury developments just outside the city limits are becoming like mini fortress cities, 'complete with encompassing walls, restricted entry points with guard posts, overlapping private and public police services, and even privatized roadways' (Davis, 1990, p.294). He also documents an increasing privatization of public space, observing that traditional 'luxury enclaves', like Beverley Hills or San Marino, are restricting access to *public* facilities to 'residents only' by using municipal regulations to 'build invisible walls' in the form of preferential parking arrangements, residential requirements for access to parks, or restricted opening times. Davis (1990, p.246) concludes from his observations that 'residential areas with enough clout are thus able to privatize local public space, partitioning themselves from the rest of the metropolis, even imposing a variant of neighbourhood "passport control" on outsiders'. Such trends highlight the dichotomy within views of city life. It is a place of excitement but it is also a place of danger. It is a place to get 'out and about' and to take advantage of all that it offers, but it is being outside on the streets that feels threatening and that leaves property unguarded. It is a place to be young, free and mobile, but it is 'the young who riot'. This dichotomy is played out in the new spatial arrangements.

The barrel-shaped bus bench, Downtown, Los Angeles: designed to deter sleepers

The shopping mall is the exemplar of the general trend as today's urban spaces are increasingly cordoned off by high-level security cameras, foot patrols and locked gates after hours. The built environment has become less and less *accessible* as traditional 'transitional' areas between public and private space such as street-level shops have been replaced by blank walls, dark glass frontages and curtained offices. Remaining public spaces contain 'ingenious design deterrents' against 'undesirables'. In England seats in some public spaces have been made uncomfortable, but in Los Angeles the barrel-shaped bus bench has been specially designed to make sleeping impossible, and outdoor sprinklers are randomly deployed at night as an extra deterrent to would-be park sleepers.

5.2.1   The enemy without

Against whom is it that such deterrent measures are being deployed? The new enemies, who this time will be prevented from becoming 'within', are the poor, the homeless, the vagrants, street people and all the other 'unsuitables' who are unable to measure up to the consumerist demands of the twentieth century and so who are not wanted in the new citadels of consumerism. According to Davis, in the USA there has been a 'conscious "hardening" of the city surface against the poor' (Davis, 1990, p.232). He puts this down to two interlocking trends. First, in a market-oriented economy, market provision of 'security' will inevitably generate its own demand – there is in short a consumerist 'imperative' for more security. Second, in the absence of first-hand knowledge of actual conditions in the inner city the 'white middle-class imagination will magnify the perceived threat through a demonological lens' (Davis, 1990, p.224). Between these two, the conditions are set for justifying the creation of a segregated 'defensible space' against the 'contagion' of disreputable and disorderly elements. It is a 'creation' which *necessarily requires* the destruction of accessible public space and a cordoning off of the private and 'safe' areas (see Extract 4.3).

Extract 4.3   Davis: 'The destruction of public space'

The universal and ineluctable consequence of this crusade to secure the city is the destruction of accessible public space. The contemporary opprobrium attached to the term 'street person' is in itself a harrowing index of the devaluation of public spaces. To reduce contact with untouchables, urban redevelopment has converted once vital pedestrian streets into traffic sewers and transformed public parks into temporary receptacles for the homeless and wretched. The American city, as many critics have recognized, is being systematically turned inside out – or, rather, outside in. The valorized spaces of the new megastructures and super-malls are concentrated in the centre, street frontage is denuded, public activity is sorted into strictly functional compartments, and circulation is internalized in corridors under the gaze of private police.

The privatization of the architectural public realm, moreover, is shadowed by parallel restructurings of electronic space, as heavily policed, pay-access 'information orders', elite data-bases and subscription cable services appropriate parts of the invisible agora. Both processes, of course, mirror the deregulation of the economy and the recession of non-market entitlements. The decline of urban liberalism has been accompanied by the death of what might be called the 'Olmstedian vision' of public space. Frederick Law Olmsted, it will be recalled, was North America's Haussmann, as well as the Father of Central Park. In the wake of Manhattan's 'Commune' of 1863, the great Draft Riot, he conceived public landscapes and parks as social safety-valves, *mixing* classes and ethnicities in common (bourgeois) recreations and enjoyments. As Manfredo Tafuri has shown in his well-known study of Rockefeller Centre, the same principle animated the construction of the canonical urban spaces of the La Guardia–Roosevelt era.

This reformist vision of public space – as the emollient of class struggle, if not the bedrock of the American *polis* – is now as obsolete as Keynesian nostrums of full employment. In regard to the 'mixing' of classes, contemporary urban America is more like Victorian England than Walt Whitman's or La Guardia's New York. In Los Angeles, once-upon-a-time a demi-paradise of free beaches, luxurious parks, and 'cruising strips', genuinely democratic

The other side of these changes is the relative abandonment of poor housing areas and estates – those not attractive enough to be thought worth redeveloping, whose inhabitants are unable to afford household security measures, whose local authorities have run out of cash for crime prevention measures, and where the police no longer go. Such areas form the 'spaces between the places' in the new urban map. They are passed through or by-passed by the 'respectable' citizen. They do not attract inward investment – indeed, they are more likely to be marked by the loss of public and commercial facilities, as reduced public spending or low profit margins impact upon them. Their inhabitants fail to measure up to the new model citizen: they are too poor to attract commercial services or exercise much by way of consumer choice, they are predominantly dependent on public income support rather than a wage or salary, and they are too immobile to take advantage of the city's new possibilities. Where they are mobile – where they venture into the new places – they look 'out of place' and are likely to be treated as such. Dress codes at entertainment venues, the policing of shopping areas against the 'disreputable', the 'hardening' of the city's architecture, the suburban suspicion of 'outsiders' – all aim to exclude those who 'have no business being here'.

space is all but extinct. The Oz-like archipelago of Westside pleasure domes – a continuum of tony malls, arts centres and gourmet strips – is reciprocally dependent upon the social imprisonment of the third-world service proletariat who live in increasingly repressive ghettos and barrios. In a city of several million yearning immigrants, public amenities are radically shrinking, parks are becoming derelict and beaches more segregated, libraries and playgrounds are closing, youth congregations of ordinary kinds are banned, and the streets are becoming more desolate and dangerous.

Unsurprisingly, as in other American cities, municipal policy has taken its lead from the security offensive and the middle-class demand for increased spatial and social insulation. De facto disinvestment in traditional public space and recreation has supported the shift of fiscal resources to corporate-defined redevelopment priorities. A pliant city government – in this case ironically professing to represent a bi-racial coalition of liberal whites and blacks – has collaborated in the massive privatization of public space and the subsidization of new, racist enclaves (benignly described as 'urban villages').

Yet most current, giddy discussions of the 'postmodern' scene in Los Angeles neglect entirely these overbearing aspects of counter-urbanization and counter-insurgency. A triumphal gloss – 'urban renaissance', 'city of the future', and so on – is laid over the brutalization of inner-city neighbourhoods and the increasing South Africanization of its spatial relations. Even as the walls have come down in Eastern Europe, they are being erected all over Los Angeles.

The observations that follow take as their thesis the existence of this new class war (sometimes a continuation of the race war of the 1960s) at the level of the built environment. Although this is not a comprehensive account, which would require a thorough analysis of economic and political dynamics, these images and instances are meant to convince the reader that urban form is indeed following a repressive function in the political furrows of the Reagan–Bush era. Los Angeles, in its usual prefigurative mode, offers an especially disquieting catalogue of the emergent liaisons between architecture and the American police state.

(Davis, 1990, pp.226–8)

5.3 Dreams and nightmares: urban futures

Speculations about the possible future of the city emphasize the dynamic tensions between order and disorder and between progress and crisis that have been centrally connected to the development of the modern city. The tendencies towards a new urban order, based on greater privatization, policing and exclusion, represent a new version of 'progress'. But they also create new problems: the costs of security, the erosion of public space, and the question of how to manage or control the 'excluded populations'. In the process, they create new tensions between those who belong to this new order and those who are excluded – they multiply fears about the other.

Not all 'progress' is being sought in this direction. Alternative approaches to urban renewal are more positive. They recognize that deprivation and crime remain glaringly obvious on the streets of London or Los Angeles, but stress that cities, at least 'successful' ones, offer more of an opportunity than a threat. Among the more positive approaches are those that seek to emphasize the building of communities, through valuing public space and stressing the importance of community participation in planning and development schemes. They focus on the need to 'empower' communities against the wider economic and political tendencies of globalization that threaten to overtake the city and create 'unimaginable mega-monsters' by early in the twenty-first century (Davis, 1994).

Such views of the importance of community have to confront the problem of the unstable meaning of 'community' in contemporary society. The idea of community evokes images of a more stable world in which people and place were intimately connected. These images have been undermined by social and spatial mobility but also by the more diverse senses of attachment that people now have. Communities of place coexist uneasily with communities of identity (as in references to black or minority ethnic communities, for example) which may not live in the same place. Creating communities in the face of social mobility and social diversity is a daunting task, but the problems involved need to be compared with the problems that the other vision of a new urban order might create.

In this chapter we have talked about the city in general, looking at broad themes and processes rather than trying to trace the history and patterns of development in a particular city. We have worked at this level of generality in order to be able to focus on the themes and imagery of urban order, disorder and danger. Any particular town or city will both share in these general themes and have its own particular history in which the themes are played out. These particular histories will combine wider processes (of economic, political and social development) with local conditions, choices and struggles in the making of urban order. But none of them will have escaped the recurring questions of 'what sort of urban order' and 'what sort of dangers' are at stake in the city.

Further reading

Jones (1971) and Walkowitz (1992) both provide significant historical studies of 'dangerousness' and problems of social order in nineteenth-century London, while Cohen (1981) presents important arguments about strategies of social control in the city. The Chicago School's approach to crime and the city is well exemplified in Shaw and McKay (1942) and is critically discussed in **Bottoms and Wiles (1992)** and Bottoms (1994).

Contemporary debates about the city, disorder and the underclass have been heavily influenced by the work of **Murray (1990)**, while the idea of the underclass has been subjected to critical analysis by Morris (1993). More widely, Katz (1989) provides a valuable discussion of ideas of urban poverty and social disorder.

Finally, Davis's (1990) study of Los Angeles provides a bleak but gripping account of one city's historical development and the sorts of future social order that might be at stake in the contemporary remaking of the city.

References

Auletta, K. (1983) *The Underclass,* New York, Vintage Books.

Beauregard, R.A. (1993) 'Representing urban decline: postwar cities as narrative objects', *Urban Affairs Quarterly*, vol. 9, no.2, pp.187–202.

Booth, C. (ed.) (1889–1902) *Life and Labour of the People in London,* 17 vols, London, Macmillan.

Bottoms, A.E. (1994) 'Environmental criminology', in Maguire, M., Morgan, R. and Reiner, R. (eds) *The Oxford Handbook of Criminology*, Oxford, Oxford University Press.

Bottoms, A. E. and Wiles, P. (1992) 'Explanations of crime and place', in Evans, D.J. *et al.,*(eds) *Crime, Policing and Place*, London, Routledge. (Reprinted in Muncie *et al.,* 1996.)

Campbell, B. (1993) *Goliath*, London, Methuen.

Clarke, J. (1991) *New Times and Old Enemies*, London, HarperCollins.

Cochrane, A. (1993) *Whatever Happened to Local Government?*, Buckingham, Open University Press.

Cohen, P. (1981) 'Policing the working-class city', in Fitzgerald, M., McLennan, G. and Pawson, J. (eds) *Crime and Society: Readings in History and Theory*, London, Routledge and Kegan Paul.

Coleman, A. (1990) *Utopia on Trial: Vision and Reality in Planned Housing*, Eynsham, Shipman.

Cross, M. and Keith, M. (eds) (1993) *Racism, the City and the State*, London, Routledge and Kegan Paul.

Davis, J. (1989) 'Jennings Buildings and the Royal Borough: the construction of the underclass in mid-Victorian Britain', in Feldman, D. and Jones, G.S. (eds) *Metropolis London: Histories and Representations Since 1800*, London, Routledge and Kegan Paul.

Davis, M. (1990) *City of Quartz*, London, Verso.

Davis, M. (1994) *Beyond Blade Runner: Urban Control,* Westfield, New Jersey, Open Magazine Pamphlet Series.

Deakin, N. and Edwards, J. (1993) *The Enterprise Culture and the Inner City,* London, Routledge and Kegan Paul.

Dorn, N., Murji, K. and South, N. (1992) *Traffickers,* London, Routledge and Kegan Paul.

Garreau, J. (1991) *Edge City: Life on the New Frontier,* New York, Doubleday.

Gatrell, V.A.C. (1990) 'Crime, authority and the policeman state', in Thompson, F.M.L. (ed.) *Cambridge Social History of Britain, 1750-1950*, vol. 3, Cambridge, Cambridge University Press. (Reprinted in Muncie *et al.*, 1996.)

Gilroy, P. (1987) 'The myth of black criminality', in Scraton, P. (ed.) *Law, Order and the Authoritarian State,* Buckingham, Open University Press.

Goldberg, D.T. (1993) 'Polluting the body politic: racist discourse and urban location', in Cross and Keith (eds).

Hagan, J. (1994) *Crime and Disrepute,* California, Pine Force Press.

Hall, S. (1980) *Drifting into a Law and Order Society*, London, Cobden Trust. (Extract reprinted in Muncie *et al.*, 1996.)

Hall, S. *et al.*, (1978) *Policing the Crisis,* London, Macmillan.

Harvey, D. (1989) *The Condition of Post Modernity,* Oxford, Blackwell.

Herbert, D. (1982) *The Geography of Urban Crime,* London, Longman.

Jones, G.S. (1971) *Outcast London,* Oxford, Oxford University Press.

Katz, J. (1989) *The Undeserving Poor,* New York, Pantheon.

Keating, P. (1973) 'Fact and fiction in the East End', in Dyos, H.J. and Wolff, M. (eds) *The Victorian City,* 2 vols, London, Routledge and Kegan Paul.

Keith, M. (1993a) 'From punishment to discipline? Racism, racialization and the policing of social control', in Cross and Keith (eds).

Keith, M. (1993b) *Race, Riots and Policing*, London, UCL Press. (Extract reprinted as 'Criminalization and racialization' in Muncie *et al.*, 1996.)

Lee, M. (1995) 'London: community damage limitation and the future of drug enforcement', in Dorn, N., Jepsen, Y. and Savona, E. (eds) *European Drug Policies and Enforcement,* London, Macmillan.

Mayhew, H. (1851–62) *London Labour and the London Poor,* 4 vols, reprinted 1967, London, Cass.

Morris, L. (1993) *Dangerous Classes,* London, Routledge and Kegan Paul.

Muncie, J., McLaughlin, E. and Langan, M. (eds) (1996) *Criminological Perspectives: A Reader,* London, Sage in association with The Open University.

Murray, C. (1990) *The Emerging Underclass*, London, Institute of Economic Affairs. (Extract reprinted as 'The underclass' in Muncie *et al.*, 1996.)

Newman, O. (1973) *Defensible Space,* London, Architectural Press.

Painter, K. (1992) 'Different worlds: the spatial, temporal and social dimensions of female victimization', in Evans, D., Fyfe, N. and Herbert, D. (eds) *Crime, Policing and Place*, London, Routledge and Kegan Paul.

Park, R.E., Burgess, E.W. and MacKenzie R.D. (1925) *The City*, Chicago, University of Chicago Press.

Pearson, G. (1975) *The Deviant Imagination*, London, Macmillan.

Rex, J. (1973) 'The sociology of a zone of transition', in Raynor, J. and Harden, J. (eds) *Cities, Communities and the Young*, London, Routledge and Kegan Paul.

Robins, D. (1992) *Tarnished Visions – Crime and Conflict in the Inner City*, Oxford, Oxford University Press.

Robson, B. (1988) *Those Inner Cities*, London, Routledge and Kegan Paul.

Savage, M. and Warde, A. (1993) *Urban Sociology, Capitalism and Modernity*, London, Macmillan.

Shaw, C.R. and McKay H.D. (1942) *Juvenile Delinquency and Urban Areas*, Chicago, University of Chicago Press.

Sherman, L.W., Gartin, P.R. and Burger, M.E. (1989) 'Hot spots of predatory crime: routine activities and the criminology of place', *Criminology*, no.27, pp.27–55.

Smith, S. (1989) 'The challenge of urban crime', in Herbert, D. and Smith D. (eds) *Social Problems and the City*, Oxford, Oxford University Press.

Thorns, D.C. (1972) *Suburbia*, London, MacGibbon and Kee.

Waddington, D., Jones, K. and Critchter, C. (1989) *Flashpoints: Studies in Public Disorder*, London, Routledge and Kegan Paul.

Walklate, S. (1996) 'Community and crime prevention', in McLaughlin, E. and Muncie, J. (eds) *Controlling Crime*, London, Sage in association with The Open University.

Walkowitz, J. (1980) *Prostitution and Victorian Society: Women, Class and the State*, New York, Cambridge University Press.

Walkowitz, J. (1992) *City of Dreadful Delight: Narratives of Sexual Danger in Late Victorian London*, London, Virago Press.

Whyte, W.F. (1959) *Street Corner Society*, Chicago, University of Chicago Press.

Young, J. (1992) 'Riotous rage of the have-nots', *Independent on Sunday*, 19 July.

Chapter 5
Dangerous Places:
The Family as a Site
of Crime

by Esther Saraga

Contents

1   Introduction

This chapter is concerned with examining the relationship between the 'family' and 'crime', and in particular with exploring the ways in which the family can be thought of as a dangerous place for family members, or as a 'site of crime'.

How we think about families is likely to be affected by our own personal life experience. However, images of dangerousness depend not only on personal experience, but also on the way in which events within families are socially constructed, and on what is considered 'normal'. We shall look at when, under what circumstances, and to whom certain forms of behaviour occurring within families become visible and when, how and by whom they are viewed as crimes. The chapter focuses mainly on those events within families usually described as 'domestic violence' and 'child abuse' (physical and sexual abuse and neglect). It is not concerned to provide a comprehensive account of theory and research on these different forms of violence and abuse; rather, they will be used selectively to examine a range of themes and ideas concerned with the nature and extent of crime in contemporary society.

More specifically, this chapter examines:

- The relationship between the 'private' world of the 'family' and the 'public' world of crime.

- The extent of 'hidden crime' within families.

- Changing historical definitions of abuse and violence within families.

- The role of the law in making this violence visible or hidden.

- The construction of family violence as 'crime' or 'non-crime'.

2   Public and private

2.1   Family as a place of safety

Conventionally, the social world is understood as divided into separate public and private spheres, with the 'family' situated firmly within the private domain. It is seen as a place of close intimate personal relationships and a haven from the rigours of the public world (of social activities such as work, politics and, indeed, crime). There is, of course, no one kind of family, but a great diversity of household arrangements in which people live; family forms vary historically, socially and culturally (Muncie *et al.*, 1995). The meaning of 'family' may also be very different for different people. For example, for many black people in the UK, 'family' may represent a place of safety and solidarity in the context of racism; many lesbians and gay men with children describe their households as 'families' even though most definitions of 'family' assume a heterosexual relationship at the centre of family life.

Despite this diversity, the ideology of the 'normal' family is so powerful that we nevertheless speak of, and seem to understand, what is meant by 'the family'. There is an 'image that the vision of the British family conjures up: an image of a settled, harmonious, wholesome and orderly unit, instilling the correct social values into its children, and capable of prudent housekeeping without needing the interference of the state and its army of functionaries to prop it up' (Blagg and Smith, 1989, p.23). Although this 'ideal' family is characterized by loyalty and harmony, it is accepted that some tensions may be seen as a normal part of family life, to be worked through. What is crucial is that family relationships appear to be self-regulatory; the need for the state to intervene in intimate family interactions is taken as a sign of failure.

the 'ideal' family

The 1950s family embodied the ideals of safety, security and a sense of identity

'Family' is also strongly associated with relationships of dependency, and is expected to be the place where vulnerable people can be safely dependent. 'Vulnerability' is associated with women, children, disabled and older people. It is within families that children should be looked after and socialized into good citizens, where older and disabled people are cared for, and where adult women, though responsible for the care of other family members, will themselves be protected by a male head. Men, it seems, do not need this kind of protection, but in return for being the protector, they receive care, domestic services and sexual intimacy.

So far we have described the representation of relationships within the ideal family. How is this safe private world linked to the dangerous public world of crime? In Chapter 4 we saw how the problem of crime has come to be understood as mainly an urban phenomenon, the city being linked in the popular imagination with dangerousness and crime. The family is often explicitly contrasted to this dangerous outside world, and seen as private, a place of safety and protection. This contrast has been highlighted at times when there has been a spate of murders or attacks on women and children. Certain neighbourhoods or areas of the city can suddenly become 'no-go areas' for women. For example, for five years from 1975 to 1980 before Peter Sutcliffe, the 'Yorkshire Ripper', was caught, women in the whole of West Yorkshire were advised not to go out alone. In emphasizing the danger of the public world, implicitly it is assumed that 'home' is the place which is 'safe' (Hanmer et al., 1989). By placing 'crime' within the public sphere, violence inside the private sphere of the family is either not seen, or, if seen, is not considered serious and not called 'crime'.

On the other hand, the family and crime are strongly linked in both popular and political discourses. Families are not seen as the sites of crime but as both the cause and cure of crime. Family 'breakdown', identified by such factors as high rates of divorce, illegitimacy, lone parenthood and lack of firm discipline for children, is assumed to be the cause of a range of social problems including, in particular, juvenile crime, the breeding ground for all adult crime (see, for example, Dennis and Erdos, 1992; Dennis, 1993; Murray, 1990, 1994). This family and crime nexus derives from a more general view of the family as the cornerstone of society, its natural building block. At the same time the family is viewed as fragile, at risk of breakdown, of contributing to an increase in crime. In this context the sequence of family breakdown → juvenile delinquency → criminality → moral malaise → threat to social/moral order is readily applied. It follows that the family can also be seen as the cure for crime. Restoration of traditional family values will, it is assumed, decrease crime and restore social order.

Family members may, of course, be the victims of crimes such as burglary, car theft, street attacks and racial violence, but crucially the danger is seen to come from outside the family. It is rarely accepted that crimes occur inside families. Except in cases judged as 'extreme' and exceptional, events that outside the family might be identified as criminal, may be seen as 'normal' within families. For example, if one adult assaults another in the street, it is likely to be considered a criminal act; but if a man hits his wife at home, this may be seen as a 'domestic argument'. Similarly, a parent hitting a child, depending on the extent of the violence, may be seen variously as 'normal' (discipline), an understandable reaction to dealing with a difficult child, an over-reaction to stress, or, at worst, 'cruelty', yet infant murders are more common than in any other age group (see Figure 5.1).

2.2 Family as a place of danger

The view of families as havens of safety and security has to be placed alongside the increased public awareness and recognition, since the 1960s, of acts of violence and abuse within families. Although violence against women and children was first identified as a serious social problem in the late nineteenth century, public concern at the time was short-lived and did not re-emerge until the second half of the twentieth century (section 4 will look at this in greater detail). Over four successive decades, different forms of violence have come to be identified: physical abuse and neglect of children in the 1960s, followed in the 1970s by concern about domestic violence, in the 1980s about child sexual abuse, and in the 1990s about the abuse of older people in their homes. Looked at from this viewpoint a very different image of the family emerges:

> War and riots aside, physical aggression occurs more often among family members than among any others. Moreover, the family is the predominant setting for every form of physical violence from slaps to torture and murder. In fact, some form of physical violence in the life cycle of family members is so likely that it can be said to be almost universal … If this is indeed the case, then violence is as typical of family relationships as is love.
>
> (Hotaling and Straus, 1980, p.4)

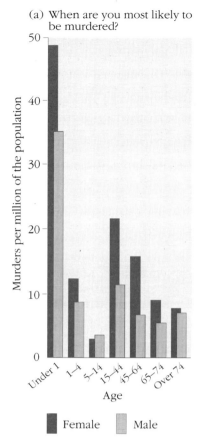

(a) When are you most likely to be murdered?

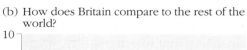

(b) How does Britain compare to the rest of the world?

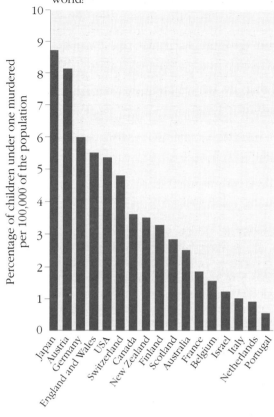

Figure 5.1 More infants are murdered than all other age groups combined (Britain, 1994) (Source: The Mail on Sunday Review, 9 October 1994, p.20)

In later sections of this chapter we shall explore the extent of such violence, and how it came to be recognized, but first we want to consider some consequences of this greater visibility. Acknowledgement of family violence has the potential to open up the private world of the family to external scrutiny, and therefore to challenge the image of the ideal family and notions of privacy. On the other hand, if we want to preserve this image intact we can deny the extent of violence in the family, or see it as exceptional, situated within a few deviant or 'dysfunctional' families.

The idea of the 'dysfunctional' family is important and will recur throughout the chapter. The ideal functional family is seen as an organic system in which all the separate parts have a particular role to play: 'The bourgeois family with its bread-winning father and dependent wife, who performs the domestic labour for the household and cares for the young and old, is seen as an harmonious organic unit successfully meeting the needs of an industrial society' (Lewis, 1986, p.32). These needs are usually described in terms of the successful socialization of children and the reproduction of national stability.

'Dysfunctional' families are those that do not conform to the traditional structure; they have 'broken down'. Almost by definition, they are assumed to be incapable of socializing their children effectively. They are characterized by abuse, neglect and lack of discipline. The families most

the 'dysfunctional' family

commonly described in this way are those seen as 'different' from the ideal: for example, lone parents, working-class or black families, lesbian or gay parents. Far from challenging the dominant views, these exceptions to the rule further strengthen the importance of the traditional ideas. So long as violence and abuse can be identified with a group of families that are different or deviant, the image of the 'normal' family can be preserved.

There is another way of trying to make sense of the apparent contradictions about the family and crime. This involves challenging the image of the traditional family, and the naturalness attributed to the distinction between public and private. First, there are numerous ways in which the state does intervene in family life, while at the same time maintaining the fiction of the private autonomous family (Lewis, 1986; Rose, 1989). Second, the 'family' is discussed as if it were homogeneous; rarely is it disaggregated – that is, broken up into its component parts. 'Usually "the family" becomes the representation of the interests of the family head, if it is a man, carrying an assumption that all family members share his interests' (Gordon, 1989, p.296). As a result, divisions of age and gender, and the associated relationships of power and dependency within the family, are rendered either invisible or natural. Violence against women and children from strangers, which are events in the 'public' domain, fits in well with everyday notions of 'crime', but there is a reluctance to extend the idea of 'crime' to the private domain of the family, even though it is here where children and older people are more likely to be attacked.

2.3 Competing perspectives on family violence

Although violence in the family has been 'rediscovered' as a social problem, there is no agreement on how it should be viewed or understood. Is it normal, pathological, criminal, or a violation of human rights? From these different perspectives arise disagreements about where responsibility for such violence lies (whether with offenders, victims or the structure of society), and about the appropriate form of intervention.

ACTIVITY 5.1

Pause for a moment and think about the kinds of violence that occur in families. How would you explain why such violence occurs? Would you adopt different explanations for different forms of violence? Is such violence criminal? Jot down a few notes of your own on these questions.

COMMENT

Violence in the family is described in a variety of different ways. You may have thought of some or all of the following:

*   *It is an inevitable part of family life*
    (slapping a child as part of discipline is acceptable to many people; for others it may be regrettable but also understandable).
*   *It is pathological*
    (those who are violent within the family must be deviant or mentally ill).

- *It is a product of family breakdown or deviation from traditional family structures*
  (in 'normal' families, everyone has an appropriate part to play, according to their age and gender. Tensions and conflicts can then be managed without violence occurring. However, if the family is 'broken' or 'deviant' then these roles are disrupted, and violence is seen as a possible outcome).

- *It is the result of social conditions*
  (physical violence and neglect are often understood as the outcome of stress, derived from material conditions such as poverty or unemployment).

- *It is a product of power inequalities of gender and generation*
  (many feminists emphasize the inequalities between men and women under patriarchy; advocates of children's rights focus on the low social status and lack of power of children and the way in which they are seen as the property of their parents).

- *It is a product of masculinity/the abuse of male power*
  (some feminists describe a 'continuum' of male violence, an extension of 'normal masculinity' – see Kelly, 1988b. In the early 1990s, attention was drawn more generally to the relationship between masculinity and crime, recognizing that most crimes are carried out by men – see, for example, **Segal, 1990**; Campbell, 1993).

It will be useful to keep these different perspectives in mind while reading the rest of the chapter. We shall return to them in the final section to examine the implications of different approaches for viewing the family as a site of crime.

3 Violence and abuse in the family

In Chapter 1 we saw some of the difficulties that arise in defining 'crime' and in establishing the extent of crime. Violence within the family is an example of 'hidden crime'. It appears very infrequently in either the official crime statistics or those gathered through victim surveys such as the British Crime Surveys.

hidden crime

Why might it be particularly difficult to collect reliable information on violence within the family?

The first difficulty arises in deciding what is 'normal' behaviour within families, and what is abusive or violent. Even if we could establish some agreement on this, knowledge about what goes on in families is hard to obtain. By their very nature, acts of violence and abuse within families are events that take place 'behind closed doors'. Those on the receiving end may not tell anyone: they may think that no-one will believe them; be frightened of retaliation from the aggressor; feel responsible for the violence themselves, or too ashamed or embarrassed to tell; or they may fear the consequences of telling – for themselves, for the aggressor or for their whole family or community. Reporting may be particularly difficult if the abuser is someone they also love and on whom they are dependent. While physical violence may result in injuries visible to an outsider, sexual violence may leave no visible signs, and may be justified by its perpetrators as an expression of love, rendering it even more hidden. Most crucially perhaps, a general reluctance to believe that family violence exists means that it remains invisible.

3.1 Terminology and definitions

domestic violence

'Domestic violence, family violence, domestic disputes, spouse abuse, wife abuse, woman abuse, battered wives, battered women … There is a plethora of terms which are used, sometimes almost interchangeably, to describe the same phenomenon' (Smith, 1989, p.1). Yet each of these terms conveys a different meaning. 'Domestic violence' does not distinguish between violence perpetrated by women or by men, even though the conclusion from research is that women are overwhelmingly the victims of such violence. On the other hand: 'the term "domestic violence"… helps to emphasize – in a way that the terms "abuse" and "disputes" do not – that what is being examined *is* violence, not arguments or minor altercations, but violence' (Smith, 1989, p.1). But how do we decide what is a normal and acceptable private dispute or altercation, and what is unacceptable? Straus *et al.* (1980) 'distinguished between "ordinary" or "normal" (*sic*) violence within the family and "severe" or "abusive violence". "Ordinary" or "normal" violence was defined as "throwing things, pushing, grabbing and slapping"' (Smith, 1989, p.11). As we shall see later, police responses to incidents of domestic violence are very much influenced by the perceived severity of the violence, whether or not physical injuries have been sustained. But the threat of violence can be extremely powerful and many women live in fear, controlled by threats rather than by actual violence.

child abuse
child sexual abuse

A wide range of terminology also exists for describing violence against children. Terms that have been used since the 1960s include: 'battered babies', 'non-accidental injury', 'failure to thrive', 'neglect', 'emotional deprivation', 'child abuse', 'incest' and 'child sexual abuse'. The word 'violence' itself is rarely used. Again, different terms convey different meanings. For example, there has been some debate about the use of the terms 'incest' and 'child sexual abuse'. Legally, the former must involve penetration, and is restricted to a particular set of family relationships. It has also been criticized for underplaying the force, threat and coercion frequently used by abusers (Allan, 1978; MacLeod and Saraga, 1988; Kelly, 1988a; Saraga, 1993).

elder abuse

Terminology to describe the abuse of older people by their carers (formal or informal) has also varied. In the 1970s reference was made in medical journals to 'granny battering'; discussions in the 1990s refer to 'elder abuse'. As with child abuse and domestic violence, it has been recognized that the abuse can take different forms – physical, emotional, sexual and neglect. In addition, many older people are robbed or cheated by carers who are supposed to be managing their money, and this is described in the literature as 'financial abuse'.

The usefulness of a new category of 'elder abuse' has been questioned. Most of the abusive acts would fit into legal definitions of crime such as common assault, grievous bodily harm, or theft. It has also been suggested that the term 'elder abuse' is unhelpful as it is too emotive, and because it restricts concern to one particular group of vulnerable adults, excluding, for example, younger adults with learning difficulties (*Community Care*, 22 July 1993, p.22).

Definitions of family violence inevitably involve judgements about what is 'normal' in family life. Let us explore this further, focusing on the boundaries between 'good parenting' and 'child abuse'. In general, what is considered good parenting is defined in terms of the dominant norms of a society, so that in the UK it is associated with the child-rearing patterns of white middle-class families. These ideas are not static, but change over time. For example, in the period following the Second World War, motherhood was idealized, and 'good mothers' were urged to stay at home with young children to avoid the 'maternal deprivation' that would result from separation. Whilst these ideas still exist, there is much greater acceptance today of alternative forms of child care for young children. In the post-war period, the majority of 'working mothers' were working class, many of whom attempted to become 'better' mothers by working part-time. Many black women who came to the UK as immigrants and 'had to leave their children behind until they were settled, or who had to work at jobs for long hours and low pay, were seen already to have failed as mothers' (Williams, 1989, p.163). Thus child-rearing practices associated with groups seen as different in terms of class, 'race' or 'culture' tend to be judged to be at best inferior and at worst abusive. On the other hand, practices associated with the British ruling class, such as sending children to boarding school at a very young age, which could be argued to be emotionally damaging to children, are unlikely to be judged in this way.

At various times particular aspects of child care may be highlighted and give rise to moral panics. In the early 1990s, for example, media attention was given to young children left at home by their parents (called 'home alone' children after a popular film of that title). In 1993, particular concern was expressed at Christmas – a time that is associated with 'family', even though child-protection agencies receive information about such children all the year round. A second example concerns the question of whether parents have a 'right to chastise' their children in whatever way they deem appropriate, including the use of physical punishments. Again in the early 1990s, 'smacking' became an issue of public controversy and debate.

ACTIVITY 5.2

What do you think might be the relationship between smacking and child abuse? It would be useful to jot down a few of your own ideas on this. Later in the chapter you will be asked to consider why physical punishment was a particular concern of the early 1990s for another reason – as a form of discipline, and whether there is a link between a lack of discipline and crime.

COMMENT

Those in favour of smacking argue that it is a necessary and effective form of discipline which teaches children right from wrong. They suggest that it is easy to distinguish between legitimate punishment and abuse: 'Surely there's a big difference between the deliberate infliction of cruelty on helpless children and a parent correcting his child the same way he was corrected? I have caned my son when necessary just as my father did to me' (a father quoted by Sinason, 1993, p.24).

Opponents of smacking and corporal punishment argue that: 'we now have the social anomaly that children are the only people who can be hit with relative impunity in their own homes' (Sinason, 1993, p.24). They argue that its supporters confuse the need to discipline and socialize children with the need to punish. They suggest that physical punishments are not necessary, and not effective, in the sense that most smacked children go on misbehaving, thus needing to be smacked more and more. They do not believe it is possible to draw clear boundaries between smacking and abuse. Smacking as a form of discipline is widespread in the UK (Newson and Newson, 1970, 1989), and Jones argues that: 'our society ... places a high premium on the infliction of pain as necessary or inevitable in the rearing of children. It seems probable that this creates a context in which child abuse is more likely' (Jones *et al.*, 1987, p.27). This is particularly the case as 'parents who injure their children ... more often than not relate the event to a concept of punishment, even when they accept that they "went too far"' (Jones *et al.*, 1987, p.27).

The cover of The No Smacking Guide to Good Behaviour – *a campaign leaflet by Penelope Leach, of End Physical Punishment of Children (EPOCH)*

3.2   Research

Research into the extent of family violence reflects many of the general difficulties, described in Chapter 1, in gaining an accurate picture of the 'true facts' of crime. We shall outline here some particular factors affecting research into violence in the family and indicate some research findings which may help you to judge for yourself whether or not the family should indeed be considered a site of crime.

Examining these factors is important not only because it helps us to interpret research findings, but also because it can shed more light on the nature of the phenomena being studied. For example, one of the first difficulties encountered is to decide what is meant by the 'extent' of violence. Research studies may give figures for the incidence of violence (the number of such acts occurring), or for its prevalence (how common it is). But attempts to count acts of violence reveal that, unlike a crime such as burglary, these forms of violence are hard to count as they are rarely experienced as discrete incidents. They are more likely to be prolonged and habitual, often lasting for years. Figures obtained will also depend on how questions are asked and who is asking them. People may be reluctant to talk about such painful experiences, or, if filling in a questionnaire, find it difficult to fit their experiences into the categories provided.

Estimates will also vary according to the definitions of violence that are used. As Smith argues in relation to domestic violence:

Sometimes in the research this is restricted to purely physical abuse resulting in bodily harm – with distinctions being drawn between levels of severity of injury – whereas, on other occasions, violence is defined as incorporating both physical and psychological abuse and sometimes sexual abuse. Problems also arise in respect of which relationships are defined as 'domestic'. Sometimes this is restricted to legally married couples living together but other research studies include co-habiting couples within their definitions and some include separated and divorced couples.

(Smith, 1989, p.7)

There have been no comprehensive studies in the UK attempting to estimate the extent of different forms of violence in the family for the population as a whole. Estimates have been obtained from a variety of sources including criminal statistics, studies of homicides and violent assaults, data collected by child-protection agencies, surveys, and child custody and divorce cases in the civil courts. The findings vary enormously. Smith (1989) suggests that it is necessary to get a composite picture from a variety of sources, since individually each has its own limitations, and each is likely to provide an underestimate.

Let us consider a few of these research findings. One source of evidence – criminal statistics – is likely to represent a very tiny proportion of violent events. As we shall see later, many such events are never reported to the police, and, even when they are, result in few prosecutions and fewer convictions (Smith, 1989). Overall, more men than women are victims of homicide (381 men compared with 228 women in England and Wales in 1990), but this gender difference changes dramatically when we consider only those homicides by spouses or co-habitees, past or present (19 men compared with 86 women) (Levi, 1994).

Highest estimates of domestic violence come from those – usually fairly small-scale – surveys carried out by feminist researchers, who have designed their studies in a way that will facilitate women disclosing personal, painful information of this kind. For example, Hanmer and Saunders (1984) interviewed 129 women in a small community in Yorkshire. Fifty-nine of the women had experienced incidents of 'threats, violence or sexual harassment' during the past year, and 21 per cent of these incidents had occurred in their own homes.

In a survey of 1,007 women, Painter (1991) found that marital rape was by far the commonest form of rape experienced, being seven times as common as rape by a stranger. Fourteen per cent of the women had been raped by their husbands, and in most of these cases violence had been used or threatened. Eighty per cent of these women said the rape occurred frequently; 84 per cent were living with their husbands when the rape took place. At that time in England and Wales such acts were not legally defined as crimes. (The crime of rape has been applied to cases involving cohabiting men and women in Scotland since 1989 and in England and Wales since 1991.) Perhaps not surprisingly, therefore, only three out of 140 victims had reported the rape to the police. The reported incidence of rape in Scotland was twice as high as in the rest of the UK, though it is not possible to say whether this is because rape is more common in Scotland, or whether the legal recognition of marital rape as a crime led to more women reporting it. In the same study Painter also found a high incidence of physical violence. Thirty-three per cent of all the women had been hit by their husbands, whereas 70 per cent of those who had been raped had also been hit – and not only as part of the sexual violence.

Official data on child abuse are available from statistics on child-protection registers held by the National Society for the Prevention of Cruelty to Children (NSPCC) or local authorities. These figures are therefore restricted to 'the cases which have been identified and notified by the professional networks' (Creighton and Noyes, 1989, p.1). Table 5.1, taken from the NSPCC report of child-abuse trends in England and Wales for 1983–87, shows the incidence of different forms of abuse in terms of the categories for registering children as in need of protection. Over these five years: 'the physical injury

Table 5.1 Number of registered children by year and reason for registration

	1983	%	1984	%	1985	%	1986	%	1987	%
Physically injured	675	(60)	707	(63)	909	(57)	938	(44)	808	(35)
Sexual abuse	51	(5)	98	(9)	223	(14)	533	(25)	640	(28)
Neglect	62	(6)	50	(4)	73	(5)	124	(6)	126	(6)
Failure to thrive	15	(1)	34	(3)	28	(2)	46	(2)	50	(2)
Emotional abuse	31	(3)	18	(2)	22	(1)	41	(2)	34	(1)
Total abused	834	(75)	907	(81)	1,255	(79)	1,682	(78)[1]	1,658	(72)
'At risk' cases	278	(25)	209	(19)	355	(21)	461	(22)	647	(28)
Accidental injuries	3		1		1		1		2	
Total registered	1,115	(100)	1,117	(100)	1,591[1]	(100)	2,144	(100)[1]	2,307	(100)
Rate per 1,000 under 15's[2]	1.16		1.16		1.68		2.32		2.50	
Rate per 1,000 under 17's	1.05		1.06		1.55		2.18		2.36	

Notes:

1   Discrepancies in totals as in original source.

2   (Office of Population Censuses and Surveys) population estimates.

Source: Creighton and Noyes, 1989, p.4, Table 1

rate increased from 0.63 per thousand children under 17 in 1983 to 0.82 per thousand in 1987, whilst *the sexual abuse rate increased from 0.08 to 0.65 per thousand children over the same period'* (Creighton and Noyes, 1989, p.5). This dramatic increase in sexual-abuse cases presumably reflects the growing awareness among professionals of such abuse, during this period.

Since 1989 such data have been collated nationally for England. In 1989, 23,000 new cases were registered; by 1993 the figure was 26,500 (Department of Health, 1994). Creighton and Noyes point out that: 'Children who come to the notice of professionals and public agencies tend to be those where the abuse cannot be disguised or where other factors give cause for concern' (Creighton and Noyes, 1989, p.1). These figures, therefore, are again likely to be an underestimate.

Higher estimates of child sexual abuse have been obtained from surveys of adults. Reviewing a range of studies in the literature, Kelly *et al.* (1991) found that figures for child sexual abuse ranged from 12 per cent to 62 per cent for women, and from 4 per cent to 31 per cent for men. Their own study showed how the definition of sexual abuse employed can have a dramatic effect on estimates of prevalence, which varied from 50 per cent to 5 per cent for women and from 27 per cent to 2 per cent for men, depending on which reported 'unwanted sexual experiences' they decided to include as 'sexual abuse'.

Research data show that, in relation to domestic violence, overwhelmingly it is women who are on the receiving end (Dobash and Dobash, 1980; Smith, 1989). Sexual abuse is also perpetrated predominantly by men (Kelly *et al.*, 1991). The relationships of physical abuse, emotional abuse and neglect to gender are less straightforward. The statistics derived from child-abuse registers show that women are involved in far more such incidents than men. However, these figures do not take account of the fact that many children live only with their mother. More careful analysis of the data shows, for example, that if men are living with children they are more likely to abuse children physically: 'natural mothers were implicated in 36% and natural fathers in 61% of the injury cases where the child was living with them' (Creighton and Noyes, 1989, p.21). In cases of neglect it is difficult to identify a perpetrator, since neglect implies an act of omission rather than commission. The fact that the NSPCC tables do name mothers as the majority of abusers in neglect cases 'can be interpreted as more of a moral judgement as to which parent should be supplying the child's needs' (Creighton and Noyes, 1989, p.22). Reported levels of child abuse are skewed in terms of class and 'race': facts that should be interpreted in the context of both the greater contact that working-class and black families have with a range of state agencies, and also the way in which definitions of abuse are judged against a norm of white middle-class life. Surveys of adult survivors certainly suggest that sexual abuse occurs in all social groups (Kelly *et al.*, 1991). The issue is less clear-cut in relation to physical abuse of children, where the greater incidence in working-class families is attributed by some authors to stress-inducing material conditions as well as being an artefact of reporting processes (see Parton, 1985, 1991).

Researching the prevalence of elder abuse is also extremely difficult. Like other aspects of family violence, it is hidden by taking place within the private realm of the family. The elderly victims are often reluctant to speak about it, and most of the carers deny that their actions are abusive. As for child abuse, evidence is derived largely from social services records, though in the case of older people there is no statutory responsibility to investigate and record such events. Research in the USA suggests that between 2 per cent and 10 per cent of people over 65 are at risk of abuse. Writers in the UK refer to 3 million being at risk (see, for example, Penhale, 1993; Eastman, 1994).

Although it is not possible to give precise figures for the prevalence of the various forms of abuse, it does seem that, for many women, children and dependent adults, home is indeed a dangerous place. If that is so, then we need to consider why this danger is hardly recognized, and to examine factors contributing to its invisibility.

4 Changing definitions: a history of visibility and invisibility

'Throughout history children have been subjected to the kind of treatment we now call abuse and neglect' (Parton, 1985, p.21). Others have argued similarly that what we consider to be domestic violence has always occurred (see, for example, Dobash and Dobash, 1980). However, violence in the family has not always been recognized as a social problem. It has only been on the agenda for public concern since the 1960s, with different forms of violence being recognized in successive decades. As each kind of abuse was recognized it was presented as if it were an entirely new problem, or at least a problem that had been permanently hidden and was being discovered for the first time.

The difficulties of finding out what goes on in 'such an intimate and private setting as the family' (May, 1978, p.135) are even greater when seeking historical evidence. It was not until the late nineteenth century that violence against women and children was first recognized as a serious social problem requiring state intervention, but the public interest did not last: 'Indeed the intermittent nature of public concern is the most striking historical feature of the problem, and is reflected in the paucity of historical research into this aspect of family relationships' (May, 1978, p.135).

It will be useful to outline some of the main features of the historical developments in the identification of, and responses to, various behaviours within families since the late nineteenth century, in order to identify some of the factors that have influenced how family violence has become visible and the form that visibility has taken. (For more detailed discussions see Gordon, 1989; Dobash and Dobash, 1980, 1992; Pinchbeck and Hewitt, 1973; May, 1978; Parton, 1985.)

4.1 The late nineteenth century

4.1.1 Child abuse

Surveying the situation of children in Britain in the late eighteenth and early nineteenth centuries, May (1978) suggests that there was a universal belief in the sanctity of parental rights, including the moderate use of chastisement. Physical punishment was probably a normal part of childhood. However, as we saw in Chapters 3 and 4 of this volume, during the nineteenth century there were growing concerns about the general level of violence in society. By the end of the century, a problem of *family* violence was identified, defined mainly in terms of 'cruelty' to children. The response of the upper-class charity workers involved with the voluntary societies was one of 'saving' or 'rescuing' these children. This historical period is particularly significant because it was during that time that a new response to family violence developed, with the establishment of Societies for the Protection of Children (SPCCs), leading to legal changes and the establishment of new 'crimes'. The first SPCC was set up in New York in 1871 following publicity about the case of Mary Ellen Wilson who had been treated very cruelly by her adoptive parents: 'She was only rescued after a judge interpreted the word "animal", under laws against cruelty to animals, to include children' (Morgan and Zedner, 1992, p.8).

Events in England were influenced directly by what had happened in the USA. The first SPCC (in Liverpool in 1883) grew out of an appeal for a dog's home, which was extended to an appeal for the protection of children, at a meeting of the Society for the Prevention of Cruelty to Animals. The National Society for the Prevention of Cruelty to Children (NSPCC) was founded in 1889 and gained its Royal Charter in 1895, 20 years after the equivalent society for animals, the Royal Society for the Prevention of Cruelty to Animals (RSPCA). As Conley comments: 'authorities were very slow to act against child abuse. In Harold Perkin's memorable phrase, the English in the nineteenth century "diminished cruelty to animals, criminals, lunatics and children (in that order)"' (Conley, 1991, p.105).

This low status of children was reflected in lenient sentences for the killing of children. For example, in a study of the criminal justice system in

Kent, Conley found that, from 1859 to 1880, of those convicted of killing adult males 55 per cent were hanged and 25 per cent served 18 months or less; for those convicted of killing children the equivalent figures were 21 per cent and 68 per cent (Conley, 1991, p.111). Sentences for killing children varied with age, with the death of a baby less than 48 hours old not being seen as very serious: 'You cannot estimate the loss to the child itself, you know nothing about it at all. It creates no alarm to the public' (St James Fitzjames giving evidence to the Capital Punishment Commission 1866, quoted by Conley, 1991, p.110).

The authorities did not wish to challenge the 'unshakeable faith in the sacred bonds between parent and child' (Conley, 1991, p.105), or the common law rights of parents. Nor did they wish to be seen to be intervening in personal or familial matters: 'The evils you state are enormous and indisputable, but they are of so private, internal and domestic a character as to be beyond the reach of legislation, and the subject, indeed, would not, I think, be entertained in either House of Parliament' (Lord Shaftesbury 1871, quoted in Pinchbeck and Hewitt, 1973, p.622). It seems that the law was only to be used when there was a clear threat to the public interest.

As a result of campaigns by the SPCCs and other voluntary organizations, various legal changes were introduced. In 1889 the Prevention of Cruelty to, and Better Protection of, Children Act was passed, through which cruelty to and neglect of children became a criminal offence for the first time. Punishment was to be 'confined to acts of wilful cruelty, that is, to acts of criminal intention, and not to cases of neglect due to ignorance, poverty, or any of the other prevailing evils of the time' (Pinchbeck and Hewitt, 1973, p.623). This 'was an essentially criminal rather than a social welfare approach' (Parton, 1985, p.35). Concern about children was very largely a result of the links made between parental cruelty and the threat of delinquency, and the wider anxiety about the disorderly nature of working-class family life.

Other campaigning organizations focused on the sexual abuse of children, particularly young girls, and there was public concern about the sale of young girls into prostitution, and a desire expressed by the social purity movements 'to protect girls from the sexual attentions of their adult male relatives, particularly in the overcrowded slums of urban areas' (Morgan and Zedner, 1992, p.10). Again, abuse was associated with the 'dangerous classes'. The 1885 Criminal Law Amendment Act raised the age of consent for sexual intercourse from 13 years to 16 years. The aim was to deter men from abusing mainly working-class girls, but it also led to greater surveillance of these girls, who could be legally defined as in moral danger and incarcerated 'for their own good'.

The 1885 legislation was seen to provide inadequate protection for girls within their own families: 'But it was also felt that incest was particularly heinous because of the bonds of kinship that it violated and that it therefore required a unique form of sanction' (Smart, 1989, p.53). In 1908 the Punishment of Incest Act was passed. For the first time sexual relations between people within families were treated as crimes by the law. Definitions of incest within this law were restricted to certain sexual acts and to particular blood relations. Step-daughters were explicitly excluded from protection, suggesting that the main concern was with 'the "unnaturalness" of the offence rather than the question of an abuse of authority or the exploitation of a minor' (Smart, 1989, p.54). Although this law made it possible to prosecute men for incest, it was rarely used. In 1956 these two Acts were consolidated into the 1956 Sexual Offences Act, and they remain the basis for such criminal prosecutions today.

4.1.2 Violence against wives

conjugal violence

By the middle of the nineteenth century in Britain there was also considerable public concern about violence against wives. Conjugal violence 'was depicted as one facet of the generalized "savagery" of the uncivilized masses, reflected in their brutal sports and pastimes, and the frequency of street brawls in which women often participated' (May, 1978, p.142). Two groups campaigned around this issue: law-enforcement agencies concerned about the general level of violent crime, since 'a man who assaulted his wife might easily attack others or transfer his aggression to the streets' (May, 1978, p.143); and feminists agitating for the emancipation of women. No specific laws were enacted to criminalize violence against wives, though such assaults could be included within the 1861 Offences Against the Person Act.

In practice, 'judges … did little to challenge the patriarchal privilege of legitimate chastisement of wives' (Dobash and Dobash, 1992, p.155). This reluctance reflected the belief that men had usually been provoked, as well as concerns about disrupting the marriage bond. These views were challenged by women's groups, resulting in the first changes in the law. In 1878 the first of the Matrimonial Causes Acts offered a civil remedy to women. They could obtain a separation order if their husband was convicted of *aggravated* assault and if they were considered in *grave* danger. Witnesses to a parliamentary committee in 1874, hearing evidence on violence against children and wives, 'expressed some concern for brutally assaulted wives but voiced little concern for women experiencing "ordinary" assaults' (Dobash and Dobash, 1992, p.157). Domestic violence was treated with ambivalence. Women might be seen as provoking the attack, or taking advantage of the new laws to bring malicious complaints or disgrace to their husbands, since the disgrace appeared to stem from the public knowledge of the event rather than from the violence itself. The abuse might also be 'legitimate chastisement' by the husband.

right to chastise

IN 1877, A MAN COULD BEAT HIS WIFE WITH A STICK – IF IT WAS NO THICKER THAN HIS THUMB

SO WHAT'S CHANGED?

WOMEN'S AID FEDERATION (ENGLAND) LTD
PO BOX 391, BRISTOL, BS99 7WS
TEL: 0272 428368 (helpline) 0272 420611 (admin)

Attitudes to those on the receiving end of violence were structured through gender, class and 'race':

> In order to merit protection a woman had to be obedient, submissive, and incapable of defending herself. Chivalry was reserved for those women who both needed and deserved protection – a relatively select group. The right to protection was based on the assumption that women were weaker, softer, and generally very different from the strong men who protected them. Therefore protection was often reserved for middle class women. While it was possible for a working class woman to be respectable, some of the more delicate aspects of the feminine ideal were clearly beyond her.

> (Conley, 1991, p.71)

'A man of "good character" could usually chastise an "immoral" or "irritating" wife or girlfriend with relative immunity' (Conley, 1991, p.79). Most judges subscribed to the view that: 'a good man had the right to beat a bad woman' (Conley, 1991, p.80) and for the violence to be truly wicked the women had to be defenceless. The men who were not of good character were those from the 'dangerous classes' or immigrants. Even feminist social reformers such as Frances Power Cobbe, who campaigned vigorously on this issue, saw men who assaulted their wives as 'predominantly Irish immigrants who were distinct from the civilized English males who were the "natural" inhabitants of Britain' (Dobash and Dobash, 1992, p.235).

Women were seen as the property of men: 'A respectable woman belonged to one man, going from her father's possession to that of her husband' (Conley, 1991, p.77). A woman who did not fulfil her expected role might expect to be chastised. Thus adultery, failure to do all the cooking and cleaning, working outside the home, being verbally abusive or drunk, were all seen as extenuations for the violence. To a considerable extent domestic violence was seen as a normal part of marriage.

ACTIVITY 5.3

Many of the developments described here laid the foundation for responses to family violence today. Before continuing, make a few notes on what seem to be the key points. You will be able to check your response as you read on.

COMMENT

Although the laws passed at the end of the nineteenth century have laid the basis for criminal prosecutions, the definitions and understanding of different forms of family violence have undergone many changes in the intervening period. For example, although 'cruelty' is the forerunner of our term 'child abuse', 'it is subtly but importantly different … The former was a moralistic notion directing attention to the cruel culprit … more than to the victim' (Gordon, 1989, p.20). This moral tone reflected the social movements that drew attention to the problem: 'It shared the feminist emphasis on illegitimate male power, the moralism characteristic of the social purity (anti-drinking, anti-prostitution) campaigns, and the socially elite assumptions of both' (Gordon, 1989, p.20). Views of culprits were structured not only through gender, but also through 'race' and class. They were seen as primarily the 'disorderly working class' and 'immigrant poor'. As mentioned above, to a large extent men were seen as having the right to chastise their wives and children, so that both child abuse and domestic violence were seen as normal parts of family life.

4.2 From 1900 to the 1960s

Concern at the end of the nineteenth century was focused on saving children, but by the beginning of the twentieth century violence against women and children was de-emphasized. Instead, the focus was on the standards of family life, amidst increasing concern with 'national efficiency' and children as 'national assets' (May, 1978, p.155). Brutalized or neglected children represented a 'wastage' of national resources, and eugenic concerns about the quality of the 'race' lay behind much of the alarm about incest.

Gordon (1989) describes the development in the USA of a new group of middle-class 'experts' – professional social workers – who set the standards of family life. In the UK, too, this was a period of welfare reforms characterized by 'much more direct state intervention which for women meant an attempt to regulate and supervise their domestic lives' (Williams, 1989, p.151) and by the professionalization of different types of social work, especially in child welfare and probation, giving these experts the authority to define the nature and consequences of family violence.

neglect   Attention shifted from cruelty to the neglect of children, with little or no attention paid to wife beating and incest. Previous feminist concerns were seen now as moralistic and unscientific, in contrast with the scientific judgements of the new experts, particularly psychologists. The idea of a male crime of wife beating was replaced by the idea of mutual violence between husband and wife induced by stressful conditions. Sexual assaults were seen to occur at the hands of 'perverted strangers'. The focus of concern also shifted away from the perpetrator of the assault towards the 'victim' who was likely to be seen as both sexually delinquent and criminal. Gordon (1989) analyses these changes in the context of the decline of feminism, though we can see how developments within welfare and the growth of particular kinds of professional expertise also played an important role.

The more general concerns about 'national efficiency' directed attention to the distinction between, on the one hand, state support for respectable working-class families and, on the other hand, reinforcement of the state's power to prosecute cruel parents and to take over parental responsibility from the 'disreputable'. Responsibility for intervention had shifted from the Poor Law and philanthropic societies to the state in the form of local authorities. Their role was defined in terms of social welfare as explicitly preventative, with coercion held in readiness for those who would not conform to the moral standards of family life. The 1908 Children Act consolidated previous legislation and remained essentially unchanged until 1933. Although concerned with cruelty and neglect, its prime focus was delinquency: 'In effect cruelty and neglect were not conceptualized or legislated for as independent from delinquency' (Parton, 1985, p.38).

In 1933 the Children and Young Persons Act established for the first time the 'welfare principle' which has continued up to the 1990s to inform all state intervention in relation to children:

> Every court in dealing with a child or young person who is brought before it, either as an offender or otherwise, shall have regard to the welfare of the child or young person and shall in a proper case take steps for removing him from undesirable surroundings, and for securing that proper provision is made for his education and training.

(Children and Young Person's Act, 1933, s.44(1))

Parton (1985) suggests that two central themes from the nineteenth century continued up until the Second World War. The goal of intervention was as much to prevent delinquency as to protect children, and the primary way of acting in the interests of the child's welfare has been to remove the child from his or her home. Cruelty and neglect were subsumed into more general concerns about delinquency, and both child abuse and delinquency were seen to result from family or environmental circumstances. Children, as victims or offenders, whether considered deprived or depraved, were to be treated the same. As a result, it has often been difficult to distinguish between these two categories of children. Though described in terms of welfare, the emphasis on removal of children can be seen as a legal version of the nineteenth-century strategy of 'rescue'. Clear gender differences were apparent in the use of care orders to protect children. Girls were more likely to be seen to be in 'moral danger', whereas boys were more likely to be seen as criminal or at least potentially criminal.

Although domestic violence was addressed by the Suffragette movement, it became marginalized in relation to the central issue of securing the vote for women, which, it was assumed, would allow them to address all other problems. The dominant public view was that the problem of violence against wives no longer existed.

Experiences during the Second World War had a significant impact on views of the family, leading to what was seen as a more positive and supportive approach. Evacuations had produced evidence of wide-scale neglect and deprivation. The major concern about children shifted to those in public care, leading eventually to the 1948 Children Act, described as the last in a series of post-war statutes that together 'represented a "family charter", which strengthened and supported the family as never before' (Pinchbeck and Hewitt, 1973, p.651).

The emphasis in the post-war welfare policies was to maintain the stability of the family. Motherhood was idealized, and primary concern about child abuse focused on 'emotional deprivation' caused by mothers going out to work. As we saw in section 3.1, working-class and black women were particularly likely to be labelled as 'bad mothers'.

The aim of policy and practice was not to punish parents but to act in the best interest of children and, wherever possible, to try to maintain them in their family. But the primary concern continued to be with delinquency, as reflected in a series of government reports and resulting in the Children and Young Person's Act 1969 which abolished the previously used distinction between 'deprived' and 'depraved' children. As Parton says: 'any reference to children as victims was lost. It is almost as if it was assumed that a conflict of interest between child, parents and the state had disappeared and the nineteenth century problems of cruelty and neglect had been virtually abolished' (Parton, 1985, p.45). Sexual abuse was almost entirely invisible.

'Wife beating' was seen as part of a general picture of 'problem families'. The women were portrayed as 'bad mothers, bad managers, slatternly and probably nagging or vituperative wives' (Wilson, 1983, p.87). They were probably responsible for provoking the violence or even seeking it out, and they were seen as being in need of treatment themselves. The relationship between state and family was based on the ideal of the nuclear family with traditional gender roles: 'within this paradigm wife beating was easily seen as merely an extreme form, although rather an unfortunate one, of *appropriate masculine* behaviour '(Wilson, 1983, p.87).

4.3   The 'rediscovery' of family violence

Since the 1960s there has been a gradual rediscovery of different forms of violence and abuse within families. In the 1960s abuse of children in the form of 'battered babies' was 'discovered' by the medical profession who constructed such abuse as a 'disease' resulting from family breakdown. The initial discovery was followed, during the next three decades, by a series of scandals concerning children who died at the hands of a parent or step-parent or while in the care of the local authority. Although the adults concerned were prosecuted, the main responsibility for intervening in cases of child abuse remained with social workers, and each scandal resulted in a public inquiry leading to a tightening up of the welfare policies and practices (Parton, 1985, 1991; Frost and Stein, 1989).

Gordon (1989) associates this new visibility of family violence with the development of various radical social movements (civil rights, student and women's movements), all of which, in different ways, challenged the sanctity of family privacy and the separation of public and private spheres. The women's movement has been particularly influential in bringing to public attention the violence and abuse associated with men, so that, during the 1970s, both rape and domestic violence were recognized again. Feminists campaigned simultaneously on three fronts: first, demanding that the state take these forms of violence seriously; second, in the absence of action to protect women, setting up self-help forms of protection through organizations such as Rape Crisis and Women's Aid; and, third, researching into the prevalence of violence against women and children.

Kelly and Radford emphasize the role of feminism in naming and defining violence against women and children:

> Concepts which are now commonplace simply did not exist before the present wave of feminist activism, for example, domestic violence, sexual harassment, child sexual abuse. While these behaviours undoubtedly existed – they were revealingly described by first wave feminists as 'unspeakable outrages' ... – what women lacked were social definitions. Names provide social definitions, make visible what is invisible, define as unacceptable what was accepted; make sayable what was unspeakable ...

> (Kelly and Radford, 1990, p.40)

In 1975 a report by a House of Commons Select Committee on Violence in Marriage established the abuse of women within their homes as a social problem. However, it was not to be treated as a crime. The major form of intervention advocated was that offered by Women's Aid, to be backed up by welfare services. Legal remedies were to rely on injunctions to keep the man away from the woman, a remedy within the civil law. The criminal justice system was not seen to be relevant to helping women in these situations.

When sexual abuse of children re-emerged on to the public agenda in the 1980s, it was largely as a result of campaigning by women's organizations concerned with rape and domestic violence. As with physical abuse and neglect, child-protection agencies rely on social welfare policies and practices to protect children who have been sexually abused, often removing children from their homes. The distinction between respectable and disreputable families has continued through professional discourses of 'dangerous' or 'dysfunctional' families in which abuse occurs.

A feminist demonstration in the 1980s against violence against women

There has been much public and political concern about the role of social workers in relation to child abuse. When children have died at the hands of a parent or step-parent, social workers have been condemned for doing too little, too late. On the other hand, in relation to the child sexual abuse investigations of the 1980s – for example, in Cleveland, Rochdale and Orkney – social workers were blamed for removing children from their families unjustifiably. These 'scandals' had a major impact on the new Children Act 1989 for England and Wales. Parton suggests that this Act addresses the major tension identified at all periods since the late nineteenth century: 'how can we devise a legal basis for power to intervene into the family which does not convert all families into clients of the state?' (Parton, 1991, p.2). The Act attempted to strike a new balance between the contradictory needs to protect children from danger, and the family from unwarrantable intrusion into its privacy, by encouraging local authorities to work 'in partnership' with parents and by making professionals (especially social workers) more accountable to families and to the courts.

In the early 1990s, a 'new' form of family violence, described as one of the last myths of family life to be exposed, became visible: the abuse of older people in their homes by formal or informal carers. Although known before this time – for example, in the 1970s – it was not recognized as a social problem. In 1991 the Health Secretary, Virginia Bottomley, stated: 'I don't frankly think that abuse against the elderly is a major problem' (quoted in *Community Care*, 6 May 1993, p.17), and until 1993 this was the formal government response. However, in the context of the 1990 NHS and Community Care Act, there is more pressure for older people in need of care to receive that care from relatives in their own homes. The Act emphasizes the need to support carers, acknowledging the stress involved for them, but it does not consider that there might be a need to protect those being cared for.

In 1993, the Social Services Inspectorate issued guidelines for social workers, and a junior minister helped to launch a campaign entitled 'Action on Elder Abuse' based at the voluntary agency Age Concern. It is interesting to note that most publicity on elder abuse has been given to revelations of scandals involving older people in residential care, and it is worth considering whether the existence of abuse in these settings is easier to accept.

ACTIVITY 5.4

Look back over this brief account of the history of violence in the family. Do any patterns emerge? Make a few notes on what seem to you to be the issues that are most significant for understanding the changing visibility of violence within the family.

COMMENT

Issues that arose for me include:

- Changing definitions of family violence and explanations of its causes.
- Changing ideas on what constitutes 'normal' family life.
- Changes in who are considered to be the 'experts', and what is seen as the appropriate form of intervention.
- The absence of reform of the criminal law since the nineteenth century, and the emphasis on civil law or 'welfarist' solutions.
- A focus on the protection of vulnerable individuals rather than on the criminalization of offenders.
- The distinction between two kinds of working-class families: 'respectable' and 'disorderly'.
- The primary focus, in discussions of child abuse, on the protection of society from delinquency.
- The tension between the need to control violence and the need to protect family privacy.
- The importance of feminist movements in highlighting certain kinds of violence.
- Changing representations of 'victims' and 'offenders', and the way in which these are structured through class and 'race'.
- The low status of children.

4.4 Learning from history

The history of the visibility and the invisibility of family violence can be read in various different ways. First, many historians have used 'their "evidence" to demonstrate the "progress" that has been made, particularly during the twentieth century … the historical changes … are seen as essentially natural, self-evident and benevolent' (Parton, 1985, p.21). However, we have also seen – for example, in the nineteenth century – that many of the reforms were primarily concerned with keeping public order, preventing delinquency or monitoring families. The early child-protection agencies wanted to promote a particular set of family values and to encourage more acceptable lifestyles, more concerned with reforming parenting than with protecting children (Frost and Stein, 1989). Thus a second reading of the history focuses on state intervention in relation to child abuse as a form of social control, involving monitoring and surveillance of working-class families in particular: 'The concern about child abuse justifies State employees literally crossing the threshold of the homes of those with children considered to be "at risk". Thus the child-abuse issue helps to define the "good" family and the boundary of State intervention in households' (Frost and Stein, 1989, p.48). According to this reading, 'the extension of social regulation to the lives of children actually had little to do with recognition of their rights. ... The apparent humanity, benevolence, and enlightenment of the extension of protection to children in their homes disguised the extension of surveillance and control over the family' (Rose, 1989, p.123).

Seen as 'social control', state intervention into families has been criticized by both left and right as an invasion of privacy, and by feminists for masking the realities of 'family life' in which women and children are on the receiving end of a great deal of violence. The study by Gordon (1989) presents a third, feminist, reading of the history (see Extract 5.1 overleaf).

In what ways is a feminist reading of the history of state intervention different from a 'social control' view?

Gordon 'insist[s] that an accurate view of this "outside" intervention into the family must consider, as the clients so often did in their strategic decisions, both external and familial forms of domination' (Gordon, 1989, p.299).

This kind of feminist analysis of the historical developments helps us to understand the significance of the 'public/private' split which places a homogeneous family unit within the 'private' sphere, hides power differences and conflicts of interest between family members, renders invisible violence within families, and constructs those on the receiving end as merely passive victims, rather than as actors, able to resist, struggle and shape their own lives.

5 The role of the law in defining violence in the family

Feminists and civil rights activists have tried to use the law as an instrument for change, to improve the lives of women and children. In particular, the campaigns of the social reform movements of the nineteenth century resulted in the enactment of new laws that criminalized certain behaviours for the first time. Criminal prosecutions in relation to violence in the family are still governed by these laws, together with a complex body of case law. The campaigns since the 1970s have demanded that these laws be enforced.

5.1 Dual jurisdictions: the criminal and civil law

Violence within the home has been regulated, if at all, via the use of civil legal proceedings and welfare policies and practices, rather than by use of the criminal justice system. There is a general consensus that the criminal law is not appropriate for dealing with 'family matters'. Let us consider the implications of this in relation to domestic violence and child sexual abuse.

Since 1976, in England and Wales (1981 in Scotland), women have been able to seek redress through the civil courts, through the granting of injunctions and exclusion orders. In practice, after the passing of the

Extract 5.1   Gordon: 'Social control and the "powers of the weak"'

Neither positive nor negative appraisals of social control [from the first use of the phrase in 1901 to the 1970s] had gender or generational analyses. Both, in fact, continued a patriarchal usage in identifying 'the family' that was being invaded with a male-dominated, father-dominated form of family. If one uses family violence as the key instance of social control, an issue that contained an inherent critique of patriarchal domination, then new questions arise and the evaluation of intervention must be more complex.

For example, the critique of social control, both left and right, frequently points to the violation of civil liberties as evidence of the dangers of intervention into family privacy. ... but before condemning the very enterprise of intervening into the family, one must ask: Whose privacy? Whose liberties? ... Until recently it was customary for law-enforcement officials to decline to guarantee such liberties to battered women, for example. Children did not usually even get as far as telling their story to law officers, so removed were they from access to their 'rights'. Thus one man's loss in privacy was often another's (frequently a woman's) gain in rights.

...

Futhermore, ... clients often wanted this intervention. While the definitions of family violence and its remedies have reflected the biases of dominant groups – have been unfair, discriminatory and oppressive – family violence remains as a problem experienced by its participants. The clients did not consider their sufferings inevitable. The power of labelling, the representation of poor people's behaviour by experts whose status is defined through their critique of the problematic behaviour of others, co-exists with real family oppressions. ...

In historical fact, most of the invitations for intervention came from women and secondarily children. In other words, the inviters were the weaker members of family power structures. Social work intervention has not been a process that can be expressed simply in class terms, as the rich against the poor. In their struggles to escape the control of a patriarchal family, women not only used the professions and the state but helped build them. The social work/social control establishment did not arise out of the independent agenda of the ruling class, or even of the middle class. Rather it developed out of conflicts that had gender and generational as well as class 'sides'.

When critics of social control perceive social work simply as unwanted intervention, and fail to recognize the active role of agency clients, it is in

Domestic Violence and Matrimonial Proceedings Act and its Scottish equivalent, the Matrimonial Homes (Family Protection) (Scotland) Act, it was found that the police were reluctant to support criminal prosecutions and encouraged women to seek civil solutions, even though in practice these were hard to obtain and were largely ineffective unless a 'power of arrest' was attached to them (Dobash and Dobash, 1992).

This emphasis on the civil law was written into the 1976 Act. Witnesses to the Parliamentary Select Committee of the House of Commons on Violence in Marriage in the 1970s, did not see the criminal justice system as relevant to helping women in situations of domestic violence. Hanmer (1989) argues that the attitudes of the police and their evidence to the Select Committee were important influences on this approach. She quotes the Association of Chief Police Officers of England, Wales and Northern Ireland:

> Whilst such problems take up considerable police time during say, 12 months, in the majority of cases the role of the police is a negative one. We are, after all, dealing with persons 'bound in marriage', and it is important, for a host of reasons, to maintain the unity of the spouses. Precipitated action by the police could aggravate the position to such an extent as to create a worse situation than the one they were summoned to deal with. The 'lesser of two evils' principle is often a good guideline in these situations.

(Select Committee, 1975, p.366, quoted in Hanmer, 1989, p.91)

large part because they conceive of the family as a homogeneous unit. ... Shorthand expressions attributing behaviour to an aggregate such as the family would be harmless except that they often impose particular cultural norms about what 'the family' is, and mask intrafamily differences and conflicts of interest. Usually 'the family' becomes a representation of the interests of the family head, if it is a man, carrying an assumption that all family members share his interests. (Families without a married male head, like single-parent or grandparent-headed families, are, in the common usage, broken, deformed, or incomplete families.) Among the clients in family-violence cases, outrage over the intervention into the family was frequently an outrage over a territorial violation, a challenge to male authority; or, expressed differently, an outrage at the exposure of intrafamily conflict and of the family head's lack of control. Indeed, the interventions actually were more substantive, more invasive, when their purpose was to change the status quo than if they had been designed to reinforce it. The effect of social workers' involvement was sometimes to change existing family power relations, usually in the interest of the weaker family members.

...

Social work interventions in family-violence cases rarely changed assailants' behaviour, but they had a greater impact on victims. The main factor determining the usefulness of casework was the activity of clients: those who sought help and knew what they wanted were more likely to get it. This is why, ironically, the child-protection agencies contributed more to help battered women, defined as outside their jurisdiction, than abused children. Modern urban society gave women some opportunity to leave abusive men because they could earn their own living. In these circumstances, even a bit of material help – a referral to a relief agency, a positive recommendation to the courts regarding child custody – could turn their aspirations for autonomy into reality. Moreover, women could get this help despite class and ethnic prejudices against them. ... Children would need more than money to escape abusive parents.

At the same time, in this society of great inequality, interventions against family violence have been and continue to be discriminatory. Class privilege brings with it immunity from discovery and/or intervention. Not only have poor, working-class, immigrant and black people been discriminated against, but so too have women, despite the feminist influence in stimulating anti-family-violence intervention.

(Gordon, 1989, pp.293–8)

Generally, domestic violence was seen as trivial compared to 'more serious matters' such as traffic offences and theft. The police believed that in most cases the prime responsibility for this problem should lie with social services and counselling agencies. Their own role should be to take 'positive action at the time, to give advice, to keep the peace, and most of all to prevent injury' and 'as often as not play a conciliatory role ...' (Select Committee, 1975, quoted in Dobash and Dobash, 1992, p.150). Police and judicial representatives saw no need for big changes, and thought more serious penalties might be counterproductive. The police seemed to maintain the nineteenth-century distinction between 'normal' and 'exceptional' violence, arguing that, in exceptional cases of extreme violence, they did intervene, and that existing legislation was adequate for these purposes. The Lord Advocate of Scotland argued that: 'Sentences of imprisonment could well have an adverse effect upon the family by removing the "breadwinner", and imposing heavy fines will likewise reduce the "purchasing power" of the family and place the burden of subsidizing such families on the taxpayer' (Select Committee, 1975, quoted in Dobash and Dobash, 1992, p.151).

The police were reluctant to get involved in civil law matters and to powers of arrest being attached to injunctions; the use of injunctions in this way could be seen as offering preferential treatment to women. Other representatives argued that the criminal justice system must also protect men from false accusations from women.

In this way the focus on the civil law is thought to strengthen the idea that violence against women within the home is fundamentally different from violence in the street, and that it is essentially a private matter: 'The existence of civil law remedies thus has *obstructed* the recognition of violence in the home as a criminal offence' (Edwards, 1990, p.155).

At the time of writing there are proposals to reform the law on domestic violence to extend ideas on the nature of domestic/family relationships that should be covered by the civil law provisions (see *The Guardian*, 6 June 1994, reproduced opposite).

How might these propositions affect the position of women on the receiving end of domestic violence?

The use of criminal proceedings in relation to child abuse is also controversial:

> The fact that it occurs primarily within the family has led to the belief that criminal prosecution is not a particularly appropriate response. The development of a separate system for dealing with child abuse which focuses on the welfare of the child rather than the prosecution of the offender may well obscure the fact that a criminal offence has often been committed. The tendency to marginalize children as victims of crime is reinforced by the use of the term 'abuse' rather than 'assault'.
>
> (Morgan and Zedner, 1992, p.20)

Criminal proceedings are not thought to be in the best interests of children who have been sexually abused. It is argued that it is extremely difficult to mount a prosecution. The lack of visible evidence in most cases means relying on the evidence of children, who are not deemed to be reliable witnesses, and who might be further traumatized by the experience in court.

Since the late 1980s, some changes in criminal procedures have been introduced, such as videotaping children's evidence. These were intended to ease the situation of children in court and to increase the likelihood of securing a conviction, but they have proved very controversial. On the one hand, they have not been seen to reduce the trauma for children; and, on the other hand, they have raised fears about reductions in civil liberties for the accused which can be hidden by an emphasis on the rights of children (Woodcraft, 1988).

What do you think is the significance of the focus on civil, rather than criminal, law proceedings in dealing with violence in the family?

5.2 Law enforcement

It will be clear from your earlier reading in this book that whether or not certain behaviours are treated as 'crimes' depends upon many factors other than the written law. The failure of the criminal justice system, especially the police, to take action in what they called 'domestics' was one of the main targets of the feminist campaigns of the 1970s: 'Police did not usually arrest men for assaulting their wives or cohabitees, rarely offered assistance to

Aid for domestic violence victims

Clare Dyer
Legal Correspondent

THE Government is to reform the law on domestic violence to protect a wider range of victims and make it easier to arrest perpetrators.

The changes, announced yesterday by Lord Mackay, the Lord Chancellor, will extend protection now covering only spouses and cohabitees to a range of people linked by domestic or family relationships.

Where violence has occurred or been threatened, courts will normally be required to attach a power of arrest to an order forbidding one party from molesting the other. This allows the police to arrest the person breaking the order. At present, many judges are reluctant to attach such a power to domestic violence injunctions.

The measures, to be introduced 'when a suitable opportunity occurs', will implement most of the recommendations of a Law Commission report two years ago. They will rationalise an area of the law widely criticised for inconsistencies, loopholes and anomalies.

Critics have pointed out that the present law gives little protection to former wives and ex-cohabitees, although those most likely to resort to violence include ex-partners who refuse to acknowledge that a relationship is over.

Relationships to be covered by the new measures are:
- Spouses and ex-spouses
- Present and former cohabitees
- People who live or have lived in the same household
- Certain close relatives
- Co-parents of a child
- Parties to a family court case

People linked by these relationships will be able to apply for non-molestation orders against each other, stopping specific behaviour or 'molestation' generally. This would include serious pestering or harassment as well as violence. Children will also be protected.

Former and current spouses and cohabitees, and others in the prescribed relationships with a legal right to occupy the home – for example, as joint owners and tenants – will be able to apply for occupation orders, giving one party the right to live there and excluding the other.

Spouses and others with a legal right of occupation will be able to apply to exclude the other indefinitely. Otherwise, occupation orders will be for a maximum of six months, renewable for six months at a time.

In cases of actual or threatened violence, courts would be required to attach a power of arrest to an order, unless the applicant or child would be adequately protected without such a power.

At present, most domestic violence injunctions do not include a power of arrest. Of nearly 26,000 non-molestation injunctions granted in 1992, only 9,660 had a power of arrest attached, and in the North-east fewer than one in six.

The Government has rejected a Law Commission recommendation that police should be given power to apply for orders on behalf of victims too cowed by violence to act themselves. The commission recommended that the remedies should also be available to those once engaged to each other and those in, or formerly in, a sexual relationship. But the Government has decided their inclusion would pose problems of definition and proof, and would not be justified.

(*The Guardian*, 6 June 1994, p.4)

women and sometimes denigrated them for seeking protection within the law. Judges, prosecutors and other criminal justice personnel also failed to deal with the violence in a meaningful manner' (Dobash and Dobash, 1992, p.146). Women's agencies see 'violence against women in the home ... as the crime least likely to elicit a positive police response' (Hanmer, 1989, p.117). In contrast, 'the crimes of violence police are most likely to respond positively to are those that involve strangers to the woman' (Hanmer, 1989, p.118).

A decision on whether to act, or how to act, depends upon the discretion of the individual officer or officers present at the time. Factors that increase the likelihood of an arrest by the police include the presence of children or older people, visible signs of injury, threats or violence against the police, court injunctions with powers of arrest, a woman not seen to 'deserve' violence, the legal status of the partnership, and the man already being known to the police or wanted for another crime (Hanmer, 1989; Dobash and Dobash, 1992).

Women's expectations of the likely response they will get may well discourage them from reporting violent incidents. Estimates of the proportion of domestic violence reported vary from 2 per cent in the research by Dobash and Dobash (1980) to 71 per cent in research by Pahl (1985). But women in the latter study were already living in refuges, so for these women the police may be a last resort. In a study of domestic violence in London's black communities, Mama found that 'police may be particularly insensitive, and on occasion brutal, towards black women' (Mama, 1989, p.182). Reluctance by black women to call in the police, even when they had been badly beaten and had no-one else to turn to, was influenced by (a) the men concerned having been harassed or brutalized previously by the police; (b) their own experiences of racist attitudes and treatment from the police; and (c) experience of the police carrying out other agendas such as surveillance of a particular household. In some cases domestic violence incidents were turned into immigration matters, resulting in the victim being deported.

As a result of pressure from feminist campaigns both nationally and locally, since the late 1980s the Home Office and several police forces have formally made domestic violence a priority. However, research carried out by a local community group, Southall Black Sisters, found that little had changed in practice despite this policy change. Lewis and Shah (n.d.) argue that black women's experience of police involvement in relation to domestic violence has to be understood within the wider framework of 'over-' and 'under-' policing of black communities. Southall, they suggest, has been 'remapped' by the police as an area of criminality, resulting in over-policing of, in particular, black young men in relation to 'gangs' supposedly involved in drugs and immigration offences, but 'under-policing' of racial attacks and domestic violence. These have been down-played or turned into 'non-crimes'. Police argued that, in order to be able to police the area effectively, they had to keep the sympathy of the community leaders, and therefore they could not always intervene in domestic violence cases, despite this remaining formally a high priority. They claimed that intervention into a private family would cause conflict with community leaders because of the importance of the patriarchal family structure in Asian communities. In addition, police were publicly heard to talk about 'the supposed higher tolerance of older Asian women' (Lewis, 1993) who were therefore in less need of protection.

over- and
under-policing

Edwards found more generally that: 'conventional police wisdom … accommodates its stereotypes of real and legitimate or false and illegitimate victims' (Edwards, 1989, p.92). These stereotypes have both 'race' and class dimensions:

> police may be less willing to protect poorer women and black women, whom they may perceive as less deserving. … Police officers generally come to regard domestic assault as a 'normal' occurrence in run-down inner-city neighbourhoods, where victims because of their powerlessness or culture may be seen to have forefeited their right to protection. For example, domestic violent assault committed against Asian women by Asian men is often seen as 'a family matter'.

> (Edwards, 1989, p.92)

It appears that the police response to domestic violence is crucial in determining which acts are criminalized and which are treated as non-crimes. Police responses are further reinforced by the responses of the Crown Prosecution Service, magistrates and judges (Smith, 1989). In addition, the class and 'race' stereotypes operate to locate domestic violence in disorderly working-class/black families, thus ignoring violence by middle-class men; at the same time, these stereotypes are used to justify non-intervention for black and working-class women (Edwards, 1989).

Despite the limitations of the police response, many feminists continue to campaign for more effective policing of domestic violence, while recognizing the contradictions in their position:

> if we make a demand of just intervene and enforce the law … [the police] may be able to use it to enforce other agendas … or they may not enforce the law because they've got other agendas … But, at the end of the day what women say time and time again is at two o'clock in the morning when he comes home and he's assaulting me the police are the only people that are open and that I am able to turn to immediately and therefore … in the short term what we are arguing is the police should enforce the criminal law and should do it all the time and should do it effectively.

> (Lewis, 1993)

5.3 The law as a site of struggle

In criticizing the lack of protection offered to victims of domestic violence, some feminists have argued that the lack of legal regulation is part of the problem. The law is seen to play an important symbolic role: 'a society which presses for changes without at the same time expressing and codifying these sentiments within its legislative framework cannot effect any real change' (Edwards, 1990, p.148). Thus the campaign to criminalize rape within marriage was seen as very important symbolically, despite the recognition that, in practice, it was not likely to lead to many prosecutions.

In the 1990s feminist pressure contributed to the Zero Tolerance campaign, a public hoarding advertising campaign, initially in Edinburgh, but adopted later in many other cities in the UK. This campaign stressed that domestic violence should be seen as a crime. (The Edinburgh campaign also included sexual abuse.) In October 1994 the Home Office launched its own awareness campaign – 'Domestic Violence is a Crime – Don't Stand For It' –

consisting of leaflets, posters and a cinema commercial. While welcoming the publicity about domestic violence, some feminist organizations criticized the government for not providing the resources of refuges, policing and other services needed to protect women: 'this campaign denies the Government's responsibility for women suffering violent crime in the family' (Women Against Rape, quoted in *The Guardian*, 25 October 1994).

Given the authority of law and its symbolic importance, we can see why some feminists have wished to locate abuse and violence against women within such a discourse. However, use of the law is also recognized as problematic and limited as a mechanism for change as it 'tends to frame issues in terms of individual pathology and, consequently, to offer individual remedies' and because 'the law has traditionally encompassed *men's* accounts of events because it is men who both legislate and then interpret the law' (Gelsthorpe and Morris, 1990, pp.143, 144).

Some feminists believe that the law is so saturated with patriarchal beliefs and structures that it cannot embody discourses and practices which represent women's experiences of violence (see Smart, 1989). Others see the law as a legitimate site of struggle even though: 'The law not only reflects but also constructs a very limited definition of sexual violence, and thereby plays a significant role in denying or trivializing women's experience of male sexual violence' (Kelly and Radford, 1990, p.39). In addition, 'the law plays the central role in constructing "what counts" as crime, and in the case of sexual violence (unlike, for example, public order offences) it focuses almost entirely on extremes, thereby discounting many women's experiences' (Kelly and Radford, 1990, p.41). As a result, only a proportion of women's complaints are seen as legitimate, and 'the law suggests that clear distinctions can be made between violence and not violence, and thereby between abusive and "normal" men' (Kelly and Radford, 1990, p.41):

> While the protection of women is an objective shared by all women at various points on the political spectrum, deep divisions are evident as to how it is best achieved. … Left-wing feminist idealists totally reject the notion that reforms in policing policy and practice can have any real effect on providing protection from violence, since the state and its institutions (including the law and the police) are oppressive and coercive. Indeed, some regard attempts to reform policing as fundamentally dangerous, a tampering which works to help the state and its police in providing them with legitimation while coercion continues as before. The left-wing feminist realist position, while not endorsing the law and police, recognizes that the law and police are here to stay. The problem, then, is to strike a balance between controlling the excesses of male violence without opening the door to further excess of state power, surveillance and control.
>
> (Edwards, 1989, p.237)

Woodcraft also describes some of the contradictions raised for feminists by the issue of violence in the family:

> For those of us working as self-styled radical lawyers, issues of crime and punishment are on the whole quite clear. We defend the accused against the powers of the state… . We argue against harsh sentences. In particular we argue against imprisonment because we see this as an ineffective method of dealing with offenders… .

(a)

(b)

(c)

Poster campaigns of the 1990s against child abuse and domestic violence, produced by
(a) the Edinburgh Zero Tolerance Campaign;
(b) the Association of London Authorities' Zero Tolerance Campaign; and
(c) the Home Office

Then we are confronted with crimes against women and children. As feminists, we have a particular perspective on the root cause of such offences – that is, the position of women in our society. ...We want the child protected... . Are we prepared ... to say ... that we must use the sanction of criminal proceedings? ... Should we not support any action by the state which seems for once to take the issue seriously, which punishes the individual offender and makes an example of him in order to discourage others?

(Woodcraft, 1988, p.125)

On the other hand, she argues:

In a situation where the efficacy of criminal proceedings can be challenged – on the basis of their damaging effects on individual victims and the wider lack of effect in changing the behaviour of society at large – we must ask what price we are paying when we push for the use of criminal sanctions. The price seems to be more nails in the coffin of civil liberties. This cannot be the best we can do to protect children from abuse. As feminists we must be prepared to look further for ways of dealing with an insidious social wrong which is daily committed against children in their homes.

(Woodcraft, 1988, p.130)

An important area of feminist struggle around the law has focused on the situation of women convicted of murder for killing their violent husband or male partner. In July 1995 Emma Humphries, sentenced to life imprisonment 10 years earlier for the murder of her violent lover, was released from prison when her murder conviction was replaced by one of manslaughter by the Court of Appeal. This outcome followed an active campaign by the organization Justice for Women. The significance of this case lay in the acceptance by the Court, that not only events immediately prior to the killing, but also cumulative abuse should be regarded as possible 'provocation' (see *The Guardian*, 8 July 1995, reproduced opposite).

6 Family violence: crime or non-crime?

In this final section we return to the competing perspectives on violence in the family, discussed in section 2.3, to see how they construct violence in the family as crime or non-crime. (You might find it helpful to look back at section 2.3 at this point, to remind yourself of these perspectives.)

6.1 Professional discourses: violence as pathology

When violence within the family first became recognized as a social problem in the nineteenth century, it was described in moral terms. The early part of the twentieth century saw a shift from moral to scientific judgements, associated with the rise of new professional 'experts', particularly within social work and psychiatry, who constructed family violence within psychological, medical and psychiatric discourses, as a mental health problem. In 1979 two new categories – 'battered spouse' and 'battered woman' – were added to the International Classification of Diseases: Clinical Modification Scheme, compiled in the USA as a list of 'all known diseases and related entities' (Dobash and Dobash, 1992, p.213). This can be seen as the transformation of 'complex social, cultural and political issues into psychological syndromes' (Dobash and Dobash, 1992, p.215).

mental health discourses

Court attempts to soften law on provocation

Clare Dyer reports on legal repercussions of Emma Humphreys's appeal case victory

THE Court of Appeal's decision yesterday to quash Emma Humphreys' murder conviction 10 years ago and substitute manslaughter is its latest attempt to mitigate the harshness of the law on provocation.

The defence reduces murder, which carries a mandatory life sentence, to manslaughter and allows the judge complete freedom in sentencing.

Traditionally a plea of provocation could only succeed when the defendant killed as a result of a 'sudden and temporary loss of self-control'. This led to the assumption that even if a woman had suffered repeated batterings over years, only the 'last straw' could count. If this was trivial, the provocation defence failed, because a reasonable person would not have killed in reaction to it.

In Emma Humphreys' case, the judges have made it clear for the first time that cumulative provocation can be taken into account in deciding whether a reasonable person would have acted as the defendant did.

Lord Justice Hirst speaks of 'several distinct and cumulative strands of potentially provocative conduct building up until the final encounter'. This included long-term cruelty, her partner's drunkenness early in the evening and his threat of making her take part in a gang bang.

Just before the killing he taunted her about her pathetic attempt at slashing her wrists – the 'trigger' put forward at her trial as causing her to snap – and took off his clothes, apparently preparing to rape her yet again.

Yesterday's ruling, together with the appeal court's judgment three years ago when it freed Kiranjit Ahluwalia, have removed some of the more obvious injustices of the law. In the case of Mrs Ahluwalia, who poured petrol over her brutal husband as he lay sleeping in bed, the judges removed the need to show that the defendant acted immediately. It extended the defence to cases where anger was not sudden but boiled up over a period. The defendant still had to act in 'hot blood' but not necessarily in haste.

It is not clear whether the law has moved far enough to secure the release of Sara Thornton, who has had one appeal turned down but whose case was recently referred back to the appeal court by the Home Secretary, Michael Howard. She was convicted of murder five years ago for stabbing her brutal husband, Malcolm, while he slept. Andrew Ashworth, professor of criminal law at King's College, London, said of yesterday's judgment: 'It will widen the concept of provocation and it begins to undermine the idea of suddenness which was so insisted on in Thornton.'

The judges who rejected Sara Thornton's appeal said: 'There is no suggestion that she had reacted suddenly and on the spur of the moment, deprived of her self-control, to the provocative statements made by the deceased. On the contrary, she always insisted that she had gone to the kitchen to cool down and had cooled down.'

A growing number of lawyers and psychiatrists argue that the law on provocation ignores the effects of years of abuse on a woman's psychology. Helena Kennedy QC, who has defended several battered women, believes the impulsive reaction which makes someone blind with rage is a male behaviour pattern.

The Ahluwalia judgment also opened the way for the courts to hear evidence that the defendant was suffering from battered woman's syndrome, a form of post-traumatic stress disorder. In the United States, this amounts to a plea of self-defence which, if successful, entitles the woman to an acquittal. Psychologists claim that years of subjection to systematic violence induces a state of 'learned helplessness' in which the woman believes she has no choice but to kill her abuser to preserve her life.

Campaigners for the abolition of the mandatory life sentence for murder, including the past and present Lord Chief Justice and most senior judges, point out that the legal contortions over provocation would become unnecessary if judges were free to fit the sentence for murder to the circumstances of the crime.

(*The Guardian*, 8 July 1995)

[At the time of writing, Sara Thornton, whose case is mentioned in this article, had been released on bail pending an appeal to be heard later in 1995.]

It is very easy to effect this transformation. In the 1970s, the Women's Aid movement used the term 'battered woman' deliberately as a powerful emotive phrase that emphasized women's experience of severe and persistent violence. It was also seen as preferable to gender-neutral terms such as 'domestic violence'. However, this same term came to be used as a 'disease' category (seen by most professionals and even some campaigners as a breakthrough in acknowledging the occurrence of such violence), and the associated term 'battered woman syndrome' was coined to describe the psychological effects of battering on the woman.

One effect of this was to shift the focus of explanation for the violence away from the man on to the woman. In the UK, the recommendations of the House of Commons Select Committee on Violence in Marriage were based on the idea that the causes of domestic violence were psychological (Dobash and Dobash, 1992). Despite the fact that no research has been able to find psychological characteristics that reliably distinguish women who have been on the receiving end of violence from those who have not, battered women continue to be constructed in terms of their own psychopathology. They are described variously as violence-prone, 'addicted to violence' (through experiences in childhood, or even in the womb), 'masochistic', or suffering from 'learned helplessness'. What these characterizations have in common is that they identify 'the primary roots of victimization in the background of the victim and not in the offender' (Dobash and Dobash, 1992, p.223).

At least partly because of the impact of women's campaigns, and the entry into the welfare professions of many feminists who had previously worked within voluntary organizations such as Rape Crisis and Women's Aid, the predominant discourses blaming women have been challenged and there has been a greater focus on the offenders, but they, too, are largely constructed as psychopathological. Violence may be seen as a clinical condition arising either from a psychobiological disorder such as an abnormal blood glucose level, or as a psychological disorder arising from bad experiences in childhood – the 'cycle of violence'. In either way, men are not seen as being in control of their actions.

Constructions of child abuse have also been predominantly within psychological and medical discourses. Since the 1960s, when 'battered babies' were rediscovered, physical abuse of children has been constructed as a disease. Professional discourses on child sexual abuse speak of the 'diagnosis' of a disorder from symptoms (Parton, 1985; MacLeod and Saraga, 1991). Children are less likely to be seen as directly responsible for violence inflicted on them, although young girls may still be described as provoking sexual attacks, or of being seductive. Parental abusers have been described as 'immature' or having 'poorly controlled aggression', resulting from emotionally deprived childhoods; they are assumed to require therapeutic intervention.

'Lack of control' is cited in particular in relation to sexual violence by men. Perpetrators of child sexual abuse are frequently described in terms of 'addiction': 'as long as the "whisky bottle" is within easy reach that is, the child is readily available, the addiction continues ... if one form of alcohol, in the form of the original victim, is removed but substitutes remain, in the form of other children, then a new victim replaces the first one' (Fawcett, 1989, p.2). Other explanations also seem to remove blame from the offender. For example, the cycle of violence described earlier is an accepted 'truth' in most professional circles, despite contrary evidence (Waterhouse et al., 1993).

The failure of models of individual psychopathology to be able to distinguish abusers from non-abusers and/or victims from non-victims, led many professionals to turn instead to the growing field of family systems theory for explanations of violence, and to family therapy for forms of intervention (Bentovim *et al.*, 1988). In family systems theory, the whole family, rather than the individuals within it, is the unit of attention and analysis. In one of the most influential forms of this approach, violence is seen to be a 'symptom' of something that has gone wrong in the family as a whole. In this case there are no victims or abusers. In incidents of domestic violence, the woman is seen as culpable and responsible, along with her male partner.

When applied to child abuse, even when the violence has been perpetrated by the father, the mother is seen as at least sharing the responsibility. There has been a great deal of 'mother blaming' in the literature on child abuse: 'The couple act as one in the abuse of the child … the "failure to protect" behaviour of the partner with the passive role is at least as crucial and pathological as the role of the aggressor' (Dale, 1984, p.21), and: 'Maternal responsibility seems inescapable' (MacLeod and Saraga, 1991, p.41).

Feminist criticisms of, in particular, mother blaming, have led to some modification of these ideas. But professionals adopting a family systems approach continue to use gender-blind terms such as the 'battering couple', 'battering families' and 'sexually abusing families' which suggest that the 'couple' or the 'family', rather than the abuser, is abusive. Power relations of gender and age within families are ignored, as is the wider social and cultural context in which these power relations are constructed.

Criticisms of this approach have come from many sociologists who attempt instead to understand such violence in social structural terms. In particular, physical violence is seen as a response to frustration and stress arising from social and material conditions including unemployment, bad housing and poverty. This kind of explanation has been used to account for the apparent greater incidence of physical child abuse in working-class families. However, it fails to account for the majority of poor parents who do not abuse their children, and the occurrence of abuse in more affluent families, nor can it explain why children should be the target of such frustration-induced violence (Parton, 1991; Saraga, 1993).

There are three important consequences of these mental health discourses. First, we have seen that responsibility for the abuse is shifted away from the perpetrator, and frequently the victims (women and even children) share responsibility. Second, the voices of the women and children involved are silenced. Experts speak for them and see them as a homogeneous category, all suffering from the same psychological disorder. They are rendered defenceless and passive, classified in a rigid way that gives no space for individual experience or experience that is structured through 'race', class, culture or religion. Third, by describing the violence as individual pathology, it is constructed as non-crime.

6.2 Feminist discourses: violence as a product of power and gender relations

Feminist explanations of violence in the family have focused in particular on those forms of violence associated with men. Far from being pathological, '[domestic] violence is seen as intentional behaviour chosen by men as a tactic or resource associated with attempts to control and dominate women' (Dobash and Dobash, 1992, p.248). Evidence from studies of child sexual abusers is cited to support the argument that, far from being out of control, abusers plan the abuse carefully, and often 'entrap' children over a period of time (Conte *et al.*, 1989).

masculinity

There is more than one feminist approach to family violence, but, typically, male violence is explained in terms of the construction of masculinity and the power relations between men, women and children in society:

> The seeds of wife beating lie in the subordination of females and in their subjection to male authority and control. This relationship between women and men has been institutionalized in the structure of the patriarchal family and is supported by the economic and political institutions and by a belief system, including a religious one, that makes such relationships seem natural, morally just, and sacred.

> (Dobash and Dobash, 1980, p.33)

male sexuality

Within the patriarchal family, male sexuality is constructed as powerful, dominant and controlling, but at the same time experienced as 'driven' and 'out of control', to be controlled by women. Sexual abuse is understood as an expression of masculinity, of men's need to be powerful and dominant: 'Crucially, feminists argue that these characteristics of sexuality are not peculiar to abusers, but part of "normal" male sexuality ... they refuse to link abuse to the "abnormal", sick or "deprived", but see it as intimately connected with *normal* relations between men, women and children within society' (Saraga, 1993, p.70). However, feminists differ on their views of male violence, some seeing it as part of a continuum of masculine behaviour; others believing that it must be understood within a wider context of class, 'race', gender and generational relations within society (see Extract 5.2).

Feminist perspectives also emphasize the importance of listening to the experience of the victims of abuse, challenging the power of professionals to define their experiences for them as the symptoms of a disease with a medical prognosis. What is so remarkable is that, despite the enormous physical and emotional suffering, women and children are rarely passive. Domestic violence leads to 'determination, action and bravery' (Dobash and Dobash, 1992, p.230). Gordon (1989) describes the way in which women on the receiving end of severe violence actively sought help for themselves and their children from the state agencies, even if it meant risking losing their children.

Feminist accounts of child sexual abuse have similarly demonstrated that even small children are rarely entirely passive, even in the face of assault against which they are physically quite unable to defend themselves. In limited ways they may resist what is happening – for example, by cutting off their feelings, pretending to be asleep, telling someone, and, when older, by running away (Kelly, 1988b).

survivors

In rejecting the characterization of women as passive victims in these circumstances, feminist discourses tend to speak of 'survivors' rather than 'victims' in order to emphasize their active agency. Survival is not a prognosis, but a journey to recovery – one in which the survivor plays an active role, whatever therapeutic help they may or may not seek. Making the abuse visible, naming it as abuse and rejecting self-blame are important parts of that journey.

Extract 5.2   Segal: 'Continuities and discontinuities in men's use of sexual violence'

There is a ... development in feminist thinking on sexual assault which ... directs us towards seeing all men as perpetrators of violence, and all women as its victims. This is the feminist extension of the definition of 'male violence', whereby it is seen as not only general and pervasive, but occurring along a 'continuum of sexual violence'. The continuum ranges from the everyday abuse of women in pornographic images, sexist jokes, sexual harassment and women's engagement in compliant but unwanted marital sex, through to the 'non-routine' episodes of rape, incest, battery and sex murder. Elizabeth Stanko, for example, groups together a wide selection of such behaviour from men towards women as threatening or violent, arguing that they all serve to remind women of their vulnerability to men: 'Try as they might women are unable to predict when a threatening or intimidating form of male behaviour will escalate to violence' [Stanko, 1985, p.1]. In her recent, clear and comprehensive overview of work on male sexual violence, Liz Kelly adopts a similar position. She makes three key points which she presents as the background to her own research: most women have experienced sexual violence; the different forms of violence are connected along a continuum of abuse; sexual violence occurs in the context of men's power and women's resistance [Kelly, 1988, p.1]. This means, she argues, that rape is but one of the ways men maintain power through sexual violence. It is men's 'taken for granted' use of aggression – for example, in sexual harassment in workplaces – which enables men's gender power to override other power relations like that between teacher and pupil [Kelly, 1988, p.27]. And it is the limited definitions of sexual violence, she adds, which have enabled men individually and collectively to benefit from distinctions between a so-called 'deviant' minority of men and the 'normal' majority [Kelly, 1988].

Such feminist extensions of notions of sexual violence have real advantages. There is no doubt that men's intrusive staring, touching, sexist joking and worse is not only often extremely discomforting for women, but also consolidates sexual hierarchy, affirming in men a shared sense of themselves as the dominant, assertive, active sex. Similarly, the so-called 'harmless' acts of flashing, grabbing of breasts or obscene phone calls are not only frightening in their sudden violation of women's immediate personal space, but can induce a more chronic sense of fear in women – turning public places into hostile environments. Furthermore, there is truth in the feminist reflection that what gross and petty acts of sexual intrusion have in common is the sexist myths to which they give rise, and which seek either to render them harmless or, when regarded as more serious, to blame women for not preventing their occurrence.

Nevertheless, there are problems both with the idea that the high incidence of unreported rape suggests all men are guilty, and with the notion of a continuum of men's sexual violence, from heterosexual acts initiated by them (rather than women) through to acts of rape and sex murder. At least, there are problems if we are seeking to understand the causes, and prevent the occurrence, of men's use of violence. Although absent from most feminist writing on men's violence, there is evidence that there are significant differences not only between men who commit sexual assault on women and other men, but between different types of violent men – and between different types of violent acts – and their meanings. Rather than ignoring these differences, the endeavour to understand them seems to me crucial to tackling the problems of violence and to finding the appropriate variety of solutions to prevent men from resorting to them.

References

Kelly, E. (1988) *Surviving Sexual Violence*, Cambridge, Polity.

Stanko, E. (1985) *Intimate Intrusions: Women's Experience of Male Violence*, London, Routledge and Kegan Paul.

(Segal, 1990, pp.243–5)

6.3 Family, crime and discipline

'For over a century there has been a consensus that there must be some limits placed on the treatment family "heads" can mete out to their dependants. But setting and enforcing those limits encounters a fundamental tension between civil liberties and social control' (Gordon, 1989, p.4). We have seen how this tension has affected legal and policy developments and that intervention into the most private aspects of family life has been tolerated by identifying a group of deviant, abusive families.

The Children Act 1989 refers to parental 'responsibilities' rather than 'rights'; yet the right of parents to chastise their own children in whatever way, within limits, they choose is still seen as natural. In December 1991, shortly after the Act came into effect, the UK ratified the United Nations (UN) Convention on the Rights of the Child, which included the protection of children from physical violence in the privacy of their own homes. Several European countries have banned the use of physical punishments by parents, but in the UK it is not illegal. In 1992, the Scottish Law Commission decided not to recommend that it be outlawed completely.

In January 1995 a UN committee set up to monitor progress on the Convention carried out the first international audit of children's rights in the UK. It accused the UK government of repeatedly violating the Convention, and its criticisms included the continued legality of corporal punishment in private schools, and the failure to introduce a legal ban on smacking at home. In response, John Bowis, the government health minister responsible for children, claimed that the UK had a very good record on children's welfare, saying: 'Other nations have been beating a path to our door to find out how to perform. We stand high in respect throughout the world in this field and British parents know that' (quoted in the *Daily Mail*, 28 January 1995, p.2) (see also the extract from the *Daily Mail*, 28 January 1995, reproduced below).

HOW DARE THE U.N. LECTURE US

By JOHN DEANS, Chief Political Correspondent

MINISTERS were outraged last night after a United Nations committee accused Britain of failing its children.

The lofty lecture came from a panel dominated by Third World countries such as Brazil and the Philippines, where youngsters endure appalling poverty.

Its members urged Britain to ban smacking in the home, give pupils expelled from school an automatic right of appeal and rethink plans to set up new detention centres for persistent young offenders, which they said would break international laws.

The eight-page report accused Britain of seriously breaching the spirit of the UN Convention on Children's Rights, which it signed in 1991.

It was greeted with furious indignation at Westminster. Iain Duncan-Smith, a Tory member of the Commons Health Committee, said: 'All these supra-national groups – from Brussels to the UN – are stuffed full of meddling do-gooders who would do better concentrating their efforts on the parts of the world where youngsters find it difficult even to survive.'

(*Daily Mail*, 28 January 1995, p.1)

The issue of parental discipline came into the public arena in 1993 and 1994 when an English local authority, Sutton, took off its register a childminder who refused to undertake not to smack children in her care. Arguments about this case centred on the right of parents to decide how their children should be disciplined, and on the link between physical forms of punishment and child abuse discussed in section 3.1. The High Court ruled against the local authority, upholding the rights of the parents and the childminder.

parental discipline

ACTIVITY 5.5

Before continuing, test your understanding of notions of discipline and causes of crime by making some notes on the following questions:

1   Why do you think the issue of physical punishments as a form of discipline was of such concern in the early 1990s? (Part of your response to this might, of course, reflect your answer to Activity 5.2 in section 3.1.)

2   What is the link between the discipline of children and concern about crime?

COMMENT

In order to understand this link we need to return to the ideas about the family described in section 2 of this chapter. Increasing concern about the rise of crime has been accompanied by assumptions that parents are responsible for their children's behaviour, and indeed that the major cause of crime is lack of discipline of children. For many conservatives, especially members of the 'New Right', strict discipline of children is not only essential for the prevention of crime and delinquency, but more generally for the maintenance of social order. The High Court ruling on the right of the childminder to smack the children in her care was approved of by the government health minister: 'What the court did was to underscore common sense' (quoted in *The Guardian*, 17 March 1994, p.1).

Supporters of these views are very resistant to seeing corporal punishment as child abuse. They are concerned that too much publicity about child abuse, and discussion of children's rights, is dangerous because it is likely to undermine children's respect for authority. For this reason, Overton suggests that: 'conservatives have preferred to cling to pathological explanations for abuse – individual "rotten apples" and dysfunctional families' (Overton, 1992, p.76).

Lack of discipline is linked in these arguments to an increase in lone-parent families: 'We have produced a generation of fatherless children. No father to support them, discipline them and set an example' (Peter Lilley, writing in the *News of the World*, quoted in *The Guardian*, 23 May 1993, p.63). 'Discipline' is seen as a key issue for controlling crime. In 1993, the Prime Minister, John Major, argued that children should be instilled with fear of punishment for wrong doing:

> It is a simple lesson we want people to learn from a very young age. If you do wrong you are likely to be caught, and when you are caught you will be punished ... We need to encourage a greater sense of self-discipline if we are to get down to tackling the roots of crime.

(Quoted in *The Guardian*, 13 November 1993, p.3)

The discipline of children is thus the focus of many debates about the causes of crime. It brings families and parental authority centre-stage in asking where the responsibility for crime lies.

7   Conclusion

This chapter has explored the extent to which the family can be considered to be a dangerous place, in particular for women and children but also for older people. In doing so it has illustrated many of the general themes identified in Chapter 1. We have seen how difficult it is to define abuse and violence within the family, the limitations of legal definitions, and the way in which definitions have changed with socio-economic circumstances. In addition, an analysis of family violence, within a broader discussion of the problem of crime, challenges traditional definitions of what constitutes 'crime'.

Although violent events within the family were first recognized as major social problems over one hundred years ago, for the majority of the years in between they were invisible, and despite the current 'rediscovery' of the pervasiveness of such violence, they remain largely 'hidden crimes'. There would seem to be a range of reasons for this. At a personal level it can be very hard to accept that the family can be a place of danger. Many of us feel a need to experience the family as the ultimate haven and place of support and safety. At a social level, the reluctance to 'see' the family as a site of crime has to be understood in a wider context of the relationship between the family and the state:

> In Western societies, the ideas of peace and security and harmony are still so strongly associated with the institution of the family that it has been exceedingly difficult to deal with the fact that many people are horribly abused within the home ... Despite overwhelming evidence to challenge it, the myth of family bliss and security survives almost totally intact.
>
> (Dobash and Dobash, 1980, p.7)

A consequence of this myth is that, at times of visibility, the dominant concern about violence within the family has been the need to preserve the private nature of 'family' and to maintain social order. Increasing anxiety in the 1990s about the rise of crime has been accompanied by assumptions that parents are responsible for children's behaviour, and indeed that the major cause of crime is inadequate child-rearing and lack of discipline of children. So, violence and abuse are situated within a group of dysfunctional, dangerous, disreputable families, an 'underclass' characterized at the present time in terms of illegitimacy and fatherlessness (**Murray, 1990**, 1994). These families, which are often constructed in terms of both class and 'race', are assumed to be both abusive and criminal.

In analysing the social construction of family violence, this chapter has also demonstrated the roles played by the 'victims' themselves in putting family violence on to the public agenda, in constructing definitions and influencing the forms of intervention. Recognition of this reminds us that a discussion of this kind can never be purely academic: 'to call family violence political is not to deny that each subjective experience of it is wholly personal and unique' (Gordon, 1989, p.292). Feminist organizations and campaigns have played a central role in making violence within the family visible. They have argued in particular for the need to listen to the voices of those on the receiving end of violence, and to recognize the courage, strength and determination that many survivors have shown.

Feminists have viewed the law and criminal justice system not simply as patriarchal and repressive agencies, but as areas of struggle, often demanding that domestic violence and child abuse be seen and responded to as crimes, but also recognizing the contradictions in these demands. In these ways an analysis of the family as a dangerous place and as a site of crime also is capable of challenging traditional and common-sense ideas on what constitutes 'crime'.

Further reading

Discussions of violence in the family will not be found in this form in criminological texts, though they are increasingly discussed under the heading of 'hidden crime', or 'victims' (see, for example, Maguire *et al.*, 1994). The most useful discussions of domestic violence and child abuse as 'crime' can be found in the work of Edwards (1989, 1990), Smart (1989) and Gelsthorpe and Morris (1990). These same texts will also provide information on debates among feminists, particularly about the role of the law. The majority of feminist work in this area is found in non-criminology texts such as Hester *et al.* (1995). Useful texts on domestic violence include: Stanko (1985), Yllo and Bograd (1988), Dobash and Dobash (1980, 1992), Hanmer *et al.* (1989), Mama (1989) and Radford and Russell (1992). Many aspects of child sexual abuse are discussed in a volume of *Feminist Review* (1988), in Wilson (1993) and in Kennedy and Kelly (1992). To consider different feminist discourses on male violence see Kelly (1988b) and **Segal (1990)**. Gordon (1989) provides one of the most interesting and thorough feminist historical accounts of family violence in the USA. No such equivalent text exists for the UK, but aspects of the history of family violence can be found in Dobash and Dobash (1980), Pinchbeck and Hewitt (1973) and May (1978). Analyses of the role of the state in relation to family life are found in Lewis (1986), Rose (1989), Parton (1991) and Muncie *et al.* (1995). The specific experiences of black women and children can be found in Mama (1989) and Wilson (1993). Orthodox perspectives on child abuse are found mainly in the social work and psychiatric literature: for example, Bentovim *et al.* (1988) and Jones *et al.* (1987). Discussions of elder abuse are also found within social work literature: for example, Eastman (1994).

References

Allan, L.J. (1978) 'Child abuse: a critical review of the research and theory', in Martin, J.P. (ed.) *Violence and the Family*, Chichester, Wiley.

Bentovim, A., Elton, A., Hildebrand, J., Tranter, M. and Vizard, E. (eds) (1988) *Child Sexual Abuse Within the Family*, London, Wright.

Blagg, H. and Smith, D. (1989) *Crime, Penal Policy and Social Work*, Harlow, Longman.

Campbell, B. (1993) *Goliath: Britain's Dangerous Places*, London, Methuen.

Community Care (1993) 'Elder abuse: break the silence. What next?', *Community Care*, 22 July.

Conley, C.A. (1991) *The Unwritten Law: Criminal Justice in Victorian Kent*, Oxford, Oxford University Press.

Conte, J.R., Wolf, S. and Smith, T. (1989) 'What sexual offenders tell us about prevention strategies', *Child Abuse and Neglect*, vol.13, pp.293–301.

Creighton, S.J. and Noyes, P. (1989) *Child Abuse Trends in England and Wales 1983–1987*, London, National Society for the Prevention of Cruelty to Children.

Dale, P. (1984) 'The danger within ourselves', *Community Care*, 1 March, pp.20–2.

Dennis, N. (1993) *Rising Crime and the Dismembered Family*, London, Institute of Economic Affairs, Health and Welfare Unit.

Dennis, N. and Erdos, G. (1992) *Families without Fatherhood*, London, Institute of Economic Affairs, Health and Welfare Unit.

Department of Health (1994) *Health and Personal Social Services Statistics for England*, London, HMSO.

Dobash, R.E. and Dobash, R.P. (1980) *Violence Against Wives: A Case Against Patriarchy*, Shepton Mallett, Open Books.

Dobash, R.E and Dobash, R.P. (1992) *Women, Violence and Social Change, London*, Routledge.

Eastman, M. (1994) *Old Age Abuse,* London, Chapman and Hall.

Edwards, S. (1989) *Policing 'Domestic Violence': Women, the Law and the State*, London, Sage.

Edwards, S. (1990) 'Violence against women: feminism and the law', in Gelsthorpe and Morris (1990).

Fawcett, J. (1989) 'Breaking the habit: the need for a comprehensive long term treatment for sexually abusing families', in NSPCC *The Treatment of Child Sexual Abuse*, London, National Society for the Prevention of Cruelty to Children.

Feminist Review (1988) 'Family secrets: child sexual abuse', no.28, January (Spring special issue).

Frost, N. and Stein, M. (1989) *The Politics of Child Welfare*, London, Harvester Wheatsheaf.

Gelsthorpe, L. and Morris, A. (eds) (1990) *Feminist Perspectives in Criminology*, Buckingham, Open University Press.

Gordon, L. (1989) *Heroes of Their Own Lives: The Politics and History of Family Violence, Boston 1880–1960*, London, Virago.

Hanmer, J. (1989) 'Women and policing in Britain', in Hanmer *et al.* (1989).

Hanmer, J. and Saunders, S. (1984) *Well-Founded Fear*, London, Hutchinson.

Hanmer, J., Radford, J. and Stanko, E.A. (eds) (1989) *Women, Policing and Male Violence: International Perspectives*, London, Routledge.

Hester, M., Kelly, L. and Radford, J. (eds) (1995) *Women, Violence and Male Power: Feminist Research, Activism and Practice*, Buckingham, Open University Press.

Hotaling, G.T. and Straus, M.A. (1980) 'Culture, social organization and irony in the study of family violence', in Straus, M.A. and Hotaling, G.T. (eds) *The Social Causes of Husband–Wife Violence*, Minneapolis, MN, Minnesota University Press.

House of Commons Select Committee on Violence in Marriage (1975) *Report from the Select Committee on Violence in Marriage,* London, HMSO.

Jones, D.N., Pickett, J., Oates, M.R. and Barbor, P. (eds) (1987) *Understanding Child Abuse,* London, Macmillan.

Kelly, L. (1988a) 'What's in a name?: defining child sexual abuse', *Feminist Review,* no.28, January (Spring special issue), pp.65–73.

Kelly, L. (1988b) *Surviving Sexual Violence,* Cambridge, Polity.

Kelly, L. and Radford, J. (1990) 'Nothing really happened: the invalidation of women's experience of sexual violence', *Critical Social Policy,* issue 30, vol.10, no.3, pp.39–53.

Kelly, L., Regan, L. and Burton, S. (1991) *An Exploratory Study of the Prevalence of Sexual Abuse in a Sample of 16–21 Year Olds,* London, Child and Woman Abuse Studies Unit, University of North London.

Kennedy, M. and Kelly, L. (guest eds) (1992) 'Disability and child abuse', *Child Abuse Review,* vol.1 (special edition).

Levi, M. (1994) 'Violent crime', in Maguire *et al.* (1994).

Lewis, G. (1993) *Domestic Violence: Issues of Intervention,* Audiocassette Tape 3B, D311 Family Life and Social Policy, Milton Keynes, The Open University.

Lewis, G. and Shah, S. (n.d.) *Dangerous: Armed and Extremely Dangerous: Women and Policing,* unpublished paper.

Lewis, J. (1986) 'Anxieties about the family and the relationships between parents, children and the state in twentieth century England', in Richards, M. and Light, P. (eds) *Children of Social Worlds,* Cambridge, Polity.

MacLeod, M. and Saraga, E. (1988) 'Challenging the orthodoxy: towards a feminist theory and practice', *Feminist Review,* no.28, January (Spring special issue), pp.16–55.

MacLeod, M. and Saraga, E. (1991) 'Clearing a path through the undergrowth: a feminist reading of recent literature on child sexual abuse', in Carter, P., Jeffs, T. and Smith, M. (eds) *Social Work and Social Welfare Yearbook 3,* Buckingham, Open University Press.

Maguire, M., Morgan R. and Reiner, R. (eds) (1994) *The Oxford Handbook of Criminology,* Oxford, Oxford University Press.

Mama, A. (1989) *The Hidden Struggle: Statutory and Voluntary Sector Responses to Violence Against Black Women in the Home,* London, London Race and Housing Research Unit.

May, M. (1978) 'Violence in the family: an historical perspective', in Martin, J.P. (ed.) *Violence and the Family,* Chichester, Wiley.

Morgan, J. and Zedner, L. (1992) *Child Victims,* Oxford, Clarendon.

Muncie, J., McLaughlin, E. and Langan, M. (eds) (1996) *Criminological Perspectives: A Reader*, London, Sage in association with The Open University.

Muncie, J., Wetherell, M., Dallos, R. and Cochrane, A. (eds) (1995) *Understanding the Family,* London, Sage.

Murray, C. (1990) *The Emerging Underclass*, London, Institute of Economic Affairs. (Extract reprinted as 'The underclass' in Muncie *et al.*, 1996.)

Murray, C. (1994) *Underclass: The Crisis Deepens,* London, Institute of Economic Affairs.

Newson, J. and Newson, E. (1970) *Four Years Old in an Urban Community*, Harmondsworth, Penguin.

Newson, J. and Newson, E. (1989) *The Extent of Parental Physical Punishment in the UK*, London, Association for the Protection of All Children Ltd.

Overton, J. (1992) 'Child abuse, corporal punishment, and the question of discipline: the case of Mount Cashel', *Critical Social Policy*, issue 36, vol.12, no. 3, pp.73–95.

Pahl, J. (ed.) (1985) *Private Violence and Public Policy*, London, Routledge and Kegan Paul.

Painter, K. (1991) *Wife Rape, Marriage and the Law: Survey Report: Key Findings*, University of Manchester, Department of Social Policy and Social Work.

Parton, N. (1985) *The Politics of Child Abuse*, Basingstoke, Macmillan.

Parton, N. (1991) *Governing the Family: Child Care, Child Protection and the State*, Basingstoke, Macmillan.

Penhale, B. (1993) 'The abuse of elderly people: considerations for practice', *British Journal of Social Work*, vol.23, no.2, pp.95–112.

Pinchbeck, I. and Hewitt, M. (1973) *Children in English Society Volume II: From the Eighteenth Century to the Children Act 1948*, London, Routledge and Kegan Paul.

Radford, J. and Russell, D.E.H. (eds) (1992) *Femicide: The Politics of Women Killing*, Buckingham, Open University Press.

Rose, N. (1989) *Governing the Soul*, London, Routledge and Kegan Paul.

Saraga, E. (1993) 'The abuse of children', in Dallos, R. and McLaughlin, E. (eds) (1993) *Social Problems and the Family*, London, Sage.

Segal, L. (1990) *Slow Motion: Changing Masculinities, Changing Men*, London, Virago. (Extract reprinted as 'Explaining male violence' in Muncie *et al.*, 1996.)

Sinason, V. (1993) 'When discipline comes back-handed', *The Guardian*, 3 April, p.24.

Smart, C. (1989) *Feminism and the Power of Law*, London, Routledge.

Smith, L.J.F. (1989) *Domestic Violence: An Overview of the Literature*, London, HMSO.

Stanko, E. (1985) *Intimate Intrusions: Women's Experience of Male Violence*, London, Routledge and Kegan Paul.

Straus, M.A., Gelles, R. and Steinmetz, S.K. (1980) *Behind Closed Doors*, New York, Anchor.

Waterhouse, L., Carnie, J. and Dobash, R. (1993) 'The abuser under the microscope', *Community Care*, 24 June, p.24.

Williams, F. (1989) *Social Policy: A Critical Introduction*, Cambridge, Polity.

Wilson, E. (1983) *What Is To Be Done About Violence Against Women?* Harmondsworth, Penguin.

Wilson, M. (1993) *Crossing the Boundary: Black Women Survive Incest*, London, Virago.

Woodcraft, E. (1988) 'Child sexual abuse and the law', *Feminist Review*, no.28, January (Spring special issue), pp.122–30.

Yllo, K. and Bograd, M. (eds) (1988) *Feminist Perspectives on Wife Abuse*, London, Sage.

Chapter 6
Hidden and Respectable: Crime and the Market

by Mary Langan

Contents

1 Introduction

The familiar image of crime presented in newspaper reports, television police series, courtroom dramas, whodunnits and 'law and order' speeches is that of violence against people or offences against property. Murder, rape, assault, theft, burglary, vandalism: these are the offences that dominate public discourse about crime and haunt the popular imagination.

Closely associated with the stereotypical crime comes the archetypal criminal: young, male, unemployed, poorly educated, likely to be black, and certainly a member of the 'underclass'. As Levi (1987, p.14) observes, a reliance on Home Office criminal statistics leads to the conclusion that crime is 'primarily an activity conducted by working-class juveniles against motor vehicles, households and shops' (see also Chapter 1 of this volume).

Though 'crimes of the street' remain at the forefront of public attention, what have become known as 'crimes of the suites' have led to official investigations and sanctions, as well as attracting wider media and academic recognition. In Britain this was largely the result of a series of major frauds and financial scandals that emerged in the City of London from the late 1980s onwards.

The following were some of the most notorious cases:

- the collapse of the investment managers Barlow Clowes in 1988 left 17,000 small, mainly elderly, investors short of a total of £200 million, and managing director Peter Clowes was subsequently imprisoned for fraud;

- the Guinness–Distillers affair, which culminated in criminal convictions for three senior Guinness executives for insider dealing and other offences in September 1990;

- the closure of the Bank of Credit and Commerce International in July 1991 after the misappropriation of around £10 billion was exposed;

- following the mysterious death of publishing tycoon Robert Maxwell in November 1991, it was revealed that around £500 million had disappeared from his employees' pension funds;

- in May 1993 Asil Nadir jumped bail and fled to Northern Cyprus to escape criminal charges arising from the collapse of his Polly Peck International empire and the disappearance of some £450 million.

*Another unacceptable face of capitalism?
Asil Nadir jumped bail in 1993, with creditors
short of £450 million*

Violations of civil and even criminal codes by apparently respectable persons are not confined to the world of business and high finance, and nor are their consequences only to be recorded in sums of money. In Britain in the late 1980s there was a spate of disasters leading to major loss of life and serious injuries, in which criminal neglect of safety standards and regulations by public authorities and private companies was commonly alleged and occasionally proved. These included:

- the sinking of the *Herald of Free Enterprise* passenger ferry at Zeebrugge in 1987 (192 deaths);

- the Piper Alpha North Sea oil rig fire in 1988 (168 deaths);

- the capsize of the *Marchioness* pleasure boat in the Thames in 1989 (51 deaths).

In this chapter we move beyond the sorts of offences that commonly engage the attention of the police and the courts – not to mention journalists, politicians and the public – to consider a range of offences which have rarely been the major concern of criminologists. When we discuss 'ordinary' crime we feel that it is something familiar from our day-to-day experience, it is easily recognizable, clear-cut and straightforward. By contrast, offences committed by financiers and businessmen, by corporations or even by small firms, by employees, entrepreneurs or professionals, often appear remote, difficult to perceive, complex and obscure.

Not only does the state deal differently with white-collar offenders and 'ordinary' criminals, but there is also a marked difference in public attitudes. Whereas murderers and burglars provoke hostility and condemnation, public opinion on fraudsters, embezzlers and tax evaders is more ambivalent.

Our discussion of corporate crime is organized as follows. Section 2 examines issues in corporate crime: we begin by raising some of the themes raised by the study of white-collar offences that have wider relevance to the debate about crime. Section 3 considers the diversity of white-collar crime by surveying some of the wide range of offences that may be considered to fall within this category. In section 4 we examine the distinctive characteristics of corporate crime, while in section 5 we move on to review various theories about what makes respectable people breach laws and regulations. Section 6 looks at the issue of regulation: what are the particular methods used to prevent corporate offences, and to deter and punish white-collar offenders? Finally, in section 7 we examine the debate about how corporate crime can be curbed.

2 Issues in corporate crime

Throughout this book we have consistently questioned the idea that 'crime' is a site characterized by sharp, unproblematic contrasts. It is not a straightforward matter to distinguish between criminal and non-criminal, guilt and innocence, wrong and right. This chapter moves on to a sphere in which even deeper shades of grey predominate. Though a closer look into the shadows of corporate crime raises many questions, trying to answer them may help to throw light on some of the wider issues about how society defines crime and how it deals with different sorts of offences. In this section we indicate some of the themes to which we will return in the course of the

corporate crime

chapter. We can divide the problems that arise from the study of corporate crime into three areas:

- problems of definition: if we are going to expand the category of 'crime' to include corporate offences as well as familiar criminal acts, then what are the consequences for our understanding of 'crime' in general?

- problems of social context: what is the relationship between corporate crime and the wider operation of market forces and the profit motive?

- problems of regulation: can corporate crime be controlled by the customary informal mechanisms, or should there be a greater application of criminal sanctions?

2.1   What constitutes a crime?

From our brief discussion so far it is already clear that not all crime can be subsumed under lurid tabloid headlines and that criminals may not be as easily recognizable as viewers of popular television dramatizations and real-event reconstructions might think. It emerges that not all killing or avoidable death is defined as murder, and not all those responsible for deaths face criminal prosecution.

It also appears that many sorts of injury to the person are not regarded by the official authorities as criminal offences and that there are many ways in which people can be deprived of their property that are not treated by the criminal justice system as theft.

Once we look at a wider range of offences against individuals or the public it becomes clear that crime is not defined by the character or consequences of any particular action, but by whether it is judged to be in *white-collar* violation of the criminal law. Whilst some white-collar offences, such as fraud *crime* or insider dealing, may be commonly defined and treated as criminal, other offences, particularly those relating to the health and safety of employees, consumers and the public, are only likely to be viewed as breaches of more or less informal regulatory codes. As a result of such violations, corporate entrepreneurs may be sued for damages and subjected to various financial sanctions, but they are unlikely to face criminal prosecution, no matter how serious the consequences of their actions (Burrows and Hiram, 1995). The tendency to label many such offences as 'accidents' reflects the emphasis on motivation in the definition of a criminal act. In ordinary crime the key issue is to prove intent to cause harm; white-collar offences may result in harm, but because this was not the primary intention of the offender such actions do not usually come to the attention of the criminal justice system.

In some cases, most conspicuously in major disasters, public opinion may be shocked by the spectacle of large-scale death and injury. Survivors and relatives of victims of such tragic events often express the view that somebody must be to blame and should therefore be liable to prosecution. Yet it is often so difficult to ascertain what went wrong and to attribute individual responsibility that no prosecution can be sustained. In such cases people may condemn the criminality of individuals at various levels of the corporate hierarchy in an appeal to a higher morality than that enshrined in the law. But in the eyes of the law, it may well appear that no crime, or even offence, has been committed.

2.2   What is the relationship between crime and the market?

Once we shift the focus of our attention from the street or home to the boardroom, office or other workplace, the close association between various offences and commercial enterprise is inescapable. All forms of trade inevitably create the possibility of fraud; the greater the scale of commercial activity, the greater the scope for dishonest practices. The expansion of manufacturing industry and the parallel growth of credit and the finance sector in nineteenth-century Britain were accompanied by a rising incidence of major frauds and other offences against employees, competitors, consumers and the public (Robb, 1992).

The growing bureaucratic complexity of the modern enterprise and the separation of ownership and control following the transition from family firms to those with publicly held shares, with prices regulated through stock exchanges, have facilitated large-scale corporate crime over the past century. These developments make it impossible for the old-style entrepreneur to supervise corporate affairs directly. The resulting division of labour makes it possible for individuals at any level of the hierarchy to engage in illicit activities. The concentration and centralization of capital into larger and larger units administered by professional managers means that the modern company offers corrupt executives the prospect of big rewards for relatively little risk, making corporate crime an attractive option for some.

bureaucratic complexity

Tendencies towards monopoly and periodic recession in the modern era have expanded the range of corporate wrongdoing. Attempts to fix prices and thus contain competitive rivalries among a small number of large firms operating in the same market have provoked state intervention, through informal regulations or formal legislation, in an attempt to uphold the principles of the free market. Meanwhile, periods of economic crisis have intensified competitive rivalries, increasing pressures towards sharp practice and illegality.

Since the onset of the world-wide recession of the 1980s, western and indeed many former Communist governments have pursued a policy of deregulation, reining back state intervention and promoting market forces in all spheres of economic activity. The deregulation of the London Stock Exchange in the 'Big Bang' of October 1986 marked a decisive opening up of the City of London to international money markets. Whatever the effect of these policies in reviving industry, there can be little doubt that the relaxation of controls on the financial sector in Britain appeared to increase the scale of fraud and corruption, leading to the collapse of banks and destabilizing other institutions, such as the insurance brokers Lloyds.

deregulation

The close association between commerce and crime suggests that the link is not merely that enterprise offers opportunities for the unscrupulous. The market assumes equal exchange, yet it creates the possibility of unequal exchange, by fraud or deception. The most fundamental dictate of the market – 'buy cheap, sell dear' – implies a competitive pressure to gain an advantage over a rival or customer. The market itself has no means of distinguishing whether this is achieved by fair means or foul. The spectrum of practices that stretches from legitimate competition, through sharp practice to overt fraud is inherent in market relations. The shades of grey that we have noted in the sphere of corporate offences originate in market forces. The personal characteristics of the corporate criminal – charm, aggression, ambition, cunning, ruthlessness – are difficult to distinguish from those of the successful entrepreneur. Indeed, it is striking that many individuals convicted of major white-collar crimes – Guinness executive Ernest Saunders, US car salesman John De Lorean, Mike Miliken, the 'junk-bond king' of Wall Street – were successful businessmen before they turned to crime.

2.3   How should corporate crime be regulated?

It is immediately apparent that the state authorities deal differently with ordinary and white-collar crime. Furthermore, the differences in the way that different sorts of violation are defined and treated appear to bear little relation to the scale of the offence or the damage caused. Thus being responsible for killing one person with a gun or knife is likely to lead to a lengthy spell in prison; being responsible for the deaths of hundreds by ignoring safety regulations is unlikely to lead to any conviction at all. Stealing a car, housebreaking or shoplifting may lead to a stiff fine and, if repeated, imprisonment, even though the value of the goods taken might amount to, at most, a few thousand pounds. By contrast, defrauding shareholders or creditors of millions is less likely to be detected and prosecuted and therefore to result in a custodial sentence.

The contrast between the coercive mode of regulation of ordinary crime through the criminal justice system and the strategy of seeking to secure the compliance of companies and individuals with more or less voluntary and informal codes of practice is at the centre of a long-running debate about the control of white-collar offences.

self-regulation On the one side stand those who uphold a system of self-regulation. While perhaps supporting some measures to improve it, they oppose more intrusive proposals, not least because of the potentially adverse effect on legitimate enterprise. On the other side stand those who condemn what they consider to be the indulgent and lenient responses of the authorities towards white-collar crime and the resulting ambivalence in public attitudes. They demand the extension of criminal legislation, enforced by the police and the courts, into the sphere of white-collar crime.

3   The diversity of corporate crime

The classic definition of white-collar crime was formulated by the American sociologist Edwin Sutherland in 1949 (see Extract 6.1).

Some commentators have broadened Sutherland's definition by bringing in offences committed lower down the occupational hierarchy, including any crime committed in the course of legitimate employment or any abuse of occupational role (Shapiro, 1990; Quinney, 1977).

To illustrate the range of corporate crime, it is useful to identify five categories of offence:

- large corporate crime: offences by legitimate companies, which may affect a wide range of victims, including employees, consumers, the wider public, the environment, other firms, the state, other states;

- large-scale criminal corporations: major frauds and other illicit activities perpetrated by big-time entrepreneurs or criminal syndicates;

Extract 6.1   Sutherland: 'The problem of white-collar crime'

[My] thesis … , stated positively, is that persons of the upper socio-economic class engage in much criminal behaviour; that this criminal behaviour differs from the criminal behaviour of the lower socio-economic class principally in the administrative procedures which are used in dealing with the offenders; and that variations in administrative procedures are not significant from the point of view of causation of crime …

These violations of law by persons in the upper socio-economic class are, for convenience, called 'white-collar crimes'. This concept is not intended to be definitive, but merely to call attention to crimes which are not ordinarily included within the scope of criminology. White-collar crime may be defined approximately as a crime committed by a person of respectability and high social status in the course of his occupation …

The significant thing about white-collar crime is that it is not associated with poverty or with social and personal pathologies which accompany poverty.

If it can be shown that white-collar crimes are frequent, a general theory that crime is due to poverty and its related pathologies is shown to be invalid. Furthermore, the study of white-collar crime may assist in locating those factors which, being common to the crimes of the rich and the poor, are most significant for a general theory of criminal behaviour …

The financial cost of white-collar crime is probably several times as great as the financial cost of all the crimes which are customarily regarded as 'the crime problem' …

This financial loss from white-collar crime, great as it is, is less important than the damage to social relations. White-collar crimes violate trust and therefore create distrust; this lowers social morale and produces social disorganization. Many of the white-collar crimes attack the fundamental principles of the American institutions. Ordinary crimes, on the other hand, produce little effect on social institutions or social organization.

(Sutherland, 1949, pp.9–10, 12–13)

- small-scale criminal firms: petty frauds committed by dealers, tradesmen, businessmen or professionals against consumers, creditors or clients;
- occupational crime: offences committed by individuals taking advantage of their position of employment, the gravity of the offence largely depending on the status of the employee;
- other white-collar crime: offences committed by middle-class individuals outside the sphere of employment, notably tax evasion and insurance frauds.

Let's look at each of these categories in more detail.

3.1   Large corporate crime

Violations of the civil or criminal law, or of other regulatory codes, are commonly committed by large and otherwise legitimate corporations in the course of their commercial activities. The crimes of large corporations may be subdivided according to their victim, though in practice there is often considerable overlap.

3.1.1 Offences against employees

In the drive to reduce costs, meet deadlines and increase profits, companies may breach employment contracts and health and safety regulations at the expense of the workforce. Corporate offences against employees most commonly come to public attention when they lead to death or injury at work.

In Britain more than 400 people die every year as a result of accidents at work and at least the same number die of occupationally acquired diseases such as pneumoconiosis and asbestosis (Health and Safety Commission, 1993). Since the early 1980s the recession has produced a steady fall in fatal injuries because it has severely restricted activity in some of the most dangerous sectors, notably construction and mining. Nevertheless, in Britain in 1992 some 28,000 people suffered serious accidents and 140,000 minor injuries. According to Croall (1992), two-thirds of fatal accidents involved some management violation of the Heath and Safety at Work Act and three-quarters were blamed on management. Yet less than 40 per cent of workplace deaths resulted in prosecution.

For example, the deaths of 168 workers on the Piper Alpha oil rig in the North Sea in 1988 were subsequently attributed to the weakness of both safety regulations and their enforcement in an industry characterized by hazardous conditions and intense time pressures dictated by market forces (Clarke, 1990a; Carson, 1982). Long before the Piper Alpha fire, North Sea oil had acquired a reputation as one of the most dangerous spheres of employment in British industry. The Piper Alpha disaster followed similar earlier incidents in the North Sea, one on Sea Gem in 1965 which led to 13 deaths, and another on the Alexander Kielland rig in Norwegian waters which led to 123 deaths. Was this a natural disaster, an accident or a crime?

The burnt-out shell of the Piper Alpha oil rig in which 168 people died: a natural disaster, an accident or a crime?

3.1.2   Offences against consumers

The selling of defective products is as old as the market, but modern capitalism has greatly expanded the scope for offences against the consumer. These extend from fraudulent advertising, through inferior design, manufacture and maintenance, to the defiance of regulations designed to protect the welfare of those who purchase a particular commodity or service.

Whereas in the past the sale of adulterated bread or watered-down beer and spirits probably caused minor upsets or irritation to a small number of people, the mass marketing of defective foodstuffs or of dangerous consumer goods in modern society may have catastrophic consequences. In Spain in 1987 the consumption of cooking oil contaminated with toxic chemicals killed 259 people (Croall, 1992). The sale of the Ford Pinto in the USA in the 1970s, when the company was fully aware of its mechanical defects, may have led to between 500 and 900 deaths (**Box, 1983**).

The defective manufacture and negligent operation of mass transportation systems involving air, rail, sea or road have led to numerous disasters with loss of life and serious injury to passengers. The report of the Sheen inquiry into the capsize of the passenger and freight ferry the *Herald of Free Enterprise* at Zeebrugge in March 1987, which resulted in the deaths of 154 passengers and 38 crew members, blamed the ferry owners P&O Ferries International Ltd for failing to provide a safe operating system and the assistant bosun for falling asleep on the job (Wells, 1993, pp.44–8). Though the Director of Public Prosecutions was pressed to institute a 'corporate manslaughter' prosecution, this could not be sustained. Similar acts of culpable negligence were exposed as the causes of the signal failure that led to the Clapham rail disaster, which killed 35 people in 1987, and the sinking of the pleasure boat *Marchioness* as a result of a collision with another vessel on the Thames in 1989.

3.1.3   Offences against the public

The potential danger to the public and the environment resulting from industrial development has grown with the scale of corporate enterprise and with the toxicity of some of the products and by-products of modern production processes. The extraction and consumption of traditional sources of energy – coal, oil, gas – has always been a dirty and dangerous business, but the accelerated pace of such activities in modern times has caused levels of pollution with global consequences. The most widely exploited alternative to fossil fuels, nuclear power, has the potential to be even more dangerous, with risks of leakage as well as toxic waste. Any corporate irresponsibility in this area, in parallel with the potential to endanger the public and the environment, could make a lethal combination.

'Accidents' resulting from similar sets of circumstances, perhaps without the same catastrophic consequences, are always possible throughout modern industry. Disasters associated with explosive and toxic chemicals have become familiar news items. An explosion at Flixborough near Scarborough in England in 1974 killed 28 people and injured another 89. The release of dioxin at Seveso in Italy in 1976 caused widespread pollution and an epidemic of disfiguring chloracne among local children.

In their detailed account of the catastrophic release of toxic gases at the Union Carbide factory at Bhopal in India in 1984, Pearce and Tombs (1993)

Bhopal, 1984: thousands died, and tens of thousands are still awaiting compensation from the US chemical giant Union Carbide

expose the poor design of the plant, its inappropriate siting near a shanty town, its inadequate safety systems, the lack of a proper emergency plan, and the generally run-down conditions that prevailed. They conclude that 'despite public commitments to health, safety and environmental protection ... Union Carbide created, or allowed to develop, the conditions whereby an accident was possible' (p.207). Furthermore, the company 'had not taken the steps necessary to mitigate the effects of any accident'. Compensation claims were still outstanding a decade after the disaster.

3.1.4 Offences against other firms

The competitive struggle to maximize profits or to survive sometimes drives entrepreneurs to transgress various rules and regulations in order to gain advantage over their rivals. Industrial espionage is as old as capitalism, and attempts to fix prices in markets dominated by a few large firms are as old as anti-monopoly legislation. In a famous case in the USA in the 1960s, GEC and Westinghouse, two of the largest companies in the heavy electrical supply industry, were convicted of flagrant price fixing in violation of the Sherman Act of 1890 (Geis, 1987).

The speculative financial boom of the late 1980s provided the conditions for a wide range of sharp practices shading into overt fraud – and massive rewards for successful operators. The background to the Guinness–Distillers affair, which was exposed in 1986, was the trend for corporations to look to 'mergers and acquisitions' in the City rather than invest in a stagnant real economy. In takeover bids, and in the closely associated activities of corporate raiding and asset stripping, all of which flourished in the 1980s, the dividing line between business and crime is one which many, not least the City's own regulatory bodies and the courts, find difficult to define.

Guinness's takeover bid for Distillers was fiercely contested and, as Clarke (1990a, p.176) observes, 'contested bids are the most prone of all to abuse, since not only is the target company resisting the bid, but there are two (rarely more) bidders chasing the shares'. To strengthen its own position in relation both to Distillers and to a rival bid from the Argyll group, Guinness spent £25 million in arranging for friends and associates to buy up its own shares and thus bolster its share price. At the same time it bought up a decisive tranche of Distillers' shares at an inflated price it could not have honoured to all the shareholders. Both these manoeuvres were considered in breach of Stock Exchange regulations and, in 1991, of the criminal law. Chief executive Ernest Saunders and two associates were convicted and received prison sentences.

3.1.5 Offences against the state

The high level of state intervention in economic life in modern society creates a range of points of contact between government officials and corporations at which corrupt practices may occur. Corporate tax evasion is probably the biggest single cause of lost revenue to the government, but it is usually dealt with by informal means and rarely comes to the courts.

Companies may bribe government officials to secure important contracts, as the aerospace firm Lockheed did in the USA on a grand scale in the 1960s and 1970s. Firms may pay off officials in central and local government or other regulatory bodies to ignore breaches of various regulations. On the other hand, as in the scandal surrounding sales to Iraq of engineering equipment with potential military use by the British firm Matrix Churchill shortly before the Gulf War in 1990, government ministers may discreetly encourage companies to act in defiance of controls (and then try to hide behind civil servants and 'official secrecy' regulations) (Norton-Taylor, 1995; see also Chapter 7 of this volume).

Companies may cultivate close links with politicians and civil servants to secure government initiatives that are considered to be in the company's interests. The line between legitimate lobbying and corruption may be a fine one. The resignation of US vice-president Spiro Agnew in 1973, after revelations that he continued to receive the gifts from companies that he had enjoyed as governor of Maryland even after he became vice-president, indicated the extent of such practices in the USA. President Nixon granted Agnew immunity from prosecution, thus avoiding a trial in which, it was believed, similar offences by others in high places would have been exposed. Newspaper revelations in Britain in 1993 and 1994 that MPs had accepted payments for asking parliamentary questions in pursuit of various commercial interests were followed by a series of similar scandals, giving rise to widespread concern over the extent of 'sleaze' in public life.

In Britain the trend towards the privatization of formerly nationalized industries and public services has opened up enormous scope for bribery to secure contracts and other sorts of corruption. In January 1994 the public accounts committee of the House of Commons published 'a damning catalogue of public impropriety, fraud and mismanagement' in government departments, health authorities and newly established quangos such as the Property Services Agency, the National Rivers Authority and Civil Service Catering (*The Guardian*, 28 January 1994).

Major multinational companies have frequently combined their economic activities overseas with political interference in other countries to secure what they regard as favourable conditions for their commercial activities. This may mean acting as an agent for the foreign policy of their country of origin. Examples include the involvement of the United Fruit Company in bringing down the Arbenz government in Guatemala in the 1950s, the role played by Tiny Rowland's Lonrho company in evading sanctions against Ian Smith's white minority regime in Rhodesia in the 1960s, and the activities of the telecommunications firm ITT in undermining the Allende government in Chile in the early 1970s.

Political interference by American firms is by no means confined to the Third World. There have been scandals about payments to politicians in many European countries and Japan, leading to ministerial and even prime ministerial resignations.

3.2 Criminal corporations and big-time criminals

fraud

Whereas the offences considered above are committed by respectable national and transnational companies that are often household names, there is another type of firm which is in essence a criminal corporation. Though it may have a legitimate façade, its main activity is fraud. Such operations are sometimes fronted by one flamboyant individual, or they may provide a more discreet cover for a criminal syndicate.

The origins of major financial fraud lie in the emergence of a vast banking network, linked to the growth of insurance, stocks and credit, in the years following the industrial revolution in Britain in the mid nineteenth century (Robb, 1992). The scope for such activities and the scale of fraud they can perpetrate expanded enormously in the globalized financial world that emerged in the 1980s.

One consequence of the spate of major fraud in the City was the establishment in 1987 of the Serious Fraud Office (SFO). By 1991 it was investigating some 56 cases involving a total value of £1.6 billion (Croall, 1992, p.29). However, the SFO suffered early setbacks when its attempts to bring further charges in the Guinness affair collapsed in February 1992.

Another feature of the large-scale corporate crime sector is the tendency for more old-fashioned criminals, such as armed robbers, to move upmarket. They are attracted by the promise of rich pickings (and lower risks) in the white-collar sector and the growing effectiveness of security systems in deterring old-style armed robbery and safe-cracking (Levi, 1987). Thus, for example, the 1985 Brinks-Mat gold bullion robbery was carried out by veteran criminals, who discovered that it was possible to melt down gold worth £26.5 million and to exchange it for cash over the counter in London banks. Exercising the traditional discretion to respectable customers, the bankers asked no questions, even though they had to apply specially to the Bank of England for extra £50 notes.

The Bank of Credit and Commerce International (BCCI), which was closed down in July 1991 with outstanding debts of around £10 billion and more than 300,000 creditors world-wide (30,000 in Britain), is the classic example of a modern 'megafraud' (Adams and Frantz, 1992; Kochan and Whittington, 1991). Founded in 1972 by Agha Hassan Abedi from Pakistan, the bank always had close links to the Gulf state of Abu Dhabi. The bank's central offence was to use small investors' deposits to speculate on the stock markets and to make loans to customers, real or fictitious, who lacked the collateral to back them. Losses were concealed by taking out fictitious loans and raising around $600 million in unrecorded deposits, which were transferred from account to account and from one country to another.

Illicit business organizations in various forms have long flourished in providing more or less prohibited services in the spheres of drugs, sex, gambling and blood sports (Burden, 1990). In modern times the largest and most complex criminal business with global interconnections has developed around the production, transportation and marketing of cannabis, heroin and cocaine (Henman et al., 1985). The scale of this trade has made it a major economic and political influence, particularly in a number of Third World supplier countries. In November 1994 the United Nations hosted a three-day ministerial conference in Naples on the activities of the international crime syndicates, which it considered a growing threat to democracy. According to UN experts, such 'crime multinationals' were turning over a total of $750 billion a year, more than the economic output of most countries, and most of it laundered through banks (*The Independent*, 22 November 1994). If decisive action was not forthcoming, these booming 'businesses' would gradually corrupt and 'criminalize' the formal institutions of the global economy.

3.3 Petty criminals and corrupt professionals

While the big-money fraudsters have seized the limelight in recent years, the petty frauds perpetrated by a wide range of corrupt businesspeople and professionals at the corner shop or garage, in the street market and in the pub, in the small workshop or office, have carried on apace. Indeed, as recession turned to slump in the early 1990s, the squatted High Street shop and the car boot sale indicated a new variety of enterprises of dubious legality.

This category ranges widely, and though it includes many who might not often be seen in a white collar, it also includes many who are quite capable of earning a white-collar income. Such offences and offenders are not only of interest in themselves, but because they constitute an important link, in terms of outlook at least, between corporate crime and more familiar sorts of criminality (Sutton and Wild, 1988; Croall, 1989).

The classic petit-bourgeois crime is the long-firm fraud. This is well described by Levi (1984, p.321) as 'a business which orders substantial quantities of goods on credit at a time when the owners of that business either intend not to pay for them or suspect that, as things stand at present, they may not be able to pay for them'.

long-firm fraud

Levi distinguishes three subtypes: the 'pre-planned' fraud in which the company is set up with the deliberate intention of defrauding creditors; the other extreme of a legitimate company which continues to trade in a high risk situation; and the intermediate 'slippery slope' case in which a legitimate business slides into fraud, often in response to market difficulties. In the latter case, the result may be a fraud of the 'long-firm' type, or indeed any sort of fraud. As Levi (1984, p.332) indicates, the difficulty with curbing 'the long-firm fraud' is that it 'would require laws and levels of regulatory personnel that would be anathema to many business people and professionals'.

The most familiar types of small-scale business crimes are the sale of defective goods or the provision of unsatisfactory services. Street traders claiming that falsely hall-marked cheap jewellery contains precious metals, corner shops selling outdated foodstuffs, mechanics and other tradesmen who charge for jobs they have not done, car salesmen who tamper with mileometers, restaurants serving contaminated food in dirty kitchens – these are typical examples of petty offences against the consumer carried out by staff in small businesses.

As Sutton and Wild (1988) emphasize, such entrepreneurs have a precarious existence in the niches of the market not occupied by the big corporations. They offer a highly motivated workforce, often family-based, and have a tenacious ideological commitment to free enterprise and its potential rewards.

A wide range of frauds are perpetrated against various official agencies. For example, the murder of two Ministry of Transport officials in Stockport in November 1993 drew public attention to a multi-million pound trade in MOT test certificates, which the two men were investigating. According to the

Retail Motor Industry Federation, some 154,400 test certificates were stolen in 1992; the going rate for fraudulent certificates was between £30 and £50, reaching up to £1,000 for heavy goods vehicles (*The Guardian*, 24 November 1993).

Local authorities are the victims of extensive rackets involving housing benefit cheques, resulting in losses of £20 million in 1992 (mostly in direct payments to corrupt landlords). False claims for student grants, false accounting, payroll frauds and fraud involving contractors and planning permission accounted for additional losses of around £12 million (HMSO, 1993).

Another type of petty fraud is that carried out by professionals either in collaboration with their clients – as in the case of accountants and lawyers who assist in disreputable activities against some third party – or against the client, which is possible in any professional relationship. Such conduct may include malpractice, when the client receives a professional service below the standards to which they are entitled, or fraud, when the client is required to pay in excess of a reasonable fee for the service provided.

3.4 Occupational crime

A wide range of offences are committed by individuals taking advantage of their positions as employees in a private company or public service. The character and scale of such offences depends largely on the nature of the employment and on the employee's status in the managerial hierarchy. The greater the responsibility borne by any particular employee, particularly in the handling of money, the greater the scope for negligence or criminality.

The question of responsibility for offences carried out in the course of routine employment often makes it difficult to distinguish between corporate and occupational crime. At one end of the spectrum stand the employees who take advantage of opportunities provided at work in clear violation of corporate policy and practice. At the other stands the employee who is genuinely 'only obeying orders', or at least in good faith carrying out duties within a corporate framework in which bending and breaking regulations has become commonplace and accepted.

This is usually, but not always, a distinction of status. More senior employees have greater autonomy and opportunity to violate regulations and perpetrate fraud, and the potential rewards may be substantial. Those at the lower end of the hierarchy are under greater pressure to conform to established practices, they have limited opportunities to commit offences, and their capacity for substantial fraud without detection is less.

corporate liability

The fact that it is obviously in the interest of any individual accused of offences relating to their occupational duties, especially those in executive positions, to seek to establish corporate liability, means that it is sometimes difficult to establish where the burden of responsibility lies. Individuals at different levels of the hierarchy are likely to commit different sorts of offences. Thus those at a higher level are more likely to be responsible for breaching regulations affecting the welfare of other employees, consumers, the public and the environment, other firms and the government, though sometimes the enterprise itself may be the main loser. Junior employees are more likely to engage in illicit activities to the detriment of the company itself, though the welfare of consumers and the public may be jeopardized as a result.

At lower levels of the occupational hierarchy, white-collar crime shades off into blue-collar crime, and major fraud gives way to petty theft and deception. At this level too a distinction may be drawn between what are commonly regarded as 'perks' of the job, justified by the familiar shrug and excuse that 'everybody's at it', and systematic frauds, which may involve the misappropriation of substantial sums of money over a period of time. All these distinctions are easier to theorize than they are to perceive in the real world of work, where shades of grey predominate.

Occupational offences at the lower end of the spectrum, though a common cause of summary dismissal and criminal conviction, rarely attract much publicity because they are so commonplace. The character of these offences varies greatly according to the nature of the occupation and the employee's status. Typical examples are the fiddling of expenses claims and the pilfering of petty cash; the theft of everything from company products to light bulbs, toilet rolls and stationery. In all retail outlets, short-changing and over-charging customers are commonplace. Employees who sell their labour in units of time may devise ways of illegitimately reclaiming minutes or hours, by outwitting whatever mechanism is used to monitor time-keeping or by fitting diverse domestic or leisure activities into the working day.

It is clear that few employees could honestly claim never to have committed offences in the workplace. On the other hand, any of these offences can be developed into substantial rackets, perhaps involving groups of employees in defrauding their employers of substantial sums over long periods of time. Computer access to financial systems may give relatively junior employees the scope to commit major fraud. A senior officer at the SFO reported to a conference on computer crime in London in October 1993 the case of a systems analyst who had been foiled in an attempt to transfer assets valued at £1.6 million to an account in Spain (*The Independent*, 25 October 1993).

Many employers ignore much petty fiddling and pilfering, regarding these almost as wage costs or operational overheads, indulging the popular view of these as the perks of the job. A study of routine fiddles conducted by workers engaged in bread delivery revealed that these were generally regarded as compensation for inadequate pay levels (Ditton, 1977). At the same time, recognizing the need to keep such activities under control, employers may periodically stage a clamp-down or purge and make an example of some individual as a general deterrent.

3.5 Middle-class crime

Following Sutherland, much of the academic discussion about 'white-collar' crime has focused on the areas we have considered as 'corporate' crime and, to a lesser extent, as 'occupational' crime. Here we consider a range of offences which may be committed by 'a person of respectability', but which fall outside corporate or occupational crime. These are offences committed by middle-class individuals outside of their employment or occupational role, notably tax evasion and insurance fraud.

Tax evasion is the archetypal middle-class crime (Deane, 1981; Cook, 1989; Croall, 1992). Though it accounts for an enormous loss of state revenue, it is widely regarded sympathetically and treated leniently by the authorities. With prosecutions running at less than 500 a year (compared with

8,000 for social security benefit fraud) the risks involved in tax evasion are low and the rewards high (Cook, 1989).

Insurance fraud is another booming sphere of middle-class criminality. Offences in this field vary enormously in scale, from the householder who adds a few extra items to losses sustained in a flood, fire or burglary, to those who routinely make small claims for household maintenance costs following a major storm, simply to reclaim the premium, and to those who stage fires at home and business premises for fraudulent purposes. According to Clarke (1989), such frauds are concentrated in the travel, motor, home and business contents area and commonly involve arson.

By the late 1980s there were signs of the growing concern of insurance companies at the rising scale of fraud. One indication of this concern was the public launch of the Motor Industry Anti-Fraud Register. Another was the development of better and more open co-operation between the police and the special investigation units run by the fire service.

ACTIVITY 6.1

Read the article 'Auditors place £36bn value on hidden economy' from *The Independent*, reproduced below, and then answer the following questions:

1   How can you explain the apparently low level of resources put into detecting tax evasion compared with the energetic pursuit of social security fraud?
2   Why are social security 'scroungers' condemned while tax evaders are generally ignored, if not envied and admired (see Carlen and Cook, 1989; Cook, 1989)?

Auditors place £36bn value on hidden economy

by Donald Macintyre

The 'hidden economy' is worth more than £36bn a year and is costing the country several billion pounds a year in lost tax, according to a National Audit Office report published today.

Not only the self-employed but also 'employees, the unemployed, the retired, students and house-wives' are all contributing to the hidden economy – defined as 'activity which is not made known to the tax authorities'.

The report by Sir John Bourn, the Comptroller and Auditor General, identifies among the worst offenders building workers, car salesmen, market traders, guest house owners, bookkeepers and auditors, insurance agents and brokers, scrap dealers and road haulage contractors.

But the report also reveals that the 109,000 largest employers in the country were late with 62 per cent of their monthly PAYE returns. This suggests many big firms are hanging on to tax payments deducted from employees until the last moment to maintain cash balances.

The report, which will be considered by the Public Accounts Committee in the New Year, shows that the amount collected from ghosts – people for whom no tax records exist – and moonlighters – registered taxpayers with undeclared jobs – has grown significantly because of a big collection drive.

Over the last five years it has risen £35.1m to £86.5m in 1992–93, despite staff shortages. But total 'compliance' enforcement by the Inland Revenue in 1992–93 yielded some £4.6bn of which £1.7bn was directly related to the hidden economy. But because 'Schedule D' compliance work, forcing ghosts and moonlighters to pay, is time consuming and less cost-effective than some other forms of tax collecting activity, switches of staff to more productive areas mean that a total of 42 tax districts currently have no one carrying out Schedule D compliance.

The NAO recommends that the Inland Revenue should carry out further analysis to examine the most cost-effective way of allocating resources.

(*The Independent*, 3 December 1993)

4 Characteristics: deconstructing corporate crime

Despite the diversity of corporate crime, it is possible to identify a number of common features (Croall, 1992). These characteristics help to clarify the distinctions between 'white-collar' crime and more familiar forms of criminality, and help to explain why such offences are regarded differently by society and treated differently within the criminal justice system.

4.1 Low visibility

When somebody is stabbed and deprived of their wallet while walking down the street, it is clear to all involved – and to a wider public notified through the media – that a crime has taken place. In the case of, for example, the Guinness bid to take over Distillers, the offences of which several Guinness executives were subsequently convicted were not at all apparent to many of those closely involved, let alone to the public at large. As we have seen, even in the less spectacular and much more common event of a 'long-firm' fraud, the distinctions between misfortune, incompetence and criminality may be far from obvious.

The fact that corporate crimes are carried out under the cover of normal occupational routines helps to hide them from public view. The image of respectability projected by large corporations with familiar brand name products and highly publicized commitments to charitable trusts and other good works may also disguise their transgressions of laws and regulations. As we have seen, the fine line between aggressive business tactics in a competitive market and overt criminality may in practice be a difficult one to perceive, particularly by those with high personal stakes in corporate success.

The essentially 'private nature' of corporate crime also contributes to its invisibility. By contrast with 'crimes of the streets', 'crimes of the suites' take place out of public view and, generally, out of the glare of publicity. Whereas the media focus on conventional crime and criminals, relatively little attention is paid to corporate crime. This may sometimes be attributable to corruption (as in the case of the failure of the Italian media to expose the role of the Mafia in politics and big business) or it may be the result of intimidation (as in Robert Maxwell's notorious use of libel law to prevent the exposure of his fraudulent activities by investigative journalists).

Levi (1987, p.13) has commented thus on the media's attitude to white-collar crime: 'The general relative media neglect of business crime compared with other forms of crime is explicable more by laziness, investigative cost, the invisible nature of the crime and the deviousness of its progenitors, and by the difficulty of presenting it simply in the human terms expected by mass audiences, than by any elite conspiracy to suppress it.'

Do you agree with this assessment? Is there any other explanation of media neglect of white-collar crime than Levi's alternatives of circumstantial factors and conspiracy?

4.2 Complexity

When a house is burgled, the offence is not only transparent, it is also straightforward – one person has forcibly entered another's house and seized their property. In the case of corporate crime the offence is often more complicated, particularly in terms of the process of appropriating money or goods, which may involve numerous transactions among different agents over a considerable period of time.

Major frauds, such as those involving the BCCI or Robert Maxwell, are characteristically highly complex. These cases involved large numbers of individuals (with varying degrees of awareness and culpability) and a network of companies and bank accounts engaged in interlinked deals and transfers of assets over several years. Teams of expert investigators have spent years (and many millions) in attempting to unravel these megafrauds in the hope of pursuing prosecutions and securing the return of at least some of the misappropriated funds.

Complexity is not, however, peculiar to criminal corporations, but is a characteristic feature of bureaucratic organization within the modern company. Trends towards recession that re-emerged in the world economy in the early 1980s, together with the aggressively anti-state, pro-market ideology characteristic of the Reagan/Thatcher years on both sides of the Atlantic, have further complicated the organization of commercial activity. The withdrawal of state controls from national markets and financial systems was a response to economic stagnation which sought to accelerate the global circulation of capital and commodities. However, together with the parallel trend towards the privatization of industry and services, it also increased the scope for fraud and corruption.

The deregulation of the money markets took place in tandem with the development of computer and information technologies, enabling instantaneous communication and round-the-clock trading on the world's major money markets. All these trends create greater scope for illicit activity of a complexity mirroring that of the system itself, and with the offer of high rewards.

4.3 Diffusion of responsibility

The difficulty of pinning the blame for the crimes of the powerful on any particular individual becomes clearest when the question of culpability for a major disaster arises. For example, inquiries into responsibility for the deaths that occurred in the *Herald of Free Enterprise* and *Marchioness* disasters variously attributed blame to individual crew members on duty at the time of the incident, their commanding officers, the companies owning and operating the boats, and the regulatory authorities. Though various prosecutions were initiated against individual crew members, by the state authorities and privately by relatives of the deceased, none succeeded.

It is noteworthy that, in terms of media attention and judicial procedures, the only individuals identified as potentially culpable were the crew members in charge of the boats when the incidents took place. Neither the press nor the courts identified individual company executives or members of the regulatory authorities as bearing any personal responsibility for these disasters.

The Marchioness *the morning after: though 51 people died, nobody was convicted of any offence*

The diffusion of responsibility for corporate crime is a consequence of the complex division of labour and hierarchical structure of the large firm, which makes it difficult to determine who is responsible for a particular offence. As Croall (1992, pp.12–13) argues, 'this is particularly the case with organizational offences which may involve neglect or deliberate flouting of many regulations covering health, safety, quality control, information or sales practices'. Furthermore, 'at all levels of the chain of responsibility … individual employees can deny responsibility by claiming that they were only "following orders" or that their orders were ignored' (p.13).

The attribution of responsibility is further complicated by the fact that many corporate crimes do not result from any malign intent (*mens rea* in legal terms), but rather from neglect of regulations. The difficulty of proving that the corporate offender consciously intended to inflict the harm that resulted from his actions (or failure to act) means that in law such offences can rarely be considered criminal. Thus whatever the scale of death or injury that results, the state regards such corporate wrong-doings as 'quasi' crimes committed against a vaguely defined 'public welfare', whereas 'real' crimes are directed, intentionally, against individuals (Wells, 1993, pp.5–8).

4.4   Diffusion of victimization

Whereas it is usually apparent when somebody has been robbed or murdered, the victims of corporate crime may not even be aware of the offence. This is most obvious in the case of company violations of anti-pollution regulations, which may affect vast numbers of people, but often (though by no means always) to a relatively small and scarcely perceptible degree. Thus while the immediate local impact of the Chernobyl nuclear power station explosion in 1986 was lethally clear, its wider consequences, in terms of an increased incidence of radiation-related malignancies and other disorders over a wide area of Northern Europe, will only become apparent over several decades. Periodic disasters draw public attention to the more mundane corporate neglect of environmental safeguards that are prejudicial to public health on a small scale, but are commonplace and may well result in a considerable excess morbidity and mortality in the long term.

Similarly, the losses to any particular individual resulting from petty frauds perpetrated against a large number of consumers or creditors may be relatively small, even though the gain to the fraudsters may be considerable.

Again, it is only the more spectacular frauds resulting in substantial losses to relatively large numbers of people that bring to public attention the fact that we all have to pay the price of more mundane white-collar crime – in higher prices, insurance premiums, taxes, etc. – as well as suffering inferior consumer goods and services.

ACTIVITY 6.2

Read the article 'Arrests follow £1bn mortgage fraud probe' from *The Guardian*, reproduced below. Which characteristic features of corporate crime are present in this case?

Arrests follow £1bn mortgage fraud probe

by Michael Gillard

Scotland Yard has begun making a series of arrests in what is described as Britain's biggest ever mortgage fraud, involving property deals totalling more than £1 billion and losses to the banks and building societies involved of up to £100 million.

A number of those involved were arrested and charged with various offences last Thursday and Friday. Other participants are expected to be charged early this week.

A total of 19 company directors, lawyers, bank and building society officials, valuers and loan brokers are likely to be charged. The defendants are expected to appear in court for the first time later this month.

The arrests follow an investigation lasting more than two years by Scotland Yard Fraud Squad detectives into a maze of interlocking deals involving 200–300 homes, commercial properties, pubs and a football ground in London and the South-east which were to be sold or redeveloped.

A senior Yard detective described the case as 'the most complex mortgage fraud ever investigated'. The largest previous cases involved less than £10 million.

The biggest victim is understood to be Barclays Bank. It has been alleged in the High Court that a £70,000 Hansel and Gretel style cottage was built at no cost in the garden of a Barclays manager by the company at the centre of the fraud. The cost was to be 'lost' in that of a nearby office development. The manager has denied the cottage was a gift.

National Westminster, Royal Bank of Scotland, the Cheltenham & Gloucester and several other building societies are among the other victims.

Scotland Yard was called in following information received from a solicitor, Guy Lucas, who ran a sole-partner practice, R Lucas & Sons, in Harrow but had a more impressive office near London's Regent's Park.

Lucas went to the police in March 1991. He later went into hiding, saying he was in fear of his life. He has been the subject of disciplinary proceedings by the Law Society.

Lucas acted on behalf of the company at the centre of the police investigation, the Harrovian Group, which collapsed in November 1991 with a deficit of £15 million. Harrovian, based in Harrow, was a family company headed by hotelier William Johnston.

Detectives discovered that multiple mortgages – in one case 14 – had been obtained on the same properties. Loans were obtained with inflated valuations. Lenders were also misled into believing they were financing 'dummy' sales.

Banks and building societies relied on solicitors' undertakings – a normal practice – to pay off non-existent mortgages.

Over the four years that the fraud operated, millions were allegedly siphoned off by those involved. But as the property market slumped, more and more money was required to cover up the fraud by making mortgage payments and financing purported sales.

Many lenders have sued the Law Society for compensation. Several valuers have also been sued in multi-million pound cases.

The Harrovian affair has resulted in the biggest ever claim against the Law Society's compensation fund, put at up to £10 million.

'We have been paying out on quite a slab of claims', a Law Society official confirmed yesterday. The Law Society has contested many claims on the basis of either contributory negligence or complicity in the frauds. Often lenders made no effort to check on the properties they were financing.

(*The Guardian*, 10 April 1994)

5 Explanation

Why do people, many of whom are relatively well-off, engage in the sort of offences we have described above? As we have already indicated in the introduction, the study of white-collar crime and criminality may help to encourage a wider questioning of traditional 'common-sense' theories of conventional crime and criminality. Let's look more closely at four approaches to explaining corporate crime.

5.1 Individual pathology

Just as in theories of conventional criminality, the focus of much of the early discussion of white-collar and corporate crime focused on individual pathology. Highly publicized cases of major frauds and financial offences perpetrated by high-profile individuals such as Robert Maxwell and Ernest Saunders in Britain have reinforced the popular view that such offences are committed by particular types of personality. Such individuals are characterized as greedy and ruthless, with a lack of scruple in exploiting others, and often a propensity to gamble for high stakes. Yet, as we have noted, these are the very personality traits widely considered to be conducive to success in the competitive world of private enterprise.

Robert Maxwell: a charismatic, flamboyant and successful entrepreneur, but he defrauded thousands of their pensions

In the immediate post-war period the American sociologist Marshall Clinard (1946) emphasized such personality traits among individual violators of the law in his studies of black marketeers, while Lane (1953), in his study of 'why businessmen violate the law' in New England, identified the 'more personal characteristics' of the offenders.

Individualistic theories of corporate deviance tend to find favour with both the authorities and public opinion. As Doig (1984) has argued, official investigations into corruption often tend to pin the blame on particular 'rotten apples' in an otherwise healthy barrel. This approach offers convenient scapegoats while limiting further investigations which might reveal both more extensive corruption and a closer relationship between legitimate and illegitimate operations than it would be comfortable to recognize or make public.

247

In a sense, the study of white-collar crime emerged out of a critique of individualistic criminological theories. In his pioneering work in the 1940s, Sutherland noted that 'conventional' crimes were largely committed by people of lower social class and that contemporary explanations of criminality emphasized poverty, social conditions and personality traits. It was immediately apparent that there was a weak correlation between white-collar crime and poverty. Hence Sutherland (1949, p.6) argued that 'social and personal pathologies are not an adequate explanation of criminal behaviour'. In pursuing wider cultural and structural explanations of white-collar crime, Sutherland paved the way for the development of post-war criminological theory in this area.

5.2 Company pathology

After the closure of the Bank of Credit and Commerce International in July 1991, the governor of the Bank of England described it as 'rotten right through' (quoted in Croall, 1992, p.60). The Sheen inquiry into the Zeebrugge disaster similarly condemned the parent company, P&O Ferries International, declaring that 'from top to bottom the body corporate was infected with the disease of sloppiness' (quoted in Wells, 1993, p.34). The fact that many of the offences we have been considering are committed by individuals working within corporate structures raises the question of the role of the organization itself in illicit behaviour. The focus of inquiry shifts from 'rotten apples' to the character of the barrel.

One of the main themes of Sutherland's theory of white-collar crime was the contribution of 'differential association' to deviant behaviour. He argued that criminal behaviour was 'learned in association with those who define such behaviour favourably and in isolation from those who define it unfavourably, and that a person in an appropriate situation engages in such criminal behaviour if, and only if, the weight of the favourable definitions exceeds the weight of the unfavourable definitions' (Sutherland, 1949, p.234). In other words, individuals who work in organizations in which rule-breaking is commonplace and accepted, tend to adopt such deviant behaviour patterns themselves.

Some have argued that the commitment of capitalist corporations to profit maximization makes them inherently 'criminogenic' (Gross, 1978). Pressures to raise production levels, increase sales and outwit competitors, etc. drive the hierarchy to cut corners on quality control, health and safety, and compliance with environmental and public health regulations. In his influential early study of retail pharmacists in the USA, Quinney (1964, p.14) concluded that 'prescription violation is related to the structure of the occupation and the differential orientation of retail pharmacists'. Pharmacists who were more concerned with the 'business' side of their activities were more likely to engage in violations than those who emphasized the more 'professional' aspects of their work.

The fact that there is considerable variation among large companies concerning their record of convictions for corporate violations confirms the importance of the culture within organizations. According to Clinard and Yeager (1980), around 40 per cent of large corporations have a clean sheet, indicating internal regimes unsympathetic to illicit activity.

At the other end of the spectrum there are clearly firms in which top management either encourage or turn a blind eye to illegality. As a result, a culture of 'everyone is at it' prevails, and new employees are rapidly socialized into deviant practices that are accepted as routine.

While some commentators have focused on how the culture of a particular firm can encourage or facilitate crime, others have identified the ways in which the social organization of work offers opportunities for the violation of the basic trust that is essential in the relationship between provider and consumer (Shapiro, 1990). Occupations clearly vary widely in the opportunities they provide, depending on the character of the industry or service and the employee's status. Mars (1982) has categorized occupations according to the opportunities for illegitimate activity they offer, dubbing them 'hawk' jobs, 'donkey' jobs, 'wolfpack' jobs and 'vulture' jobs as a way of reflecting the sorts of animal behaviour adopted by individuals in particular jobs. He also indicates occupations that are particularly 'fiddle-prone', such as hotel and catering and professional services.

The lowest level of organizational influence on criminal behaviour is the subculture of the workplace. Whatever the dominant ethos of the company, fiddling and pilfering, idling and absenteeism, even sabotage, may become a familiar and accepted part of day-to-day working life in a particular workshop, office or factory. In some workplaces such activities on a small scale are tacitly approved as perks, but sometimes they develop into extensive rackets which ultimately conflict with corporate goals and provoke criminal sanctions.

In all workplaces some workers may refuse to engage in illicit activities, indicating the influence of wider social forces beyond the workplace in conditioning the propensity of any particular individual to commit crime, whatever the culture of the organization or the workplace. Attempts to explain such differences in behaviour emphasize the 'neutralization of social controls' through the use of various justifications – such as assertions of loyalty to the firm, or that 'business is business', or dislike of government interference – which are more effective for some than others (Nelken, 1994, p.368). These 'control' theorists also argue that the difference between rule-breakers and the rest is that deviants have less of a stake in the existing social structure in terms of property, family or status.

5.3 Social disorganization

Sutherland, putting white-collar crime in a wider social context than the individual and the company, pointed to what he called 'social disorganization' as an important contributory factor. By this he meant a lack of standards or a conflict of standards in society which resulted in a loss of moral restraint. In turn, white-collar crime violates trust among individuals, and it 'thus lowers social morale and produces social disorganization' (Sutherland, 1949, p.13). For Sutherland, this breakdown in civilized standards within American firms was the result of the ascendancy of monopoly capitalism over free competition and the replacement of small family firms by large impersonal bureaucratic corporations.

Following the work of Sutherland's contemporary Merton, there have been various attempts to explain corporate crime as a deviant adaptation to the 'strain' on an individual in a corporate hierarchy (Nelken, 1994, p.368). Executives and managers are under intense pressure to fulfil both company and personal standards of success. Yet many experience structural obstacles – resulting from various restrictions on equal opportunities or merely from the operation of market forces – to realizing their aspirations for self-improvement.

Writing in the USA in the Great Depression of the 1930s, Merton pointed out the tension created by the 'ceaseless striving for more encouraged by the American dream' (quoted in Taylor, 1994) at a time when many of the institutional means of individual advancement were blocked. Given the weakness of moral consensus governing economic activity, some people responded to such 'strain' by deviant adaptations. Merton characterized white-collar crime as an 'innovative' response to the strain of conforming to cultural imperatives to maintain profitability. The immediate source of the pressure on the individual may vary: it may come from developments in the national economy, or from imperatives on particular industries or firms.

5.4 Radical perspectives

In the 1970s and 1980s radical criminologists sought to locate the problems of white-collar and corporate crime within a wider critique of modern capitalism and the social conflicts that it generates (Pearce, 1976; **Box, 1983**). These authors maintain that when companies encounter obstacles to maintaining profitability by legitimate means, particularly in periods of recession, they resort to illicit methods of the sorts we have already reviewed. They argue that such corporate crime is an inevitable corollary of the capitalist economy, especially when profits are in jeopardy.

Other radical commentators have emphasized the close relationship in general between the spirit of capitalist enterprise and corporate criminality. For Mars (1982, p.49), 'there is only a blurred line between entrepreneurality and flair on the one hand and sharp practices on the other'. In particular in periods of recession, when entrepreneurs are under intense competitive pressures, the boundaries between legitimate and illegitimate measures to reduce costs and maximize profits inevitably become blurred. It is also inevitable that the boundaries will be set differently by company executives keen to cut some corners, and by employees who may be obliged to work more intensively and perhaps at greater risk to health and safety. Consumers and the wider public may take a different view again, according to the nature of the enterprise and the consequences of violations of established codes of practice.

In addition, this perspective stresses the important functional role that organized crime has played in the development of capitalist economies world-wide. Luttwak (1995) reminds us of the crucial and highly complex part that local criminal groupings played in the post-war re-establishment and remarkable recovery of the West German, Italian and Japanese economies. He also maintains that a similar beneficial process is presently playing itself out in the crypto-capitalist economies of Eastern Europe. In Russia, for example,

> Local mafias act in many places and many ways to resist the excessive concentrations of economic power brought by government corruption, or rather by the prevalence of under the table joint ventures between Russian government officials and new private firms run by ex-officials – including the very highest officials and the very largest firms. They are, in effect, competitors which use physical force, or more often just the threat of force, usefully to offset the monopolistic market power in a still lawless economy.

(Luttwak, 1995, p.7)

As a result of the affinity between the spirit of enterprise and a readiness to bend the rules to guarantee profits, there is widespread moral ambivalence about white-collar offences. For many entrepreneurs the state and its laws are often regarded as imposing illegitimate restraints on the free operation of the sovereign laws of the market. As Benson (1985, p.588) observes, 'criminal behaviour can then be characterized as being in line with other higher laws of free enterprise'. For the typical small businessman, tax evasion is not so much an offence or a crime as a gesture of defiance against unwarranted state intrusions.

6 Regulation

The distinctive features of the regulation of corporate crime are:

*   informality, including 'self-regulation', voluntary guidelines, civil courts
*   a low risk of detection
*   a low risk of prosecution
*   more lenient sanctions

Let's look at each of these features more closely.

6.1 Informal regulation

Though some of the violations we have considered above, such as major fraud, come under the jurisdiction of the criminal justice system, many corporate crimes are regulatory offences. These include violations of health and safety, environmental health, or trading standards regulations, which are monitored by a variety of statutory, non-statutory or quasi-autonomous regulatory agencies. Because of the problem of proving 'malign intent' (*mens rea*) it is difficult to pursue criminal prosecutions against individuals (and even more difficult against companies), even though their neglect or evasion of particular standards or regulations may have caused major injury or loss of life.

regulatory offences

Even in the sphere of major fraud, the instinct of private enterprise for informal self-regulation – as manifested in the London Stock Exchange or Lloyds – remains powerful. Traditionally companies have jealously protected their commercial independence against outside interference, even at the cost of accepting a certain level of loss through fraud or other illicit practice. Many commentators have noted the gradual and piecemeal development of legislation against fraud. Such legislation has been introduced in the face of fierce resistance from defenders of business like the American judge who insisted that 'any interference with the operation of the natural laws of greed was subversive of liberty' (quoted in Geis and Mcier, 1977, p.11).

As Levi (1984, p.332) observes, 'to generate commercial control measures which would reduce the actual risk of being defrauded would require laws and levels of regulatory personnel that would be anathema to many business people and professionals'. In this spirit, Levi (1986, p.394) notes that, 'until 1980, the attitude to commercial fraud taken by all British governments could best be described as benign neglect'. McBarnet (1984, p.232) identifies an 'unholy trinity' of law, state and capitalist interests which has ensured that the balance between the needs of industry and the protection of the public remains firmly in favour of the *laissez-faire* policy of minimal intervention.

The problem with all informal forms of regulation is that they assume a consensus on norms of business practice that, if it ever existed, no longer does. Regulatory agencies are highly vulnerable to strategies of collusion and subversion, particularly by the sorts of entrepreneurs responsible for large frauds and other forms of financial malpractice.

In the course of the 1980s, however, fraud in the City reached such a scale as to threaten the survival of several banks, and even Lloyds itself suffered damaging losses. One result was the tightening up of informal systems of regulation. Another was the formation in 1983 of the Fraud Trials Committee under Lord Roskill, whose 1986 report recommended the formation of the Serious Fraud Office and reforms of criminal procedure including preparatory hearings to disclose the outlines of the case to all concerned and the abolition of the right to jury trial in complex fraud cases (Levi, 1986). The collapse of a series of cases brought by the SFO in the early 1990s, often after prolonged and vastly expensive investigations and court proceedings, intensified pressures for legislative reform. The paucity of successful prosecutions for insider dealing – running at an average of less than two a year through the 1980s – led to new provisions to proscribe it in the Criminal Justice Act of March 1994.

ACTIVITY 6.3

Read the article 'Britain fails to come to grips with suspicious share deals' from *The Independent*, reproduced opposite. Why has the Stock Exchange had such difficulty in dealing with brokers who violate its rules? How would legislation help?

6.2 Lower risk of detection

The characteristic features of corporate crime (considered in section 4) make it more likely that the offender will escape detection. The character of the regulatory machinery also helps to make such offences much less risky than conventional crimes like burglary or armed robbery. The most elementary difference is that whereas the police patrol the streets and have increasingly sophisticated methods of surveillance of *public* areas, it is difficult for anybody to see what is going on in the *private* spaces of corporate life.

The corporate sector has its own private security systems and 'watchdogs' of various sorts. Indeed, the police has a team dedicated to financial crime. However, the fact that in 1985 only 538 of Britain's 120,000 police were allocated to the Fraud Squad is a reflection of its priorities (Levi, 1987, p.14).

Regulatory agencies maintain teams of inspectors, but usually their numbers are small in relation to their responsibilities, and their powers of investigation are limited. The Health and Safety Inspectorate is a good example of a regulatory body with too few staff and too limited powers to monitor standards effectively in an area where, as we have seen, violations cause hundreds of deaths and major injuries every year. It is noteworthy that in the drive to curb public spending, the numbers of inspectors were reduced substantially in the 1980s. In the wave of privatization and deregulation in the 1980s, the inspectorate was targeted for removal from the public sector and has been stripped of many of its powers.

Britain fails to come to grips with suspicious share deals

by Heather Connon

Any irritation on Lord Archer's part at the Department of Trade and Industry's delay in releasing its verdict on whether he insider dealt in the shares of Anglia Television would be understandable.

The transactions that aroused the Stock Exchange's suspicion occurred in January; the DTI appointed inspectors on 8 February. It took them more than five months to produce their report, which was delivered to the DTI this week. There is still no indication of when the DTI will announce the outcome.

That may seem an inordinately long time to study three transactions, establish whether Lord Archer or his associates dealt in Anglia shares, and if so whether it was because they knew something they shouldn't. Yet this inquiry was dealt with more swiftly than most such investigations – if they are started at all.

The City's attitude to insider dealing has moved on dramatically since Sir Martin Jacomb, then chairman of the stockbroker Barclays de Zoete Wedd, described it as a victimless crime in 1986. Now institutional shareholders describe it as theft – and they know that they, and the pensioners and private shareholders they represent, are the victims. Those who buy or sell ahead of price-sensitive announcements are robbing law-abiding shareholders of profits, or inflicting losses on them.

Nevertheless, many in the City believe it is still rife. There is growing frustration at the apparent inability of the Stock Exchange to track down the offenders, at the delays in the investigation process, and at the difficulty in securing convictions when cases are actually brought to court.

In the past five years, the Stock Exchange has referred 52 suspicious cases to the DTI. It is responsible for deciding whether the allegations warrant further investigation – usually done by independent inspectors. In the same period 25 of these were appointed.

These numbers are tiny compared to the number of suspicious price movements seen in the market each week.

On Wednesday, for instance, after its share price had halved to 6p in a matter of days, the property adviser de Morgan was forced to confirm bid talks had been aborted. And last week Castle Communications disclosed it was in bid talks after its shares had soared.

These cases may already be on either the Stock Exchange or the DTI's list but the City doubts it. And in any case only 52 people have been tried, and just 23 convicted, in the 34 cases brought since the legislation was introduced in 1980.

Tighter legislation, introduced by the Criminal Justice Act on 1 March, may help – or it may just lead to more confusion, since it brings far more people into the insider net.

The best place to start improving matters is probably the Stock Exchange, where a 20-strong surveillance team is responsible for monitoring suspicious trades.

'Their credibility has been destroyed', one institutional investor said, pointing to Tiphook, where Paul Myners, chairman of the fund manager Gartmore, took the rare step of publicly calling for reform of the exchange's procedures because of their lack of success. 'They have no enthusiasm for investigation – they just go through the motions'.

A growing number of people believe that responsibility for monitoring all forms of market misconduct should no longer rest with the Stock Exchange.

Indeed, the regulator, the Securities and Investments Board, in a recent paper suggested that it should take on the responsibility for market surveillance. It argues markets are becoming increasingly complex, and more international. Effective surveillance will, therefore, increasingly depend on co-operation with other market regulators, like the London International Financial Futures Exchange and the London Traded Options Market, as well as with their counterparts overseas.

The exchange insists that it has never had any problem in getting co-operation from other regulators, although some suggest surveillance staff frequently have trouble even in persuading colleagues in other departments to talk to them.

Passing the responsibility up to the SIB would put a bit more distance between practitioners and regulators, which may give it more credibility.

But it would also need the exchange's co-operation and adequate resources: the 20 surveillance staff pale into insignificance compared with the huge resources available to the Securities and Exchange Commission in the US.

That has led some to suggest that Britain should have a Government-backed SEC-style market regulator. They compare the SEC's successful $100m fine and 22-month prison sentence for Ivan Boesky with the £25,000 fine and 12 months suspended for Geoffrey Collier, the Morgan Grenfell merchant banker who is still Britain's most famous offender.

British governments, however, tend to be less than effective regulators. So others suggest that insider dealing should become only a regulatory offence, which could be dealt with by the SIB or the exchange. Punishment would be a fine and disqualification from trading.

That would speed things up – there would be no need for time-consuming DTI reports or decisions by ministers. It would also remove the stringent evidence requirements needed to secure criminal conviction.

Leaving it to regulators is half-way to accepting that it is a victimless crime, though. A better solution may be to make it a civil offence, where less weighty evidence is required. In the US, it can be either – and the SEC will focus its energy only on criminal prosecution for cases involving large sums, or where there is evidence of a series of offences.

But letting regulators punish dealers would be unpopular unless there were radical changes to the surveillance system. As information is the key, that would be a good place to start. The rules permitting disclosure of large trades to be delayed by 90 minutes, or even up to five days, keep information from the market and should be abolished.

Most people in the City will be able to tell you which stockbrokers are regularly associated with suspicious deals. Immediate publication of all trades, and who carried them out, would disseminate that information more widely.

And that goes for companies too. The less time information is kept confidential, the fewer insiders are created.

(The Independent, 22 July 1994)

253

Another example of a watchdog lacking in bite is the Insolvency Service, an agency run by the Board of Trade, which appoints receivers to insolvent companies and is supposed to maintain a public register of directors found to be unfit to run a company. An inquiry by the National Audit Office, published in October 1993, revealed that more than 40,000 directors, 90 per cent of those suspected to be unfit to run a company, had escaped disqualification by the official receivers since 1986 (HMSO, 1993). The report complained of delays, inaction and incompetence, including failing to record on public registers nearly half the directors who had been barred from holding office. The report confirmed that the Insolvency Service had been simply overwhelmed by the wave of bankruptcies since 1986 and as a result was failing to do its job of protecting the public from unfit entrepreneurs.

Regulatory agencies usually deploy a mixture of reactive and proactive investigative techniques, but the emphasis is always on securing compliance with regulations rather than detecting offenders. Though environmental health and trading standards inspections are always unannounced, other agencies provide advance notice of inspection. This gives companies the opportunity to tighten up their procedures and also allows them to revert to their illicit practices the following day. The close relationship between regulatory agencies and the companies they regulate provides ample scope for collusion if not frank corruption.

6.3 Lower risk of prosecution

compliance

As we have seen, the emphasis of the authorities concerned with the crimes of the powerful is on securing compliance rather than inflicting punishment. This approach is particularly clear in the sphere of tax evasion. Though such crimes are common, the chances of detection are low, and on detection the chances of facing criminal charges are also low (Deane, 1981).

According to Deane, every year in Britain around 100,000 people make settlements with the Inland Revenue after they have been discovered fiddling their taxes; less than 200 are convicted. From his survey of such cases, Deane concluded that the risks of prosecution were increased if the defendant acted in collusion with others, if they were reluctant to admit their offence or made incomplete disclosures, if the case involved forged documents, if they had a professional adviser (accountant or lawyer), and if the offence had been repeated over many years.

A later survey comparing the official responses to tax evasion and social security fraud revealed a dramatic difference. Whereas in 1986–87 around 8,000 social security claimants were prosecuted, the figure for tax dodgers was 459 (Cook, 1989). In dealing with social security fraud the authorities

coercion

emphasized coercion, policing the poor and deterrence by prosecuting some and intimidating the rest. By contrast, their approach to tax evasion emphasized compliance, a concern to spare the feelings of the offender, and deterrence by exemplary prosecutions of a few.

Croall (1992) suggests that the policy of reserving prosecution for a minority of more serious offences or more blameworthy offenders has a wider applicability in relation to white-collar crime. Levi (1987, p.183) notes the low prosecution rate in relation to commercial fraud and observes that, by contrast with conventional crime, bringing criminal charges is generally regarded as the last resort in such cases. He also notes the emergence of a process of 'litigation' between defence lawyers and regulatory personnel, particularly in the USA.

In his account of 'attorneys at work' in defending white-collar crime cases in the USA, Mann (1985, p.4) emphasizes the 'potential for early action by a defence attorney to prevent the issuance of a formal criminal charge'. By contrast, in dealing with street crime, lawyers generally assume that their client is guilty and that conviction is likely and therefore enter a process of plea bargaining to minimize the sentence. Lawyers in the emerging speciality of white-collar crime also assume their client's guilt, but also that the state has not enough evidence to convict. The object of legal representation is to control access to information in such a way that government investigators and prosecutors are prevented from concluding that the client warrants criminal prosecution (Mann, 1985, pp.5–8). By entering a substantive defence before any charge is made, the defendant can often be saved from the public embarrassment of an indictment.

6.4 More lenient sanctions

Persistent offenders who steal £1 go to prison; persistent insider dealers who steal £10m pay back the money – perhaps in addition to a substantial fine – on the rare occasions that they are caught ... for the greatest things, the law provides no remedy.

(Levi, 1987, p.357)

In November 1993 Roger Levitt, a City 'financial adviser' whose firm collapsed in 1990 with debts of £34 million, was sentenced to 180 hours of community service (see Chapter 1). While the leniency of this punishment provoked a public outcry, it appeared to confirm Levi's point. Elsewhere he observes that 'except for professional people who steal from their clients' accounts – who are almost always sent to jail – fraudsters enjoy a low rate and average length of imprisonment, and a low average size of fine and compensation' (Levi, 1989, p.106).

Croall (1992, p.123), however, argues that when it comes to sentencing, there is little evidence of a clear class bias. Class advantage operates at every stage of the judicial process to prevent the respectable offender from being convicted. Thus powerful criminals can use their resources to avoid detection and prosecution and to secure out-of-court settlements. If they eventually do face criminal proceedings, they can afford good lawyers and can appear in court as honest and respectable businessmen. The prevailing prejudices that white-collar crime is not really serious and that the white-collar criminal is not a danger to the public all work to their advantage. It is often easier to disguise the persistent character of white-collar crime and the dishonest intent of the offender.

In passing sentence the judge may sympathetically take into account the damage to a respectable reputation resulting from conviction and hence impose a lesser sentence than might be considered appropriate for a conventional criminal of lower social class who had little reputation to lose. On the other hand, the judge may consider that somebody of elevated social status should be expected to maintain higher standards of behaviour and thus impose a harsher sentence. Thus Deane (1981) notes the tendency for a high proportion of major tax offenders who are convicted to be imprisoned and that professional advisers are as likely as anyone to face prison.

For Levi, the difficulty of judging whether the sentences imposed on those found guilty of commercial fraud are more lenient than those imposed on conventional criminals arises from the difficulty of making comparisons. Is robbing somebody of a small amount at gunpoint a more or less serious crime than defrauding them of a great deal more through the stroke of a pen? Like Croall, Levi (1987, p.313) concludes that 'commercial elites enjoy a structural advantage from the reporting, policing and prosecution processes, so that the practical significance of the post-conviction sentencing process, for members of the upperworld, is comparatively minor, at least at present'.

ACTIVITY 6.4

The spoof letter from the police to an adolescent burglar reproduced below reflects the differential response of the criminal justice system to conventional and white-collar crime:

> Dear G E Rald,
>
> We should like to take this opportunity to inform you that on 12th of March this year you were seen entering empty handed into the private premises of Ms P C Edwards of Convent St, Folkestone, and leaving shortly afterwards with your hands full.
>
> In our opinion, this constitutes a violation of the Theft Act 1968 subsection 32 (c) and we would be grateful if you would consider the following advice: please stop going down Convent St and entering houses without the owners' permission.
>
> We should warn you that next March 12th another police constable will be on foot duty in Convent St, and should he notice a repetition of your behaviour, we shall have to consider the possibility of taking even more stringent action than we have on this occasion.
>
> **(Box, 1983, p.50)**

List the key differences between the way the authorities seek to regulate white-collar crime and their methods for curbing burglaries.

COMMENT

As Box observes, there could be a public outcry if the authorities dealt with familiar types of criminality in the same way that they approach white-collar crime. The official response to the crimes of the powerful is consistent with some of the themes we have considered above: such violations are often not regarded as 'real' crime and are not treated as such at any stage in the legal process.

Box's letter illustrates how the state tries to control white-collar crime. Such offences are commonly subject either to civil courts or to non-judicial forms of regulation, rather than being dealt with by the criminal justice system. Offenders carry a lower risk of detection and, if they are caught, less chance of prosecution. The authorities tend to seek compliance with regulations and, if appropriate, financial reparation, rather than emphasizing the pursuit of punitive sanctions. If a middle-class offender is detected, prosecuted and convicted, then it is likely that he or she will receive a relatively lenient sentence, though because of the rarity of such cases it is difficult to make comparisons with sentencing for conventional crime.

7 Controlling corporate crime

The spate of highly publicized cases of major fraud and corruption over the past decade has provoked a fierce debate among criminologists – and more widely – about what should be done about corporate crime. In the aftermath of such cases as Maxwell and Nadir, there have been many statements, from politicians, journalists and academics, about the evils of white-collar crime and the urgency of doing more to prevent – and punish – them.

Levi has noted a perhaps surprising convergence on this matter between radical criminologists and regulatory authorities. The result is 'an intriguing harmony of interest ... between radical criminologists, on the one hand, and private security and self-regulatory organizations on the other, who are equally anxious to play up the costs and significance of business crime' (Levi, 1987, p.55).

Indeed, the debate about how to deal with white-collar crime has been characterized by a reversal of traditional positions on conventional crime and law and order. Conservative commentators, who generally favour more coercive strategies against conventional crime, tend to emphasize attempts to improve informal regulatory mechanisms to contain white-collar offences. By contrast, radicals who have demanded more liberal policies to deal with familiar forms of criminality, favour the more extensive and punitive use of the criminal justice system when it comes to white-collar crime. Some criminologists take up a middle position, favouring elements of both the above positions.

7.1 Compliance

Government policy-makers are preoccupied by the problem of how to prevent illicit practices in the business world without restraining legitimate entrepreneurial activity. Because, as we have seen, it is difficult to draw a clear line between crime and profit-making, the policy-makers are inclined to set the balance between restraining enterprise and preventing fraud in favour of minimizing intervention. They would rather suffer the costs of periodic frauds than tolerate state intrusions into the world of commerce. Levi (1987, p.357) exemplifies the prevailing cynicism: 'Although we may try to develop our upperworld equivalent of the punitive city we cannot try too hard: for whether they are market traders, first class chefs, or presidential advisers, those who are socially useful and create our wealth have to be allowed the occasional peccadillo.'

Another argument by those who oppose the application of criminal sanctions to white-collar crime is that, given the lack of moral opprobrium surrounding such offences, the result might be to degrade criminal law itself. Observing the relative public indifference to white-collar crime, Kadish (1963) counselled the US presidential commission on law enforcement in the 1960s against extending criminal law to cover it. He pointed to the 'danger of debilitating the moral impact of the criminal conviction and hence decreasing the overall effectiveness of the criminal law' (Kadish, 1963, p.312).

Those who favour relying on informal methods of regulating business also point out that the criminal justice system is expensive and ineffective in this area (Croall, 1992, p.145). The record of the Serious Fraud Office in the Guinness, Nadir and other cases has reinforced this view: prolonged and costly processes of investigation and litigation have rarely resulted in conviction.

The alternative to extending criminal sanctions is to improve existing regulatory systems, to make business more accountable for its activities. Clarke (1990a) outlines a range of 'prescriptive' strategies for tightening control, including the identification of violations, the accreditation of personnel, the exclusion and rehabilitation of offenders, and measures to ensure compensation. Clarke emphasizes the need to raise awareness of what is legitimate and illegitimate practice and the promotion of high standards of business and professional conduct. The recent record of illegality in high places may lead some to question his optimistic view of the prospects of self-regulation:

> In the longer term, business will continue, by small and on the micro level haphazard increments, to be made more accountable, and as part of that process, business offences will come to be increasingly carefully evaluated and the possibility for them circumscribed by ethical and regulatory innovations, and by special institutional arrangements, and the continuing perpetrators of them will be more and more likely to suffer exclusion from the market, not only as individually unacceptable, but as a threat to the common good.

(Clarke, 1990a, p.243)

7.2 Criminalization

Focusing on the sphere of large-scale corporate crime, Pearce and Tombs (1990, p.440) have argued forcefully that 'a punitive policing strategy is necessary, desirable and practicable'. They acknowledge the difficulties involved in policing corporations, but advance a number of specific recommendations. They consider that the criminal law could be used more widely against corporations and propose that it 'should be strictly and consistently enforced'. They recommend the modification of company law to make management 'accountable for safety'.

Pearce and Tombs further propose that state regulatory machinery should be funded by industry and treated as a cost of production. They call for penalties to be severe enough to act as a deterrent. Recognizing that such a set of policies would face stiff resistance from 'capital and its allies', they accept that 'ultimately it will have to be forced on corporations by other social groupings – workforces, local communities, consumers' (Pearce and Tombs, 1990, p.440).

In a similar spirit, **Box (1983)** insists that corporate crime is more serious than conventional crime and should be prioritized. However, he considers that the state and the criminal justice system have become more receptive to arguments that 'corporate crime victims deserve protection and that corporate criminals deserve sanctioning' (p.66). Box's policy proposals include a scheme forcing companies to make 'positive repentance' through advertisements that inform a mass audience of their offences and indicate their firm purpose of amendment (p.67).

Box goes on to suggest that 'serious consideration should be given to abandoning judicial practices which protect the accused from arbitrary or unjust conviction, or which ensure that they receive the benefit of the doubt'. Instead he proposes alternative judicial principles more conducive to securing prosecution and conviction. For example, the right to trial by jury 'could also be abandoned'.

Box is not reticent in drawing out the coercive logic of his proposals, calling for stiffer fines and insisting on the beneficial effects of imprisonment. However, recognizing the high risk of recidivism on return to the corporate environment, he suggests a bold alternative: ' "imprison" all or part of the offending corporation' by nationalizing it for a specific period. His proposals also include modified forms of probation order for deviant companies, community service orders – for example, a corrupt building firm could be ordered to build a hospital or some other socially utility – and adequate compensation of victims (Box, 1983, pp.72–3). He insists on the need for 'pro-active' policies to increase detection and conviction, including the use of spies, informers, entrapment and the encouragement of 'whistleblowers' (pp.73–4).

Whether or not such measures would prove effective against white-collar crime, the dangers to civil liberties – as distinct from capitalist enterprise – could be considerable. Levi (1987, pp.74–5) warns that 'liberals have reason to fear the setting of retributive punishment by popular acclamation'. He points out how, in the USA, the influence of populist pressures on the criminal justice system has resulted in harsher sentencing, not to mention the dramatic extension of capital punishment.

7.3 A middle way

Many criminologists find the compliance approach too complacent and the criminalization strategy too coercive. They favour a combination of tighter informal regulation and tougher formal punishments. This aims to achieve prevention and deterrence, whilst protecting justice and equity (see Extract 6.2).

Croall insists that white-collar crime is 'a real "crime problem" ': 'Like any other crime, it should be subject to both informal social control and such public prosecution and punishment as is necessary to both protect the public from victimisation and underline the moral unacceptability of serious white-collar offences' (Croall, 1992, p.174).

Braithwaite (1989) has further suggested a strategy of what he calls 're-integrative shaming', which seeks to reduce society's moral ambivalence over white-collar crime, but without stigmatizing offenders. He considers that stiffer penalties would signal the moral unacceptability of such offences, which could be underlined by informal mechanisms.

ACTIVITY 6.5

Read the article 'Crime without punishment' from *The Guardian*, reproduced overleaf. What are the difficulties facing the imposition of criminal sanctions on corporate wrongdoing? Can the criminal law be 'successfully adapted to control commercial delinquency'?

Extract 6.2   Braithwaite: 'Strategies for controlling corporate crime'

Let us begin with what the law can achieve. It will be argued that law enforcement can reduce corporate crime in the pharmaceutical industry, probably dramatically. The crime reduction goal can be achieved via a number of subgoals. First, deterrence – both specific (against offenders) and general (against those who witness the sanctioning of others) – can be effective. This is so because corporate offenders, with more to lose than traditional blue-collar offenders, are inherently more deterrable.

Second, the law can effectively impose rehabilitation on corporate offenders. Rehabilitation is a more workable goal for corporate criminal law than for individual criminal law because organization charts and SOPs [Standard Operating Procedures] can more easily be rearranged than human personalities.

Third, the law can readily require restitution to victims of corporate crime and reparation to the community. This is because the corporation normally has an inordinate capacity to pay, and a pool of expertise which makes possible reparatory acts of community service of enormous social value. Restitution imposed by law, particularly through the mechanism of class actions, also has invaluable deterrent effects.

These three goals can be achieved without resort to the repressive measures (imprisonment, corporal punishment, capital punishment) which have been so unsuccessful in attempts to control traditional individual crime. A wide array of sanctions – fines, restitution orders, community service orders, intervention in the corporation's management system, licence revocation, injunction, seizure, remedial advertising – all have important places in the armouries of regulatory agencies.

(Braithwaite, 1984, pp.290–1)

Crime without punishment

by Gary Slapper

CRIMINAL proceedings begin today against two directors of the leisure company responsible for the four children who were killed in the Lyme Regis canoe tragedy last year. In an unusual move, the company itself is also being prosecuted for manslaughter. No company, however, has ever been convicted of the crime of manslaughter in this country.

About 500 people, employees and members of the public, are killed each year through work activities. It has been clear since a case at Glamorgan Assizes in 1965 that companies can be charged with manslaughter yet, despite 19,000 deaths related to company faults since that time, the crime of corporate manslaughter remains one for which there has never been a conviction.

Workplace deaths and public disasters are investigated by the Health and Safety Executive (HSE), with the police usually playing no part after taking brief statements at the scene. Yet the HSE is only concerned with violations of the Health and Safety at Work Act 1974, not with serious crimes like manslaughter.

Each year, a few of these hundreds of fatalities are referred by the HSE to the Crown Prosecution Service, but they are invariably rejected for want of evidence. These rejections are not just symptomatic of the CPS's generally low prosecution rate, but rather are the result of the particular evidence required for cases of corporate manslaughter.

To convict a company of manslaughter it is necessary to prove that at least one of its directors, or someone who was a 'controlling mind' of the company, was 'grossly negligent' about an obvious risk of death or injury.

In larger companies, the problem is that the knowledge of several partly culpable directors cannot be aggregated.

It is not enough to prove that, between them, the directors were aware of the facts which, when pieced together, constituted the fatal danger. That was one of the points on which the prosecution of P & O European Ferries failed after the sinking of the *Herald of Free Enterprise*. Another problem with wanting the law to be as severe with companies who kill as with, say, drivers who kill, is what should be done with those which are convicted. Companies, as Lord Thurlow once remarked, have 'a soul to damn but nobody to kick'.

Directors, can, of course, be prosecuted individually (although only one has ever been convicted of manslaughter arising from work conditions) but this can lead to

Whose crime is it anyway? ... 192 died in the Herald of Free Enterprise disaster, but P&O directors were acquitted of manslaughter

people being made scapegoats for wider organizational recklessness.

When a company is criminally culpable the question arises as to the most suitable sanction.

Fines are arguably not always appropriate. Last year the record for a fine against a construction company was broken when the Channel Tunnel consortium TML was fined £200,000 after it admitted failing to ensure the safety of a worker who was crushed to death between trains.

One problem is that the burden of fines may be inappropriately borne by shareholders, or, if the fine affects the company very badly, by employees who are eventually made redundant, or by consumers.

A dramatic illustration of this effect arose recently. Manchester City Council was fined £25,000 for a 'disastrous programme' of ineptitude in wrongly fitting gas heaters in council properties resulting in one resident's death and which jeopardized the lives of 800 others.

Who will ultimately bear the burden of the £25,000 fine (remembering one cannot insure against criminal liability)? The answer is the Manchester council tax payers, including the relatives of the man who died and the 800 people endangered by the council.

The fine was necessary to register the gravity of the offence, but could the money have been better used to fund improved safety training or equipment?

Another sanction which could be used against companies is known as 'corporate probation', which has been available in the US since 1987. The judge can compel the senior management of a company to change how the way it devises and implements safety procedures.

As with personal probation, conditions can be imposed by the court; for example insistence on certain safety procedures and the employment of safety staff.

There was no evidence, though, that companies which have been technically disgraced by a conviction and such sanctions, or by a huge fine for a very serious wrong, are lowered in the estimation of the public. In 1987, for example, BP was fined £750,000 after an incident in which three of its workers were killed. This was a major news item at the time yet there is no evidence of any consumer boycott of BP products as a result.

The seriousness of company recklessness which results in injury and death is now more clearly recognized by the public. Accidents at work and the impact of resulting health bills costs industry and the state up to £15 billion a year. Most accidents are preventable and are usually linked to cost-cutting measures, which, evidence suggests, increase during a recession.

The question is whether the criminal law and sentencing can now be successfully adapted to control commercial delinquency.

(*The Guardian*, 1 February 1994)

8 Conclusion: crime and the market

The aim of this chapter has been to extend our study of crime in general by looking at a particular sphere of rule-breaking behaviour that is often not considered criminal, either by the law or by public opinion. Much corporate and white-collar crime remains hidden because it is carried out by apparently respectable persons in the course of their routine commercial activities.

Far from corresponding to the familiar stereotype of the criminal, many of those convicted on charges of major fraud, insider dealing or other such offences were formerly regarded as being of good character, with a stable family background and often possessing substantial means. Indeed, many such offenders had previously won recognition and success through their entrepreneurial flair. The distinction between the sort of offences they commit and the fiercely competitive activities customarily carried out by individuals and companies under the pressure of market forces appears to many to be one of degree, rather than a question of principle. There is, in other words, an intimate link between the capitalist market-place and white-collar crime. It is striking that the trend towards the deregulation of market forces in the 1980s was accompanied by a rising scale of offences by both companies and well-placed individuals.

The difficulty of differentiating between the pursuit of legitimate commercial advantage and rule-breaking profiteering goes some way towards explaining the differential response of the authorities and public opinion towards white-collar and 'ordinary' crime. It also helps to explain the difficulty in regulating such offences, given the traditional hostility of the entrepreneur towards state interference. The debate about whether measures to strengthen informal methods of self-regulation will be enough to curb the rise of white-collar crime, or whether tougher sanctions under the criminal justice system will be required is certain to continue.

Further reading

Levi's claim that 'business crime has been neglected by most academics and activists on the Left as well as those on the Right' (Levi, 1987, p.207) may have been true a decade ago, but is less so today. A number of useful general surveys of this subject, as well as some detailed studies of particular aspects of the problem, have recently appeared.

As in all such discussions, it is always worth returning to the classic texts, and Sutherland's (1949) pioneering book is available in a more recent 1967 edition. The subsequent development of American work in this area is well documented in the collection edited by Geis and Meier (1977).

Croall (1992) provides a good general introduction to the subject in a British context, and Nelken (1994) explores some of the continuing controversies in the criminological study of white-collar crime. For more detailed studies it is well worth consulting some of the works of Levi (1987, 1991a and 1991b) on the financial sector, Clarke (1990a and 1990b) on business crime and insurance, and Wells (1993) on corporate liability for the consequences of disasters. On the contrasts between tax evasion and social security fraud, see Cook (1989) and Deane (1981).

For controversies about regulation, see the debate between Pearce and Tombs (1990, 1991) on the one side, and Hawkins (1990) on the other in the *British Journal of Criminology*, which reveals both their differences and, perhaps more importantly, what they have in common. From Australia, Braithwaite (1985) provides a comprehensive survey of the debate. For a radical perspective on 'crimes of the powerful', the writings of Pearce (1976), Pearce and Tombs (1990) and **Box (1983)** are helpful.

References

Adams, J.R. and Frantz, D. (1992) *A Full Service Bank: How BCCI Stole Millions around The World,* New York, Simon and Schuster.

Benson, M.L. (1985) 'Denying the guilty mind: accounting for involvement in a white-collar crime', *Criminology*, vol. 23, no.4, pp.583–604.

Box, S. (1983) *Power, Crime and Mystification*, London, Tavistock. (Extract reprinted as 'Crime, power and ideological mystification' in Muncie *et al.,* 1996.)

Braithwaite, J. (1984) *Corporate Crime in the Pharmaceutical Industry,* London, Routledge and Kegan Paul.

Braithwaite, J. (1985) 'White-collar crime', *Annual Review of Sociology*, vol. 11, p.1025.

Braithwaite, J. (1989) *Crime, Shame and Re-integration,* Cambridge, Cambridge University Press. (Extract reprinted as 'Reintegrative shaming' in Muncie *et al.,* 1996.)

Burden, T. (1990) 'Crime: why don't economists have much to say about it?', *Journal of Interdisciplinary Economics*, vol. 3, pp.209–21.

Burrows, N. and Hiram, H. (1995) 'The official control of foodstuffs', in Daintieth, T. (ed.) *Implementing EC Law in the United Kingdom: Structures for Indirect Law,* Chichester, Wiley.

Carlen, P. and Cook, D. (eds) (1989) *Paying for Crime,* Buckingham, Open University Press.

Carson, W.G. (1982) *The Other Price of Britain's Oil,* Oxford, Martin Robertson.

Clarke, M. (1989) 'Insurance fraud', *British Journal of Criminology*, vol. 29, no.1, pp.1–21.

Clarke, M. (1990a) *Business Crime: Its Nature and Control,* Cambridge, Polity.

Clarke, M. (1990b) 'The control of insurance fraud: a comparative view', *British Journal of Criminology*, vol. 30, no.1, pp.1–23.

Clinard, M.B. (1946) 'Criminological theories of violation of wartime regulations', *American Sociological Review*, vol. 11, pp.258–70.

Clinard, M.B. and Yeager, P.C. (1980) *Corporate Crime,* New York, Free Press.

Cook, D. (1989) *Rich Law, Poor Law: Differential Responses to Tax and Supplementary Benefit Fraud,* Buckingham, Open University Press.

Croall, H. (1989) 'Who is the white-collar criminal?', *British Journal of Criminology*, vol. 29, no.2, pp.157–74.

Croall, H. (1992) *White-Collar Crime,* Buckingham, Open University Press.

Deane, K.D. (1981) 'Tax evasion, criminality and sentencing the tax offender', *British Journal of Criminology*, vol. 21, no.1, pp.47–57.

Ditton, J. (1977) *Part-Time Crime: An Ethnography of Fiddling and Pilferage*, London, Macmillan.

Doig, A. (1984) *Corruption and Mismanagement in Contemporary British Politics*, Harmondsworth, Penguin.

Geis, G. (1987) 'The heavy electrical equipment anti-trust cases of 1961', in Ermann, M.D. and Lundman, R.J. (eds) (1987) *Corporate and Governmental Deviance: Problems of Organizational Behaviour in Contemporary Society*, Oxford, Oxford University Press.

Geis, G. and Meier, R.F. (eds) (1977) *White-Collar Crime*, New York, Free Press.

Gross, E. (1978) 'Organizations as criminal actors', in Braithwaite, J. and Wilson, P. (eds) *Two Faces of Deviance: Crimes of the Powerless and Powerful*, Brisbane, University of Queensland Press.

Hawkins, K. (1990) 'Compliance strategy, prosecution policy and aunt sally: a comment on Pearce and Tombs', *British Journal of Criminology*, vol. 30, no.4, pp.444–66.

Health and Safety Commission (1993) *Annual Report 1992/93*, London, HSE Books.

Henman, A., Lewis, R. and Mayon, T. (1985) *Big Deal: The Politics of the Illicit Drugs Business*, London, Pluto.

HMSO (1993) *The Insolvency Service Executive Agency: Company Director Disqualification*, report of the Comptroller and Auditor General, London, HMSO.

Kadish, S.H. (1963) 'Some observations on the use of criminal sanctions in enforcing economic regulations', reprinted in Geis and Meier (1977).

Kochan, N. and Whittington, B. (1991) *Bankrupt: The BCCI Fraud*, London, Gollancz.

Lane, R.E. (1953) 'Why businessmen violate the law', reprinted in Geis and Meier (1977).

Levi, M. (1984) 'Giving creditors the business: the criminal law in inaction', *International Journal of the Sociology of Law*, vol.12, pp.321–33.

Levi, M. (1986) 'Fraud in the courts: Roskill in context', *British Journal of Criminology*, vol. 26, no.4, pp.394–401.

Levi, M. (1987) *Regulating Fraud: White-Collar Crime and the Criminal Process*, London, Tavistock.

Levi, M. (1989) 'Sentencing white collar-criminals', in Carlen and Cook (1989).

Levi, M. (1991a) 'Pecunia non olet: cleansing the money-launderers from the temple', *Crime, Law and Social Change*, vol.16, pp.217–302.

Levi, M. (1991b) 'Regulating money laundering: the death of bank secrecy in the UK', *British Journal of Criminology*, vol. 31, no.2, pp.109–25.

Luttwak, E. (1995) 'Does the Russian mafia deserve the Nobel prize for economics?', *London Review of Books*, vol.17, no.15, p.7.

McBarnet, D. (1984) 'Law and capital: the role of legal form and legal actors', *International Journal of the Sociology of Law*, vol. 12, pp.231–8.

Maguire, M., Morgan, R. and Reiner, R. (eds) (1994) *The Oxford Handbook of Criminology*, Oxford, Clarendon.

Mann, K. (1985) *Defending White-Collar Crime: A Portrait of Attorneys at Work*, New Haven, Yale University Press.

Mars, G. (1982) *Cheats at Work: An Anthology of Workplace Crime*, London, Allen and Unwin.

Muncie, J., McLaughlin, E. and Langan, M. (eds) (1996) *Criminological Perspectives: A Reader*, London, Sage in association with The Open University.

Nelken, D. (1994) 'White-collar crime', in Maguire *et al.* (1994).

Norton-Taylor, R. (1995) *Truth is a Difficult Concept: Inside the Scott Inquiry*, London, Fourth Estate.

Pearce, F. (1976) *Crimes of the Powerful: Marxism, Crime and Deviance*, London, Pluto.

Pearce, F. and Tombs, S. (1990) 'Ideology, hegemony and empiricism: compliance theories of regulation', *British Journal of Criminology*, vol. 30, no.4, pp.423–43.

Pearce, F. and Tombs, S. (1991) 'Policing corporate "skid rows": a reply to Keith Hawkins', *British Journal of Criminology*, vol. 31, no.4, pp.415–30.

Pearce, F. and Tombs, S. (1993) 'Union Carbide and Bhopal', in Pearce, F. and Woodiwiss, M. (eds) *Global Crime Connections: Dynamics and Control*, London, Macmillan.

Quinney, R. (1964) 'Occupational structure and criminal behaviour: prescription violations by retail pharmacists', reprinted in Geis and Meier (1977)

Quinney, R. (1977) *Class, State and Crime*, Harlow, Longman.

Robb, G. (1992) *White-Collar Crime in Modern England: Financial Fraud and Business Morality, 1845–1929*, Cambridge, Cambridge University Press.

Shapiro, S.P. (1990) 'Collaring the crime, not the criminal: reconsidering the concept of white-collar crime', *American Sociological Review*, vol.55, pp.346–65.

Sutherland, E.H. (1949) *White-Collar Crime*, revised edn 1967, New York, Holt, Rinehart and Winston.

Sutton, A. and Wild, R. (1988) 'Small business: white-collar villains or victims?', in Findlay, M. and Hogg, R. (eds) *Understanding Crime and Criminal Justice*, Sydney, Law Book Co.

Taylor, I. (1994) 'The political economy of crime', in Maguire *et al.* (1994).

Wells, C. (1993) *Corporations and Criminal Responsibility*, Oxford, Clarendon.

Chapter 7
Political Violence, Terrorism and Crimes of the State

by Eugene McLaughlin

Contents

1 Introduction

The previous chapter explored the complex dimensions of the problem of crimes of the economically powerful. This chapter is also concerned with the relationship between power and crime, but will pursue a different trajectory. Here we will examine the vexed question of political crime, especially the problem of violent political crime – both against the state and by the state. We begin in section 2 by distinguishing political violence from other forms of violence, and move on to confront the crucial issue of the precise relationship between the state and violence. At this point we look briefly at the body of national and international law that defines the exceptional circumstances when the state can legitimately employ force.

The latter part of section 2 asks whether there are moments when citizens or subjects can use violence against the state. Here we also have to consider how states respond to those who proclaim that their violence and law-breaking is motivated by higher political and moral ideals. Should states recognize that politically motivated offenders are different from common criminals? What would such recognition imply for the processes of criminal justice?

In section 3 we consider the questions: What is 'true' terrorism? and: Who are the 'real' terrorists? Here and in section 4 we will analyse how and why only certain actions and actors are so defined and the import and implications of such labelling. In addressing these thorny questions we begin to see how, transnationally, the monopoly of violence and force wielded by the state can be used to victimize, in some cases in an endemic manner, the citizenry through gross human rights violations such as routine repression, torture, judicial murder and genocide.

One point in particular needs to be made clear at this juncture: these 'crimes of the state' (which might also include war crimes) are not imaginary or hidden crimes. They constitute the stark facts of everyday life for millions of people – and have a massive impact, corrupting governing institutions, subverting the democratic process and undermining all notions of the rule of law, civil liberties and human rights.

Sections 5 and 6 consider what can be done to control political violence and terror, particularly that practised by delinquent, criminal or homicidal states. Here we are forced to think very carefully about the relationship between crime and the political process; the functioning and effectiveness of the criminal law in this particular area; and specifically whether the discourses, logics and procedures of the criminal law are able:

- To provide satisfactory protection to citizens from arbitrary and illegal state violence and guarantee the upholding of civil liberties and human rights.

- To provide adequate and meaningful justice and reparation for those who have been the victims of state criminality.

- To hold the state (or governments or regimes) and its agencies to account in the way that it holds non- or sub-state actors to account.

- To deal objectively with those non- or sub-state actors who argue that their violent law-breaking is consciously motivated by 'higher' political, ideological or moral reasons.

The areas considered in this chapter have, in the twentieth century, been regarded as the province of such disciplines as political science, human rights and international law, along with investigative journalism, and have only recently begun to be readdressed by criminology. As a result, in the sections that follow, much of the examination of the issues involved is exploratory and formative, rather than definitive. However, if social injury or harm, as discussed in Chapter 1, is used as a defining feature of crime in any way at all, then the 'ultimate' forms of social injury discussed here should be placed firmly and centrally on the criminological agenda. As our examination covers fairly extensive ground, it is possible to give little more than an overview in the space we have – to highlight issues and questions and point to ways in which they might begin to be addressed and theorized. But it is our hope that the least this will do is encourage a refocusing of the 'problem of crime' beyond the more familiar criminological concerns and thus a reworking and expansion of the criminological imagination.

2 Theorizing violence: meanings and contexts

ACTIVITY 7.1

It is almost impossible to read a newspaper or novel, listen to the daily news or watch a film or drama without confronting multiple representations of violence. Before reading this section, think about how the word 'violence' is presented in these media. To gain a clear understanding of this concept, reflect closely and critically on the following questions:

- Are all forms of violence outlawed?

- Is violence always portrayed in a negative manner?

- What are the causes of violence?

- What is the 'purpose' of violence?

- Why are we fearful of and fascinated by violence?

- Is violence a constituent part of the human condition?

- Is there a stereotypical representation of a violent person?

- Who is most likely to be a victim of violence?

- What is the difference between violence and force?

As these questions underlie a key theme of this chapter, you might find it helpful to make a few notes on your responses which you can then expand or refer back to as you progress through the following sections.

Surveying the myriad theological, legal and philosophical debates on how human violence should be conceptualized is beyond the scope of this chapter. However, we need to take account of the following points. First and foremost, like many concepts employed for both descriptive and analytical purposes, 'violence' has an impreciseness that makes it difficult to delimit. Norman (1995) argues that it is one of the most confused, emotive and subjective terms in our moral language. Foucault (1980) holds that there is a

rhetoric of violence

'rhetoric of violence' which classifies certain behaviours, events and individuals as violent. This rhetoric produces and reproduces objects and subjects *of* violence and structures 'violence' as a seemingly coherent, unproblematic fact. And, yet, as Armstrong and Tennenhouse (1989) note, careful and balanced historical and empirical interrogation indicates that, embedded in events and actions that are perceived and understood as 'violence', are highly variable, abstract, contingent, complicated and conflicting conceptions of social and moral order.

Certain writers contend that the only way to produce a precise and unambiguous definition is to concentrate on the archetypal *public* representation – that is, the infliction of serious or irreparable *physical* damage or injury instrumentally or impulsively wrought by a 'dangerous stranger' upon the body of another human being. However, other analysts have expanded its meaning to cover: the destruction of property; the threat of violence; damaging psychological processes, such as domination, humiliation and degradation; and the violent processes intricately woven into the very texture of the social order, such as those related to enduring poverty, discrimination and socio-economic exploitation. Skolnick, for example, believes that: 'Less dramatic but equally destructive processes may occur well within the routine operation of "orderly" social life ... indifference, inaction, and slow decay that routinely afflict the poor are far more destructive than the bomb in the night. High infant mortality rates or rates of preventable disease, perpetuated through discrimination, take a far greater toll than civil disorder' (Skolnick, 1969, p.5). Bourdieu (1977) agrees, arguing that we need

symbolic violence

to acknowledge the 'symbolic violence' which is impressed and continually reproduced in dominant socio-economic relations.

Second, we must recognize that only certain forms and categories of violence are defined as illegal and subject to regulation. Acts of criminal violence normally encompass discrete events and actions that have beginnings and ends and involve individuals who deliberately physically damage or destroy other human beings in a specific location at a specific time. Murder, assault, rape and robbery are the paradigmatic interpersonal crimes of violence that hold a hegemonic and exemplar position in public and legal discourse and imagination. The unintended structural, social or economic violence that concerns Skolnick (1969) and Bourdieu (1977) does not fall straightforwardly within the domain of the criminal law or the process of criminalization.

Third, the causes of, and solutions to, human violence have troubled and divided the academic mind. Socio-biology, anthropology, psychology, psychiatry, theology, philosophy and sociology have all studied the act iself, the perpetrators, the victims, motivational factors and the social context in which it occurs and have presented very different explanations for the root causes of violent forms of human aggression. Some feminists have sharpened the focus by stressing the crucial, inextricably interwoven concrete connections between aggression, sex and gender across time, place and culture (Hanmer and Maynard, 1987). The thrust of this fundamentally important argument is that what needs to be brought to the fore and addressed are micro and macro questions of violent masculinities and the male monopoly of violence (see Chapter 5, section 6.2), and class/gender relations (see, for example, **Segal, 1990**).

Fourth, as we have seen earlier in this book and as we will see in the course of this chapter, violence is not always unequivocally condemned. It is generally perceived to be a *prima facie* moral transgression and mark of atavistic evil – undesirable and unacceptable in a civilized society. It 'dehumanizes', debases and brutalizes both perpetrator and victim. But this is not the entire storyline:

> Violence is characteristic of a natural energy, something that overflows the bounds of institutions and habits, canons of behaviour and rules of etiquette. Violence belongs to what is spontaneous and powerful; and since the spontaneity is that of nature ... it is both something terrible and dangerous and, at the same time, a source of life sacred, a refreshment ... That the violent processes of nature are sources of strength and creativity, as well as of destruction, gives the idea of violence a certain fascination; for what promises to fortify and enrich our existence promises also to destroy it.

> (Cameron, 1970, p.24)

This 'force of nature' argument leaves us in no doubt that human societies can exhibit deeply ambiguous and often contradictory reactions to violence. We need only think, for example, about the ambivalent but (for many) irresistible emplacement of violence in late modern popular culture and how cinematic and 'pulp' fiction representations and simulations of 'thrill kill' violence or 'ultra-violence without consequences' are capable of triggering both critical artistic praise and moral condemnation.

Perhaps it is this belief that certain categories of violence are productive, positive and inevitable that has generated the endless attempts to explain away violence, irrespective of whether or not it is legal. As we shall see in this chapter, it has been obscured, mystified, valorized, redefined and, in certain instances, rendered socially acceptable by various transformative procedures:

transformative procedures

> Violence has cloaked itself in the garments of some means of making it legitimate. In defence of violence, man has insisted that he was provoked beyond human endurance; he has stated that he was not responsible by reason of insanity; he has pointed out that he acted only in self-defence; he has claimed that honour and manhood required violent response; he has maintained that he never intended to produce the outcome that occurred; he has said that what he did was for the ultimate good of society; and he has felt, if not said, that his actions were inescapably necessary given the situation in which he has found himself.

> (McNeil, 1966, p.155)

2.1 Theorizing political violence

Philosophers, legal scholars and political theorists have devoted a great deal of time to answering the question: Is it normatively possible to distinguish between 'political' violence and other forms of violence? According to Nieburg, the term refers to: 'acts of disruption, destruction, injury whose purpose, choice of targets or victims, surrounding circumstances, implementation, and/or effects have political significance, that is, tend to modify the behaviour of others in a bargaining situation, that has consequences for the social system' (Nieburg, 1969, p.13). He also identified two forms of political violence: state-sanctioned violence (violence by the state) and internal violence against the state.

political violence

2.1.1 Violence by the state

the modern state

Max Weber maintains that there is one characteristic above all others that marks out the form, structure and procedures of the modern state:

> Ultimately one can define the modern state sociologically only in terms of the specific *means* peculiar to it, as to every political association, namely the use of physical force … Of course force is certainly not the normal or the only means of the state – nobody says that – but force is a means specific to the state. Today, the relation between the state and violence is an especially intimate one … we have to say that a state is a human community that successfully claims the *monopoly of the legitimate use of physical force* within a given territory.
>
> (Weber, 1970, p.77)

The exceptional power and potency of the state, irrespective of its specific social, political or ethnic formation, or spatial and temporal setting, lies in its *colonization, monopolization* and *domestication* of physical force. And we need to pose a question which should be central to criminology: Why does the state claim such a unique right or privilege? Tilly (1985) points out that violence on a sometimes unimaginable scale has been the critical element in the conception and forging of all modern nation-states. Moreover, to persist as a sovereign politico–legal–spatial entity and centre of power, the state must possess the requisite coercive powers to be able to enforce its internal commands, provide a security umbrella for the citizenry and, in doing so, restrain subject–citizens from resorting to violence to resolve their own private disputes. Its monopoly of physical violence, in the final instance, is the *de facto* foundation of internal social order and, as Poulantzas has argued: '*permanently underlies the techniques of power and mechanisms of consent: it is inscribed in the web of disciplinary and ideological devices; and even when not directly exercised, it shapes the materiality of the social body upon which domination is brought to bear*' (Poulantzas, 1978, p.81).

state violence
official force

The modern state's custodianship of violence is, in theory, regulated and controlled and can only be deployed within clearly defined parameters. Internally, state violence is transformed into 'official force' by being harnessed and bound by the rule of law, the constitutional civil and human rights of the citizenry and through its *institutionalization* in policing and military bureaucracies which are governed by what Weber (1970) defined as *rational–legal rules*, and by hierarchical procedures, disciplinary instructions and codes of honour. For violence or force by state agencies and officials to be considered legitimate it must only be used in the last resort and only when all avenues of rational persuasion, peaceful resolution and social defence have been exhausted. Just as important, it must also be minimal in application (see Figure 7.1).

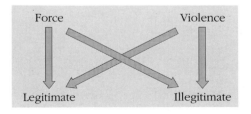

Figure 7.1 The difference between force and violence

Externally, the state's right to resort to violence is also regulated. Warfare – the ultimate form of deliberately organized mass killing, maiming and destruction – between states is a rule-governed and ordered activity. It is recognized and formally framed by a tangle of international 'laws of war' which cover both when states can resort to armed conflict (*jus ad bellum*) and the actual conduct and practice of warfare (*jus in bello*). Significantly, 'war', a highly problematic concept in itself, is not a 'crime', being seen, like some forms of state-sanctioned violence, as inevitable and morally justified in certain circumstances (see Hinde and Watson, 1995). All states have inalienable rights and, indeed, duties under international law to use armed force in certain exceptional 'just war' circumstances – for example, to resist aggression, protect their territory, defend their cultural and ethnic integrity and fulfil internationally recognized treaty obligations. Hence, there are clearly identifiable moments when states can assert the ultimate right in this context – the right and freedom to kill and destroy.

But all is not fair in war. Detailed international agreements, rules, declarations, conventions, resolutions and protocols seek to restrain, moderate, regulate and 'civilize' the kind and degree of violence resorted to in times of war (Rosenblad, 1979; Roberts and Guelff, 1982; Best, 1983; Detter De Lupis, 1987; Reisman and Antoniou, 1994). According to Rosenblad (1979), the following humanitarian precepts traditionally underpin this particular set of laws:

- The 'principle of distinction' which asserts that armed conflict ought to be conducted exclusively by readily identifiable combatants. The cornerstone of the law of armed conflict is that unarmed and uninvolved civilians are not legitimate targets.

- The 'principle of proportionality' which claims that all loss of life and damage to property should be strictly comparable to the military advantage likely to be gained.

ACTIVITY 7.2

What forms of behaviour and actions do you think are outlawed by the laws of war? For what reasons? Again, this question underlies a key theme of the chapter and it might help to consolidate your thoughts on this if you make, perhaps in tabular form, a note of your response before reading on. Does your answer here build on any part of your response to Activity 7.1?

The International Military Tribunal at Nuremberg (1945–46) opted for a seemingly straightforward criminal justice, rather than political or military, approach to produce the basic definition of what constituted a *war crime*.   war crime
This, according to the Tribunal, comprised: the murder, ill-treatment or torture, or deportation to slave labour or for any other purpose, of civilians of or in occupied territory; the murder, ill-treatment or torture of prisoners of war; the killing of hostages; the plunder of property; the wanton destruction of human settlements; and devastation not warranted by military necessity. Members of the armed forces and civilians who violate these laws are guilty of committing war crimes and can be *individually* judged and, where appropriate, punished by international or national courts and military tribunals. This is the case whether or not such war crimes have been ordered by a political leader or by commanding officers. Individuals accused of war crimes cannot absolve themselves of criminal responsibility by citing an

crime of
obedience

official position or that they obeyed superior orders – that is, the *crime of obedience* Conversely, commanding officers are responsible for violations carried out by their troops unless they self-evidently attempted to suppress them. At a general level, war crimes are *acts that retain their essential criminal nature even though they are committed by individuals in time of war and/or under orders.*

Just as significantly, the Tribunal created two new additional categories of crime to encompass aggressive and destructive forms of behaviour that were beyond the scope of the human imagination and resultant from the advances made by weapons manufacturers. A *crime against peace* was established to cover the planning, preparation, initiation or waging of a war of aggression, or a war in flagrant and unjustified violation of international treaties.

crimes against
humanity

Finally, there was the first formal acknowledgement of *crimes against humanity* in international law. These inhumane crimes were defined as the:

> murder, extermination, enslavement or deportation, and other inhumane acts committed against any civilian population, before or during the war or persecutions on political, racial or religious grounds in the execution of or in connection with any crime within the jurisdiction of the Tribunal, whether or not in violation of the domestic law of the country in question.

> (International Military Tribunal, 1947, vol.1, p.11)

genocide

In 1948 the United Nations (UN) named this crime 'genocide' when it created a convention on the Prevention and Punishment of the Crime of Genocide which stressed that it was a crime in peacetime as well as in war to seek systematically and deliberately to eradicate, or attempt to eradicate, a national, ethnic, racial or religious group by mass murder. This was defined as the ultimate crime and the gravest of all *violations of human rights*. This convention, which predated the UN Universal Declaration of Human Rights by one day, also crucially established that genocide was not a *private* nation-state issue but a matter of *public* international law. Under it, states have a legal obligation, besides that of not committing genocide themselves, to take action considered appropriate for the prevention, suppression *and* punishment of genocide commited by other states (Kuper, 1981).

Torture of combatants, prisoners of war and non-combatants was formally outlawed by the 1948 Universal Declaration of Human Rights, the 1949 Geneva Conventions Relative to the Treatment of Prisoners of War and Relative to the Protection of Civilian Persons in Time of War, and the 1950 European Convention for the Protection of Human Rights and Fundamental Freedoms. In 1984, the United Nations adopted a Convention Against Torture and Other Cruel, Inhuman or Degrading Treatment or Punishment. This made torture a crime triable anywhere and not only in the country in which it was committed. Moreover, according to Article 2[2] of this Convention: 'No exceptional circumstances whatsoever, whether a state of war or a threat of war, internal political instability or any other public emergency, may be invoked as a justification of torture'. Europe has also drawn up its own Convention for the Prevention of Torture and Inhuman or Degrading Treatment or Punishment, 1987, and a Committee for the Prevention of Torture, created under the aegis of the Convention, has the right to visit any site within the territory of a signatory to the Convention where citizens are being detained. In addition, section 134 of the 1988 Criminal Justice Act makes torture anywhere in the world an offence in the UK punishable by a life sentence.

Before closing this discussion it is important to note that the criminal justice approach and the stress on *individual*, as opposed to collective, responsibility championed by the Nuremberg Tribunal was deemed by many jurists to be inappropriate (Smith, 1977). As Smith (1977) and Cesarani (1992) point out, the legality of the trials was questioned because the defendants were being held to account for crimes which were new, having been created *ad hoc* and ex-*post facto*. There was also unease about the prosecuting authorities' rejection of the defence 'I was only obeying orders'. Could the international community seriously expect professional soldiers to disobey superior orders and risk a military court martial? If not, then what would be the point of passing a law that would never be obeyed? In addition, the fact that only 177 Nazis were indicted, with 25 being sentenced to death and 20 to life imprisonment, threw up as many questions as it answered. Holding these few individuals to account for the slaughter of millions would:

- Generate accusations ranging from tokenism and scapegoating to the conducting of show trials.

- Transform defendants into victims and even martyrs.

- Perpetuate the myth that such actions were the result of the machinations of a few evil individuals rather than the logical outcome of clinically planned state policies and processes which were ideologically approved by significant sections of German society.

In addition, what punishment could the Tribunal possibly pass which could be seen as fitting retribution given the nature and sheer scale of these crimes and act as a deterrence to others? Finally, how would the international community reform, and indeed rehabilitate, the guilty society in which the crimes occurred in order to prevent them from happening again? What would be an appropriate act of communal purification and cleansing? Clearly, there are 'natural limits' and constraints to attempts to apply the logic of criminal justice to the area of war crimes, crimes against humanity and crimes against peace.

Survivors of Auschwitz during the first hours of the concentration camp's liberation by soldiers of the Soviet Army, 27 January 1945. Colonel Telford Taylor, US Prosecutor at Nuremberg, stated: 'Crime has been piled upon crime ... until we are in danger of losing our sense of proportion. We have heard so much of mass extermination that we are likely to forget that simple murder is a capital offence' (quoted in Cesarani, 1992, p.178)

2.1.2 Violence against the state

Two interrelated questions, above all others, lie at the centre of discussions of the internal use of violence against the state. First, we have to ask ourselves whether violence can ever be defined as a legitimate means of settling political disputes or grievances. Are citizens under an a priori moral obligation to comply with the law and accept the exisiting social order no matter how unjust or oppressive, if no means other than violence would overthrow it? The second question that has perplexed legal systems is how to classify and deal with those who do resort to violence for political reasons. In particular, should the category of *political* offender be formally recognized by the state?

The right to resort to violence

Certain theorists, such as Arendt (1961), Sharp (1973) and Wehr *et al.* (1994), argue that only reason, rational debate and compromise can resolve political grievances and that challenging the state's monopoly of violence inevitably results in intense misery and suffering and very often compounds the existing injustice. Direct action that is violent in nature can provide the authorities with the justification to escalate and intensify authoritarian clampdowns, unleash merciless vendettas and create a culture of coercion which has a destabilizing or corrosive influence on the body politic, civil society and social relations. Consequently, violence against the state can only be rightly embarked upon when the following moral criteria have been met.

First, a fundamental and profound injustice or oppression that afflicts a significant proportion of the population must exist (this is the argument of the 'just cause'). The classic example given is being forced to live under a tyrannical or totalitarian regime. Second, all lawful, constitutional and non-violent methods, processes of negotiation and means of protest, dissent and resistance, including civil disobedience, must have been tried and demonstrably found wanting. Violence must be a last resort. Third, the violence should be defensive (reactive) rather than aggressive (proactive) in nature and must remain only one part of a wider political struggle. Fourth, the forms and levels of violence resorted to must be proportionate and strictly limited, and due deliberation needs to be given to limiting the extent and seriousness of the violence. Fifth, those advocating such a strategy must demonstrate that violence can correct the injustice or end the oppression. It must always be a means to a negotiable end, and restraint and self-control must be exercised to ensure that violence does not become a self-contained nihilistic end in itself (Harris, 1989).

Other political theorists, however, have argued that such an 'exceptional circumstances' conceptualization is highly problematic because it severely curtails the circumstances under which the citizenry can resort to violent protest. For example, it could be argued that it is virtually impossible to meet the second criterion because there will always be some method of protest that remains untried. These theorists believe that immediate and unconditional resort to violence has been a powerful catalyst for change, and central, in many geographical settings, to the achievement of basic human rights and justice. Expressed in another way, violence and the threat of violence are (to paraphrase Karl Marx) the 'midwives to the birth of a new society'. Moreover, in situations of colonial domination and oppression, using violence is deemed to be cathartic:

Violence alone, violence committed by the people, violence educated and organized by its leaders makes it possible for the masses to understand social truths and gives the key to them …

At the level of individuals, violence is a cleansing force. It frees the native from his inferiority complex and from his despair and inaction; it makes him fearless and restores his self-respect.

(Fanon, 1967)

The political criminal

Schafer has noted incisively that: 'The never ending stream of political criminals indicates that political crime is no ordinary crime and its history no ordinary history … [it is] pivotal to the understanding of criminology, and maybe even truly critical to understanding law and the whole normative system of the society' (Schafer, 1974, pp.2, 8). And it is certainly a far larger subject than we can deal with here. However, it is important to think about how tolerant the state should be towards those who challenge its political authority and power.

political crime

In Western Europe in the course of the nineteenth century, internal politically motivated crime came to be redefined as an offence against the state (*lèse-nation*). Historical analysis suggests (see, for example, Langbein, 1977; Gatrell, 1994) that, prior to the French Revolution, most crimes against political rulers were defined as 'treason' or, in Roman law, crime against sacred authority (*lèse-majesté*). This encompassed acts of betrayal, challenges to political authority and legitimacy, sedition, assassination, hindrance of the official function and usurpation of the state's powers. Significantly, it also included conspiracy as well as the actual deed. Those accused of politically motivated crimes were likely to suffer gruesome public punishment (including judicially regulated torture), much more exacting than that sanctioned against ordinary common criminals. As Foucault (1979) has commented, the more reasoned, rational and selfless the act, the less pardonable it was deemed to be.

But with the above-mentioned shift, the political offender came to be viewed in certain countries as the *beau ideal*, motivated neither by private avarice nor by vindictiveness but by principled, public *representative* considerations such as opposing autocratic regimes in the name of liberal democracy or championing the cause of nationalism or idealistic social reform:

> It may … happen that in the course of committing these Crimes, and with a view to facilitating the commission of them, other acts are done which, in everything but the accompanying Motive, are not distinguishable from ordinary Crimes. A question, then, may be presented whether these Acts ought to be treated as (1.) ordinary Crimes, and no more nor less, regard being had only to the Intention and not to the Motive; or (2.) as merely incidents to or aggravation of the Political Offence, regard being had to the Motive, and not to the Intention; or (3.) as Acts qualified by reference both to the Intention and to the Motive, and so, as *sui generis*, being punishable on principles founded on the special views of Political expediency.

(Sheldon Amos in 1872, quoted in Radzinowicz and Hood, 1990, p.404)

It was the recognition that the use of violence could be politically progressive both in intent and outcome that prompted the change in official attitude (including the attitude of European criminology) towards the political offender in certain European jurisdictions. The principle that such offenders should be dealt with 'politically' – that is, leniently – rather than in accordance with the strict provisions of the criminal law, found its place in several European penal codes. As Vidal wrote in the early years of the twentieth century:

> Whereas formerly, the political criminal was treated as a public enemy, he is today considered as a friend of the public good … his criminality cannot be compared with that of the ordinary malefactor, with the murderer, the thief, etc. The criminality has not at all the same morality. It is only relative, dependent on time, place, circumstances, the institutions of the land, and it is often inspired by noble sentiments, by disinterested motives, by devotion to persons and principles, by love of one's country. In conclusion, the criminality is only passing.

> (Quoted in Ingraham, 1979, p.35)

In England, which was controversially hospitable to political fugitives and European exiles by offering them a 'safe haven', the challenge posed by Fenians and Suffragettes, who committed acts which were clear breaches of the criminal law in the furtherance of political objectives, generated heated discussion about whether the concept of 'political offender' should be explicitly acknowledged in law.

In the 1860s, there was parliamentary debate about whether Britain was deviating from international convention in treating Fenian prisoners charged with treason-felony more harshly than common criminals on the grounds that they were much more of a threat to the interests of the state:

> We are in great danger of being shamed before the world. Our Russells and Gladstones, amid the plaudits of the nation, have called foreign despotisms to account again and again for a treatment of political convicts, which though very ugly in its details, was looking to its results, essentially less terrible than that to which the Fenian prisoners are now subjected. They have maintained, or used such language that they seemed to maintain, that political prisoners should not be treated as common convicts; and we have all cheered them on while doing so, thanking God that we were not as the inhuman Neapolitans and Austrians. If we were right in this, are we right in treating the Irish political convicts as common felons?

> (*The Lancet*, 1866)

Fenian offenders informed the courts that they regarded their trials as political and themselves as soldiers of Ireland. They considered their offence to be of a special character, implying in their view no moral culpability, and status engaged in a series of protests when their political status was not recognized by the courts or the penal authorities. This in turn brought further exceptional punishment, and accompanying public protest and campaigns for a political amnesty argued that the prison authorities were trying to break, through torture, the political resolve of the Fenian prisoners (Hopper, 1984).

During the passage of the 1877 Prison Act, Irish and Liberal MPs tried to resolve the issue by recommending that the government establish a penal regime, similar to the *custodia honesta* prison regimes on the Continent which were run on the principle that deterrence or reform should play no part in the penal life of political offenders because it was recognized that it was not possible to discourage ideologically committed offenders.

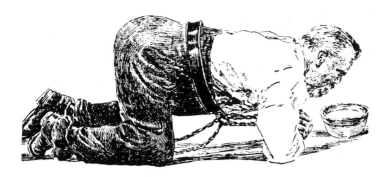

The Fenian Jeremiah O'Donovan Rossa, under temporary strict punishment regime, handcuffed with his hands behind his back and in chains, often naked, had to eat his food off the floor in a dark cell in Chatham jail, 1868–69

The Suffragettes, because of the 'direct action' tactics they used during the 'Women's War' (1905–10), also raised the question of whether they should be treated as political offenders. They refused to recognize the legitimacy of court proceedings, asserting that they were not under any a priori obligation to accept the laws promulgated by a male political establishment and demanding that they be treated as political prisoners:

> If it were the custom to treat political offenders as ordinary offenders against the well-being of society are treated, we should not have complained if we were treated like that; but it is not the international custom to do it, and so, for the dignity of the women of the country, and for the sake of the consciences of the men of the country, and for the sake of our nation amongst the nations of the earth, we are not going to allow the Liberal government to treat us like ordinary law-breakers in future.

(Pankhurst, 1931, pp.134–5)

In prison, they launched a campaign of resistance in the form of disobedience, riot and hunger strikes. In turn, they had to endure strip-searching, hosings, beatings, being placed in canvas straight-jackets and solitary confinement and being forcibly fed. In an attempt to break the deadlock, Keir Hardie, then leader of the Independent Labour Party, introduced a Prison (Political Offence) Bill to achieve treatment as *de facto* political offenders for Suffragettes. However, it was blocked by the Home Office.

In the case of both the Fenians and the Suffragettes we see why certain observers believed that the wisest course of action was to treat political offenders differently. It was clear that political offences were beyond the grasp of the conventional criminal justice system and, indeed, posed a fundamental challenge to its legitimacy. Political offenders tested to the limit the questions: What is crime? and: Who are the real criminals? They demanded that the acts be considered in terms of intention rather than in terms of the acts themselves. In addition, there was every possibility that those who considered themselves to be political prisoners would, through their resistance to the process of criminalization, and re-presentation of themselves as victims and martyrs, gain considerable public sympathy with demands for clemency or outright amnesty.

Ingraham (1979, p.288), however, notes that the First World War brought a significant change in the attitude of the European powers towards political crimes and political criminals which became evident during the following decades in the more repressive laws sanctioned to deal with them. European nation-states returned to using the death penalty for crimes which were political in nature (treason, espionage and insurrection) (see also Burk, 1982).

What caused these changes? There are no clear-cut answers to this question, but various external and internal reasons have been put forward. First, two world wars, escalating anti-colonialist struggles and the rise of transnational ideologies of communism, anarchism and fascism re-centred anxieties about treason, espionage, sabotage, conspiracy and subversion. Second, a profound reordering of the state and civil society took place. The processes of governance were democratized, political and industrial rights were legally recognized and the concurrent 'institutionalization' of political conflict occurred. Such transformations reinforced the view that political disputes could be resolved, and meaningful change and reform could be realized gradually, through rational discourse, debate and compromise. Finally:

> In addition to this new and measurable enmity and vulnerability, the state had acquired other characteristics during the latter part of the [nineteenth] century. Those aspects of national community that had begun the century by seeming so abstract in the thought of Hegel and so non-political in that of Herder had become by the end of the century far more concrete and political. Indeed, organic nationalism was a product of the end of the century when, in Eugene Weber's phrase, peasants turned into Frenchmen, as did petit-bourgeois and others, and in other states passions turned many more English people into Englishmen, Rhinelanders, Saxons, Prussians, and Bavarians into Germans. The identification of the state with the ethnic national community, supported by other propaganda and legislation, constituted in the early twentieth-century state a very different organism from the abstract State of the Enlightenment and its nineteenth century successors, the eclectics, classicists, utilitarians and positivists. Now the state, like the law, represented, indeed personified, a people, and it was operated according to the people's will; those who opposed it, whether ordinary criminals or political criminals, opposed the will of the people, and gradually the political criminal came to be regarded as more dangerous – and more repulsive – than the ordinary criminal.
>
> (Peters, 1985, p.120)

What might viewing political offenders in this way suggest in terms of shifting definitions of crime and criminality and changing perceptions of social order?

3 Deconstructing the problem of 'terrorism'

terrorism

In the course of the twentieth century, the 'political criminal' was transformed into the 'arch-criminal' – the 'terrorist'. Such a transformation posed a whole new set of definitional questions. From the late 1960s onwards, terrorism was elevated to the status of primary threat to peace and stability because it had the capacity to disrupt and paralyse, on a transnational scale, virtually every aspect of life. According to Paul Johnson:

Terrorism is the cancer of the modern world. No state is immune to it. It is a dynamic organism which attacks the healthy flesh of the surrounding society. It has the essential hallmark of malignant cancer; unless treated, and treated drastically, its growth is inexorable, until it poisons and engulfs the society on which it feeds and drags it down to destruction.

(Johnson, 1986, p.31)

When respondents were asked in a 1986 *New York Times*–CBS poll to list the most pressing problems facing the USA, reference to the Middle Eastern/Mediterranean 'terrorist' threat surpassed *all* other domestic and foreign issues (Livingston, 1994). In the UK during the 1970s and 1980s, the media was saturated with reports of national and global 'terrorist' incidents, ringing condemnations of atrocities that were said to plumb new depths of savagery and bestiality, and solemn promises that there would be no hiding place for those who had planned and executed such evil acts. Very soon it began to be possible to provide seemingly definitive answers to the questions: What is terrorism? and: Who are terrorists?

ACTIVITY 7.3

Make a note of what you think are the defining features and images of terrorism. You will need to consider the following questions:

- What are acts of terrorism?

- Whom does terrorism target?

- What are its objectives?

- What type of person carries out such acts?

- Which political ideologies, organizations and countries are readily associated with terrorism?

- What are the differences between those labelled as terrorists, guerrillas, freedom-fighters and political criminals?

Analyse how you have reached your conclusions. Was the media an important source of your information?

COMMENT

Commentators such as Hogan and Walker (1989) have questioned why, in the late twentieth century, we use the terms 'terrorism' and 'terrorist' rather than using the terms 'political violence' and 'political offenders'. They believe it is because the former terms have much wider ideological meanings and resonances. In this commonplace usage:

- Terrorism is defined as violence that deliberately targets and 'frontlines' civilians who have no chance of defending themselves ('soft targets').

- It is conducted by sub-state groups and is revolutionary in nature.

- Its perpetrators, who are pathologically deranged, fanatical or 'cultish' individuals, operate in a clandestine manner with the support of a minority of 'rogue' states who use them to advance their own geopolitical interests.

- Its perpetrators should be treated as common criminals.

However, if we critically examine certain of these defining features closely, we see that it is a highly problematic endeavour to attempt to draw clear boundaries around who the terrorists are and to distinguish between terrorism and orthodox forms of warfare. Indeed, by reflecting critically on its essential features, it is possible to produce an extensive reconstruction and reconceptualization of the problem of terrorism.

3.1 To terrorize innocent civilians?

Terrorists, according to writers such as Sterling (1981), Netanyahu (1986), Wilkinson (1986) and Lodge (1988), aim and intend to generate shock and spread fear and insecurity by deliberately murdering, maiming and menacing innocent, defenceless and unsuspecting bystanders. The rationale underpinning carefully staged and choreographed displays of reckless and savage violence is that, if no-one in particular is the target, no-one can feel safe. Thus, the terrorist act is a form of symbolic communication aimed at terrifying an audience much wider than the immediate victim (the so-called 'magnifying effect'). These are the features, it is argued by terrorologists (that is, those who study terrorism), that mark terrorism out as being manifestly different from conventional warfare and, indeed, from the actions of freedom-fighters:

> In seeking to destroy freedom and democracy, terrorists deliberately target non-combatants for their own cynical purposes. They kill and maim defenceless men, women and children. They murder judges, newspaper reporters, elected officials, government administrators, labour leaders, policemen, priests and others who defend the values of civilized society. Freedom fighters, in contrast, seek to adhere to international law and civilized standards of conduct. They attack military targets, not defenceless citizens. Non-combatant casualties in this context are an aberration or attributable to the fortunes of war. They are not the result of deliberate policy designed to terrorize the opposition.

> (US President George Bush, quoted in Brogan, 1992, p.543)

And we can all, for example, recall the carnage and devastation caused by no-warning bomb and gun attacks in various parts of the world during the 1980s and 1990s.

However, this very broad conceptualization is deficient in several respects. First, as Taylor (1993) has noted, officially designated terrorists repeatedly deny that they primarily target civilians and in certain instances have publicly apologized for what they define as 'military actions' that have gone disastrously wrong, killing innocent bystanders. And, second, they argue, in classic 'just war' tradition, that physical force is used only in so far as no other methods are available or effective. Their violence has a specific and identifiable purpose and is measured by its likely achievement.

Conversely, studying accounts of conventional twentieth-century military campaigns and wars reminds us that the difference between terrorist atrocities and the conduct of conventional war (irrespective of what the previously discussed laws of war state) may not be so clear-cut. For instance, in 1938 Winston Churchill announced that, if war with Germany was declared, it would be no part of British policy to breach the 'principle of distinction' because:

In the first place, it is against international law to bomb civilians as such and to make deliberate attacks upon civilian populations. That is undoubtedly a violation of international law. In the second place, targets which are aimed at from the air must be legitimate military objectives and must be capable of identification. In the third place, reasonable care must be taken in attacking those military objectives so that by carelessness a civilian population in the neighbourhood is not bombed.

(Quoted in Best, 1994, p.200)

However, the realities of waging total war turned out to be much more complicated, especially when it was realized that adhering strictly to the rules was resulting in heavy casualties among Allied air crews. Operational difficulties resulted in a dramatic redefinition of what constituted a 'legitimate target': the military targets could encompass not merely military forces and installations, but also factories engaged in the manufacture of military supplies and key lines of communications. The presence of civilians would not, therefore, rule out attacks on factories, ports, airports, railway stations, roads or dams. Moreover, if significant military installations were sited in densely populated urban areas, they could also be viewed as legitimate targets.

It was this policy shift that created the lasting controversy about the legality or otherwise of the Allies' 'saturation bombing' of German cities and the dropping of 'Little Boy' and 'Fat Man' (the atom bombs) on Japan in 1945. One historical interpretation presents these as among the greatest operations of the Second World War. They hastened the end of a conflict in which the Nazis and the Japanese had broken all the laws of war and shocked the conscience of humankind by using conquered populations as slave labour; ruthlessly abusing prisoners of war; massacring and mutilating non-combatants; authorizing mass rape; conducting grotesque medical experiments; and systematically murdering millions in history's greatest example of industrialized, ultra-efficient 'conveyer belt' genocide. The Allied bombings were unquestionably horrific but, according to the moral philosopher Michael Walzer (1977), a lowering of moral and legal standards was necessary because this was *the* 'supreme emergency' situation. The violence deployed was for *the* ultimate 'good war' or just cause: namely, the defence of civilization.

However, there are others who believe that sacrosanct war myths and memories must be challenged, and claim that those responsible for masterminding and sanctioning the 'war within a war' strategy should have been held to account before a court of law for the slaughter of civilians on an unprecedented scale. They allege that Britain and the United States, like Germany, had breached the rules of war by deliberately incinerating German and Japanese cities which had no significant military or industrial installations. Vera Brittain, one of the most outspoken critics of the bombing of German cities and an advocate of consistent and unwavering commitment to universal moral and legal clarity, asserted that:

The tortures to which we have subjected civilians, including children, in our 'saturation raids' far exceed the sufferings caused by poison gas between 1914–18. I venture to prophesy with complete confidence that the callous cruelty which has caused us to destroy innocent human life in Europe's most crowded cities, and the vandalism which has obliterated historic treasures in some of her loveliest, WILL APPEAR TO FUTURE CIVILIZATION AS AN EXTREME FORM OF CRIMINAL LUNACY.

(Brittain, 1944, p.116)

The critics maintain that the 'without mercy' 'anti-city' bombings were specifically calculated to terrorize and produce a stupefying effect on the morale of the civilian population. Giddens argues, for example, that: 'the atomic bombs dropped on Hiroshima and Nagasaki, were nothing more nor less than a concentrated application of terror, designed to shock Japan into surrender' (Giddens, 1985, p.33). And with regard to the bombing of Germany, there is evidence to suggest that certain sections of the British War Cabinet, the Air Staff Command, and even aircrews, became increasingly troubled when forced to reflect upon the morality of the saturation bombings and the possibility that they could be held to account under the international laws of war. In 1945, for example, Churchill stated:

> It seems to me that the moment has come when the question of bombing of German cities simply for the sake of increasing the terror, though under other pretexts, should be reviewed. Otherwise we shall come into control of an utterly ruined land ... I feel the need for more precise concentration on military objectives ... rather than on mere acts of terror and wanton destruction, however impressive.

(Quoted in Saward, 1985, p.382)

Determined efforts were made to exclude the contentious issue of the saturation bombing strategy from the agenda of the Nuremberg war crimes tribunal by announcing that, because all sides had used such tactics, it would be impossible to enforce the rules of war. This 'closing of the books' bequeathed two notable legacies, the first of which was an important question as to whether the 'victors' justice' could ever be truly impartial. Was it only the victors in a given war who had the right to define what a war crime was and to pass judgement on who was and who was not a war criminal? Did the commission of atrocities by a defeated nation in a war preclude its civilians from claiming the status of victim in relation to atrocities committed by a victorious nation?

A second, lasting legacy of the bombing initiative was the precedent it unintentionally set. The law of war in this area had been broken with impunity and the principle of distinction literally obliterated. Consequently, it would be very difficult morally to condemn or take punitive action against any future targeting of civilians:

> Various terrorist groups have from time to time defended their indiscriminate killing of civilians by saying that they were only following the precedent established by the British in World War Two ... This is what might be called the *nemesis effect* of violating the war convention, even in a worthy cause: such a departure often returns to haunt those originally responsible for it. Others pursuing a far less just end now find it convenient and possible to wrap themselves in the mantle of legitimacy when they employ those new techniques of violence, which often are directed at the very society that originally introduced them.

(Garrett, 1993, p.200)

Although assurance was given that Dresden, Hiroshima and Nagasaki were exceptional deviations from the 'norm', the deliberate targeting of non-combatants and the civilian infrastructure became the centre-piece of military strategy in the second half of the twentieth century. As we have seen, killing civilians took on its own military rationale, namely to terrorize and demoralize. Let us consider another concrete situation. As Ely (1993) notes, by the time the undeclared and illegal, and therefore unattributable, bombing of Laos (which commenced in 1965) ceased in 1973, the United States Air Force had dropped almost 800,000 tonnes of bombs with the destructive effect of 25 Hiroshima-style nuclear explosions. The stated rationale of this carpet bombing was to obliterate the physical and social infrastructure and it is estimated that at least 150,000 civilians were killed and tens of thousands maimed. Many critics argue that the whole of the Vietnam war should be defined, first and foremost, as a 'war of terror' because American forces resorted to saturation bombing and to using napalm, white phosphorous, 'search and destroy' missions, free-fire zones, 'body-count' operations and ecocidal chemicals. In the process they killed 1,350,000 civilians (Falk *et al.*, 1971; Karnow, 1983; Bilton and Sim, 1993).

View from the town hall tower over the ruins of Dresden, 1945

Hence, it is probably fair to conclude that the indiscriminate and systematic frontlining of unsuspecting civilian populations is not the sole preserve of officially defined terrorist campaigns. Indeed, some would argue that, by comparison with the breadth and varieties of violence used by conventional armies, these groupings have been remarkably restrained in this respect. The totalizing nature of late twentieth-century wars, in conjunction with the methods through which war is now conducted and the lethal nature of the hyper-sophisticated weaponry available, means that there is the distinct possibility that 'collateral damage' – that is, mass civilian casualties – will continue to be excessive.

3.2   Revolutionary in intent?

The problem of terrorism becomes even more complicated when we critically evaluate the common assertion that terrorism is practised by extremist revolutionary groups and individuals committed to seizing power from governments or states. A plethora of books on terrorism have tended to concentrate on the exploits of what they describe as the 'high priests' of revolutionary terrorism: groups such as the Irish Republican Army (IRA), Euskadi Ta Askatasuna (ETA), African National Congress (ANC), Palestine Liberation Organization (PLO), Hezbollah and Islamic Jihad. However, this representation of what terrorism is conflates very different political struggles and runs the risk of draining them of their political meaning and specificity. For example, many of the groups mentioned above were or are demanding some form of national self-determination or autonomy from or within existing nation-states.

Chomsky (1991) and Herman (1993) also emphasize that such a 'bottom-up' conceptualization fails to recognize the critical linkages that can exist between the state, the status quo and terrorism. Indeed, according to these writers, there is simply no overstating the degree to which states, because of their monopolization of violence, have the potential to become malignant epicentres of terrorism. In recent years the US government has published an annual inventory of foreign states alleged to be the criminal paymasters of international terrorism (see, for example, US Department of State, 1995). Those named on this list (Libya, Iran, Iraq, Cuba, North Korea, Nicaragua, South Yemen and several Eastern European states) were 'outed' for secretly providing finance, weaponry and logistical support and also for providing terrorists with a safe haven before and after their acts of violence. Being designated as a terrorist state meant that countries were defined as invalid for most kinds of US aid and committed the US government to opposing the granting of loans from multilateral financial institutions such as the International Monetary Fund and imposing trade embargoes and global freezing of assets.

Missing from the 'outing', according to Herman and Chomsky, were those Western and pro-Western paymasters who, in the global Cold War fight against communism, covertly, and often illegally, spent billions of dollars equipping and training networks of right-wing groupings in many parts of the world. Groups such as UNITA in Angola, the Contras in Nicaragua, the Mujahadeen in Afghanistan and Renamo in Mozambique relied on terror, for example, to stage right-wing revolutions.

This is perhaps the place to point out briefly how sections of the Western media have come under particular criticism for limited vision, distortion, selective indignation, outright misrepresentation and falsification and for uncritically reproducing – often in the form of visual clichés – the official 'What is terrorism?' and 'Who are the terrorists?' storyline. As Hall has argued of news 'framing' generally:

> Some things, people, events, relationships always get represented: always centre-stage, always in a position to define, to set the agenda, to establish the terms of the conversation. Some others sometimes get represented – but always at the margin, always responding to a question whose terms and conditions have been defined elsewhere; never 'centred'. Still others are always 'represented' only by their eloquent absence, their silences, or refracted through the glance or gaze of others.

(Hall, 1986, p.9)

Livingston (1994) describes in detail how, in the 1980s, those groupings which did not pose a threat to the US geopolitical interests were much more likely to be categorized by the American media as freedom-fighters, liberation movements, rebels, armed militias, guerrillas and partisans. And there was considerable bias when it came to identifying what were and were not acts of terrorism. Livingston's extensive research indicates that the actions of pro-American or anti-communist groups, no matter how indiscriminate and horrific, were likely to be denied through defining them as being purely retaliatory or accidental in nature. Because these groups managed to evade the official label of terrorism, their activities attracted considerably less condemnatory media comment and coverage. This particular media framing, Livingston argues, should be defined as a 'crime of omission' and had an important knock-on effect for victims of terrorist violence. The deaths of a large number of people were essentially ignored, down-played or disqualified while other victims were elevated to the status of what he calls 'super-victim', with due outrage and sympathy being accorded to their suffering. Therefore, political considerations defined victims as being worthy or unworthy of media recognition and created a 'hierarchy of victimization'. Researchers have noted a similar tendency in the British media's reportage of the Northern Ireland conflict where the actions of the IRA were much more likely to be labelled as 'terrorism' than were the actions of their Loyalist counterparts (Miller, 1994).

crime of omission

hierarchy of victimization

ACTIVITY 7.4

Research indicates that the state's involvement with terror does not stop at sponsorship. Pause here for a moment and think about other ways in which a state could terrorize its own citizenry. Why might it do this and what might the effects be? Make a few notes on this before you continue. These questions are essential to an understanding of terrorism and its consequences and will be looked at further in the following sections. You will be able to compare your response with ours as you read on.

Research suggests that state-directed terror can take several often interrelated forms. First, states, although they have experienced very different forms and degrees of political conflict, have displayed a remarkable similarity in their response in order to restore 'law and order': a mixture of surreptitious negotiations and *repressive* or *enforcement* terror strategies. Criminal justice procedures can be streamlined; core civil liberties and legal rights and safeguards 'temporarily' restricted, circumvented or suspended; media censorship or control imposed; and special courts established to hasten 'terrorist' detention, convictions or executions. States are also able to promulgate draconian and sweeping 'emergency' legislation to extend the surveillance and investigative powers of security and policing agencies. They can upgrade the coercive and intelligence capacity of these agencies through rearmament and reorganization and let loose 'the dogs of war' in the form of covert military or paramilitary counter-insurgency or 'terrorist detection units' to terrorize the 'terrorists' into submission or negotiated solutions (Wolf, 1987).

The crucial point about counter-terror strategies, according to Wolf (1987), is that once they are unleashed they develop a momentum of their own and there is every possibility that those fighting terrorism eventually resort to proactive terror, or undeclared 'dirty tricks' and secret wars. In many situations, for example, where counter-terrorist measures have been resorted to, state-directed or 'independent' pro-state 'death squads' and 'counter-gangs' have surfaced. These have a tendency to operate with very broad definitions of who are suspected terrorists, subversives, undesirables, degenerates, 'intransigents', 'social deviants' and enemies of the state, and to act as judge, jury and executioner. In South Africa, conclusive evidence finally emerged that state-sponsored right-wing death squads had been responsible for the assassination of political opponents and many of the civilian massacres in the townships and on commuter trains (Africa Watch, 1991). Israel's secret services also employed assassins in the 'war' with their Palestinian enemies (Taylor, 1993). And throughout the duration of the Northern Ireland and Basque conflicts, it was repeatedly claimed that sections of the security forces had established, financed, armed and colluded with pro-state terrorist groupings engaged in 'retaliatory' or 'copycat' killings to terrorize the 'terrorists' and supporters into submission or cessation of activities (Taylor, 1993). Counter-terror campaigns and vendettas also have a tendency to outlive the 'terrorist' opposition by finding new political enemies and new social threats (Mason and Krane, 1989).

torture

Torture is the second type of terror practised by states and is regarded as the ultimate form of individualized terror. As was noted in section 2.1.1, according to international law, torture is illegal in all circumstances. However, at the close of the twentieth century its use remains commonplace and, as a consequence of the lucrative global market in 'internal security' equipment, technologies of political and social control and 'law-enforcement' expertise, it is undergoing constant refinement and modernization (Lashmar, 1995). According to Ackroyd *et al.* (1977, pp.230–4), state torture is practised for the following reasons:

- To elicit information. As we shall see later in section 5.1, the quest for the 'truth' is the classic *post hoc* justification for torture.

- To prepare enemies for 'show trials' and public confessions and testimony. The classic example remains Stalin's show trials of 1936–38 during which former leaders of the Bolshevik Party were forced to admit guilt to charges of which they were innocent.

- To terminate, or even reverse, the political effectiveness of the detainee by making her or him afraid of re-experiencing the suffering.

- To create a 'culture of terror' and a 'dialectic of fear' permeating every milieu of society and the national psyche.

In this last scenario, as noted by Amnesty International (1984), Scarry (1985) and Rejali (1994), torture transforms the victim's body into a political text and inscribed on it is the omnipotence of the state and an all-too-visible warning for dissident groups or whole communities. The intention is to make the costs of political opposition or resistance too high to be contemplated. According to Rodley: 'the typical victim will be a political opponent of the government – violent or non-violent, a real force for change or a minor irritant to the regime – seized by the security forces' (Rodley, 1987, p.9). And because torture is being used to intimidate and silence the general population, innocent surrogate targets are as effective as political activists:

> the state takes upon itself the right to impose, through violence, its definitions of reality and correct behaviour throughout the whole field of human action. As terror penetrates the sinews of every organization and association in social life, people are numbed into subservience and repress any independent thought or impulse to action. Life becomes pervaded by the symbols of the all powerful state and its agents and tools of repression – the political police, their weapons and prisons, and their wider cultural manifestations, all conveying the ever-present threat of violent reprisal for transgressions of all types. A culture of terror develops in which no-one is to be trusted.

(Bushnell *et al.*, 1991, p.9)

In parts of the world where states are permanently at war or in conflict with sections of their own citizenry, or undergoing revolution or counter-revolution, key state agencies have been secretly transformed into fully fledged bureaucratic instruments of terror, complete with networks of clandestine torture and death centres which operate with standardized instrumentation, routinized operating procedures, divisions of labour, rational administrative structures, and professionals whose specialist knowledge is utilized to keep people alive for as long as is deemed either useful or necessary:

> Although death squads and torture groups may torture victims, only states have the resources to torture systematically. States possess the financial and human resources to sustain a torture complex. Further, they can rely on support from other sectors of society to provide technical support (hospitals and mental asylums) and information (universities, unions, the criminal undergrounds).

> (Rejali, 1994, p.134)

Disappearance – that is, extra-judicial arrest or abduction of alleged critics and opponents, usually followed by their torture, secret execution and burial – is the third form of state terrorism. Its origins lie in the Second World War when the Nazis passed a 'Night and Fog' decree, under which anyone deemed to be a threat to security was 'ghosted' to Germany under cover of night. It re-emerged in various Latin American states in the post-war period. For example, between 1976 and 1983 under the military dictatorship in Argentina, it is estimated that between 10,000 and 30,000 people were 'disappeared' in a pre-planned 'dirty war' against terrorism (Pitman, 1986). General Iberico Saint Jean, Governor of Buenos Aires Province, explained the rationale of the Argentinian state during this time: 'First we kill all the subversives; then, their collaborators; later, those who sympathize with them; afterward, those who remain indifferent; and finally, the undecided' (quoted in Morgan, 1989, p.126). There is evidence that the Argentinian authorities also learned from previous reigns of terror in Latin America:

disappearance

> There would be none of the evidence of mass slaughter which followed Pinochet's seizure of power in Chile and none of the international outcry which it provoked. There would be no mass imprisonment as in Uruguay, where left-wing suspects had converted other prisoners and even prison guards to their cause, and there would be no possibility of such prisoners being released under a general amnesty only to start their campaign again, as happened in Argentina under Perón's predecessor, President Cámpora. There would be no evidence and no one would be able to prove who was responsible. The murderous campaign would be concealed from Argentina and the world.

> (Fisher, 1989, p.180)

And only states have resorted to the fourth, most extreme, kind of internal terror – namely, concerted and co-ordinated *genocide*. Chalk and Jonassohn (1990), Kuper (1991) and Rummel (1995) have detailed how states and governing classes can conceive and preside over *systemic* mass murder leading to or bordering on outright genocide to establish or maintain political power or to acquire wealth, land and resources. This tool of public policy can also be practised to realize a multitude of ideological objectives such as spreading terror among real, 'imagined' or potential class, ethnic or political enemies; redressing past victimizations; or socially engineering 'brave new worlds'.

genocide

In the aftermath of the Holocaust, the outcry from the international community was 'never again'. And yet genocide has remained a feature of the post-war period. In 1966, the year after General Suharto seized power in Indonesia, the military dictatorship murdered between 500,000 and one million people (Crouch, 1978). Since then, according to various Amnesty International annual reports, large numbers of people have been killed in suspicious circumstances and many political prisoners have served, or continue to serve, long prison sentences imposed after unfair trials. Hundreds of other people have been arrested and held without charge or trial and the 'torture of political detainees and criminal suspects [has been] common, in some cases resulting in death'. There have been reports of extra-judicial and judicial executions, and the 'fate of possibly hundreds of Acehnese and East Timorese who [have] "disappeared"' remains unknown (see, for example, Amnesty International, 1995, p.160). After the Indonesian invasion and annexation of East Timor in 1975, an estimated 200,000 out of a total population of 700,000 were killed (Budiardjo, 1991). During the Khmer Rouge's reign (1975–78), Kampuchea (now Cambodia) was transformed into:

> a 'vast concentration camp' a 'gigantic prison' and a 'state of barracks socialism', where rivers of blood flow and a ruthless and systematic policy of genocide is being carried out with respect to the country's own people. A special course aimed at the construction of a historically unprecedented society had been proclaimed – a society without cities, without property, no commodity–money relations, without markets, and without money, without families. Those who are dissatisfied with the new regime are being 'eradicated', along with their families, by disembowelment, by beating to death with hoes, by having nails banged into the backs of their heads and by other cruel means of economizing on bullets.
>
> (Quoted in Kuper, 1991, p.25)

It is estimated that between one and two million people died in the 'killing fields' as a result of the conditions of life, state-initiated massacres and prison-based execution programmes.

In April 1994, the killing of President Juvnal Habyrimana plunged Rwanda into another genocidal civil war. The slaughter cannot be put down to random, irrational acts of savagery: the killings began with lists and targets and the planned elimination of all political opponents. One month later, around half a million people, mostly minority Tutsis, had been murdered. The aim of this Hutu violence was not to drive the Tutsis out of the country but to wipe them out (see, for example, McGreal, 1994; Africa Watch, 1995).

In Europe, 'ethnic cleansing' in Bosnia in the 1990s also took state-initiated terror to its logical conclusion. The defining logic, as Vulliamy (1994) argues, was not just to win a war or to gain territorial advantage, but to eradicate all trace of those whose presence would violate the ethnic and cultural integrity of the new nation-state (see Extract 7.1). This was why approximately 85 per cent of those killed in the conflict were civilians. Mass rape was resurrected as a deliberate weapon of war in the Serb/Muslim/Croat conflict. As you read Extract 7.1, note how Vulliamy stresses that genocide is as much to do with eradicating all traces of history, memory and culture as it is with killing human beings.

ARE THOSE WHO CANNOT OR WILL NOT ACKNOWLEDGE, REMEMBER AND CONFRONT THE PAST
CONDEMNED TO REPEAT IT?

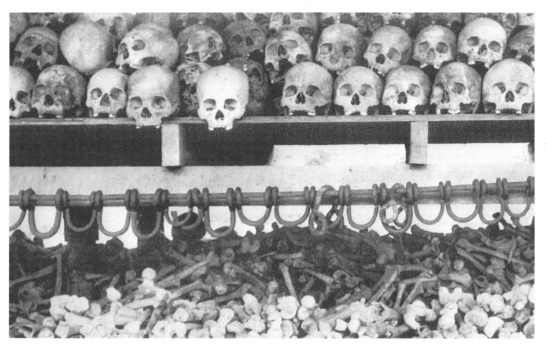

A display outside Phnom Penh burial pits for victims of Kampuchea's Khmer Rouge regime.
8,985 remains were found at this site. The iron shackles were used to bind the victims

'Remembering Rwanda', London, Palm Sunday 1995

Extract 7.1 Vulliamy: 'Genocide in our lifetime'

Mohammed Curac, Mayor of Travnik, said some weeks prior to an attempt to kill him by blowing up his car: 'Look at the way this war is being conducted: it has become city-cidal, culture-cidal, history-cidal, memory-cidal, dignity-cidal, economicidal – in short, genocidal. Our parents' generation bore witness to the Holocaust against the Jews. That was on a different scale. I think this is what genocide looks like in our lifetime.'

In January 1993, the Chief Rabbi of British Jewry, Jonathan Sacks, added his cogent voice to the call for military intervention in Bosnia, saying: 'There are some crimes which, because they are crimes against humanity, implicate us all, and we are sometimes morally responsible for what we fail to prevent as well as for what we do. I wonder if future generations could ever forgive us if we, who have lived through the century of the Holocaust, did not rise up and prevent the beginnings of a second Holocaust.'

Among the declared ambitions of modern Europe is to make sure that nothing like the Nazi persecutions should ever be repeated. But the characteristics of genocide, its tone, its dictionary definition, its component parts, can be revived without a second Auschwitz or Dachau. And some of those characteristics have undoubtedly hallmarked the crushing of Bosnia's Muslims in the eighteen months since April 1992 … . Europe is not now menaced by a grand and lunatic quest for supremacy like Hitler's, but it is fragmenting into a plethora of fiercely harboured ethnic identities. And genocide in this Europe will be a more localized, parish-pump, grubby business – but genocide nevertheless.

The Bosnian government has established a war crimes commission under the leadership of a lawyer, Mirsad Tokaca, who argues that what has happened to Bosnia's Muslims meets the various internationally recognized definitions of genocide. He cites mass ethnic cleansing,

the murders in the camps and mass rape. 'We know we cannot solve anything,' he says, 'we are here only to get facts, documents and testimonies, to prepare data for an international court, if there ever is one.'

One important facet of genocide, though less costly in human terms than the main tranches of Tokaca's submissions, can be seen by anyone who drives through the towns from which Muslims have been 'cleansed' by the Serbs: the obliteration of historical identity and memory, and of an entire culture, as expressed in architecture, in religious buildings or historical records. All this has gone, systematically destroyed. …

A rump Bosnia in the form of a Muslim state, probably an ugly political creature, will be born out of the war in order to accommodate the victories of the other two factions and the sentence of the 'international community'. The first generation to grow up in this bereft, crowded, mono-ethnic state will know only too much about how it came to be, and about the suffering which their parents – who never wanted or asked to live in such a place – went through at its inception. The country into which they should by rights have been born, Bosnia-Herzegovina, will have ceased to exist, shattered and blown asunder.

This next generation will grow up seeped in the recent history and memory of that destruction, with goodness knows what outcome. But they will never see an Ottoman minaret and may never see a Bogomil tomb. The tangible, visible and rich history of their people and its strange hybrid culture down the centuries, of their curious and inimitable place at a fulcrum between the Orient and Western Europe, will have been decimated. And that is the underlying purpose of genocide, on whatever scale, and of warfare of a particular, singular and intolerable kind.

(Vulliamy, 1994, pp.352–3, 356–7)

3.3   The mind of a terrorist?

What kind of person could do such a thing? This is the question that immediately comes to mind when watching the emergency services clearing up after the latest no-warning 'terrorist' bomb explosion, gun or suicide attack. Many of the most influential textbooks on terrorism assert, in answer to this question, that the 'terrorist' is the pathological 'other' who glories in remorseless, senseless, brutal, random violence. He or she is either criminally insane (Pearlman, 1991) or a cold-blooded thug addicted to psycho- or sociopathic violence (Walzer, 1975). In this narrative, such individuals cynically use politics as an excuse for their barbaric actions:

> I believe that with the Provisional IRA and some of the Middle-Eastern groups, it is nothing really to do with a political cause any more. They are professional killers. That is their occupation and their pleasure and they will go on doing that. No political solution will cope with that. They just have to be extirpated.

> (British Home Secretary Douglas Hurd, quoted in Rolston, 1991, p.171)

It may be the case that individuals can be cited who fit the stereotype. However, Giddens maintains that, at a general level:

> This sort of characterization is usually far from the truth. Most groups purporting to use violence to further their ends have a coherent philosophy about why they act as they do. Controversial though their ideas may be, these groups are not normally composed of people who claim to value violence for its own sake.

> (Giddens, 1989, p.368)

Arblaster (1977) and Morgan (1989) argue that the 'terrorist psychology' concept is an opportune way of evading political complexities. Most 'terrorist' groupings, they argue, have political representatives and go to great lengths to reject the terrorist-criminal label and, as mentioned in section 3.1, assert that they were forced to resort to violence because of the impossibility of achieving meaningful political change through peaceful means:

> The time comes in the life of any nation when there remain only two choices: submit or fight. That time has now come in South Africa ... We shall not submit ... The liberation organizations have consistently followed a policy of non-violence – because we prefer peaceful change to civil war, but our patience is not endless. The government has interpreted our peacefulness as weakness but government force will no longer be met by non-violence. The choice is not ours ... It has been made for us by the government, which has answered every peaceable demand for rights and freedom with force. Umkhonto we Sizwe will be at the frontline of our defence.

> (Nelson Mandela in 1961, quoted in Pinchuck, 1994, pp.92–3)

We also need to pose the question: Are those who are officially labelled 'terrorists' any more 'psychopathological', for example, than soldiers in conventional armies? It is argued that, in order to justify their murderous deeds, 'terrorists' depersonalize and dehumanize their victims, but Duster (1971) and Kelman and Hamilton (1989) maintain that dehumanization, desensitization, 'conscience narrowing', 'dissociation', indifference and demonization are also an inescapable part of military socialization generally and one of the reasons why 'guilt-free' or 'sanctioned' atrocities can occur.

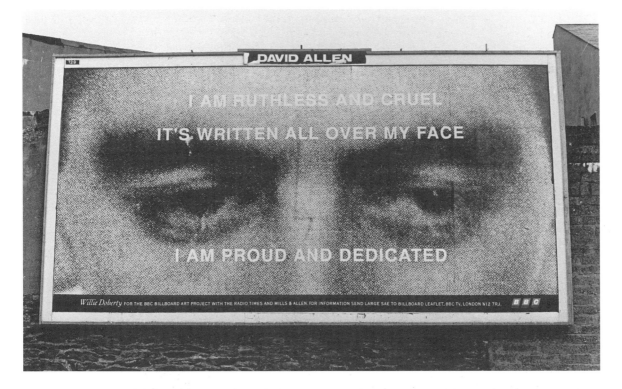

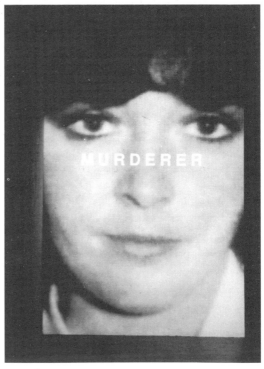

'The same people and the same activities look very different from opposing points of view. What one party sees as terrorist gunmen, another sees as fearless freedom fighters' (Mackie, 1977, p.238)

Dehumanization involves constructing rational mental frameworks which deny and deprive the 'enemy' of their humanity by distancing or excluding them from the moral and cognitive universe. The enemy or 'other' is:

> deprived of the two qualities essential to being perceived as fully human and included in the moral compact that governs human relationships: *identity* – standing as independent, distinctive individuals, capable of making choices and entitled to live their own lives – and *community* – fellow membership in an interconnected network of individuals who care for each other and respect each other's individuality and rights.

(Kelman and Hamilton, 1989, p.19)

dehumanization

Dehumanization also rules out the idea of innocence and can therefore counteract moral contradictions, doubts and ambiguities. The less-than-human 'enemy' is seen to be guilty and to have precipitated and be deserving of her or his victimization. The process of 'enemy creation' can be taken one step further if racist ideologies can be mobilized. So, for example, American soldiers in Vietnam were searching for and destroying stereotypical 'dinks', 'gooks', 'dopes' and 'slopes', and the Serbians were ethnically cleansing 'gypsies', 'filth' and 'animals'. The Khmer Rouge used non-human designation – blue and green scarves – to identify those to be killed, in much the same way as the Nazis used coloured triangles for political prisoners (red), criminals (green), social deviants (black), Jehova's Witnesses (violet) and homosexuals (pink), and the yellow star to identify the Jews, the *Untermenschen*. In Rwanda, the Tutsis were described as 'inyenzi' (cockroaches). In these circumstances moral restraints against killing and personal responsibility can be effectively neutralized.

enemy creation

Kelman and Hamilton (1989) argue that the process can be self-perpetuating once set in motion. Soldiers can, for example, come to view their victims in 'body-count' terms and 'are reinforced in their perception of the victims as less than human by observing their very victimization' (Kelman and Hamilton, 1989, p.19). During the Vietnam war, a platoon of American troops entered My Lai village on 16 March 1968 as part of a 'counter-terrorism' mission. By the time they left four hours later approximately 500 unarmed villagers had been killed in an atrocity that was not acknowledged publicly until late 1969. In Extract 7.2 it is important to notice how one of the participants repeatedly uses the word 'just' in his version of what happened.

ACTIVITY 7.5

In this context, what do you think this repeated use of the word 'just' might signify? Keep this question in mind as you read Extract 7.2 and make a note of your response. What also might it signify in terms of the thinking behind the arguments used, in a court of law, to justify such actions? You will be able to check your thoughts further on this when you come to section 5.1.2.

Extract 7.2   Bilton and Sim: 'My Lai, Vietnam'

I went to turn her over and there was a little baby with her that I had also killed. The baby's face was half gone. My mind just went. The training came to me and I just started killing. Old men, women, children, water buffaloes, everything. We were told to leave nothing standing. We did what we were told, regardless of whether they were civilians. They was the enemy. Period. Kill. If you don't follow a direct order you can be shot yourself. Now what am I supposed to do? You're damned if you do and you're damned if you don't. You didn't have to look for people to kill, they were just there. I cut their throats, cut off their hands, cut out their tongue, their hair, scalped them. I did it. A lot of people were doing it and I just followed. I just lost all sense of direction.

I just started killing any kinda way I can kill. It just came. I didn't know I had it in me. After I killed the child my whole mind just went. It just went. And after you start it's very easy to keep on. The hardest is to kill the first time but once you kill, then it becomes easier to kill the next person and the next one and the next one. Because I had no feelings, no emotions. Nothing.

I just killed. I wasn't the only one that did it; a lot of people in the company did it, hung 'em, all types of ways, any type of way you could kill someone that's what they did. That day in My Lai I was personally responsible for killing about twenty-five people. Personally. I don't think beforehand anyone thought that we would kill so many people. I mean we're talking about four to five hundred people. We almost wiped out the whole village, a whole community. I can't forget the magnitude of the number of people that we killed and how they were killed, killed in lots of ways.

Do you realize what it was like killing five hundred people in a matter of four or five hours? It's just like the gas chambers – what Hitler did. You line up fifty people, women, old men, children, and just mow 'em down. And that's the way it was – from twenty-five to fifty to one hundred. Just killed. We just rounded 'em up, me and a couple of guys, just put the M-16 on automatic, and just mowed 'em down.

(Quoted in Bilton and Sim, 1993, pp.130–1)

Another example of how methodical official dehumanization can be is provided by research on the training and 'enculturization' of state torturers. Although popularly depicted as psycho-sexual sadists, research into the 'world of the torturer' indicates that, more often than not, they are state employees – 'securocrats' – who undergo harsh specialist training and group socialization and who, by and large, regard their work with professional detachment. As Crelinsten argues:

> first, the torturer is doing a *job*, he is 'doing torture'; second, he is supposed to do it well, 'mastering torture'; third, he is supposed to achieve certain results ('making them talk'), i.e., obtaining confessions, breaking the enemy's will; fourth, the central method used to achieve these results is inflicting pain ('making them hurt'); fifth, the people upon whom this pain is inflicted are defined as 'enemies'. The information, the confessions, and, ultimately, the broken people, are the end products of the torturer's work. It is these end products by which he is judged as skilled or unskilled, deserving of promotion or dismissal, considered indispensible or expendable. It is this *judgement* or *assessment* of the torturer's work that leads us to the final feature of the torturer's world: the torturer is working in an institutional context, within a hierarchy in which others, his superiors and their superiors and their superiors, decide who is an enemy, what needs to be known, and what must be done to know it.

(Crelinsten, 1993, p.40)

It is important to note here the emphasis on the *institutional* context. The making of a torturer would appear to have less to do with 'individual psychology' and more to do with the social and political order in which the torture is enabled to take place. In discussing 'factors contributing to the creation of a torturer', Gibson refers to a number of studies, particularly of the Nazi regime, which likewise make it clear there is no one 'type of person' who is more likely to become a torturer:

> It might be comforting to assume that torturers are, in fact, peculiar monsters who can be explained away as the sort of freaks of nature who commit mass murders in periods of insanity. However, the conclusions ... show clearly that this is not the case: They hold that, although it is true that, in some situations, deranged and sadistic individuals have committed acts of torture for pleasure, in most cases in which torture is committed at the instigation of government officials, the torturers can best be described as normal individuals. ...

> The conclusion of these studies is that individual personality characteristics and background information about individuals, by themselves, cannot distinguish individuals who will commit torture or other cruel acts from those who will not.

(Gibson, 1990, p.78)

So what are the factors that contribute to the creation of a torturer? Stover and Nightingale state that: 'An alarming aspect of contemporary torture is the emergence of military or police training programs that instruct security personnel in interrogation techniques that amount to torture' and refer in particular to evidence elicited from torture trials held in Greece after the collapse of the military dictatorship in 1974, and to evidence in Argentina of 'training and *modus operandi* of torturers and executioners, known as "task forces" who worked in hundreds of secret detention centers run by the military and police between 1976 and 1983' (Stover and Nightingale, 1985, p.11). Let us take the case of Greece which is one of the most well-documented instances of the training of torturers.

In her study, Haritos-Fatouros has described the procedures whereby selected recruits to the Greek military police during the years of military rule between 1967 and 1974, were taught 'obedience in its extreme form ... obedience to the "authority of violence"' (Haritos-Fatouros, 1993, p.142) in a process described by Crelinsten generally as following a pattern of:

> *progressive* features of training ... [in which] [t]he subject (the conscript/recruit/torturer-to-be) is progressively desensitized while the object (the subversive/Communist/terrorist/victim-to-be) is progressively dehumanized, objectivized, stripped of any identity except the demonizing labels of the dangerous enemy who will take your life if you do not protect yourself.

(Crelinsten, 1993, p.56)

This process involved 'turning the normal behaviour of an army recruit into the deviant behaviour of a torturer' (Haritos-Fatouros, 1993, p.143). Haritos-Fatouros documents (pp.149–57) how, on being drafted at the age of 18 into military police training camps, recruits to be trained as torturers were initially selected principally on the strength of their own and their family's 'anti-communist feelings and actions'. They then underwent several months of military police training which tested, *inter alia*: 'ability to endure beating of all kinds and exercises to exhaustion ... [and] obedience to the demands of authority, even of the most illogical and degrading kind' (p.149). This training placed particular importance on an initiation process which involved not only an 'initiation beating' and the swearing of 'allegiance to the totemic-like symbol of authority used by the junta' (p.150), but also 'harsh treatment … [which] produced high levels of stress' (p.154). These factors 'bound' the individual recruit to the group, a process which was built on in other ways in later training to produce what Crelinsten has described as the 'breaking down of the previous, civilian identity of the new recruit and building up a new identity based upon an identification with the military subculture, its ideology, and its internal structure and worldview' (Crelinsten, 1993, p.54).

As mentioned above in relation to other agencies in other circumstances, Haritos-Fatouros identified the important role played by language in depersonalizing people and altering perception of torture techniques. For example, recruits would use nicknames to hide their own identities, they gave nicknames to prisoners, and torture techniques would be described in almost jocular fashion, such as 'tea party with toast'.

Training involved both brutal and brutalizing procedures and degrading acts which had little meaning to the recruit, but: 'Obedience without question to an order without logic was the ultimate goal' (Haritos-Fatouros, 1993, p.155). Desensitization of recruits themselves was required to the point where, in the words of one: 'We had to *learn* to *love* pain' (p.156). This learning to 'love pain' was a gradual process. Exposure to torture was built up, first, by initial contact with prisoners through, for example, the bringing of food; then by giving prisoners 'some blows'; watching the torturing of prisoners by others, and beating prisoners if they moved; before, finally, recruits began carrying out full acts of torture themselves.

desensitization

As with the studies referred to by Gibson (1990) above, Haritos-Fatouros similarly concluded that: 'if the proper learning procedures are applied under the right circumstances, any individual is a potential torturer. An explanation that has recourse to the presence of strong sadistic impulses is inadequate; to believe that only sadists can perform such violent acts is a fallacy and a comfortable rationalization to ease our liberal sensibilities' (Haritos-Fatouros, 1993, p.159).

To consolidate your understanding of this section, can you summarize the main ideas concerning the concept of terrorism? Do you think that it serves any useful analytical purpose to continue to use such a term?

4 Reconstructing and reordering the problem of 'terrorism'

What can we conclude from our survey of the supposedly unproblematic defining features of terrorism? Overall, it can plausibly be argued that terrorism should be defined, first and foremost, as a powerful, hyper-invested *ideological censure* which, if successfully applied, can play a decisive role in forming and inflecting public understanding of deep-seated and complicated political conflicts (see Chapter 1, section 2). And as we have seen, it has been deployed in a highly selective manner. There is more likelihood that the violence of the powerless will be defined as 'terrorist' than will the violence of the state. Indeed, such is the power of the censure that academics and journalists who have challenged the reigning orthodoxy by publishing critical analyses of terrorism, or by pointing the finger at state terrorism, have been

ideological
censure

'unveiled' as 'fellow travellers' and accused of providing terrorists with lethal 'ideological bullets'. Edward Said, for example, because of his association with the PLO, has been publicly denounced in the USA as a 'professor of terrorism' and charged with spilling ink to justify the terrorists' spilling of blood (see, for example, Alexander, 1989).

This raises the central question of whether social scientists should use the terms 'terrorism' and 'terrorist'. Hitchens (1986) and Wieviorka (1993) argue that we should not because, in doing so, rather than referring to an analytical category, we are using a polemical device – as we might use a hall of distorting mirrors – which clouds reality, debases public discourse and makes rational discussion of war, revolution and the causes of political conflict impossible. Morgan agrees: 'The murder exists. The fear exists. The grief exists. But, yes the terrorist *is* a figment of our imagination – and more, a figment of our lack of imagination' (Morgan, 1989, p.33).

From this perspective, we must recognize that there is a continuum or spectrum of socio-politically motivated violence. To bolster their argument that these terms are 'explanatory fictions', these writers could cite the many historical examples of officially defined and labelled 'terrorists' becoming rehabilitated as 'freedom-fighters' and, eventually, reborn as peace-makers and respected leaders of nation-states; and of successful 'terrorist' campaigns being redefined and remembered as wars of liberation or independence. In Palestine, for example, Britain eventually reached a settlement with the leaders of Irgun Zvai Leumi, the Jewish 'terrorist' organization responsible for many atrocities, including the no-warning bombing of the King David Hotel in Jerusalem in July 1946 in which over 70 people were killed (Bowyer-Bell, 1976). The founder of Irgun Zvai Leumi, Menachem Begin, was awarded the Nobel Peace Prize in 1978, approximately 30 years after he was removed from the list of Britain's most wanted terrorists. The most obvious examples of the late twentieth century are Nelson Mandela of the African National Congress, Gerry Adams of Sinn Fein and Yasser Arafat of the Palestine Liberation Organization: 'The sight of Israel's Prime Minister, Yitzhak Rabin, reluctantly taking the proferred hand of PLO chairman, Yasser Arafat, as if blood were still on it, was one of those moments in history when "terrorist" becomes "statesman" and the world knows a potentially momentous change is at hand' (Taylor, 1993, p.320).

Other writers argue that we should retain the terms but deploy them in a much more careful, judicious manner. We need, according to Hobsbaum (1972), to acknowledge from the outset that not all politically inspired acts of anti-state violence are legitimate and that anti-state groups are capable of engaging in torture, mutilation and arbitrary killings. Detonating no-warning car bombs in busy shopping areas, machine-gunning a packed pub, launching 'human bombs' against the security forces and torturing people are acts of unacceptable savagery. But as Arblaster has noted, in pursuit of objectivity and analytical precision we need a 'double picture' and a *co-extensive* definition of terrorism:

> to recognize on the one hand that terrorism is a regular feature of most modern wars, and on the other that the type of terrorist campaign waged by the Provisional IRA, or by certain Palestinian organizations, is a form of war. Even the fact that such wars are undeclared does not differentiate them from American operations in Vietnam and Cambodia, which were also undeclared wars.

(Arblaster, 1977, p.418)

299

Reduced to its essentials, the uncomfortable reality is that, as we have seen earlier in this chapter, terror can be used by a variety of political actors in order to effect social change, deter change or undermine political change. Consequently, states and governments and sub-state groupings, of all ideological configurations, are capable of resorting to terror in the pursuit of socio-political and military objectives:

> Any understanding of terrorism that pictures governments as completely legitimate and rational and 'terrorists' as completely illegitimate and irrational must be flawed. Governors and terrorists are both involved in the pathology of societies that have broken down to the point where politics has been wholly or partly replaced by violent action.
>
> (Woolacott, 1995, p.20)

A third perspective, to be found in the work of Chomsky (1988, 1991) and Herman (1982, 1993), argues that a full and accurate analytical grasp of what true terrorism is and who the real terrorists are can only be achieved through reconstructing and *reversing* the official gaze. In this controversial 'state-terrorist' perspective, only states can be truly terrorist because, as discussed in section 3.2, only they have the 'wholesale' capacity to deploy 'terror' as a systematic, multi-layered mode of domination and governance. Restricting the use of the term in this way would allow for recognition that states can have *chronic* criminogenic and homicidal tendencies and capacities:

> The great mass murderers of our time have accounted for no more than a few hundred victims. In contrast, states that have chosen to murder their own citizens can usually count their victims by the carload lot. As for motive, the state has no peers, for it will kill its victim for a careless word, a fleeting thought, or even a poem.
>
> (Dr Clyde Snow, quoted in Amnesty International, 1993, p.1)

So far we have restricted our attention to discussing and clarifying important definitional issues. If we accept that a variety of 'players' resort to terror for a variety of political and military reasons, then we must ask what can be done to control the most extreme form of this criminal violence. In the following section we will concentrate on discussing the nature and efficacy of contemporary responses to the problem of state violence.

5 Controlling state terror

During the 1980s and 1990s, Western governments assured their citizenry and the international community that there would be no hiding place for those they defined and labelled as 'terrorists'. Any deviation from this fundamental principle, in the form of trade-offs, concessions or negotiations, would, it was argued, encourage other 'criminal gangs' to attempt to hold nation-states to ransom. Bombings, shootings or hostage-taking were followed by statements informing the public that there will be 'no deals with the men of violence', 'no surrender to extremists', 'no hiding place for the terrorists', that 'their crimes will not be forgotten or go unpunished' and that 'terrorism will never win'. Israel relentlessly pursued its enemies, British special forces successfully ambushed and 'neutralized' IRA active service units, France sensationally extradited 'Carlos the Jackal' – 'the world's most wanted terror chief' – from

Sudan, and strenuous efforts were made to bring to trial two Libyans accused of plotting the 1988 Lockerbie bombing, in which all the passengers aboard a Pan Am flight were killed. However, we now need to consider the issue of whether the same time and effort is used to apprehend and punish those who have participated in state-orchestrated or pro-state terrorist actions that are serious criminal offences and prima facie violations of international law.

5.1 Internal regulation and control

There are significant difficulties in attempting to call to account those responsible for upholding the law, safeguarding civil liberties and guaranteeing human rights in the way that non-state actors are called to account. It should be borne in mind, from the outset, that states can and do use the law to deny individuals or social groups basic human rights. Nuremberg laws passed by the Nazi state, for example, stripped the Jews of their citizenship, removed their status as individuals before the law, and denied them their civil rights by passing new laws which placed them outside the German race and, ultimately, the human race. Through redefining the Jews as 'non-human' the Nazi law effectively paved the way for their extermination (Finkielkraut, 1992). In addition, citizens of the Nazi state, who gave shelter to Jews or aided their passage out of the country, were committing criminal acts.

5.1.1 The problem of denial and justification

Cohen's (1993) seminal work documents how states accused of torture or murder can mobilize what he describes as a litany of denials and justifications for their actions:

> The standard vocabulary of official (government) denial weaves its way – at times simultaneously, at times sequentially – through a complete spiral of denial. First you try 'it didn't happen'. There was no massacre, no one was tortured. But then the media, human rights organisations and victims show that it does happen: here are the graves; we have the photos; look at the autopsy reports. So you have to say that what happened was not what it looks to be but really something else: a 'transfer of population', 'collateral damage', 'self-defence'. And then – the crucial subtext – what happened anyway was completely justified – protecting national security, part of the war against terrorism.

(Cohen, 1993, p.102)

Cohen (1993) also details how states can deploy carefully crafted techniques of neutralization that are very similar in nature to those that **Sykes and Matza (1957)** argue are used by juvenile delinquents. These are ready-made justifications which protect the accused from self-blame and the blame of others, namely:

techniques of neutralization

* denial of responsibility;
* denial of injury;
* denial of victims;
* condemnation of condemners;
* appeal to higher loyalties.

Through these vocabularies, the accused state or state officials can present themselves as more sinned against than sinning. The complexities of the situation can be stressed and explained, as can the need to contextualize the 'incident'.

ACTIVITY 7.6

Consider the following 'ticking bomb' 'justification'. Sieghart (1985) claims that states have sometimes presented such an argument to justify the sacrificing of human rights. What do you think of it as a statement? What crucial factors does it ignore?

> Suppose you know that some terrorists have planted a bomb somewhere. You don't know where, but you do know that it is timed to go off six hours from now, and that when it does it will kill or maim many innocent people. Suppose at that point you catch one of the terrorists. Surely you are entitled to do everything you can to get him to tell you where that bomb is, so that you can save all those innocent victims, even if it means causing a guilty man some temporary pain?

(Sieghart, 1985, p.112)

COMMENT

Sieghart (1985, p.113) contends that this argument ignores at least four crucial factors:

1   You may *think* the person you have caught is a 'guilty' terrorist who knows where the bomb is, but you may well be wrong; if you are, you will be torturing an innocent person.
2   Confessions made under torture are seldom reliable; more often than not the victim will say *anything* to make you stop.
3   Presumably, you are trying to protect the high values of your society from the 'evil' people who are attacking them. But what kind of values do you expect to develop in a society whose own government deliberately violates human rights and tortures its own people?
4   Once you accept – as you are doing here – that a good end will justify even the most evil means, where are you going to stop? How long will it be before you are locking up some of your own people in concentration camps, putting others in front of firing squads, or unleashing death squads in the name of 'law and order', national security or the 'public interest'?

5.1.2   The problem of official inquiries and criminal prosecutions

A further response that states might make is to appoint official judicial investigations to uncover the 'truth' of serious allegations. However, as Extract 7.3 details, official inquiries can operate, in times of serious political and social conflict, to maintain the legitimacy of the state and preserve the 'good' name of its agencies and serve, through a prolonged process of deconstruction, reconstruction and depoliticization of events, to obscure the truth rather than uncover it.

In the first years of the Northern Ireland conflict, for example, there were four major official inquiries into controversial events or incidents: the

Cameron Commission and the Scarman Tribunal into various aspects of the 1968–69 disturbances; the Compton inquiry into allegations, against the security forces, of physical brutality and torture in 1971; and the Widgery Tribunal into 'Bloody Sunday' when soldiers of the Parachute Regiment shot dead 14 civilians during a mass civil rights demonstration in 1972. However, Extract 7.3 suggests that a serious question mark hangs over their approach, analysis and ideological balance.

Extract 7.3 Boyle et al.: 'The failure of offical inquiries'

First, the terms of reference were usually interpreted in such a way as to exclude certain broader issues from the scope of inquiry. This was particularly true of the Widgery Tribunal, which was established by a Parliamentary motion to inquire '… into a definite matter of urgent public importance, namely the events on Sunday 30 January [1972] which led to loss of life in connection with the procession in Londonderry on that day.' These terms were taken by Lord Widgery to exclude consideration of the important issues of Army/government relationships and the source of the orders for 30 January. Yet he devoted two full introductory pages to a description of the security situation in Londonderry over the previous six months, indicating the pressures under which the Army was operating. This was apparently based entirely on Army evidence. There was no similar description of the strains the people of Derry were experiencing. This one-sided approach to his terms of reference lessened the credibility of the rest of Lord Widgery's report.

Secondly, the conclusions which the various reports drew from their findings, with the possible exception of Cameron and Scarman, were not always in accord with what might have been expected from an objective assessment of those findings. The Compton Report … based its rejection of the allegations of brutality by security forces on a thoroughly unconvincing distinction between brutality and ill-treatment. Lord Widgery made a generally favourable assessment of the conduct of the paratroops in Londonderry which it is difficult to justify in terms of the specific findings he made over the various individual incidents with which he was concerned, notably the 'reckless' shooting in the Glenfada Flats area. And in reaching even these findings Lord Widgery appeared to have placed undue credence on Army evidence and to have distrusted all other sources. It was in any event the overall assessments of the various reports

rather than the detailed findings which attracted most attention, and gave rise to the widespread feeling that the actions of the security forces were being 'whitewashed'. Assessments of this kind must remain a matter of opinion, but the Compton and Widgery reports certainly failed to persuade either the Roman Catholic community or uncommitted observers that their assessments had struck the right balance.

Thirdly, there was the question of delay. This applied primarily to the Scarman Tribunal which stretched over two whole years and finally reported nearly three years after the events into which it was inquiring. It is hardly surprising that after such a long delay the impact of the report was virtually nil in terms of restoring confidence in the impartiality of the RUC [Royal Ulster Constabulary], in so far as that was a valid finding. By that time an entirely new set of disputed incidents and allegations had taken over from those of 1969.

Finally, and perhaps most important, was the fact that no action was taken to deal with those cases in which the various reports found the security forces or individual soldiers or policemen to have been seriously at fault. The most notorious instances in this respect were the findings of ill-treatment/brutality against those involved in the arrest, detention and interrogation of some of the persons arrested in August 1971, and the finding over the Glenfada Flats incidents, in which four civilians were shot dead, that on the balance of probability 'when these four men were shot the group of civilians was not acting aggressively and that the shots were fired without justification' [H.C. 220, para. 85, April 1972]. It was widely agreed that in these cases the actions by the security forces constituted the criminal offences of assault or manslaughter, if not murder.

(Boyle et al., 1975, pp.127–8)

But the matter does not end here. Even if a public inquiry forcefully declares that a state-initiated atrocity has occurred, this is not the same as holding that state or its employees to account. There is a repetitive world-wide pattern of criminal investigations being aborted because of lack of evidence, witnesses mysteriously withdrawing their evidence or disappearing, charges not being pursued beyond a certain point and defendants being acquitted either at the original trial or on appeal. In the rare instances when officials are then found guilty, human rights organizations, such as Amnesty International (1993), argue that the punishments meted out are rarely commensurate with the crimes committed. Normally, those involved can present their own version of what happened or claim that their only crime was obedience in carrying out orders, and many states, irrespective of the Nuremberg Tribunal ruling, seem to sympathize with and accept this particular plea. Let us go back to the My Lai massacre (see Extract 7.2). Despite the indisputable evidence of a massive official cover-up, only 25 soldiers were charged in relation to the atrocity and only one – Lt Calley – was court-martialled. Although Calley was found guilty and sentenced to life imprisonment, he spent exactly three days in a military jail before being transferred to house arrest and quickly parolled. Throughout the trial, Calley pleaded the 'crime of obedience' – that is, that his only crime was loyalty and patriotism:

> I was ordered to go in there and destroy the enemy. That was my job on that day. That was the mission I was given. I did not sit down and think in terms of men, women and children. They were all classified the same, and that was the classification that we dealt with, just as enemy soldiers … *I felt then and I still do that I acted as I was directed, and I carried out the orders that I was given and I do not feel wrong in doing so.*

> (Quoted in Bilton and Sim, 1993, p.335, emphasis added)

My Lai massacre scene: bodies of women and children lie on the road leading out of My Lai village, March 1968

ACTIVITY 7.7

Do you think that charging only 25 soldiers and court-martialling only one represents justice in this case? The issue of 'crimes of obedience' raises important moral and philosophical questions. Before reading on, think back to the beginning of section 2.1.2 and the question of whether citizens are under a categorical imperative to comply with the law and accept the existing social order no matter how unjust or oppressive. In the light of what you have read so far, how would you answer this question? Make a few notes on what you think are the implications of an individual pleading the 'crime of obedience' and, if found guilty, serving the kind of sentence finally served by Lt Calley. What of the individual's superiors who gave the orders? Apart from the reasons outlined briefly above, under what other circumstances might there be an apparent reluctance or inability to hold perpetrators of gross human rights violations to account?

As Cohen (1995) has pointed out, prosecution difficulties can persist in countries where an oppressive regime has given way to a functioning democratic one which has irrefutable evidence of monumental human rights violations. The crucial issue for successor governments is how to confront and explicate the crimes of the past committed by 'intimate enemies'. There are very few situations in which the transfer of political power is unproblematic and very few new governments are in a position to prosecute and punish without having to consider the political consequences. Political realism tends to prioritize the restoration of stability and social order over justice and this requires a certain national amnesia if it is to succeed. To facilitate the difficult and lengthy process of peace-making and reconciliation and the healing of wounded societies, to prove impartiality, avoid further bloodshed, placate still powerful military machines and establish the political stability necessary for the transition to be successful, compromises are accepted. A considerable re-embroidering of the past takes place in which 'everyone' was guilty of 'something' and 'we must learn to forget'; *de jure* or *de facto* amnesties and pardons are declared which exonerate specific categories of offences, along with promises that there will be no 'witch hunts' or mass prosecutions for past crimes. Leaders of the old regime may also be allowed to go into political exile. This is, in effect, a form of *decriminalization* and human rights groups (see, for example, Amnesty International, 1993) argue that it is employees of the former state who benefit the most. And, as Walsh has argued, this airbrushing and attempted forgetting of history may not work: 'What seems beyond doubt, though, is that unsettled and unforgotten grievances do not simply go away. They rankle, divide and remain nearly impossible to put to rest. Amnesties can help wipe the slate clean, but more times than not, the blood stains, like those on Lady MacBeth's hands, cannot be so easily scrubbed into invisibility' (Walsh, 1995, p.29).

As an illustration of this, let us consider what happened after the military rulers were dislodged in Argentina in 1983. A National Commission on Disappeared People (CONADEP) was established and, as Fisher (1989) and Guzman Bouvard (1994) have detailed, faced considerable difficulties in trying to establish what had happened during the military's rule. It gathered 50,000 pages of evidence from survivors and families but elicited little information from the military itself. Eventually, five of the nine military leaders brought to trial were convicted and sentenced to prison terms, but the nature of the crimes with which they were charged made court proceedings extremely difficult:

As in Nazi-occupied territories, the Argentine phenomenon of *disappearance* constituted a form of state sponsored torture that unleashed terror not only on the *disappeared* but also on society as a whole. It was a crime with no legal recourse. After the fall of the junta, when the military trials were trying those responsible for the Dirty War, many of these people could not be sentenced for murder because there were no bodies as evidence and no laws that covered this practice. *Disappearance* means just that: no proof remains of the whereabouts or the death of a person, who has lost his or her legal and social identity.

(Guzman Bouvard, 1994, p.41)

After 1986, in an attempt to neutralize the threat of a coup, a series of presidential decrees effectively brought the accounting to a halt. The *Ley de Punto Final* (a 'full stop' law) held that, after April 1987, no more claims of human rights violations against the military would be heard by the courts. This was followed by the passing of an even more significant 'law of due obedience' in 1987, which absolved all soldiers and officers beneath the rank of colonel of responsibility for virtually any actions they had committed in the 'war against subversives'. Tarnopolsky (1994) estimates that around 40 officers could still have been tried for serious human rights

The Mothers of the Disappeared: hundreds of women (many wearing the symbolic white headscarf) march in the Plaza de Mayo in Buenos Aires, demanding that the government reveal what happened to the thousands of people who disappeared during the 'dirty war' in Argentina

abuses when in 1988, facing more political problems, including rumoured military coups, President Raul Alfonsin announced a general amnesty. His successor, Carlos Saul Menem, an outspoken opponent of the amnesty while running for political office, changed his mind when he was elected. In 1990, he pardoned the five senior military officers already sentenced, together with 280 other members of the armed forces – which meant that all crimes committed during the 'war against subversives', for which prosecutions were still outstanding after the passing of the laws of 1986 and 1987, had now been pardoned (Cohen, 1995, p.30). Opponents of this amnesty, however, continued to campaign for information on the whereabouts and fate of the thousands of people who had 'disappeared', and in October 1994 the wall of military silence began to crumble when ex-naval officers publicly admitted that: 'the navy had used torture as a "tool" in the fight against subversion' and that: 'so-called "task groups" that were engaged in the clandestine operations of the "dirty war", including torture and extrajudicial executions, were an intrinsic part of the navy's operations' (Amnesty International, 1995, p.60). These admissions, however, did not lead to due public acknowledgement or reparation for past atrocities. Although the Senate Committee, before which they had been made, subsequently refused promotion to the officers concerned, President Menem, in criticizing this decision, 'said that it was better to forget the past' (Amnesty International, 1995, p.60).

5.2 External regulation and control

Those concerned about particular states or those who are not satisfied with the outcome of official state investigations, can, in theory, seek international intervention or request independent human rights bodies to examine abuses. The bodies established in the post-war period have, in principle, altered the relationship between the individual and the state by formally recognizing inviolable universal human rights and enhancing the ability of the individual to place the state in the role of defendant in order that it will be held accountable for its actions. Being publicly shamed before an international audience may, at the very least, embarrass states and governments and force them into doing something about their human rights record. However, it is very difficult for any of these international avenues to deliver substantive justice, even in the most obvious cases where human, civil or legal rights have been flouted on a mass scale. As Weiss *et al.* argue: 'Since 1948, the central problem has not been the abstract codification of norms; the problem has been in marshalling sufficient political will to deal with concrete violations of internationally recognized human rights ... In other words, human rights treaties are widely accepted in law and widely violated in practice' (Weiss *et al.*, 1994, pp.162, 166).

There have been persistent complaints since the Second World War that the international community has shown remarkable reluctance to act decisively against blatant human rights violations and crimes committed during armed conflict. There are many complex legal, political and constitutional reasons for the prevailing reluctance to intercede and to get to grips with this problem, most of which are tied up with the fact that the decisions and actions of the relevant international bodies are determined by its member states.

The European Convention on Human Rights, backed up by a Commission and Court (in Strasbourg), obliges those states *who are signatories to it* to respect basic rights and freedoms of their citizenry. However:

> the rights and freedoms contained in the convention and protocols are ... not absolute. The rights are most of the time qualified by statements such as 'except in accordance with law and justified by the public interests in a democratic society' or 'except when is necessary in a democratic society in the interests of national security, public safety or territorial integrity'.
>
> (Hurwitz, 1981, p.139)

These qualifications mean that there is ample space for states to derogate legally from the Convention. However, many would argue that it is precisely during national emergencies that citizens need added international protection from the state, rather than allowing the state to do as it sees fit. What is more, the European Commission on Human Rights, which deals with the vast majority of complaints and petitions, has also been accused of adopting a slow and cumbersome 'conflict-management' approach to state violations, by (a) attempting to achieve 'friendly' settlements; (b) being more concerned to prevent future recurrences rather than punishing past actions; or (c) being unwilling to apportion blame and guilt (see, for example, Clements, 1994; Harris *et al.*, 1995).

If we consider the nature of the United Nations we find a law-enforcement entity whose competence and jurisdiction is seriously compromised by the fact that it is first and foremost a forum of states and does not have its own military, police, prisons or judiciary, and by highly politicized 'protect-your-own' voting by states. This has impacted negatively on its powers, capabilities and effectiveness. Despite the various supranational conventions and laws of war and human rights mentioned previously, non-interference in the internal affairs of sovereign states has been the fundamental guiding principle of the United Nations since the Second World War. Kuper (1981) argues that this 'radical non-interventionist' principle has effectively blocked the United Nations from responding effectively to massacres verging on outright genocide during this time. It is worth keeping in mind that, when the United Nations Declaration of Human Rights was adopted in 1948, many states did not sign and those that did declared that the principles were not legally binding. The United Nation's interventions, irrespective of the seriousness of the situation, have generally been restricted: (a) to areas in which the consent of the territorial states in question has been secured or where all semblance of governance has collapsed; and (b) to providing humanitarian and social aid to alleviate and soften the suffering of civilian populations. As a result, as Alston (1994) has argued, transparently delinquent and chronically criminal states have not been held to account except when outrageous violations have concurred with the immediate political interests of one of the geopolitical blocs. In addition, many states reject interference from a Western-dominated 'human rights' international community, which they regard as operating with double standards, and complain that a handful of powerful states have enjoyed a considerable degree of the *de facto* indemnity from systematic scrutiny of their human rights record.

It was not until 1994, after considerable feet-dragging, that the United Nations established, at the Hague, an 'International War Crimes Tribunal for the former Yugoslavia', the first since the Nuremberg and Tokyo Trials, to try those accused of serious breaches of the Geneva Convention and crimes against humanity. Progress was seriously hindered, however, because no permanent international court existed; there was little prison accommodation for suspects and the initial budget could not cover the 'nuts and bolts' of a thorough investigation – that is, the employment of legal, administrative, forensic and medical expertise; mass grave exhumations and post-mortems; the identification and extradition of suspects and safe passage of witnesses to trials; and the recording and transcription of tens of thousands of pages of interviews and testimony (see, for example, Bunting, 1994).

Moreover, given that the conflict was ongoing, few believed that it would succeed in bringing those who had planned and overseen war crimes, breaches of the Geneva Convention and genocide to trial. The Serbians, the key suspects, refused to co-operate with it, denying that atrocities had ever happened and arguing that it was biased. In addition, those states and international bodies seeking a negotiated solution to the conflict, needed the co-operation of people – like President Slobodan Milosevic of Serbia and the Bosnian Serb leader, Radovan Karadzic and his military leader General Ratko Mladic – who had been identified and defined as major war criminals. It also became clear, as Vulliamy (1995) has argued, that intentionality and direct culpability would be difficult to prove because the majority of prosecutions would be dependent on witnesses. Very little documentary evidence was available. Warrick (1994) estimated that to prosecute a camp commander for crimes against humanity or prove that rape camps existed would require the personal testimony of hundreds of witnesses who no longer lived in the country or who were too afraid or ashamed to give evidence. As Bosnian prime minister Haris Siladzic has commented on the lack of action against the Serb leaders in the conflict generally: 'You know how it is these days. If you kill one man you get sent to prison, if you kill 200,000 they call you to Geneva for peace talks' (quoted in *New Statesman and Society*, 2 December 1994, p.9).

Given the apparent difficulty of holding to account those responsible for war crimes and genocide, how might citizens be protected against such atrocities?

6 What can be done about state violence?

So how can state violence be reduced, controlled or eliminated? As the previous discussion has made clear, there are no simple or straightforward answers to the problem. Campaigning groups such as Human Rights Watch (for example, 1991), Amnesty International (for example, 1993) and the Independent Commission on International Humanitarian Issues (1986) argue that strong and resolute steps must be taken to make the protection of human rights and civil liberties an integral part of governance. This effectively means embedding nation-states in a web of substantive non-negotiable obligations, duties and responsibilities which will make them accountable to international bodies and thus consistently and firmly locate the rights of the individual and civil society *above* the interests of states.

First, all states should be forced to demonstrate, through independent comprehensive and relentless monitoring, surveillance and evaluation, that international human rights standards and conventions are formally recognized in and ratified by their legal systems. Citizens must be made aware of their internationally guaranteed human rights and civil liberties and have substantive and unqualified means of redress. In addition to this target hardening, there is the need to change the ethical climate of state agencies and officials. The organizational, operational and occupational sub-cultures which generate powerful pressures on members to conform, irrespective of whether the conformity is right or wrong, must be challenged. Through institutional democratization and the use of rewards and sanctions, the 'crimes of obedience' syndrome must be broken.

Second, the international community must develop effective and sophisticated preventative and predictive policies by establishing early-warning systems and risk assessment patterns and typologies based upon the lessons learnt from previous crisis situations. Strategies which concentrate only on helping the victims and survivors should be regarded as a failure of policy. A central part of a proactive strategy would be studying why some state formations are more prone to such criminal activity than others.

Third, in countries where human rights violations and war crimes have taken place, 'right to truth' commissions should be established to investigate what really happened. Such commissions have been set up most notably in

Chile, El Salvador, Burundi and South Africa (see, for example, Ensalaco, 1994; Johnson, 1994; Cohen, 1995). Unlike the official inquiries mentioned in section 5.1.2, these provide those who have suffered persecution the space to be heard and understood through giving testimony to what happened, and to have their victimization and hurt recorded, memorialized and officially recognized; they also provide an opportunity for the whole community to be involved in the grieving process. In addition, the commissions should attempt to persuade state officials and employees to come forward and confess their involvement, give details of their crimes and open official archives. This can be a particularly sensitive issue and is likely to be opposed by those who continue to argue that a balance must be struck between accounting for the past and building for the future. In this version of the conflict everyone was guilty of abuses and raking over the past would only re-open old wounds.

Fourth, state killers and indeed 'killer states' – just like any other 'common criminal' – must be subject to criminal prosecution to help establish confidence in an international rule of law: 'One of the main factors contributing to these "barbaric realities" is the phenomenon of impunity: as long as the agents of repression believe that they can kidnap, torture and murder without fear of discovery or punishment, the cycle of violence will never be broken' (Amnesty International, 1992, p.1). If prosecutions do not take place a clear message is relayed to states and officials that violating human rights will be tolerated and those who do so will not be held to account. In effect, they are being told that serious crime pays. In addition:

- There should be inadmissability of pleas made on the grounds of obeying higher authority; following military orders; for reasons of national security; or acting under 'emergency' legislation.

- Actions should not be cloaked by statutes of limitation.

- Suspected war criminals should be excluded from amnesty decrees and should not be allowed refugee status or a right to political asylum.

- A state's 'right' to assert the right of derogation, or to insert blanket 'exceptional circumstances' clauses into international human rights legislation should be outlawed.

- A properly resourced and staffed permanent international criminal court which is (a) completely independent of global political bodies; and (b) empowered to pursue, across state borders, those who have committed human rights violations, should be established.

- Laws covering organizational criminal liability and individual responsibility for organizational conduct should be strengthened.

- As part of a stategy of prevention, (a) signs of pre-delinquency (for example, the taking over of state power by authoritarian or extremist governments and regimes) should be monitored for; and (b) research on the ways in which state structures and practices can systematically generate unlawful and pathological processes, should be conducted.

- In the view of campaigning groups, the overall aim must be to subordinate national states to an international rule of (human rights) law.

Do you think that it is hopelessly idealistic to assert that an international rule of law can be constructed and *absolutely* placed above political considerations?

Finally, efforts must be made to regulate and 'design out' the means of violence. Kuper maintains that: 'If the great powers do not themselves directly engage in the internal conflicts of small nations ... they do not hesitate to supply the contending parties with the sophisticated arms for mutual annihilation' (Kuper, 1981, p.17).

States and companies are supposed to abide by national and international export treaties and controls to prevent weapons reaching states that are violating human rights and ruling through 'terror'. However, in practice this means overcoming the reservations that states, armaments manufacturers and university research and development groups have about agreements that limit this multi-million pound area of trade. They want the maximum freedom to develop and nurture new markets for their products. As a consequence, there is considerable disinformation about which nations are honest dealers and which are breaking the law by trading with proscribed regimes. Generally, it is impossible to know how closely states adhere to the rules and laws governing sales. We can explore this briefly by looking at three recent cases of illegal arms dealing.

illegal arms dealing

The Iran–Contra scandal surfaced in 1986 when it was revealed that members of the Reagan administration in the USA had secretly sold weapons to the Iranian government in the hope that it would use its influence to gain the release of US hostages in Lebanon. The considerable profits generated from the sale were passed on to the Nicaraguan Contras. This action caused a scandal because it was illegal to sell arms to Iran, it was unlawful to fund the Contras beyond the limits set by the US Congress and it was US state policy not to negotiate with 'terrorists' (see Chambliss, 1989).

In the early 1990s two court cases shed light on the British state's attitude to arms control treaties and regulations. In November 1992, the trial of three executives of Matrix Churchill, a machine tool company, who had been accused of illegally exporting defence-related equipment to Iraq, collapsed in sensational circumstances. As the trial progressed, a very different picture was revealed to the one presented by the prosecution, exposing how government ministers and their officials broke the law relating to the transfer of weapons to Iraq in order to protect the UK's own machine tools industry, promote good relations with a key economic power in the Middle East (Iraq had the potential to be the world's second biggest oil producer and the UK could expect favoured status), and compliment the US government's decision to restabilize the Middle East by supporting Iraq against Iranian Sh'ite 'fundamentalism'. Ministers and civil servants effectively subverted the government's professed policies by privately 'loosening' the rules whilst stating in public that they were firmly in place. It became apparent that if Customs and Excise had not decided to prosecute some of the businesses involved in these exports, the 'relaxation' of the guidelines would never have been uncovered (see Leigh, 1993; Norton-Taylor, 1995).

In November 1994, a High Court ruling stated that the UK government's decision to spend £234 million in aid money on the Malaysian Pergau dam project was illegal. At the heart of the Pergau Dam affair was the British state's illegal use of scarce aid resources to secure highly profitable arms contracts for the British defence industry. Research carried out by the World Development Movement (1994) indicated that Pergau was not an isolated case. It argues that, in the 1980s, British companies identified South East Asia, because of its successful industrialization, as the fastest-growing defence market in the world, and attempted to secure major contracts for integrated packages of military hardware and training. The UK government and the defence industry successfully used diplomatic initiatives, ministerial visits, military hardware displays and generous financial incentives to wrest business away from the Americans. British exports of military equipment to Asia and the Far East rose from £73 million in 1985 to £306 million in 1989.

What is remarkable is that, in all three cases, state officials who broke the law were not prosecuted, which poses the question of whether this reaffirms that states can break the law, whether national or international, with relative impunity. It also highlights the conflicting interests of the campaigns for states to recognize and protect the human rights of their citizens, and a state's military, political or commercial interests which cause many to violate the various international declarations and conventions discussed earlier in this chapter. As Jongman has written in relation to torture, but which might equally apply to other forms of gross human rights violations:

> The real problem is how to actually enforce these prohibitions. Despite the international consensus expressed in numerous declarations, treaties, conventions and accords, the actual binding power of the prohibition is disputed, even by member governments which appear to be obligated. The rhetoric of universal human rights is not backed up by real powers of enforcement against sovereign states. Nor can there be effective international sanctions against a state which is, in effect, committing crimes against its own as well as international laws.

> (Jongman, 1993, p.165)

7 Conclusion

In the course of our discussion on political violence, terrorism and the state we have covered many issues. At the core of the chapter lies a series of questions: What is political violence? What is a political offence? What is terrorism? Who are the terrorists? and: What can be done to curb political violence and terrorism? In considering these questions we have been forced to consider the nature of the state and its monopoly of violence.

Events occurring in the twentieth century have thrown into stark focus various problems of the state. The first of these is the fact that in many parts of the world 'the state, like an unchained beast, has ferociously attacked those who claim to be its master: its own citizens' (Bushnell *et al.*, 1991, p.7). If the state decides to use its monopoly in a criminal manner, the citizenry quickly find out that states are not necessarily safe places in which to live. Indeed, they are places of ultimate insecurity and risk because there is very little protection available from an 'unchained' state. This leads us to a second problem, namely, the problem of the individual's relationship to the state, its authority, its laws and the appropriate response to offensive or unjust laws or rule. Key questions remaining are: How far must the citizenry always comply with domestic law? and: Is civil disobedience, violent protest or rebellion ever justified?

Clearly, as this chapter has shown, those who choose to go against the law run the risk of having their motives disregarded, or worse denied, by the state. They also run the risk of being labelled as extremists and, eventually, as 'terrorists'. Once this occurs, those with the grievance may be defined as being 'beyond the pale' and as 'enemies within'. Their criminalization will be secured. As we have seen, states readily turn to the criminal law to control threats to their own authority. However, those states which consistently move beyond the remit of national and international law to protect their own interests seem to be able to do so with impunity or, at most, with moral condemnation. It is perhaps for this reason that, in the twentieth century, political crimes against the state have come to be defined as 'terrorist' atrocities and that the criminological gaze has rarely dwelt on those criminal actions perpetrated by the state itself. If this remains the case then criminology will become the poorer for accepting such limitations to its agenda. The study of crimes of the state is not only politically sensitive, it also carries the potential for a radical rethinking of the meaning of 'dangerousness', 'risk' and 'safety'; the nature and extent of 'victimization'; and the parameters of how the 'problem of crime' might be constituted.

Acknowledgement

In writing this chapter we are indebted to Stanley Cohen, Professor of Criminology at the Hebrew University of Jerusalem, for a series of influential seminars on human rights and crimes of the state, given by him in London and Milton Keynes during 1994; and to Fiona Harris, currently undertaking doctoral research in the Faculty of Social Sciences at The Open University, for her comments on earlier drafts of this chapter and her contribution to the discussions on torture.

Further reading

Whilst many criminological textbooks might include sections on the political criminal, the concept of political crime is usually limited to those who challenge state authority. Turk (1982), for example, maintains that crimes committed by the state should not be identified as political crime. It was not until the beginning of the 1970s that definitions of crime – such as that formulated by the Schwendingers (1970) – were capable of reversing the label and applied 'criminality' to various state practices, oppression, discrimination and the violation of human rights. Even so, much of the material discussed in this chapter is rarely to be found in the standard criminological literature. Questions of human rights are more likely to be addressed in the publications of campaigning organizations such as Amnesty International (for example, 1993), Human Rights Watch (for example, 1991) and Africa Watch (for example, 1991) – though an accessible theoretical overview of how states approach international human rights issues can be found in Donnelly (1993). However, they have recently entered the criminological discourse through the seminal work of **Cohen (1993**, 1995). From outside the criminological orthodoxy, Chomsky (1988, 1991), a professor of linguistics, outlines the forces behind international political crimes by the state; Giddens (1985), a political sociologist, examines the nature and extent of state-sanctioned violence in times of war; and the social psychologists Kelman and Hamilton (1989) explore the meaning of crimes of obedience. All of these latter readings suggest radically new departures for a criminological agenda.

References

Ackroyd, C., Mangolis, K., Rosenhead, J. and Shallice, T. (1977) *The Technology of Political Control*, Harmondsworth, Penguin.

Africa Watch (1991) *The Killings in South Africa: The Role of the Security Forces and the Response of the State*, London, Africa Watch.

Africa Watch (1995) *Not So Innocent: When Women Became Killers*, London, Africa Watch.

Alexander, E. (1989) 'Professor of terror', *Commentary*, vol.88, no.2, pp.49–50.

Alston, P. (1994) 'The United Nations human rights record: from San Francisco to Vienna and beyond', *Human Rights Quarterly*, vol.16, no.2, pp.375–90.

Amnesty International (1984) *Torture in the Eighties*, Oxford, Martin Robertson/London, Amnesty International.

Amnesty International (1992) *Amnesty International Report 1992*, London, Amnesty International.

Amnesty International (1993) *Getting Away with Murder: Political Killings and Disappearances in the 1990s*, London, Amnesty International.

Amnesty International (1995) *Amnesty International Report 1995*, London, Amnesty International.

Arblaster, A. (1977) 'Terrorism: myths, meaning and morals', *Political Studies*, vol.25, no.3, pp.413–24.

Arendt, H. (1961) *On Violence*, London, Allen Lane.

Armstrong, N. and Tennenhouse, L. (1989) *The Violence of Representation: Literature and the History of Violence*, London, Routledge.

Best, G. (1983) *Humanity in Warfare: The Modern History of the International Law of Armed Conflicts*, London, Methuen.

Best, G. (1994) *War and Law Since 1945*, Oxford, Clarendon.

Bilton, M. and Sim, K. (1993) *Four Hours in My Lai: A War Crime and its Aftermath*, New York and Harmondsworth, Penguin.

Bourdieu, P. (1977) *Outline of a Theory of Practice*, Cambridge, Cambridge University Press.

Bowyer-Bell, J. (1976) *Terror out of Zion*, New York, St Martin's Press.

Boyle, K., Hadden, T. and Hillyard, P. (1975) *Law and State: The Case of Northern Ireland*, London, Martin Robertson.

Brittain, V.M. (1944) *Seed of Chaos: What Mass Bombing Really Means*, London, New Vision Publishers.

Brogan, P. (1992) *World Conflicts: Why and Where They Are Happening* (2nd edn), London, Bloomsbury.

Budiardjo, C. (1991) 'Indonesia: mass extermination and the consolidation of authoritarian power', in George, A. (ed.) *Western State Terrorism*, Cambridge, Polity.

Bunting, M. (1994) 'The evil that men do', *The Guardian*, 19 August.

Burk, K. (ed.) (1982) *War and the State: The Transformation of British Government 1914–1919*, London, Allen and Unwin.

Bushnell, P.T., Shlapentokh, V. and Vanderpool, C.K. (1991) *State Organized Terror*, Boulder, CO, Westview.

Cameron, J.M. (1970) 'On violence', *New York Review of Books*, 2 July, pp.24–32.

Cesarani, D. (1992) *Justice Delayed: How Britain Became a Refuge for Nazi War Criminals*, London, Heinemann.

Chalk, F. and Jonassohn, K. (1990) *The History and Sociology of Genocide*, New Haven, CT, Yale University Press.

Chambliss, W.J. (1989) 'State organized crime', *Criminology*, vol.27, no.2, pp.183–208.

Chomsky, N. (1988) *The Culture of Terrorism*, Boston, MA, South End Press.

Chomsky, N. (1991) *Pirates and Emperors: International Terrorism in the Real World*, New York, Black Rose Books.

Clements, L.J. (1994) *European Human Rights: Taking a Case Under the Convention*, London, Sweet and Maxwell.

Cohen, S. (1993) 'Human rights and crimes of the state: the culture of denial', *Australian and New Zealand Journal of Criminology*, vol.26, no.1, pp.87–115. (Extract reprinted in Muncie *et al.*, 1996.)

Cohen, S. (1995) 'State crimes of previous regimes: knowledge, accountability, and policing the past', *Law and Social Inquiry*, vol.20, no.1, pp.7–50.

Crelinsten, R.D. (1993) 'In their own words: the world of the torturer', in Crelinsten and Schmid (1993).

Crelinsten, R.D. and Schmid, A.P. (eds) (1993) *The Politics of Pain: Torturers and Their Masters*, Leiden, Center for the Study of Social Conflicts.

Crouch, H. (1978) *The Army and Politics in Indonesia*, Ithaca, NY, Cornell University Press.

Detter De Lupis, I. (1987) *The Law of War*, Cambridge, Cambridge University Press.

Donnelly, J. (1993) *International Human Rights*, Boulder, CO, Westview.

Duster, T. (1971) 'Conditions of guilt-free massacre' in Sanford, N. and Comstock, C. (eds) *Sanctions of Evil: Sources of Social Destructiveness*, San Francisco, CA, Jossey-Bass.

Ely, J.H. (1993) *War and Responsibility: Constitutional Lessons of Vietnam and Its Aftermath*, Princeton, NJ, Princeton University Press.

Ensalaco, M. (1994) 'Truth commissions for Chile, El Salvador: a report and assessment', *Human Rights Quarterly*, vol.16, no.4, pp.656–75.

Falk, R.A., Kolko, G. and Lifton, R.J. (1971) *Crimes of War*, New York, Vintage.

Fanon, F. (1967) *Wretched of the Earth*, Harmondsworth, Penguin.

Finkielkraut, A. (1992) *Remembering in Vain: The Klaus Barbie Trial and Crimes Against Humanity*, New York, Columbia University Press.

Fisher, J. (1989) *Mothers of the Disappeared,* London, Zed.

Foucault, M. (1979) *Discipline and Punish: The Birth of the Prison*, Harmondsworth, Penguin.

Foucault, M. (1980) *Power/Knowledge*, Brighton, Harvester Wheatsheaf.

Garrett, S.A. (1993) *Ethics and Airpower in World War Two,* New York, St Martin's Press.

Gatrell, V. (1994) *The Hanging Tree*, Cambridge, Cambridge University Press.

Gibson, J.T. (1990) 'Factors contributing to the creation of a torturer', in Suedfeld, P. (ed.) *Psychology and Torture*, New York, Hemisphere.

Giddens, A. (1985) *Nation State and Violence*, Cambridge, Polity.

Giddens, A. (1989) *Sociology*, Cambridge, Polity.

Guzman Bouvard, M. (1994) *Revolutionizing Motherhood: The Mothers of the Plaza de Mayo*, Wilmington, DE, Scholarly Resources.

Hall, S. (1986) 'Media power and class power', in Curran, J., Ecclestone, J., Oakley, G. and Richardson, A. (eds) *Bending Reality: The State of the Media*, London, Pluto.

Hanmer, J. and Maynard, M. (eds) (1987) *Women, Violence and Social Control*, Basingstoke, Macmillan.

Haritos-Fatouros, M. (1993) 'The official torturer: a learning model for obedience to the authority of violence', in Crelinsten and Schmid (1993).

Harris, D.J., O'Boyle, M. and Warbrick, C. (1995) *The Law of European Convention on Human Rights*, London, Butterworth.

Harris, P. (ed.) (1989) *Civil Disobedience,* Boston, MA, University of America Press.

Herman, E.S. (1982) *The Real Terrorist Network,* Boston, MA, South End Press.

Herman, E.S. (1993) 'Terrorism: misrepresentations of power', in Brown, D.J. and Merrill, R. (eds) *Violent Persuasions: The Politics and Imagery of Terrorism*, Seattle, WA, Bay Press.

Hinde, R.A. and Watson, H.E. (eds) (1995) *War and the Institution of War*, London, Tauris Academic Studies.

Hitchens, C. (1986) 'Wanton acts of usage', *Harpers*, September.

Hobsbaum, E. (1972) 'Terrorism', *The Listener*, vol.8, no.2256, 22 June, pp.824–6.

Hogan, G. and Walker, C. (1989) *Political Violence and the Law in Ireland*, Manchester, Manchester University Press.

Hopper, K.T. (1984) *Elections, Politics and Society in Ireland 1832–1885*, Oxford, Clarendon.

Human Rights Watch (1991) *The Killings in South Africa: The Role of the Security Forces and the Response of the State*, New York, Human Rights Watch.

Hurwitz, L. (1981) *The State as Defendant*, London, Aldwych.

Independent Commission on International Humanitarian Issues (1986) *Disappeared: Technique of Terror*, London, Zed.

Ingraham, B.L. (1979) *Political Crime in Europe*, Berkeley, CA, University of California Press.

International Military Tribunal (1947) *Trial of the Major War Criminals*, Nuremberg.

Johnson, P. (1986) 'Terrorism', in Netanyahu (1986).

Johnson, S. (1994) *Strange Days Indeed: South Africa from Insurrection to Post-Election*, London, Bantam.

Jongman, A.J. (1993) 'Torture: definition and legal instruments', in Crelinsten and Schmid (1993).

Karnow, S. (1983) *Vietnam*, London, Century.

Kelman, H.C. and Hamilton, V.L. (1989) *Crimes of Obedience*, New Haven, CT, Yale University Press.

Kuper, L. (1981) *Genocide*, Harmondsworth, Penguin.

Kuper, L. (1991) 'The genocidal state: an overview', in van den Berghe, P.L. (ed.) *State Violence and Ethnicity*, Colorado Springs, CO, University of Colorado Press.

Langbein, J.H. (1977) *Torture and the Law of Proof: Europe and England in the Ancien Régime*, Chicago, IL, University of Chicago Press.

Lashmar, P. (1995) 'No pain, no gain', *New Statesman and Society*, 20 January, pp.22–3.

Leigh, D. (1993) *Betrayed: The Real Story of the Matrix Churchill Trial*, London, Bloomsbury.

Livingston, S. (1994) *The Terrorism Spectacle*, Boulder, CO, Westview.

Lodge, J. (ed.) (1988) *The Threat of Terrorism*, Brighton, Harvester Wheatsheaf.

Mackie, J.L. (1977) *Ethics: Inventing Right and Wrong*, Harmondsworth, Penguin.

Mason, T.D. and Krane, D.A. (1989) 'The political economy of death squads: toward a theory of the impact of state sanctioned terror', *International Studies Quarterly*, vol.33, no.2, pp.175–98.

McGreal, C. (1994) 'Blood on Their Hands', *The Guardian Weekend*, 3 December, pp.40–6.

McNeil, E.B. (1966) 'Violence and human development', *Annals of the American Academy of Political and Social Science*, no.364, pp.152–65.

Miller, D. (1994) *Don't Mention the War*, London, Pluto.

Morgan, R. (1989) *The Demon Lover: On the Sexuality of Terrorism*, London, Methuen.

Muncie, J., McLaughlin, E. and Langan, M. (eds) (1996) *Criminological Perspectives: A Reader*, London, Sage in association with The Open University.

Netanyahu, B. (ed.) (1986) *Terrorism: How the West Can Win*, London, Weidenfeld and Nicolson.

Nieburg, H.L. (1969) *Political Violence*, New York, St Martin's Press.

Norman, R. (1995) *Ethics, Killing and War*, Cambridge, Cambridge University Press.

Norton-Taylor, R. (1995) *Truth is a Difficult Concept: Inside the Scott Enquiry*, London, Guardian Books.

Pankhurst, E. (1931) *The Suffragette Movement*, London, Longman.

Pearlman, R.M. (1991) *The Mind of the Political Terrorist*, Wilmington, DE, Scholarly Resources.

Peters, E. (1985) *Torture*, Oxford, Basil Blackwell.

Pinchuck, T. (1994) *Mandela,* Cambridge, Icon Books.

Pitman, P. (1986) 'Trials of the generals', *Index on Censorship*, vol.15, no.4, pp.7–10.

Poulantzas, N. (1978) *State, Power, Socialism,* London, New Left Review Books.

Radzinowicz, L. and Hood, R. (1990) *The Emergence of Penal Policy*, vol.5 of *A History of English Criminal Law*, Oxford, Clarendon.

Reisman, W.M. and Antoniou, C.T. (1994) *The Laws of War*, New York, Vintage.

Rejali, D.M. (1994) *Torture and Modernity,* Boulder, CO, Westview.

Roberts, A. and Guelff, R. (1982) *Documents of the Laws of War*, Oxford, Clarendon.

Rodley, N. (1987) *The Treatment of Prisoners Under International Law*, Oxford, Clarendon in association with UNESCO.

Rolston, B. (1991) 'The British state in Northern Ireland', in George, A. (ed.) *Western State Terrorism*, Cambridge, Polity.

Rosenblad, E. (1979) *International Humanitarian Law of Armed Conflict*, Geneva, Henry Dunant Institute.

Rummel, R.J. (1995) *Death by Government: Genocide and Mass Murder Since 1900*, Plymouth, Transaction Publishers.

Saward, D. (1985) *'Bomber' Harris: The Story of Marshall of the Royal Air Force Sir Arthur Harris*, London, Sphere.

Scarry, E. (1985) *The Body in Pain: The Making and Unmaking of the World*, Oxford, Oxford University Press.

Schafer, S. (1974) *The Political Criminal*, New York, Free Press.

Schwendinger, H. and Schwendinger, J. (1970) 'Defenders of order or guardians of human rights?', *Issues in Criminology*, vol.5, no.2, pp.123–57.

Segal, L. (1990) *Slow Motion: Changing Masculinities, Changing Men*, London, Virago. (Extract reprinted as 'Explaining male violence' in Muncie *et al.*, 1996.)

Sharp, G. (1973) *The Politics of Non-Violent Action*, Boston, MA, Porter Sargent.

Sieghart, P. (1985) *The Lawful Rights of Mankind: An Introduction to the International Legal Code of Human Rights*, Oxford, Oxford University Press.

Skolnick, J. (1969) *The Politics of Protest*, New York, Ballantine.

Smith, B.F. (1977) *Reaching Judgment at Nuremberg*, New York, Basic Books.

Sterling, C. (1981) *The Terrorist Network*, New York, Holt Reinhart.

Stover, E. and Nightingale, E.O. (1985) *The Breaking of Bodies and Minds: Torture, Psychiatric Abuse, and the Health Professions*, New York, Freeman.

Sykes, G.M. and Matza, D. (1957) 'Techniques of neutralization', *American Sociological Review*, **vol.22, no.6, pp.664–70. (Extract reprinted in Muncie et al., 1996.)**

Tarnopolsky, N. (1994) 'Argentina: fight barbarism from a wall of memory', *International Herald Tribune*, 15 December, p.4.

Taylor, P. (1993) *States of Terror: Democracy and Political Violence*, Harmondsworth, Penguin.

Tilly, C. (1985) 'War making and state making as organised crime', in Evans, P.B., Rueschemeyer, D. and Skocpol, T. (eds) *Bringing the State Back In*, Cambridge, Cambridge University Press.

Turk, A. (1982) *Political Criminality*, London, Sage.

US Department of State (1995) *Patterns of Global Terrorism 1994*, Office of the Co-ordinator for Counter-Terrorism, April 1995.

Vulliamy, E. (1994) *Seasons in Hell: Understanding Bosnia's War*, London, Simon and Schuster.

Vulliamy, E. (1995) 'In times of trial', *The Guardian*, 31 October, pp.6–7.

Walsh, J. (1995) 'Can justice ever be done?', *Time*, 22 May, pp.28–33.

Walzer, M. (1975) 'The new terrorists', *New Republic*, vol.173, no.9, pp.12–14.

Walzer, M. (1977) *Just and Unjust Wars*, New York, Basic Books.

Warrick, T.S. (1994) 'UN footdragging could make a sham of the war crimes tribunal', *International Herald Tribune*, 21 December.

Weber, M. (1970) *From Max Weber: Essays in Sociology* (trans. and ed. H.J.H. Gerth and C.W. Mills), London, Routledge.

Wehr, P., Burgess, H. and Burgess, G. (eds) (1994) *Justice Without Violence*, Boulder, CO, Lynne Rienner Publishers.

Weiss, T.G., Forsythe, D.P. and Coate, R.A. (1994) *The United Nations and Changing World Politics*, Boulder, CO, Westview.

Wieviorka, M. (1993) *The Making of Terrorism,* Chicago, IL, Chicago University Press.

Wilkinson, P. (1986) *Terrorism and the Liberal State*, London, Macmillan.

Wolf, J.B. (1987) *Anti-Terrorism Initiatives*, New York, Plenum Books.

Woolacott, M. (1995) 'Three sides to every story', *The Guardian*, 2 September, p.20.

World Development Movement (1994) *The Inquiry into the Pergau Hydro-Electric Project, the Aid and Trade Provision and Its Implication for Overseas Aid Expenditure. Evidence Submitted to the House of Commons Foreign Affairs Committee, February, 1994*, London, World Development Movement.

Acknowledgements

We have made every attempt to obtain permission to reproduce material in this book. Copyright holders of material which has not been acknowledged should contact the Rights Department at The Open University.

Grateful acknowledgement is made to the following sources for permission to reproduce material in this volume:

Text

Chapter 1: Pearson, G. (1983) *Hooligan: A History of Respectable Fears*, Macmillan Press Ltd; Dyer, C. (1993) 'Judge's comments echo "silly" remarks', *The Guardian*, 10 June 1993; 'Levittating the laws', *The Guardian*, 27 November 1993; Burrell, I. and Leppard, D. (1994) 'Fall in crime a myth as police chiefs massage the figures', *Sunday Times*, 16 October 1994, © Times Newspapers Ltd, 1994; Brummer, A. (1993) 'Crime in the city', *The Guardian*, 1 July 1993; Lewthwaite, J. (1992) 'The "killer" mistress who was at lover's wedding', *The Sun*, 7 July 1992, Rex Features; Curran, F. (1994) 'You're mad not bad', *Daily Star*, 10 December 1994, Express Newspapers plc; Scraton, P. and Chadwick, K. (1991) 'The theoretical and political priorities of critical criminology', in Stenson, K. and Cowell, D. (eds) *The Politics of Crime Control*, Sage Publications Ltd; Young, J. (1986) 'The failure of criminology: the need for a radical realism', in Matthews, R. and Young, J. (eds) *Confronting Crime*, Sage Publications Ltd; **Chapter 2:** Christie, A. (1965) *At Bertram's Hotel,* HarperCollins Publishers Ltd, copyright © Agatha Christie Limited 1965; From *Cop Killer* by Maj Sjöwall and Per Wahlöö, trans. from the Swedish by T. Teal. Copyright © 1975 by Random House, Inc. Reprinted by permission of Pantheon Books, a division of Random House, Inc.; Mosley, W. (1993) *White Butterfly*, W.W. Norton & Co., Inc. Copyright © 1992 by Walter Mosley. Reproduced by permission of Serpent's Tail; Forrest, K.V. (1993) *Murder by Tradition*, HarperCollins Publishers Ltd. Also by permission of The Naiad Press Inc.; **Chapter 4:** Park, R.E., Burgess, E.W. and McKenzie, R.D. (1925) *The City*, The University of Chicago Press, Introduction © 1967 by The University of Chicago. All rights reserved; Davis, M. (1990) *City of Quartz*, Verso; **Chapter 5:** Gordon, L. (1989) *Heroes of Their Own Lives,* Penguin. Used by permission of Viking Penguin, a division of Penguin Books USA Inc. and the Abner Stein Agency; Dyer, C. 'Aid for domestic violence victims', *The Guardian*, 6 June 1994; Dyer, C. 'Court attempts to soften law on provocation', *The Guardian*, 8 July 1995; Segal, L. *Slow Motion* © 1990 Lynne Segal. Reprinted by permission of Rutgers University Press; Deans, J. 'How dare the UN lecture us', *Daily Mail*, 28 January 1995; **Chapter 6:** Macintyre, D. (1993) 'Auditors place £36bn value on hidden economy', *The Independent*, 3 December 1993; Gillard, M. (1994) 'Arrests follow £1bn mortgage fraud probe', *The Guardian*, 10 April 1994; Connon, H. (1994) 'Britain fails to come to grips with suspicious share deals', *The Independent*, 22 July 1994; Slapper, G. (1994) 'Crime without punishment', *The Guardian*, 1 February 1994; **Chapter 7:** Vulliamy, E. (1994) *Seasons in Hell: Understanding Bosnia's War*, Simon and Schuster Ltd, © Ed Vulliamy, 1994; Bilton, M. and Sim, K. (1992) *Four Hours in My Lai*, Penguin Books, © Michael Bilton and Kevin Sim, 1992. All rights reserved; Boyle, K., Hadden, T. and Hillyard, P. (1975) *Law and State: The Case of Northern Ireland*, Martin Robertson, © Kevin Boyle, Tom Hadden and Paddy Hillyard, 1975.

Figures

Figure 1.1: Home Office Research and Statistics Department (1993) *Digest 2 Information on the Criminal Justice System in England and Wales*, © Crown Copyright. Reproduced with the permission of the Controller of Her Majesty's Stationery Office; *Figure 1.3:* Mayhew, P., Mirrlees-Black, C. and Maung, N.A. (1994) *Research Findings No. 14*, Home Office Research and Statistics Department, © Crown Copyright. Reproduced with the permission of the Controller of

Her Majesty's Stationery Office; *Figure 1.4:* Extracts from *Leicester Mercury*, 21 January 1994, Leicester Mercury Group Ltd; *Figure 1.5:* Hall, S., Clarke, J., Critcher, C., Jefferson, A. and Roberts, B. (1975) *Stencilled Occasional Papers: Newsmaking and Crime*, January 1975, © Centre for Contemporary Cultural Studies; *Figure 1.6:* Wilkins, L.T. (1964) *Social Deviance*, Routledge; *Figure 1.7:* Muncie, J. (1987) 'Much ado about nothing?' *Social Studies Review*, vol.3, no.2, November 1987, Philip Allan Publishers Ltd; *Figures 3.1 and 3.2:* Beattie, J.M. (1974) 'The pattern of crime in England 1660–1800', *Past and Present*, 62, February 1974, © World Copyright: The Past and Present Society, 1974; *Figure 3.3:* Sharpe, J.A. (1984) *Crime in Early Modern England, 1550–1750*, Longman Group Ltd; *Figure 4.1:* Park, R.E., Burgess, E.W. and McKenzie, R.D. (1925) *The City*, The University of Chicago Press, Introduction © 1967 by The University of Chicago. All rights reserved; *Figure 5.1:* 'Night and Day', *The Mail On Sunday Review*, 9 October 1994, Associated Newspapers Ltd.

Tables

Table 1.2: Mayhew, P., Mirrlees-Black, C. and Maung, N.A. (1994) *Research Findings No. 14*, Home Office Research and Statistics Department, © Crown Copyright. Reproduced with the permission of the Controller of Her Majesty's Stationery Office; *Table 1.3:* Braithwaite, J. (1989) *Crime, Shame and Reintegration*, Cambridge University Press; *Table 1.4:* Williams, P. and Dickinson, J. (1993) 'Fear of crime: read all about it?', *British Journal of Criminology*, vol.33, no.1, Winter 1993, by permission of Oxford University Press; *Table 1.5:* Hough, M. and Mayhew, P. (1983) *The British Crime Survey: First Report*, © Crown Copyright. Reproduced with the permission of the Controller of Her Majesty's Stationery Office; *Table 5.1:* Creighton, S.J. and Noyes, P. (1989) *Child Abuse Trends in England and Wales 1983–1987*, NSPCC.

Photographs / illustrations

p.11: © Alex MacNaughton; *p.26:* (top) Mary Evans Picture Library; (centre) *Illustrated London News*; (bottom) reproduced with permission from Young, P.M. (1968) *A History of British Football*, Stanley Paul; *p.30:* Commission for Racial Equality; *p.42:* David Austin; *p.46:* Curran, F. (1994) 'You're mad not bad', *Daily Star*, 10 December 1994, Express Newspapers plc; *p.48:* Sean Smith/*The Guardian*; *p.51:* Press Association; *p.71:* LWT Productions Licensing & Marketing/courtesy of Mr David Suchet; *p.78:* Kobal Collection/Warner Brothers; *p.87:* © Granada Television Limited. Reproduced with the kind permission of Ms Helen Mirren, Ms Liza Sadovy and Mr Tom Bell; *p.95:* BBC copyright photograph. Reproduced with the kind permission of Ms Siobhan Redmond; *p.96:* from *Evil Under the Sun*, a Columbia–EMI–Warner film, Ronald Grant Archive; *pp.104, 113, 132:* © The British Museum; *p.131:* Mary Evans Picture Library; *p.147:* Guildhall Library, Corporation of London/photo: Geremy Butler Photography; *p.158:* Aerofilms; *p.175:* photo: Robert Morrow; *p.185:* Hulton Deutsch Collection; *p.192:* courtesy of EPOCH/Approach; *p.198:* Women's Aid Federation (England) Ltd; *p.203:* Pam Isherwood/Format; *p. 213:* (a) © the estate of Franki Raffles/courtesy of Edinburgh District Council Women's Unit, Zero Tolerance Division; (b) © the Association of London Authorities. The Zero Tolerance logo is copyright of the estate of Franki Raffles; (c) Women's Aid Federation; *pp.228, 234, 236, 245, 247:* Popperfoto/Reuter; *p.261:* Ulli Michel/Popperfoto/Reuter; *p.275:* Popperfoto/Reuter; *p.279:* source unknown; *p.285:* AKG London; *p.291:* (top) Popperfoto/Reuter; (bottom) *The Independent*/photo: Brian Harris; *p.294:* (top) © Willie Doherty/courtesy Matt's Gallery, London; (bottom) Willie Doherty *Same Difference*. A slide text installation, Matt's Gallery, London, 1990. In the collection: Arts Council of England. Photos by courtesy of Matt's Gallery, London; *p.304:* Associated Press. Photo from *LIFE* Magazine. © 1969 Ronald L. Haeberle; *p.306:* Popperfoto/UPI.

Cover

Photograph by Nigel Francis. Robert Harding Picture Library.

Index